MO⊙N   OUTDOORS

NORTHERN CALIFORNIA BIKING

ANN MARIE BROWN

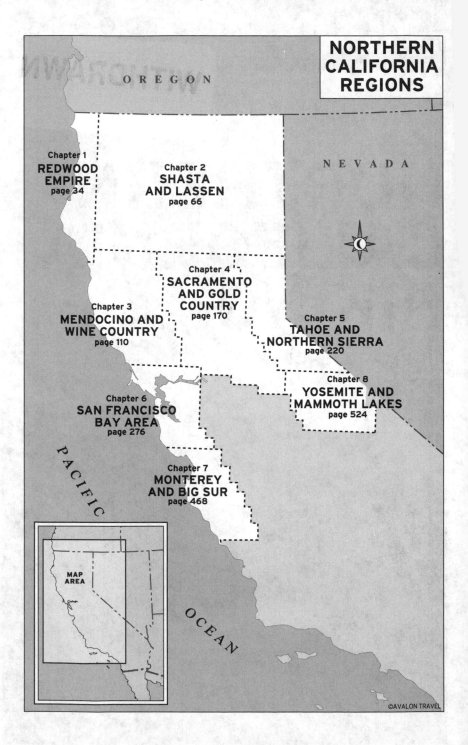

NORTHERN CALIFORNIA REGIONS

OREGON

NEVADA

Chapter 1
REDWOOD EMPIRE
page 34

Chapter 2
SHASTA AND LASSEN
page 66

Chapter 4
SACRAMENTO AND GOLD COUNTRY
page 170

Chapter 3
MENDOCINO AND WINE COUNTRY
page 110

Chapter 5
TAHOE AND NORTHERN SIERRA
page 220

Chapter 8
YOSEMITE AND MAMMOTH LAKES
page 524

Chapter 6
SAN FRANCISCO BAY AREA
page 276

Chapter 7
MONTEREY AND BIG SUR
page 468

PACIFIC

OCEAN

MAP AREA

©AVALON TRAVEL

Contents

How to Use This Book

ABOUT THE MAPS

This book is divided into chapters based on regions; an overview map of these regions precedes the table of contents. Each chapter begins with a region map that shows the locations and numbers of the rides listed in that chapter. Each ride profile is also accompanied by a detailed map that shows the bike route.

Map Symbols

——————	Road Route	○	City
- - - - - - - -	Unpaved Road Route	○	Town
- - - - - -	Trail Route	℗	Trailhead Parking
—·— ·— ·	Optional Route	Start	Start of Ride
··············	Trail	▪	Point of Interest
··············	Trail (Bikes Prohibited)	★	Natural Feature
▓▓▓▓▓▓	Divided Highway	▲	Mountain
▓▓▓▓▓▓	Primary Road	⬟	State Park
▓▓▓▓▓▓	Secondary Road	Λ	Campground
- - - - - - - -	Unpaved Road	🇶	Waterfall

ABOUT THE ELEVATION PROFILES

Each profile includes an elevation scale which approximately graphs the hills and dips on the route in height and distance. Please note that the scales on each profile are dramatically different. Scales may not always begin at an elevation of zero feet and height increments and distance can vary.

ABOUT THE RIDE PROFILES

Each profile includes a narrative description of the ride's setting and terrain. This description also includes mile-by-mile route directions, as well as information about the ride's highlights and unique attributes.

The rides marked by the BEST ◖ symbol are highlighted in the author's Best Bike Rides list.

Options

If alternative routes are available, this section is used to provide information on side trips or note how to shorten or lengthen the ride.

Driving Directions

This section provides detailed driving directions to the start of the route from the nearest major town.

Route Directions

Each profile includes a mile-by-mile listing of what to expect along the trail or road. Every major turn is noted and nearby sights or supplies are indicated where available.

ABOUT THE DIFFICULTY RATING

Each profile includes a difficulty rating. The level of difficulty for any trail can change considerably due to weather or trail conditions. Always phone ahead to check on current trail and weather conditions. The ratings are defined as follows:

1: Suitable for families with young children, novice riders, or those wanting a casual recreational ride. They include both road rides and mountain bike rides that are nearly level and are usually less than 15 miles or have shorter options. Trail surfaces are smooth and most are on bike paths where there is no vehicular traffic.

2: These rides are suitable for families with older children and for strong beginners, i.e. novices who are physically fit. Road rides are generally less than 25 miles and have little elevation gain. Off-road rides may involve some varied surfaces but don't require technical mountain biking skills. Bikers should expect to ride on dirt or grassy trails, dirt roads, and a variety of surfaces.

3: These rides are appropriate for people with solid aerobic fitness and some cycling experience. Road rides are generally less than 30 miles and involve moderate hill climbs. Mountain bike rides will require some basic technical skills, such as the ability to ride over and around rough surfaces (rocks, roots, ruts, water obstacles), descend hills, maneuver through tight turns, follow a narrow line with good balance, etc. Bikers should have moderate experience on a variety of trails, including single-track.

4: These rides are suitable for intermediate riders with excellent aerobic fitness. Road rides are generally 20-40 miles long and involve some steep hill-climbing. Mountain bike rides require technical skills, involve some steep hill climbs and descents, and call for good bike handling skills. Bikers should have solid experience on a variety of trails, including single-track.

5: These are challenging rides for experienced cyclists with excellent aerobic fitness. Road rides have several steep or prolonged hill climbs, and some routes are more than 50 miles. Mountain bike rides are technical, on a variety of surfaces and types of trails, require advanced bike handling skills, may have cyclocross sections, and generally include steep climbs and descents.

INTRODUCTION

Author's Note

When I see an adult on a bicycle, I do not despair for the future of the human race.
—H. G. Wells

It used to be that bicyclists fell into two categories: road cyclists and mountain bikers. The former spent a lot of money on bikes that weighed less than a full water bottle and black Spandex tights that fit like a second skin. They joined cycling clubs and milled around with their compatriots at coffee shops on Sunday mornings, drinking lattes and studying road maps before the day's ride.

The latter saw themselves as rebels, riding fat-tire bikes that were often splattered with mud. They wore baggy shorts and hiking boots and were frequently heard yelling "yahoo" (or something similar) as they cleaned a boulder-lined descent or bunny-hopped over a fallen log. They coined their own phrases, like "eat rocks" and "dual-boing suspension."

At different phases of my life, I have been a card-carrying member of one group or the other. I pedaled century rides on a 19-pound skinny-tire wonder—a jerry-rigged, hand-me-down relic that was coveted by other riders for its all-Campy components. I searched out long and winding country roads and rode them in the good company of friends. In my best moments, I felt like I was a member of the peloton riding in the Tour de France.

Then, after moving to San Francisco and later to Marin County, I switched over to mountain bikes and cruised around the hills and dales of Northern California. I learned the difference between serpentine and granite and schist, and what it feels like to ride on, over, and around those marvelous rocks. I spotted red-tailed hawks and golden eagles, and shared the trails with deer, bears, and bobcats. In my best moments, I felt like I was using a two-wheeled machine to get closer to nature, to travel farther than I could on foot and visit places where automobiles could not go.

It never occurred to me that the twain could ever meet—that my two bicycling selves could shake hands and coexist happily. But somewhere inside a small voice was seeking integration. Why be one thing and not the other? Why not embrace the two biking sports as one? And so this book was born. To me, the beauty of bicycling is its wind-in-the-hair, feeling-like-a-kid-again euphoria, which can be achieved on either road or trail. It is knowing that no matter what ails you in the rest of life—monotonous job, unrequited love, too much housework—all you need do is get on your bike and pedal and everything will feel better.

The 163 rides in this book, plus multiple dozens of options and add-ons, celebrate the all-in-one joy of both road biking and mountain biking. Whether you own both types of bikes or only one or the other, you will find a wealth of rides in these pages that suit your desires and ability level.

Inevitably, you'll also discover my personal biases for scenery and serenity. On trail rides, you'll find waterfalls, ocean views, redwood forests, and summit vistas. (I don't enjoy grinding out miles just for the sake of it.) On paved rides, you'll find more of the same, plus wide shoulders and as few cars as possible. (I don't like riding next to cars that fly by at 60 mph, shaving my legs with hot exhaust.) My guiding rule for choosing bike routes is this: With every ride, on road or trail, I like to return home feeling like I've done something extraordinary with my day.

Happy riding to you.

Best Bike Rides

Of the 163 road and trail rides in this book, here are my favorites in 10 categories:

(Best Butt-Kickers

Lassen Park Road, Shasta and Lassen, page 95. With 4,350 feet of elevation gain, this out-and-back ride through Lassen's volcanic landscape isn't for everybody.

Boonville's Mountain View Road, Mendocino and Wine Country, page 123. The 25-mile-long Mountain View Road runs from Boonville to the Mendocino coast and then back again, with a total 5,600-foot elevation gain.

Cavern to Cavern Loop, Sacramento and Gold Country, page 211. This loop between Murphys, Mercer Caverns, and California Caverns has a 3,800-foot elevation gain on quiet back roads that can get mighty hot in summer.

Sonora Pass Road Ride, Tahoe and Northern Sierra, page 265. If the 3,900 feet of elevation gain from Dardanelle to Sonora Pass isn't enough for you, keep riding to U.S. 395 and then turn back for a 58-mile ride with 6,600 feet of gain.

Woodside to Coast Long Loop, San Francisco Bay Area, page 424. You'll gain 5,800 feet on this 57.1-mile loop through the San Francisco Peninsula, passing redwoods, grasslands, and coastal scenery.

Nacimiento-Fergusson Road to the Mission, Monterey and Big Sur, page 512. This nearly 60-mile ride has a big climb and big descent in both directions, adding up to a total 4,200-foot elevation gain.

(Best Rides for Families

Families should also try any of the Best Paved Bike Paths.

Bizz Johnson Trail, Shasta and Lassen, page 103. The first 6.7 miles of this 25-mile-long railroad grade are easy pedaling along the scenic Susan River canyon, perfect for any kind of rider.

Quarry Road Trail, Sacramento and Gold Country, page 192. The only trail in Auburn State Recreation Area that is suitable for novice mountain bikers, this old road winds along the Middle Fork of the American River.

Sugar Pine Railway, Sacramento and Gold Country, page 214. Two stretches of this old railroad grade, one from Lyons Reservoir and one from Fraser Flat near Strawberry, make excellent easy riding for families.

Bear Valley Trail Bike and Hike, San Francisco Bay Area, page 289. This excursion in Point Reyes National Seashore is easy enough for cyclists of any ability, and leads to a spectacular coastal overlook.

Perimeter Trail and Fire Road Loops, San Francisco Bay Area, page 342. The 5.5-mile, nearly level Perimeter Trail circumnavigates Angel Island in the middle of San Francisco Bay, providing outstanding views and some interesting history lessons.

🄲 Best Rides to High Overlooks

Mount St. Helena, Mendocino and Wine Country, page 145. This 12-mile mountain bike ride takes you up a wide dirt road to the 4,343-foot summit of Mount St. Helena, where the vista on clear days expands over 200 miles.

Martis Peak Lookout and Watson Lake, Tahoe and Northern Sierra, page 231. One of the best views of Lake Tahoe and its environs can be found from the fire lookout tower atop Martis Peak, elevation 8,656 feet.

Mount Diablo Summit Ride, San Francisco Bay Area, page 380. You haven't experienced Mount Diablo's Summit Road until you've ridden it on a bike—all the way to the mountain summit at 3,849 feet, where you can see as far as the Sierra Nevada.

Mount Hamilton, San Francisco Bay Area, page 453. Climb to the top of the Bay Area's loftiest peak, Mount Hamilton at 4,209 feet, where astronomers at Lick Observatory keep a watch on the stars.

Glacier Point Road, Yosemite and Mammoth Lakes, page 529. A ride on Yosemite's Glacier Point Road takes you to one of the grandest views in the West—an overlook directly across from Half Dome and Vernal and Nevada Falls.

🄲 Best Historic Rides

Oak Bottom Channel/Great Water Ditch, Shasta and Lassen, page 82. An easy, smooth single-track along the edge of Whiskeytown Lake, this trail finishes up at the El Dorado Mine buildings, built in 1885.

Bizz Johnson Trail, Shasta and Lassen, page 103. Cyclists ride on the Bizz Johnson Trail today, but in the early 1900s thundering locomotives rumbled through the Susan River canyon, carrying heavy loads of logs and lumber.

Sacramento River Delta, Sacramento and Gold Country, page 204. As you pedal along the Delta's blue, flat-water estuaries, you can recall the days when paddle wheeler steamboats plied these waters, carrying passengers and goods from Sacramento to San Francisco.

Masonic Mountain/Chemung Mine, Tahoe and Northern Sierra, page 271. The Chemung Mine was one of several profitable gold mines near Bridgeport; its stamp mill buildings still stand.

Old Stage Road and Old Railroad Grade to East Peak, San Francisco Bay Area, page 327. Take a ride through Mount Tamalpais history on this eight-mile out-and-back on the old Mount Tamalpais Scenic Railway route, home of the "Crookedest Railroad in the World."

Perimeter Trail and Fire Road Loops, San Francisco Bay Area, page 342. Visit the many remaining buildings on Angel Island, which has had a long and varied history as a military outpost, Russian sea otter hunters' site, and immigrant detention center.

Stewartville and Ridge Trails Loop, San Francisco Bay Area, page 367. Pedal through Black Diamond Mines Regional Preserve, which from 1860 to 1906 was the largest coal-mining district in California.

Aptos Creek Fire Road to Sand Point, Monterey and Big Sur, page 482. The old railroad grade in The Forest of Nisene Marks State Park was built in 1881 and used to haul out every big redwood tree in Aptos Creek Canyon.

◖ Best Oceanfront Rides

Coastal Drive, Redwood Empire, page 45. This eight-mile stretch on gravel and pavement in Redwood National Park offers nonstop sweeping views of the ocean.

Old Haul Road/Ten Mile Coastal Trail, Mendocino and Wine Country, page 112. The Old Haul Road in MacKerricher State Park travels right alongside wide-open beaches, coastal dunes, and rocky coves north of Fort Bragg.

Golden Gate Bridge and Marin Headlands Loop, San Francisco Bay Area, page 345. Ride across the Golden Gate Bridge, visit the Point Bonita Lighthouse, and stop at Black Sand and Rodeo Beaches on this remarkable coastal loop route.

Pescadero and San Gregorio Loop, San Francisco Bay Area, page 434. Pedal south on coastal Highway 1 past Pigeon Point Lighthouse and Whaler's Cove, then loop back through the historic towns of Pescadero and San Gregorio.

Wilder Ranch Bluffs Ride, Monterey and Big Sur, page 476. Cruise along the marine terrace at Wilder Ranch State Park and view sea arches and cliffs, a seal rookery, sandy beaches, and a hidden fern cave.

17-Mile Drive, Monterey and Big Sur, page 497. A seven-mile coastal stretch of the 17-Mile Drive is full of jaw-dropping coastal scenery, plus grand mansions and golf courses, too.

❰ Best Paved Bike Paths

Hammond Trail, Redwood Empire, page 53. A 13-mile out-and-back from Mad River in McKinleyville leads to windswept Clam Beach County Park.

Sacramento River Trail, Shasta and Lassen, page 92. This 10-mile-long, paved path in Redding is the hub of a well-developed trail system in and around town, connecting to sights such as the Turtle Bay Museum and Redding Arboretum.

Eagle Lake Trail, Shasta and Lassen, page 101. Ride your bike on the south shore of Eagle Lake, the second largest natural lake in California and one of the best spots in Northern California for bird-watching.

American River Parkway, Sacramento and Gold Country, page 201. This 32.8-mile-long trail is one of the oldest and longest paved recreation trails in the United States.

Truckee River Recreation Trail, Tahoe and Northern Sierra, page 234. Lake Tahoe has several excellent paved recreation trails, but this pathway along the scenic Truckee River is the best of the lot.

Nimitz Way and Wildcat Canyon, San Francisco Bay Area, page 349. Perched on the tip of San Pablo Ridge in Tilden Park, Nimitz Way Trail offers the best views of any paved trail in the east San Francisco Bay.

Sawyer Camp Recreation Trail, San Francisco Bay Area, page 409. This trail, located in the pristine San Francisco Watershed lands near Hillsborough, travels the length of Lower Crystal Springs Reservoir and leads through marshlands to southern San Andreas Lake.

Monterey Recreation Trail, Monterey and Big Sur, page 494. This 29-mile round-trip trail runs from Marina to Pacific Grove, passing by famous Monterey attractions such as Cannery Row and the Monterey Bay Aquarium.

Yosemite Valley Bike Path, Yosemite and Mammoth Lakes, page 532. The best way to visit car-choked Yosemite Valley is to park your car and ride your bike past its spectacular granite walls and waterfalls.

❰ Best Single-Track Rides

Clikapudi, Shasta and Lassen, page 80. A popular 9.7-mile loop at Lake Shasta, the Clikapudi single-track is manageable for riders of almost any ability.

Downieville Downhill, Sacramento and Gold Country, page 180. Everyone rides these 13.7 miles of single-track as a shuttle trip—all downhill—making this the most popular single-track in the Sierra Nevada.

Pioneer Trail, Sacramento and Gold Country, page 183. If you're in or around Nevada City, this is the perfect single-track for getting a dose of the area's wonderful trail system.

Salmon Falls/Darrington Trail, Sacramento and Gold Country, page 195. If you live anywhere near Sacramento, you've probably ridden this challenging single-track on the South Fork of the American River, which leads to Folsom Lake.

Emigrant Trail, Tahoe and Northern Sierra, page 225. This 15-mile stretch of single-track runs from Stampede Reservoir to Prosser Creek Reservoir, north of Lake Tahoe.

Hole-in-the-Ground Trail, Tahoe and Northern Sierra, page 228. A loop ride near Soda Springs visits two granite-bound swimming lakes and doles out 10-plus miles of exciting single-track.

Middle Ridge Loop, San Francisco Bay Area, page 459. It isn't easy riding in this steep, hot, hilly park, but Henry W. Coe State Park is known to have some of the best single-track in the Bay Area.

Soquel Demonstration State Forest, Monterey and Big Sur, page 485. Miles of gnarly single-track in Soquel Forest twist, turn, and pitch steeply uphill and downhill through dense forests of redwoods, tan oaks, and madrones.

Lower Rock Creek, Yosemite and Mammoth Lakes, page 555. Nearly eight miles of highly technical and sometimes treacherous single-track follow the path of Lower Rock Creek near Tom's Place, south of Mammoth Lakes.

🄲 Best Rides to Waterfalls

Gold Bluffs and Ossagon Trail Loop, Redwood Empire, page 47. This loop ride in Prairie Creek Redwoods State Park travels past three tall, narrow waterfalls, including 80-foot-high Gold Dust Falls.

Fern Canyon Trail Bike and Hike, Mendocino and Wine Country, page 115. On this easy trip for families, ride a paved path and then hike to Russian Gulch Falls, a 36-foot waterfall in Russian Gulch State Park near Mendocino.

Feather Falls, Sacramento and Gold Country, page 177. A smooth and easy single-track takes you to 640-foot Feather Falls, the sixth highest freefalling waterfall in the continental United States and the fourth highest in California.

Berry Creek Falls Bike and Hike, San Francisco Bay Area, page 462. This easy-to-moderate bike-and-hike trip takes you to a 70-foot waterfall in a beautiful redwood forest at Big Basin Redwoods State Park.

Yosemite Valley Bike Path, Yosemite and Mammoth Lakes, page 532. You can practically ride to the base of Lower Yosemite Falls on this bike path in Yosemite Valley.

◖ Best Rides for Wildlife-Viewing

Gold Bluffs and Ossagon Trail Loop, Redwood Empire, page 47. Here in Prairie Creek Redwoods State Park is your best chance of sharing the trail with a 1,000-pound Roosevelt elk (or a whole herd of them).

Lake Almanor Recreation Trail, Shasta and Lassen, page 98. Lake Almanor near Chester boasts the largest summer population of ospreys in California.

Eagle Lake Trail, Shasta and Lassen, page 101. Eagle Lake, the second largest natural lake in California, is a prime spot for bird-watching, particularly for eagles and ospreys.

Boggs Lake Loop, Mendocino and Wine Country, page 136. Boggs Lake is a Nature Conservancy–managed preserve where more than 150 bird species, including bald eagles, have been recorded in winter and spring.

Point Reyes Lighthouse, San Francisco Bay Area, page 292. From December to April, spot gray whales from the Point Reyes Lighthouse coastal promontory and observe elephant seals from an overlook at nearby Chimney Rock.

Stinson Beach and Mount Tamalpais Loop, San Francisco Bay Area, page 324. From mid-March to mid-July, see hundreds of pairs of great white egrets nesting in the trees at Bolinas Lagoon Preserve.

Davenport to Santa Cruz Loop, Monterey and Big Sur, page 470. In autumn and winter, see the spectacle of thousands of monarch butterflies nesting in the eucalyptus trees at Natural Bridges State Beach.

Big Sur to Lucia, Monterey and Big Sur, page 509. Watch for gray whales, dolphins, and sea otters as you pedal down this remarkable stretch of Highway 1 south of Big Sur.

◖ Best Rides for Wine-Tasting

Annapolis Road Loop, Mendocino and Wine Country, page 130. Taste the fruits of their sauvignon blanc, pinot noir, and gewürztraminer grape crop at this out-of-the-way winery near Sea Ranch.

Geyserville Winery Loop, Mendocino and Wine Country, page 133. This road ride leads past a half-dozen major wineries in and around the Alexander Valley.

Healdsburg Westside and Eastside Loop, Mendocino and Wine Country, page 142. Visit the historic Hop Kiln Winery and more than a dozen others on this easy ramble that starts and ends in Healdsburg.

Yountville and Silverado Trail, Mendocino and Wine Country, page 160. You'll pass 10 major wineries on this Wine Country ramble and end your ride at Domaine Chandon, the champagne maker.

Monte Bello Loop, San Francisco Bay Area, page 447. Weekend wine-tasting at Ridge Winery is the reward for the ascent up Monte Bello Road in the Saratoga area.

Davenport to Santa Cruz Loop, Monterey and Big Sur, page 470. Sample the varietals at Beauregard Vineyards in the hills above Santa Cruz on this 31.4-mile road loop.

Biking Tips

BIKING ESSENTIALS

Like the Boy Scout motto says: "Be prepared." It's easy to set off on a bike ride, especially on a trail or road near your home, carrying nothing except your wallet and keys. We've all done it from time to time. But even on the shortest spin through the neighborhood or local park, it's wise to have a few items with you. Some riders carry all of the following items on every ride, some carry only some of the items some of the time. But each of these could prove to be a real lifesaver.

Helmet

They don't call them "brain buckets" for nothing. Don't get on your bike without one; many parks require them, and the ones that don't, should. Just as you wear your seat belt when you drive, wear your helmet when you ride. Make sure yours fits properly and strap it on securely. If you are a woman rider, buy a women's helmet. It will fit your head much better, and a better fit equals better protection for your head.

Food and Water

Being hungry or thirsty spoils a good time, and it can also turn into a potentially dangerous situation. Even if you aren't the least bit hungry or thirsty when you start, you will feel completely different after 30 minutes of riding.

©ANN MARIE BROWN

recumbent bicyclist on Sacramento's American River Parkway

BIKE MAINTENANCE 101

Most of us wouldn't think of neglecting the basic maintenance services our cars need. We fill up our gas tanks, clean our windshields, check our tire pressure, change the oil every few thousand miles, and even treat our cars to a complete tune-up now and then. Our bicycles need to be cared for with the same attentiveness, but too often they aren't. They sit unused in the garage all winter, then on the first sunny spring morning, we impatiently take them out for a spin without so much as checking the tire inflation.

It doesn't take the mind of a mechanic or a workbench full of fancy tools to keep your wheels in tip-top shape. A few clean rags, some lubricant, chain cleaning fluid, and simple tools like a set of Allen wrenches, a tire pump with an accurate gauge, one flathead and one Phillips screwdriver, tire levers (also called tire irons), and pliers will take care of the basics. Riders who want to do more than elementary maintenance will also want a spoke wrench, a chain tool, and a stand to support the bicycle while it is being worked on.

How often should your bike be serviced? It depends on how often and where you ride. Fair-weather riders who stick to paved trails and roads have less maintenance to do than mountain bikers who like to get out in the dirt and mud. Bikes that are ridden three or more times a week need a lot more care than bikes that rarely leave the garage. The following guidelines serve as an "average" maintenance schedule that should be sufficient for most recreational riders:

Before every ride: Check the tire pressure; if it is low, add air. While you're at it, check the tire sidewalls and treads for wear. Make sure that the treads are free of debris. Check that the quick-release levers on your wheel(s)

Always carry at least two water bottles on your bike, and make sure they are full of fresh, clean water when you head out. Add ice on hot days, if you wish. For a two- to three-hour ride, 100 ounces of water is not overkill, especially in summer. Many riders prefer to wear a bladder-style backpack hydration system, which has the extra advantage of providing room to carry a few snacks or car keys. Always bring some food with you, even if it's just a couple of energy bars. If you carry extras to share, you'll be the hero or heroine when you give them to a rider in need.

Clothing

Cycling shorts and cycling gloves will make your trip a lot more comfortable. Cycling gloves have padded palms so the nerves in your hands are protected from the pressure of leaning your upper body weight on the handlebars. Cycling shorts have synthetic chamois or other padding in the saddle area, and it's obvious what function that serves. Look for a bike short with six-panel (or greater) construction—more panels generally equals a more comfortable fit.

On the trail, weather and temperature conditions can change at any time. It are securely fastened. Squeeze both sets of brakes to see if they are working well, and check that the brake pads are squarely hitting the rims, not the tires. Spin the wheels around a few times to make sure they are properly aligned, not wobbling or out of true. Take a look at your chain and derailleurs; if they appear dry, add a touch of lubricant. Wipe off the excess with a rag. If you have clipless pedals, check that they are clean and free of debris so that you can clip in and out efficiently. And, although it seems obvious, don't forget to rinse out your water bottles and refill them.

Every 500 miles or once a month: Wipe off your bike with a rag and inspect the frame and fork for cracks or signs of wear. Clean the chain with a degreaser and then relubricate it. Check the wheel spokes to make sure that none are loose. Use a wrench to check all bolts and screws for tightness. Don't neglect the bolts on the seatpost, stem, handlebars, crank arms, and pedals. Lubricate the cables, brakes, derailleurs, and rotating points on the pedals. If you have suspension components on your bike, check the owner's manual to see how and when the shocks should be lubricated and maintained.

Every 2,500 miles or six months: Check and replace your tires and brake pads if needed. Check all cables for rust, fraying, or wear, and replace as needed. Clean the entire drive train (chain, chainrings, cassette, front and rear derailleurs) with an appropriate solvent. Replace the chain if needed.

Every 5,000 miles or once a year: Take your bike into a bike shop and let an experienced mechanic give it the once-over. For a nominal cost, you'll be able to rest assured that your bike is in great condition for another year of safe and happy riding.

may get windy or start to rain, or you can get too warm as you ride uphill in the sun and then too cold as you ride downhill in the shade. Wear layers. Bring a lightweight jacket and a rain poncho with you. Tie your extra clothes around your waist or put them in a small daypack.

Maps

Sometimes trails and roads are signed, sometimes they're not. Signs get knocked down or disappear with alarming frequency, due to rain, wind, or souvenir hunters. Get a map from the managing agency of the park you're visiting; all their names and phone numbers are listed in this book. For road rides, take along a detailed AAA or other map for the region. A GPS device can be quite handy, too, especially on road rides.

Repair Kit

How many and which tools to carry is a great subject of debate. At the very least, if you're going to be farther than easy walking distance from your car, carry what you need to fix a flat tire. Great distances are covered quickly on a bike. This is never

ACHIEVING PROPER BIKE FIT

It doesn't matter if you ride a $300 bike or a $3,000 bike – if your machine doesn't fit your body, you will be unhappy with your ride. Proper bike fit takes into account the three major areas where your bike and body connect: at your feet, hands, and seat. A bike that doesn't fit right is harder to control, and riding an ill-fitting bike for an extended period of time can lead to aches and pains in the lower back, hips, knees, neck, and shoulders.

The first element of proper bike fit is known as "stand-over height." It is easily checked by simply straddling the bike with both feet on the ground while wearing your usual biking shoes, and then bouncing up and down on your heels. If your crotch touches the frame, the bike is too big for you; you need a bike with a smaller frame size. Minimum stand-over height for riding on pavement is 2 inches. For mountain biking, minimum stand-over height is 3–4 inches.

If your bike's stand-over height is sufficient, the next thing you should check is your saddle position. Saddles can be adjusted in three directions: up and down, forward and back, and angle of tilt. The most important adjustment is height (up or down). Many people ride with their saddles too high, because they believe it gives their legs more power. Over time, this can lead to injuries of the hips, knees, or back. To test for correct seat height, take your shoes off. Have a friend hold your bike steady while you sit on the saddle and turn the pedals until one is all the way up and the other is all the way down. Your bare heel (not your toes) should rest easily on the downward pedal without having to adjust or rock your hips. Your knee should be just slightly bent. Your friend can tell you if you are rocking your hips in order to reach the pedal with your heel. If so, lower your saddle.

Forward and back adjustment, and angle of tilt, are more subjective matters. It is best to start with your seat adjusted so it is in the middle of its rails and horizontal, then make minor adjustments to see what is most comfortable for you. Some bike shops insist that the best way to make a fore/aft adjustment on the saddle is to drop a plumb

©ANN MARIE BROWN

line from the hinge of your knee to your pedal axle, but there is a simpler test: After riding for a few hours, if you find that your arms and shoulders are tired, you may be balancing too much of your weight on your handlebars and front wheel. Try moving your seat back on its rails, which will put more of your weight in your saddle.

Because many bicycle seats are narrow, hard, and just plain uncomfortable, many riders insist on tilting the nose of the saddle down to "take the pressure off." If you feel you have to have a downward saddle tilt to make your ride comfortable, consider buying another saddle. No amount of padding in your cycling shorts can make up for a poorly made or poorly fitting saddle. Women in particular should try out the wider saddles on the market, which are designed for the wider female pelvis. Many even come with a cutout section in the middle, or a foam insert, to take pressure off the pubic bone.

The next important component of bike fit is the height and angle of your handlebars, which is closely related to the adjustment of your saddle. As a general rule, your handlebars should be set at approximately the same height as your saddle. But if your torso and arms are particularly long or short, you may want to raise or lower the handlebars to accommodate your reach. Here's a simple test to check the fit of your handlebars: Standing next to your bike, touch the back of your elbow to the front of your saddle. Place your forearm parallel to the ground, with your fingers reaching toward the handlebars. Your fingertips should come within 2–4 inches of the handlebars. If the distance is greater, you are reaching too far while riding. Get a shorter handlebar stem, tilt your handlebars, move your saddle slightly

forward, or try any combination of these three adjustments. Pay attention to your hands on longer rides; if you find yourself sitting up and steering with the tips of your fingers, your "reach" needs adjustment. On the other hand, if your handlebars are too low, you will have to strain to keep your head up and your eyes on the road, and your neck and upper back will be tense or uncomfortable when you ride.

Finally, the positioning of your brake and shifting levers should be in sync with the size of your hands and fingers. If you have small hands and find it difficult to reach the brake or shift levers, change the position of the controls on the handlebars.

Women riders who are considering a new bike purchase should give some serious thought to buying a women-specific frame. Almost every major bike manufacturer now makes women-specific bikes. While some simply modify a stock "unisex" frame by switching to a shorter stem, smaller handlebars, shorter cranks, and a wider saddle, others take a more comprehensive approach, taking into account that the average woman (and there are plenty of exceptions to "average") has a shorter torso, shorter arms, and longer legs than a man of the same height. Also, a woman's hands and feet are usually smaller, her shoulders are narrower, and her hips are wider than a comparably sized man. For many female riders, having a frame that was designed with women-specific geometry makes a huge difference in terms of bike handling and power. But remember that not all women are built the same; for some, a man's frame may fit just fine. Always test-ride a variety of different types of bikes before handing over your hard-earned cash.

more apparent than when a tire goes flat 30 minutes into a ride and it takes two hours to walk back. So why walk? Carry a spare tube, a patch kit, tire levers, and a bike pump attached to your bike frame. Make sure you know how to use them.

Many riders also carry a small set of metric wrenches, Allen wrenches, and a couple of screwdrivers, or some type of all-in-one bike tool. These are good for adjusting derailleurs and the angle on your bike seat, making minor repairs, and fidgeting with brake and gear cables. If you're riding on dirt trails, carry extra chain lubricant with you, or at least keep some in your car. Some riders carry a few additional tools, such as a spoke wrench for tightening loose spokes or a chain tool to fix a broken chain.

Sunscreen and Sunglasses

Wear both. Apply sunscreen 30 minutes before you go outdoors so it has time to take effect and reapply often—at least every two hours, more frequently if you are perspiring.

Bike Lock

It comes in handy if you want to stop for anything. Many of the trails in this book combine a bike ride with a short hike or a visit to a winery, museum, or historic site. If you are planning to stop anywhere, even to use a restroom, a bike lock is valuable. Never leave your bike unlocked and unattended.

First Aid and Emergencies

Like most of life, bicycling is a generally safe activity that in the mere bat of an eye can become hazardous. The unexpected occurs—a rock in the trail, a sudden change in road surface, a misjudgment or momentary lack of attention—and suddenly, you and your bike are sprawled on the ground. Sooner or later it happens to everyone who rides. Usually, you look around nervously to see if anybody saw you, dust yourself off, and get back on your bike. But it's wise to carry a few emergency items just in case your accident is more serious: A few large and small Band-Aids, antibiotic cream, and an Ace bandage can be valuable tools. I also carry a Swiss Army knife, one with several blades, a can opener, and scissors. If I don't need it for first aid, I'll use it for bike repairs or picnics. Finally, it's a good idea to carry matches in a waterproof container and a candle, just in case you ever need to build a fire in a serious emergency.

Some riders carry a cell phone everywhere they go, but be forewarned that this is not a foolproof emergency device. You won't get cell reception in some areas, particularly in nonurban places. Carry a cell phone and hope it will work, but don't rely on it.

Always bring along a few bucks so you can make a phone call from a pay phone or buy food or drinks for yourself or someone who needs them.

MOUNTAIN BIKING BASICS

First-time mountain bike riders are always surprised at how much time they spend walking instead of riding. They walk their bike up steep grades, down steep grades, and in level places where the terrain is too rugged. Mountain bikers frequently have to deal with rocks, boulders, tree roots, sand traps, holes in the ground, stream crossings, eroded trails, and so on. Often the best way to deal with these obstacles is to walk and push your bike. Becoming familiar with these and other basics of the trail can help ensure a fun ride, instead of a frustrating one.

- If something looks scary, dismount and walk. If you are unsure of your ability to stay in control while heading downhill or your capacity to keep your balance on a rough surface, dismount and walk. It will save you plenty of Band-Aids.

- Learn to shift gears before you need to. This takes some practice, but you'll soon find that it's easier to shift before you're halfway up the hill and the pedals and chain are under pressure. When you see a hill coming up ahead, downshift.

- Play around with the height of your seat. When the seat is properly adjusted, you will have a slight bend in your knee while your leg is fully extended on the lower of the two pedals.

- Take it easy on the handlebar grips. Many beginners squeeze the daylights out of their handlebars, which leads to hand, arm, shoulder, and upper back discomfort. Grip the handlebars loosely and keep a little bend in your elbows.

- Learn to read the trail ahead of you, especially on downhills. Keep your eyes open for rocks or ruts, which can take you by surprise and upset your balance.

- Go slowly. As long as you never exceed the speed at which you feel comfortable and in control, you'll be fine. This doesn't mean that you shouldn't take a few chances, but it's unwise to take chances until you are ready.

- Experienced riders can maneuver their bikes on nearly any terrain, but good technical ability also means managing your speed. Especially when riding on trails shared by hikers, dogs, and horses, it's important to use brakes wisely. Brake before you enter turns or corners so you can ride through them *without* braking. Braking during a turn or curve causes you to lock up your rear wheel and skid or slide. Sliding lessens your control over the bike and is very destructive to the trail. Ride it; don't slide it, or you'll make yourself very unpopular with people who love trails.

• Use the front brake simultaneously and in combination with the back brake to slow you down. But don't pull too hard on the front brake or you'll go over the handlebars. Remember that 70 percent of your braking force is in your front brake.

• Learn to move your weight back and lift up your front wheel to get it over obstacles, like rocks or bumps. Otherwise, your front wheel can get trapped, causing you to fly over the handlebars. Your back wheel will usually roll over obstacles.

• Lean inside and forward into turns and curves. This keeps your center of gravity over your tires.

• On downhills, get your rear end as far back on the bike as possible—behind the seat and over the back tire if you can on extreme downhill pitches.

• When you are approaching a long, steep downhill, stop for a moment and lower your seat. You want to be able to stand on your pedals in a crouched position without the seat getting in the way.

• Never ride in mud; your tire tracks will encourage erosion. Walk your bike around muddy areas; don't ride around them and create an even wider trail.

ON THE TRAIL
Mountain Biking Etiquette

Mountain bikes are great. They give you an alternative to pavement, a way out of the concrete jungle. They guarantee your freedom from auto traffic. They take you into the woods and the wild, to places of natural beauty.

On the other hand, mountain bikes are the cause of a lot of controversy. In the past 20 years, mountain bikers have shown up on trails that were once the exclusive domain of hikers and horseback riders. Some say the peace and quiet has been shattered. Some say that trail surfaces are being ruined by the weight and force of mountain bikes. Some say that mountain bikes are too fast and clumsy to share the trail with other types of users.

Much of the debate can be resolved if bikers follow a few simple rules, and if nonbikers practice a little tolerance. The following are guidelines for low-impact,

©ANN MARIE BROWN

view from Perimeter Trail, Angel Island State Park

"soft cycling." If you obey them, you'll help to give mountain biking the good name it deserves:

1. **Ride only on trails where bikes are permitted.** Obey all signs and trail closures.

2. **Yield to equestrians.** Horses can be badly spooked by bicyclists, so give them plenty of room. If horses are approaching you, stop alongside the trail until they pass. If horses are traveling in your direction and you need to pass them, call out politely to the rider and ask permission. If the horse moves off the trail and the rider tells you it's okay, then pass.

3. **Yield to hikers.** Bikers travel much faster than hikers. Understand that you have the potential to scare the daylights out of hikers as you speed downhill around a curve and overtake them from behind, or when you race at them head-on. Make sure you give other trail users plenty of room, and keep your speed down when you are near them. If you see a hiker, slow down to a crawl, or even stop.

4. **Be as friendly and polite as possible.** Potential ill will can be eliminated by friendly greetings as you pass: "Hello, beautiful day today... " Always say thank you to other trail users for allowing you to pass.

FIXING A FLAT

There's no reason for a flat tire to ruin your ride. If you carry the proper tools with you when you ride, a flat tire will cause you only a few minutes' delay – just enough time to get out of the saddle, take a good look at the scenery, and enjoy a short breather.

Two things to keep in mind: First, remember that most flat tires are directly or indirectly caused by improper inflation (not enough air pressure). If you check your tire pressure before every ride and add air if necessary, you will have fewer flat tires. Second, make sure you are prepared to deal with a flat if you get one. Always carry a new tube, a patch kit, a set of plastic tire levers (also called tire irons), and a pump. The total weight of these items is far less than one pound.

If a tire goes flat, *stop riding immediately*, before you damage your wheel rims. Then, remove the remaining air in the "bad" tire by pressing on the valve and squeezing the tire. Take the wheel off the bike. If you have quick-release levers on your wheels, you're in luck. If not, you'll need to carry a wrench with you to release the wheel nuts. You'll also probably have to disconnect the brake cables on the affected wheel. To do so, squeeze the brakes together, then unhook the brake cable.

Now, consider the most elementary of tire-fixing facts: You don't really have a flat tire, you have a flat tube, which is the rubber circular "thing" that is inside your bike's tire. So you have to get access to that tube. Insert one tire lever between the metal rim and the exterior tire, being careful not to pinch the inner tube. Insert the other tire lever about two inches away from the first (on the same side of the wheel) and push down on both. The tire will start to pop off the rim. Work your way around the tire until one edge of it is completely off the rim. Push the valve stem through the rim and the tube will come out of the tire.

At this juncture you have two choices. If you're in a rush, you can simply replace the punctured tube with the spare tube you brought with you. Before doing so, *carefully* feel around the inside of the tire to make sure that the flat-causing glass, metal, wire, or thorn isn't still in there, or you'll get another flat as soon as you start riding. If you can't find any foreign debris, check the wheel itself for sharp spots and to make sure none of the spokes are poking through. Partially inflate the tube so that you can reinsert it into the tire. Start by inserting the valve stem into the valve hole, then use your fingers to tuck the tube into

5. Avoid riding on wet trails. Bike tires leave ruts in wet soil that accelerate erosion. This makes bikers very unpopular with park managers and other trail users. Don't ride a trail immediately after a downpour or, in places like Tahoe and Shasta, too soon after snowmelt.

6. Riders going downhill should always yield to riders going uphill on narrow trails. Get out of their way so they can keep their momentum as they climb.

Protecting the Outdoors

Take good care of this beautiful land you're riding on. The primary rules are to the tire. Don't let it twist or fold back on itself.

Work one side of the tire back onto the wheel rim, preferably using only your fingers (use your tire lever only if desperate). Then do the other side, being careful not to pinch the tube. If you are having trouble getting the tire back on the rim, let some air out of the tube. When it's back together, put the wheel back on the bike, fully inflate the tire, put the valve cap back on, and reconnect the brake cable. Voilà! You are ready to ride.

Or, if you'd rather fix the punctured tube, examine it carefully to find the hole. If you can't see it, pump up the tube and hold it close to your cheek or lips until you can "feel" the spot from which the air is escaping. Some riders swear by over-inflating the tube, which makes it easier to find the puncture. When you find it, mark the spot with a pen or tape so you don't lose it again. Now, follow the directions in your patch kit exactly. Patience and attention to detail are key to getting a good patch. Most kits come with a small file or piece of sandpaper to "rough up" the area surrounding the puncture. Don't skip this step, as it helps the patch glue to adhere. Also, make sure you wait the required time for the glue to set up before applying the patch, or it won't stick well. Apply plenty of pressure, and hold the pressure for the prescribed length of time. A properly applied patch will last forever and is often the strongest part of the tube. A tube with multiple patches can actually be stronger than a brand-new tube! Last but not least, make sure you remove the flat-causing culprit from the inside of the tire before reinserting your newly patched tube, as described above.

If you get a lot of flat tires, ask yourself if you are checking your tire inflation before you ride. If you still get lots of flats, consider installing a tire liner made of Kevlar between the tube and the tire. Or you can purchase thorn-resistant tubes, which are thicker than regular tubes. Both options will weigh down your wheels somewhat, but if you're cycling in the cactus-ridden desert, it might be worth it. A product called Slime is another good flat-fighter; it's a nontoxic solution you put inside your tires that automatically seals small punctures. Finally, Specialized makes a brand of tires called Armadillo, which are basically bullet-proof, although they do result in a somewhat harsher ride. Armadillo tires are available for both road and mountain bikes in a huge variety of styles designed for various conditions (hardpack, loam, pavement, multi-terrain, etc.).

leave no trace of your visit, to pack out all your trash, and to try not to disturb animal or plant life. But you can go the extra mile and pick up any litter that you see on the trail or road. Carry an extra bag to hold the litter you collect until you get to a trash receptacle, or just keep an empty pocket for that purpose.

If you have the extra time or energy, you can join a trail organization in your area or spend some time volunteering in your local park. Biking and hiking trails need constant upkeep and maintenance, and most of the work gets done by volunteers. Anything you do to help this lovely planet will be repaid to you, many times over.

Land of the tallest trees, dwelling place of the giants, the Redwood Empire is home to some of the largest remaining stands of old-growth *Sequoia sempervirens,* or coast redwoods. These magnificent trees grow to more than 350 feet tall and live as long as 2,000 years, contributing to one of the most unique habitat areas in California.

These behemoth trees bring people from all over the world to the Redwood Empire. Although the area boasts a rugged and beautiful coastline, quaint towns like Arcata and Trinidad, and wide, free-flowing rivers, the redwoods draw the visitors. Nowhere else in California can you gaze up at such an abundance of the world's tallest living things.

Although a redwood forest is considered to be a monosystem, many other plants live alongside the big trees, including ferns of all kinds, vine maples, huckleberry, salmonberry, and redwood sorrel. Visitors frequently say they get the feeling these woods are alive; in fact, they are more alive than almost any other place on earth. Per square inch of land surface, redwood forests have the greatest volume of living matter of any ecosystem in the world.

The Redwood Empire also features a wealth of wildlife, most notably its herds of giant Roosevelt elk. An adult male elk can weigh more than 1,000 pounds; their larger-than-life stature and huge antlers seem strangely appropriate among the giant redwoods. It's not uncommon to spot elk grazing while riding your bike, on road or trail. Although they seem gentle, give them plenty of room.

Black bears also roam the redwood forests, searching for acorns and

REDWOOD EMPIRE

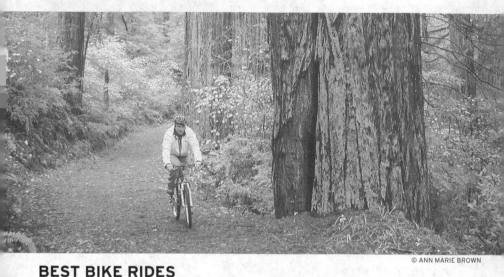

BEST BIKE RIDES

berries. Mountain lions and bobcats prefer the high grassland prairies, which are also good birding spots. The rivers and streams of the Redwood Empire, particularly the Smith and Klamath Rivers, are renowned for steelhead and salmon fishing.

No wonder these precious resources are preserved under the umbrella of Redwood National and State Parks, a co-managed park system that extends for 50 miles up the California coast and includes Redwood National Park, Jedediah Smith Redwoods State Park, Prairie Creek Redwoods State Park, and Del Norte Coast Redwoods State Park. More parks lie in the southern reaches of the Redwood Empire: Humboldt Redwoods and Sinkyone Wilderness State Parks, plus the Bureau of Land Management's King Range National Conservation Area. Clearly this is land worth protecting.

Although the area is infamous for rain, the summer months in the Redwood Empire are actually quite dry. The region receives an average of 69 inches of rain per year – almost six feet – but 90 percent of it occurs November–March. Summer can be foggy, but this dense marine layer brings life-giving moisture to the giant redwoods, allowing them to grow to their lofty heights.

Always carry extra layers when cycling in the redwoods, since fog, wind, rain, and sunshine can be encountered all in one day, or in one bike ride. Also, consider wearing yellow-tinted sunglasses when riding in the deep shade of the big trees; most riders agree that these glasses noticeably improve visibility.

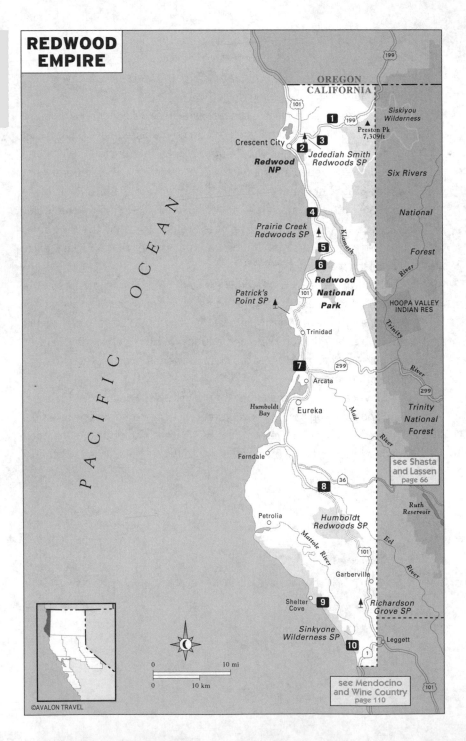

REDWOOD EMPIRE

TRAIL NAME	LEVEL	DISTANCE	TIME	ELEVATION	PAGE
1 Gasquet Toll Road	4	25 mi	5 hr	2,100 ft	36
2 Howland Hill Road	1	10.4 mi	1.5 hr	400 ft	39
3 Little Bald Hills Loop	3	18 mi	3.5–4 hr	1,900 ft	42
4 Coastal Drive	1	16.4 mi	2.5 hr	800 ft	45
5 Gold Bluffs and Ossagon Trail Loop	3	19 mi	4 hr	900 ft	47
6 Holter Ridge/Lost Man Creek Loop	4	19.5 mi	4 hr	2,200 ft	50
7 Hammond Trail	1	13 mi	1 hr	400 ft	53
8 Avenue of the Giants and Mattole Road	2	44.2 mi	4 hr	1,000 ft	55
9 Chemise Mountain	3	6.4 mi	1.5 hr	1,000 ft	58
10 Hotel Gulch Trail	3	12.6 mi	2.5 hr	2,400 ft	60

1 GASQUET TOLL ROAD
Smith River National Recreation Area, east of Crescent City

DIRT ROAD AND PAVED ROAD WITH MINIMAL CAR TRAFFIC

Difficulty: 4	**Total Distance:** 25 miles
Riding Time: 5 hours	**Elevation Gain:** 2,100 feet

Summary: Views of the Smith River and Oregon's Siskiyou Range can be seen from the lonely Gasquet Toll Road.

Gasquet (pronounced GAS-key) is one of the best small towns for outdoors enthusiasts in Northern California. Located on U.S. 199 just a few miles east of the Redwood National and State Parks and right on the Wild and Scenic Smith River, Gasquet is the main supply point for visitors to the Smith River National Recreation Area. It is home to a wonderful historic lodge and restaurant (Patrick Creek Lodge, 707/457-3323, www.patrickcreeklodge.net) and a 1950s-throwback diner serving unforgettable malts and milk shakes (She-She's, 707/457-3434). It's the kind of place where most of the talk centers on fishing (for steelhead, mostly).

©AVALON TRAVEL

© ANN MARIE BROWN

cresting the high point on Gasquet Toll Road

And it's also the start of the Gasquet Toll Road, a dirt road that in 1887 linked Crescent City with Waldo, Oregon. The road's owner, an enterprising Frenchman named Horace Gasquet, extracted a toll from stagecoach wagons on the route and made himself a wealthy man.

The road is open to cars, but you'll probably see only a handful on your ride. Today the road is purely for recreational use; it doesn't go anywhere. The surface is dirt and gravel, but it's not always hard-packed. In some areas, you'll experience minor technical challenges just from maintaining traction amid millions of small, loose rocks.

From Gasquet, the road climbs through mostly logged forests to higher, denser forests of madrone, cedar, manzanita, and toyon. By mile 9.0, the highest point of the loop, you gain great views of the Siskiyou Range in Oregon, which is snow covered much of the year. From the road's edge, you can peer down at the scenic Smith River canyon far below.

After a 2-mile downhill, at 11.5 miles you start to climb again. Finally, the road junctions with Patrick Creek Road at a picnic area with percolation ponds left from mining days. The last 3.5 miles on dirt road parallel lovely Patrick Creek on a downhill grade and bring you out behind historic Patrick Creek Lodge, a perfect stop for a meal or a drink.

To finish the loop, you must ride the final 7.5 miles on busy U.S. 199, but fortunately the road has wide shoulders and a fast, mostly downhill grade. Along the way, you might want to stop at the Botanical Trail sign on your side of the highway. Walk the 0.25-mile Darlingtonia Trail to see the unusual California pitcher plant, which traps insects and other small organisms in its cobra-like hood.

For more information, contact Smith River National Recreation Area, 707/457-3131.

Driving Directions

From U.S. 101 north of Crescent City, turn east on U.S. 199 and drive 15 miles to Gasquet. Park near the junction of U.S. 199 and Middle Fork/Gasquet Road (the Smith River National Recreation Area visitor center is 0.25 mile farther east on U.S. 199).

Route Directions

0.0 Park in Gasquet. Mileage starts at the junction of U.S. 199 and Middle Fork/Gasquet Road. Ride north on Middle Fork/Gasquet Road. *Supplies are available in Gasquet.*

0.2 RIGHT at fork, go past the Gasquet Memorial Bridge.

0.3 STRAIGHT (left fork) on North Fork Road.

0.6 RIGHT on Gasquet Toll Road. Pass the dump site; the road turns to gravel.

2.8 LEFT and head uphill at the fork.

3.0 RIGHT to stay on Gasquet Toll Road.

4.0 Road levels for next three miles.

4.9 Bridged creek crossing.

9.0 Highest stretch of the ride; great views of Siskiyou Mountains in Oregon.

14.0 RIGHT at fork with picnic area and percolation ponds; road becomes Patrick Creek Road.

14.4 STRAIGHT at junction.

15.0 Road surface turns to mixed pavement and gravel.

17.5 RIGHT on U.S. 199; Patrick Creek Lodge is on the right. *Supplies are available.*

21.6 Botanical Trail on the right. *Walk the 0.25-mile trail to see rare California pitcher plants.*

25.0 Arrive at starting point.

2 HOWLAND HILL ROAD

Jedediah Smith Redwoods State Park, east of Crescent City

DIRT ROAD WITH MINIMAL CAR TRAFFIC

Difficulty: 1

Riding Time: 1.5 hours

Total Distance: 10.4 miles

Elevation Gain: 400 feet

Summary: Old-growth redwoods and an understory of giant ferns envelope you on this easy dirt-road ride.

Howland Hill Road has one of the most incredible fern displays in the Redwood Empire, and for that reason alone you should take this easy bike ride. If that isn't enough to motivate you, consider that the ferns grow in the understory of one of the finest old-growth redwood groves in northwestern California. To ride here is to be wowed by the trees.

One negative factor may plague your trip: You'll have to deal with some car traffic on Howland Hill Road, a dirt road that is open to passenger vehicles but closed to trailers and motor homes. In summer, the region gets the heaviest traffic. For the least amount of cars and the greatest chance of seeing the majestic redwoods in peace, visit between October and May.

The route is simple: Just ride up Howland Hill Road until about a mile beyond the Stout Grove, then turn back. The final mile, as you leave the big trees, provides some nice views of the Smith River. In one direction or the other, lock up your bike at the Stout Grove parking lot and walk its 0.5-mile trail through a particularly dense grove of redwoods. The Stout Tree is the largest among them, but when trees are this big, no single giant stands out much from the other giants.

For more information, contact Jedediah Smith Redwoods State Park, 707/464-6101 or 707/445-6547, www.parks.ca.gov. or www.nps.gov/redw.

Options

If the Stout Grove has whetted your appetite for more hiking among the big trees,

an enormous stump on Howland Hill Road

check out the Boy Scout Tree Trail at mile 1.9. This 6-mile round-trip trail tunnels through another grove of immense redwoods and ends at a small waterfall.

Driving Directions

From U.S. 101 in Crescent City, turn east on Elk Valley Road and drive 1.1 miles, then turn right on Howland Hill Road. Drive 1.8 miles to a road gate (signed for Stout Grove, 4.0 miles), where there are small pullouts on the left. The pavement turns to dirt and gravel.

Route Directions

0.0 Park in the pullouts 1.8 miles up Howland Hill Road, by the gate (usually open). *Supplies are available in Crescent City.*

1.9 Boy Scout Tree Trailhead.

2.7 Bridge crossing.

4.0 Stout Grove turnoff on the left. *Lock up your bike and take this short walk through the big trees.*

4.8 Little Bald Hills Trail on the right. (See ride 3, *Little Bald Hills Loop*.)

5.2 Dirt turns to pavement. TURN AROUND.

10.4 Arrive at starting point.

3 LITTLE BALD HILLS LOOP
Redwood National Park, east of Crescent City

DIRT ROAD AND PAVED ROAD WITH MODERATE CAR TRAFFIC

Difficulty: 3

Total Distance: 18 miles (or 19.6-mile option)

Riding Time: 3.5-4 hours

Elevation Gain: 1,900 feet

Summary: This long loop through Redwood National Park passes through a variety of ecosystems, including a high grassland prairie.

Check your calendar before you set out to ride the Little Bald Hills Trail. The trail is closed every winter November–May to help prevent the spread of Port Orford cedar rot, a fungal disease that travels by spores, which can be carried on muddy bike or car tires, hiking boots, and horse hooves. The disease has taken out thousands of Port Orford cedars in Oregon and Northern California, and the National Park Service is determined to minimize its effects in Redwood National Park. That's why this trail is closed in winter and open for riding only June–October, when the ground is dry and there's no danger of spreading the cedar fungus. Fair enough.

The loop follows South Fork Road alongside the clear, aqua-colored South Fork of the Smith River, climbing ever so slightly. A right turn on dirt Little Bald Hills Trail takes you uphill through several grueling switchbacks to a high, grassy prairie fringed by firs and pines. If you've been riding your bike around the nearby damp redwood forests, it's hard to believe how dry, and even sunny and hot, it can get up here.

From the ridgeline, the rocky and sometimes narrow old roadbed makes a 1,900-foot drop over 4.5 miles back to the land of big redwoods and Howland Hill Road. A right turn brings you back to South Fork Road in a flash.

© ANN MARIE BROWN

descending through the redwoods on Little Bald Hills Loop

Even though the descent on Little Bald Hills Trail is fast and well deserved, try to keep your speed down, especially if riding in springtime. The wildflowers that bloom in these hills' dry serpentine soils put on a remarkable show. Little Bald Hills Camp at mile 12.9 is also worth a look; the small backpacking camp sits on the site of the former Murphy Ranch, where in the late 1800s a hotel served travelers along this former mining route.

For more information, contact Redwood National Park, 707/464-6101, www.nps.gov/redw.

Options

A side trip to the Stout Grove at mile 16.4 adds only 1.6 miles to your round-trip. Don't miss paying homage to these giants, including the 340-foot Stout Tree.

Driving Directions

From U.S. 101 north of Crescent City, turn east on U.S. 199 and drive 6.8 miles to South Fork Road. Turn right and park in pullouts along the first 0.5 mile of road.

Route Directions

0.0 Park in pullouts alongside South Fork Road near Tryon Bridge. Ride south on South Fork Road; Mileage begins at Tryon Bridge. *Supplies are available in Hiouchi or Crescent City.*

7.3 RIGHT on dirt connector to Little Bald Hills Trail (just before Rock Creek Bridge; may be unsigned).

12.9 Little Bald Hills Camp turnoff; camp is 100 yards away. *Water is sometimes available.*

16.4 RIGHT on Howland Hill Road; gravel turns to pavement and road becomes Douglas Park Road. *Turn LEFT at this junction for 1.6-mile optional round-trip side trip to Stout Grove redwoods.*

18.0 Arrive at starting point.

COASTAL DRIVE

BEST **⊂**

Redwood National Park near Klamath

DIRT AND PAVED ROAD WITH MINIMAL CAR TRAFFIC

Difficulty: 1   **Total Distance:** 16.4 miles (or 30.4-mile option)

Riding Time: 2.5 hours   **Elevation Gain:** 800 feet

Summary: For coast lovers, a long, mellow stretch on gravel and pavement offers nonstop ocean views.

The scenic Coastal Drive road is often missed by auto tourists traveling the Redwood National and State Parks because it's not particularly well marked at U.S. 101. On two trips here, I've shared the road with only a handful of other cars. This makes Coastal Drive a perfect thoroughfare for cyclists.

The road is a gravel and pavement mix, so mountain bikes are recommended, although some road bike tires could handle it. It begins near the small town of Klamath and heads west, winding through redwoods along the Klamath River's estuary and beyond to its mouth, before reaching the coastline and heading south. At mile 3.3 is an interesting historic site: Radar Station B-71, two concrete block buildings that were camouflaged during World War II to look like a farmhouse and barn. Shortly beyond, the High Bluff Picnic Area affords sweeping views of the ocean. Whales, sea lions, and pelicans are frequently seen.

This out-and-back ride is not without hills; a real doozy shows up around 1.9 miles as the road turns south.(This 0.5-mile stretch may require pushing your bike.) The remainder of the ride rolls up and down with a gradual uphill to Coastal Drive's junction with Newton B. Drury Scenic Parkway. You can extend the ride by pedaling on the parkway (see *Options*), but most riders are content just to turn around and enjoy Coastal Drive's Pacific scenery one more time. The way back is almost effortless.

For more information, contact Redwood National Park, 707/464-6101, www. nps.gov/redw.

Options

Ambitious riders can tack on another 14 miles out and back on the parkway to Prairie Creek Redwoods State Park's visitor center. The road leads through beautiful redwood groves, but sees moderate to heavy tourist traffic.

Driving Directions

From U.S. 101 at Klamath, drive south across the Klamath River and turn right on Klamath Beach Road/Coastal Drive. Drive two miles and park near the junction with Alder Camp Road (near the Flint Ridge Trail's east end).

Route Directions

0.0 Park near junction of Klamath Beach Road and Alder Camp Road in pullouts alongside the road. *Supplies are available in Klamath.*

1.9 Beach at mouth of Klamath River and start of steep hill.

2.3 Flint Ridge Trail on left.

3.3 Radar Station B-71.

6.8 Overlook point.

8.2 End of Coastal Drive at junction with Newton B. Drury Scenic Parkway. TURN AROUND. *Or add on a 14-mile out-and-back on the parkway to Prairie Creek Redwoods State Park's visitor center.*

16.4 Arrive at starting point.

5 GOLD BLUFFS AND OSSAGON TRAIL LOOP

BEST ☾

Prairie Creek Redwoods State Park near Orick

DIRT ROADS AND SINGLE-TRACK; PAVED ROADS WITH MODERATE CAR TRAFFIC

Difficulty: 3   **Total Distance:** 19 miles

Riding Time: 4 hours   **Elevation Gain:** 900 feet

Summary: You'll share this spectacular mountain biking trail with 1,000-pound Roosevelt elk.

Prairie Creek Redwoods State Park is a shining jewel in the Redwood National and State Park system, which includes the national park itself and three state parks, all jointly managed. Prairie Creek's resident herd of Roosevelt elk and spectacular Fern Canyon area set it a cut above the other first-class parks in the neighborhood.

But what bikers love best about Prairie Creek Redwoods State Park is the Gold Bluffs and Ossagon Trail Loop, a 19-mile loop that serves up a terrific half-day adventure for intermediate-level riders. This ride has as much to offer as a half-dozen others combined: windswept beaches, up-close encounters with Roosevelt elk, hidden waterfalls, and giant redwoods.

Most riders start at the Prairie Creek Redwoods Visitor Center, but you could also start at Fern Canyon. The loop can be ridden in either direction, but if you prefer to climb on pavement and descend on dirt, use the route directions below, which follow the loop counterclockwise. The first leg heads north on Newton B. Drury Scenic Parkway, which has a fairly wide shoulder and gentle

A Roosevelt elk crosses Davison Road on the Gold Bluffs and Ossagon Trail Loop.

uphill grade. The big redwoods lining this stretch are awe-inspiring; this is a road that every non-cyclist should at least drive.

Watch for Ossagon Trail on the left, across from and just beyond the more obvious Hope Creek/Ten Taypo Trailhead. Next comes the single-track stretch of the loop. You might push your bike over the first steep 0.25 mile uphill, but then prepare for a fast descent of 700 feet in about a mile. (Please watch for hikers.) A set of railroad-tie stair steps and a bridge over Ossagon Creek will slow you down and force you to dismount.

The trail leads to an alder thicket at the creek mouth, where you turn left and follow Coastal Trail south. The narrow path cuts through forest and opens out to a coastal prairie, the grazing grounds of Roosevelt elk. Give these animals a wide berth; although they seem gentle and disinterested in humans, you don't want to get on the bad side of a 1,000-pound creature with big antlers.

Following an inland route along the prairie's edge, you have a chance to see three 80-foot-tall, thinly streaming waterfalls that drop just a few feet off the trail, hidden in the forest. Listen for their sound and watch for their narrow spur trails. The best of the lot is Gold Dust Falls, found at 9.2 miles.

Where the trail deposits you at Fern Canyon parking area, lock up your bike and take the 0.25-mile walk into this incredible stream canyon with 40-foot-high fern-covered walls; it's like nothing you've seen anywhere else. Then follow gravel Davison Road alongside windswept Gold Bluffs Beach (watch for car traffic on the one-lane road and gravel dust in summer) to Steelow Creek Trail, your ticket back to the park campground and visitor center.

For more information, contact Prairie Creek Redwoods State Park, 707/464-6101 or 707/445-6547, www.parks.ca.gov or www.nps.gov/redw.

Driving Directions

From Eureka, drive north on U.S. 101 for 41 miles to Orick. Continue north for 5 more miles, then take the Newton B. Drury Scenic Parkway exit and turn left. Follow the signs for 1 mile to the Prairie Creek Redwoods State Park Visitor Center. Drive past the entrance kiosk to the day-use parking area.

Route Directions

0.0 Park in the day-use parking area near the visitor center. Ride back out the park road to Newton B. Drury Scenic Parkway and turn left; mileage begins there. *Supplies are available in Orick; water is available at the trailhead.*

6.1 LEFT on Ossagon Trail; steep climb uphill.

7.8 LEFT on Coastal Trail.

8.7 LEFT at fork to stay on inland trail.

9.2 Gold Dust Falls (and two other waterfalls within 0.25 mile on either side). *Gold Dust Falls is hidden a few yards off the main trail in the forest; look for a spur trail leading to it.*

10.6 Fern Canyon parking area and trailhead. *Lock up your bike and hike the 0.5-mile trail into this amazing canyon.*

10.7 Follow gravel Davison Road past Gold Bluffs Beach and campground.

15.3 LEFT on Steelow Creek Trail (previously named Jogging Trail).

17.2 LEFT on Steelow Creek Trail/Davison Trail.

18.2 Trail's end at campground's trailer dump site. Follow park road straight ahead.

19.0 Arrive at starting point.

GOLD BLUFFS AND OSSAGON TRAIL LOOP

6 HOLTER RIDGE/LOST MAN CREEK LOOP
Redwood National Park near Orick

DIRT ROAD AND PAVED ROAD WITH MODERATE CAR TRAFFIC

Difficulty: 4   **Total Distance:** 19.5 miles

Riding Time: 4 hours   **Elevation Gain:** 2,200 feet

Summary: Old-growth giants and a high ridge with ocean views are highlights of this varied ride in Redwood National Park.

The Holter Ridge/Lost Man Creek Loop is a fickle trail. Every few miles, the nature of the ride changes so dramatically that it always takes you by surprise—even if you know it's coming. And therein lies the fun of this challenging ride.

The first 1.3 miles are almost perfectly level, paralleling gurgling Lost Man Creek. A couple of bridge crossings offer eye-opening peeks into the beautiful stream canyon. Centuries-old trees are everywhere you look, moss hangs from the alders, ferns grow to immense sizes. The trail is an old gravel roadbed, smooth as silk and often covered with fallen leaves and soft needles. The only obstacles are bright yellow and green banana slugs; try to avoid squashing them as they inch across the road.

Abruptly, the old road starts to climb, and it does so on a brutal grade—1,400 feet in 2 miles. If you can't ride this grade, it's worth pushing your bike—don't bail out here. Once the trail gains Holter Ridge, the riding eases up again, with small, undulating ups and downs on a smooth gravel surface over 7 miles. Views of the coast are a fair compensation for the effort involved in getting up here at 2,300 feet above sea level. One final climb awaits around mile 10.0, but it's over in less than 0.5 mile.

Finally, paved Bald Hills Road descends from the ridgeline, passing the Lady

Riders can't help feeling awed and humbled by the big trees along Lost Man Creek Road.

Bird Johnson Grove (definitely worth a stop and a short hike) before making an incredibly fast drop to U.S. 101. Both Bald Hills Road and the highway have substantial traffic, including tourists and logging trucks, so be very cautious. Two miles later, you're back at Lost Man Creek Road, pedaling the final level stretch to your car.

For more information, contact Redwood National Park, 707/464-6101, www.nps.gov/redw.

Options

If you don't want to deal with auto traffic in the final miles of this peaceful nature ride, consider an out-and-back from the end of Holter Ridge Trail, near its junction with Bald Hills Road. The mileage is almost identical to the loop.

Driving Directions

From U.S. 101 at Orick, drive north 3 miles to Lost Man Creek Road (on the right). Turn right and drive 0.9 mile to the end of the pavement, a picnic area, and trailhead.

Route Directions

0.0 Park at Lost Man Creek Trailhead. *Supplies are available in Orick.*

1.3 Trail starts to climb steeply.

3.7 RIGHT on Holter Ridge Trail (trail simply curves to right).

10.2 RIGHT on paved Bald Hills Road. *Or turn left and ride 0.25 mile to the Redwood Creek Overlook and picnic area, a fine viewpoint on rare sunny days.*

13.8 Lady Bird Johnson Grove on your right. *Lock up your bike and walk the one-mile trail among the big trees.*

16.5 RIGHT on U.S. 101.

18.6 RIGHT on Lost Man Creek Road.

19.5 Arrive at starting point.

HOLTER RIDGE/LOST MAN CREEK LOOP

7 HAMMOND TRAIL

BEST ☾

McKinleyville

PAVED BIKE PATH

Difficulty: 1

Total Distance: 13 miles

Riding Time: 1 hour

Elevation Gain: 400 feet

Summary: A nearly level out-and-back ride from Mad River in McKinleyville leads to windswept Clam Beach County Park.

The movement to convert abandoned railroad lines to multiuse trails for bicyclists, equestrians, and anyone else under nonmotorized power has gained a lot of momentum in California, which has thousands of miles of unused railroad track. The Hammond Trail is a proud example of this movement's success: It presents a safe and easy route from Arcata to McKinleyville, grand views of the coast and rural farmlands, beach access, and a ride through a historic railroad bridge that is closed to all motorized traffic. Two short sections of the trail follow quiet neighborhood streets, but the remainder is a paved, car-free recreation trail.

The trail begins at an old railroad bridge across the Mad River, a key piece of McKinleyville's history. The original bridge on this site was a wooden covered bridge, built in 1905. When it deteriorated, it was replaced by the existing steel truss bridge in 1941. It was used by the Hammond Lumber Company for its railroad until 1961. As you cross the bridge, you gain a wide perspective on the Mad River, and you may be able to spot seals and sea otters.

HAMMOND TRAIL

CLAM BEACH DR

CLAM BEACH COUNTY PARK

PACIFIC OCEAN

CENTRAL AVE

101

AIRPORT RD

LETZ AVE

McKinleyville

MURRAY RD

Widow White Creek

CENTRAL AVE

Mad River

HILLER PARK

HILLER RD

MAD RIVER COUNTY PARK

Hammond Trail

SCHOOL RD

RAILROAD BRIDGE

Start P

MAD RIVER RD

Mad River

101

NARROW BRIDGE (NO SHOULDER)

200

0   0.5 mi

0   0.5 km

©AVALON TRAVEL

Hammond Trail passes through the farmlands of Arcata Bottoms—a Northern California version of the English countryside with green fields and grazing cows and horses. Make a stop at Roger's Market for a cool drink and, if you are brave, some fresh, locally picked mushrooms. The trail then continues north through Hiller Park, a small community park with a few trails and picnic areas. A stretch through dense coastal forest leads to Murray Road and a neighborhood of large, odd-looking houses built to resemble castles (some developer's imaginative idea). Beyond Murray Road, bikers and horses split off from hikers and follow the trail on the west side of U.S. 101 (hikers cross an environmentally sensitive area in the dunes near Widow White Creek). A 0.25-mile stretch on Letz Avenue connects to a dazzling vista point overlooking Trinidad Head to the north and the entire Mad River estuary. The trail's final stretch provides access to the brayed tan sands of Clam Beach.

For more information, contact Humboldt County Parks, 707/445-7651, www. co.humboldt.ca.us.

Driving Directions

From U.S. 101 in Eureka, drive north 10 miles to the north end of Arcata, then take the Giuntoli Lane exit and head left (west). Cross over the freeway, then turn right onto Heindon Road and drive 0.3 mile. Turn left on Miller Lane and drive 0.8 mile. Turn right on Mad River Road and drive 1.6 miles to an old steel railroad bridge.

Route Directions

0.0 Park at pullouts alongside old railroad bridge. *Supplies are available in Arcata.*

3.5 Murray Road and "castles"; bike trail splits from hiker trail to parallel U.S. 101.

5.0 Hiller Park has restrooms, picnic areas, and its own network of coastal meadow and forest trails.

6.5 End of trail at Clam Beach County Park and bridge over Strawberry Creek. TURN AROUND.

13.0 Arrive at starting point.

8 AVENUE OF THE GIANTS AND MATTOLE ROAD

Humboldt Redwoods State Park, north of Garberville

PAVED ROADS WITH MODERATE CAR TRAFFIC

Difficulty: 2   **Total Distance:** 44.2 miles (or 16.2-mile option)

Riding Time: 4 hours   **Elevation Gain:** 1,000 feet

Summary: The best of Humboldt Redwoods State Park can be seen from this road ride – a big dose of redwoods, redwoods, and more redwoods.

It's hard to resist a road with a name like Avenue of the Giants. It's even harder to resist when it's located in the third largest state park in California, Humboldt Redwoods State Park, where more than a third of 51,000 acres are ancient, old-growth redwood forests. And it's still harder to resist when you discover that the elevation gain along the entire out-and-back route is only 1,000 feet. Now if they would just block off the road to cars.

This bike ride follows the north end of the Avenue of the Giants, then takes a side trip to Mattole Road and Rockefeller Forest. Pick up a free Auto Tour pamphlet in the roadside boxes near the trailhead; nine numbered points are interpreted along the trail. The highlights range from the sublime 2.5-mile Newton B. Drury and Ralph W. Chaney Groves hiking trail (worth locking up your bike to explore) to the kitschy Immortal Tree, which survived lightning, the logger's axe, a forest fire, and the flood of 1964.

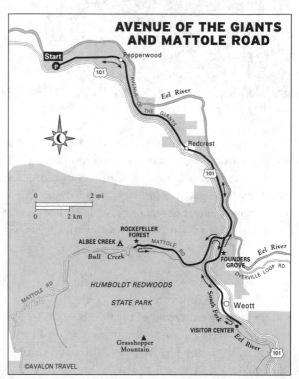

AVENUE OF THE GIANTS AND MATTOLE ROAD

Lock up your bike and admire the Rockefeller Forest on foot.

The best biking of the trip is found on narrow and less traveled Mattole Road, which winds through the largest remaining ancient redwood forest in the world: 10,000-acre Rockefeller Forest. Once on this road, a mother bear and cub lumbered across the pavement 100 feet ahead of me. This feels like primeval country.

For more information, contact Humboldt Redwoods State Park, 707/946-2409, www.humboldtredwoods.org or www.parks.ca.gov.

Options

If you want a shorter trip, try starting this ride at the end point, the Humboldt Redwoods State Park visitor center, and riding the latter half of the route in reverse: Go north on Avenue of the Giants 4.5 miles to Founders Grove (stop and visit), then north another 0.3 mile to Mattole Road. Turn left on Mattole and ride 3.3 miles to the Big Trees Area (stop and visit). Round-trip mileage will be 16.2 miles, and it's almost all level.

Mountain bikers, if you're dying to get off the pavement, two popular dirt routes begin near the Big Trees Area on Mattole Road: the grueling 17-mile Grasshopper Peak Loop and somewhat less challenging 16-mile Peavine Road Loop.

Driving Directions

From Eureka, drive south on U.S. 101 for 30 miles to the Pepperwood/Avenue of the Giants exit.

Route Directions

0.0 Park in pullouts alongside the north end of Avenue of the Giants. *Supplies are available in Pepperwood.*

2.7 Newton B. Drury and Ralph W. Chaney Groves loop trail. *Lock up your bike and walk this 2.5-mile loop through the redwoods.*

5.1 Immortal Tree.

6.6 Village of Redcrest. *Supplies are available.*

8.5 Mahan Loop Trail. *Lock up your bike and walk this 0.6-mile loop through the redwoods.*

10.7 Dyerville Bar Overlook.

10.8 RIGHT on Mattole Road at signed Albee Creek Campground Road turnoff (Rockefeller Forest).

14.1 LEFT into Big Trees Area. TURN AROUND. *Lock up your bike and walk to the Giant Tree and Flat Iron Tree.*

17.4 RIGHT (south) on Avenue of the Giants.

17.7 Founders Grove on left. *Lock up your bike and walk the 0.5-mile trail around this grove; don't miss the Dyerville Giant.*

21.1 Village of Weott. *Supplies are available one block to the left.*

22.1 Humboldt Redwoods State Park visitor center. TURN AROUND.

44.2 Arrive at starting point.

AVENUE OF THE GIANTS AND MATTOLE ROAD

9 CHEMISE MOUNTAIN
King Range National Conservation Area, west of Garberville

DIRT ROAD AND SINGLE-TRACK

Difficulty: 3   **Total Distance:** 6.4 miles

Riding Time: 1.5 hours   **Elevation Gain:** 1,000 feet

Summary: Bring your climbing legs to ascend the summit of Chemise Mountain and visit Hidden Valley, a big meadow that is often populated with grazing Roosevelt elk.

They say that the Lost Coast has two seasons: six months of rain and six months of fog. Maybe so, but if you happen to ride the trail from Hidden Valley to Chemise Mountain on a rare sunny day (best chances in spring or fall), you'll be rewarded with a view that will knock your socks off—a wide panorama of the Yolla Bolly Mountains to the east, Sinkyone Wilderness and the Mendocino coast to the south, and King's Peak to the north.

Located in the King Range National Conservation Area region of the Lost Coast (north of Sinkyone Wilderness State Park), Chemise Mountain is lined with tan oaks and madrones that have replaced the majority of the Douglas firs, which were logged. Near Chemise Mountain's summit at 2,596 feet is chaparral, including manzanita and chemise (greasewood), from which the mountain gets its name.

This is a short ride, but a difficult one nonetheless. Chances are good you'll do some walking, especially in the first 1.5 miles of highly technical single-track and nearly a dozen tight uphill switchbacks. Bring your climbing legs. After that you gain a ridge, the grade eases up, and you are rewarded with sweeping views of the Pacific coast. One more mile and you're at the summit, enjoying the view if it's sunny. Then you backtrack 1 mile and loop back via pleasant Nadelos Campground and Chemise Mountain Road.

A highlight of the ride is lovely Hidden Valley. Its large meadow, which you ride past at mile 0.3, is frequently populated with grazing Roosevelt elk. They are "extras" relocated from the herd at Prairie Creek Redwoods State Park.

For more information, contact the King Range National Conservation Area, 707/825-2300, www.blm.gov/ca/arcata/kingrange.

Driving Directions

From U.S. 101 at Garberville, take Redwood Drive 3 miles northeast to Redway, then take Briceland–Thorne Road west for 17.3 miles (it becomes Shelter Cove Road). Turn left on Chemise Mountain Road (dirt) and drive 0.25 mile to the Hidden Valley Trailhead on the right.

Route Directions

0.0 Park at the Hidden Valley Trailhead. *Supplies are available in Garberville.*

0.3 Meadow with Roosevelt elk.

0.4 LEFT at junction.

0.5 LEFT at junction (steep switchbacks ahead).

2.0 RIGHT at junction. *If you're tired, stash your bike here and walk the last 0.5 mile to the summit.*

2.6 End of trail near summit of Chemise Mountain. TURN AROUND. *Leave your bike and walk the last 50 yards to the summit.*

3.2 RIGHT at previous junction.

3.8 LEFT at junction for Nadelos Campground.

4.8 LEFT on Chemise Mountain Road at campground.

6.4 Arrive at starting point.

10 HOTEL GULCH TRAIL
Sinkyone Wilderness State Park, west of Leggett

DIRT ROAD

Difficulty: 3   **Total Distance:** 12.6 miles

Riding Time: 2.5 hours   **Elevation Gain:** 2,400 feet

Summary: See the quiet, eastern side of the Lost Coast from an old logging road that affords coastal views and a visit to virgin redwoods.

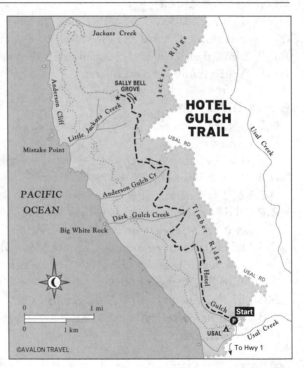

Highway 1 hugs the coast for almost the entire length of Northern California, allowing visitors easy access to glorious stretches of sea, sand, and surf. Except for one remote stretch: from north of Rockport to just south of Eureka, a land that has come to be called the Lost Coast.

The Lost Coast may be remote, but it's not forgotten. One Saturday at an REI store in the Bay Area, I stood in the checkout line with three other customers, and as we chatted, we learned that all four of us were heading separately to the Lost Coast. Lost? Hardly.

Still, this was late spring, which is the only "busy" season at the Lost Coast. From November to April, the area gets up to 80 inches of rain, which greatly reduces tourism (the area's dirt roads become impassable). In summer, the fog moves in. Autumn and spring are your best bets for a visit, and a chance to mountain bike the Hotel Gulch Trail at Sinkyone Wilderness State Park.

The trail, an old logging road, travels the park's eastern ridgeline, not the coastline, although it does supply many fine views of the coast. From the north end of Usal Campground, Hotel Gulch Trail climbs 2.6 miles to the top of Timber

© ANN MARIE BROWN

Sinkyone Wilderness State Park

Ridge at 1,200 feet, then descends for 2 miles, crossing Dark Gulch Creek and Anderson Gulch Creek. Although this area was heavily logged right up until the 1980s and the virgin trees are long gone, the landscape is dense with young forest and foliage. In a few hundred years, the giant-sized redwoods and firs will be back.

One more climb awaits around mile 5.0, shortly before the trail ends at a junction with Wheeler Road. There you turn left to visit the Sally Bell Grove of virgin redwoods. The grove was named for the last full-blooded Sinkyone Native American, a medicine woman who survived a massacre of her people.

Note that there is no piped water available at Usal Campground or anywhere near this trail. If you bring a filtering system, you can get water from the creek. Otherwise, fill your bottles in Westport or Leggett before you drive all the way out here.

For more information, contact Sinkyone Wilderness State Park, 707/986-7711, www.parks.ca.gov.

Driving Directions

From Westport, drive north on Highway 1 for 13 miles (past Rockport) and turn left on County Road 431/Usal Road (may not be signed; look for the spot where Highway 1 turns inland at milepost 90.88). The road turns to dirt after 50 yards; drive 6 miles to Usal Campground, continue over the bridge, and turn left at the Hotel Gulch junction. (From Leggett, drive southwest on Highway 1 for 14.6 miles to County Road 431/Usal Road and turn right.)

Route Directions

0.0 Park at the junction of Usal Road and Hotel Gulch Trail. *Supplies are available in Westport or Leggett.*

2.6 Summit of Timber Ridge.

5.8 LEFT at junction with Wheeler Road (end of Hotel Gulch Trail).

6.3 Sally Bell Grove. TURN AROUND. *Lock up your bike and wander among these old-growth redwoods.*

12.6 Arrive at starting point.

SHASTA AND LASSEN

© ANN MARIE BROWN

BEST BIKE RIDES

In the northeastern corner of California lies a

part of the state where most people have never set foot. Ranging from the Oregon border south to Redding and from the Nevada border west through the Klamath Mountains, this northern interior is both the least populated and least visited region of the Golden State. Yet it is bestowed with some of California's most spectacular scenery: a landscape of rugged mountains, raging rivers in steep canyons, and vast expanses of sagebrush flats and pine- and fir-covered ridges. This is the land where ospreys and eagles soar, and remnants of volcanoes sputter and fume.

Two national parks are found here, both celebrating the region's volcanic past: Lava Beds National Monument, with its 300 lava tube caves, vast volcanic cinder landscape, and western juniper forests; and Lassen Volcanic National Park, California's best example of recent geothermal activity. How recent? In May 1914, Lassen Peak began a seven-year stint of volcanic outbursts. Even today, visitors can witness volcanic action including seething hot springs, steaming volcanic vents, and boiling mud pots (springs filled with hot mud). One of the best ways to see the park is on the seat of a bike, by taking a long and strenuous ride on Lassen Park Road. The challenging climb is not for everybody, but for hearty riders, it's a once-in-a-lifetime adventure.

Then there is the 2.1 million acres of Shasta-Trinity National Forest, dominated by mighty Mount Shasta, a dormant volcano whose summit attains the lofty height of 14,162 feet. At its base is Shasta Lake, the largest reservoir in California, which is part of another federally managed parkland: Whiskeytown-Shasta-Trinity National Recreation Area. Both Shasta and Whiskeytown Lakes offer mountain bikers some of the best single-track riding in the state. In fact, Whiskeytown was the site of one of the first official mountain bike races, the Whiskeytown Downhill, originally held in 1981.

Wildlife is plentiful in the northeastern corner of the state. Black bears roam the mountainsides; herds of mule deer and pronghorn antelope migrate through the plains. Eagle Lake, the second largest natural lake in California, is one of the best spots in Northern California for bird-watching. Lake Almanor near Chester has the largest summer population of ospreys in California. Paved recreation trails at these two lakes make them accessible to families and novice riders who are camping or visiting for the day.

Relics of history can also be found here. Old gold mine sites, water ditches, and structures from the Gold Rush era are evident on Whiskeytown Lake's trails. The Bizz Johnson Trail in Susanville is built on a circa 1900s railroad grade. Where cyclists ride today, thundering locomotives once rumbled through the canyon, carrying heavy loads of logs and lumber.

The truth is, the only thing you won't find in northeast California is a crowd. And that may be the best reason of all to come here and ride your bike.

SHASTA AND LASSEN

TRAIL NAME	LEVEL	DISTANCE	TIME	ELEVATION	PAGE
1 Upper Klamath River	2	15.6 mi	2-3 hr	800 ft	68
2 Siskiyou Lake Loop	2	10.3 mi	2 hr	200 ft	71
3 Waters Gulch and Fish Loop	3	6.8 mi	1-1.5 hr	900 ft	74
4 Dry Fork Creek	3	9.6 mi	2 hr	500 ft	77
5 Clikapudi	2	9.7 mi	2 hr	400 ft	80
6 Oak Bottom Channel/Great Water Ditch	2	6.6 mi	1.5 hr	200 ft	82
7 Boulder Creek Loop	3	8.6 mi	2 hr	1,200 ft	85
8 South Fork Mountain Lookout	3	14 mi	3 hr	2,100 ft	87
9 Mount Shasta Mine Loop	3	3.1 mi	1 hr	500 ft	89
10 Sacramento River Trail	1	10 mi	1 hr	200 ft	92
11 Lassen Park Road	5	55.8 mi	5 hr	4,350 ft	95
12 Lake Almanor Recreation Trail	1	19 mi	2 hr	600 ft	98
13 Eagle Lake Trail	1	10 mi	1 hr	100 ft	101
14 Bizz Johnson Trail	2	13.4 mi	2 hr	500 ft	103

1 UPPER KLAMATH RIVER
north of Yreka

DIRT ROAD WITH MINIMAL CAR TRAFFIC

Difficulty: 2   **Total Distance:** 15.6 miles (or longer/shorter options)

Riding Time: 2-3 hours   **Elevation Gain:** 800 feet

Summary: Leave Highway 96 to the cars and trucks and pedal the old stagecoach trail on the south side of the Klamath River.

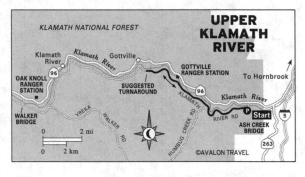

The Upper Klamath River ride is an out-and-back favored by rangers at Klamath National Forest. They suggest riding this 19-mile one-way route as a shuttle, with one car left at either end. You could do so, or follow my suggestion and simply ride out and back on the eastern 7.8 miles from the Ash Creek Bridge. Because the dirt road is quite level all the way—it ultimately loses only 500 feet during its 19-mile length—strong riders could take the entire trail out and back.

The ride follows an alternate route to Highway 96, the National Scenic Byway on the north side of the Klamath River. The "alternate" is an old stagecoach trail on the river's south side that was used by hard-rock miners blasting for gold in the late 1800s. Today it's a gravel and dirt road seldom used by car drivers except those who own homes along the road. You'll have to put up with some washboard bumps, but otherwise the riding is easy. Often the road pulls in quite close to the river; sometimes it will move away for a quarter mile or so. Highway 96 is usually visible on the river's north side, but barely noticeable with the roar of flowing water. In California, the 265-mile-long Klamath River is second only to the Sacramento River in terms of the amount of water it empties into the Pacific.

The dirt road curves westward, into an arid landscape of rocky crags, juniper, chaparral, and oaks, which eventually changes to a more lush forest. Heading west on this road, the annual rainfall increases nearly one inch per mile, and this is reflected in the foliage. The turnaround point suggested, at mile 7.8, is at a high point with a nice view of the river.

If you decide to ride the road's entire length, you'll find scenic bridges on both

© ANN MARIE BROWN

easy cruising alongside the rolling Klamath River

ends. Its eastern end is at the Ash Creek Bridge, built in 1901. Its western end is at the Walker Bridge, 19 miles to the west (the old stagecoach route continues past this point, but it becomes Walker Road). It might seem tempting to make a loop out of this ride by riding back on Highway 96, but that road is far too dangerous for bicyclists—it's busy and narrow with blind curves and no shoulder.

The Forest Service claims that this ride provides excellent chances of seeing great blue herons, muskrats, turtles, ospreys, and so on, but the only creatures I can vouch for were deer grazing on the petunias in the riverside cabin owners' yards.

For more information, contact Klamath National Forest Headquarters, 530/842-6131; or Scott River Ranger District, 530/468-5351, www.fs.fed.us/r5/klamath.

Driving Directions
From Yreka on I-5, drive north for 10 miles to the Highway 96 exit. Drive southwest on Highway 96 for 2.1 miles to its junction with Highway 263, then continue on Highway 96 for 1.9 more miles to the Ash Creek Bridge on the left. Cross the bridge and park on its far side in pullouts.

Route Directions
0.0 Park across the Ash Creek Bridge on the south side of the river in dirt pullouts. *Supplies are available in Yreka.*
7.8 High point above the river. TURN AROUND.
15.6 Arrive at starting point.

2 SISKIYOU LAKE LOOP
west of Mount Shasta City

DIRT AND PAVED ROADS WITH MINIMAL CAR TRAFFIC

Difficulty: 2   **Total Distance:** 10.3 miles

Riding Time: 2 hours   **Elevation Gain:** 200 feet

Summary: Circle around lovely Lake Siskiyou and enjoy views of Mount Shasta and maybe a swim in the lake.

If you're vacationing at Shasta Lake and all the water-skiers and loud party boats are starting to wear you down, a trip to Lake Siskiyou could be the perfect antidote. Lake Siskiyou is one of the few reservoirs in California that was built specifically for quiet kinds of recreation; the lake speed limit is 10 mph. As a bonus, the water managers leave the lake level alone even when other lakes in the area are drawn down. Deep blue and full to the brim, Lake Siskiyou is a lake for scenery lovers, surrounded by a thick conifer forest and with Mount Shasta holding court in the background.

This loop around the lake's perimeter gives you an overview of the pretty lake. It starts from the beginning of North Shore Road, although you could add on a few miles by riding from downtown Mount Shasta. (Many riders on this loop are campers at Lake Siskiyou Campground, who start right from their tent sites.)

After the first mile on North Shore Road, you reach the northern lakeshore. Several turnoffs on your left lead to dirt parking areas and shoreline access; take any of them to get an unobstructed lake and mountain view or to just sit by the water. As you ride, North Shore Road gets rougher and rockier, especially beyond the 2.5-mile mark as you move out of sight of the lake—it goes from pavement to good gravel to worse gravel to rocky dirt track. The trickiest section is the crossing of the Sacramento River at mile 4.9, which is a 100-foot-wide field of rounded rocks and boulders, with or without a lot of water running over them. Because of this crossing, this ride is best taken in late summer or fall when the

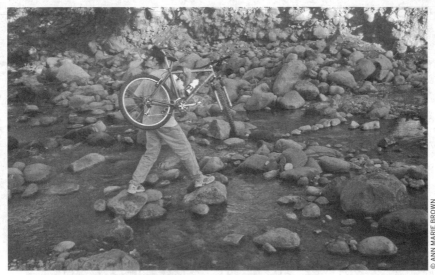

a rocky crossing of the Sacramento River on the Siskiyou Lake Loop

river level is down. The condition of the road is also better then—smoother and more tightly compacted.

Once across the river, the rest of the ride is easy. The dirt road quickly turns to pavement, and you'll pedal past the lake's campground and marina on your way back to your starting point. Watch for cars on the busier south side of the lake. You might stop for a swim at the beach near the marina, or just pause along the way and enjoy the striking view of Mount Shasta.

For more information, contact Siskiyou Lake Campground and Marina, 530/926-2618.

Driving Directions

From Redding, drive north on I-5 for 60 miles to the town of Mount Shasta, then take the central Mount Shasta exit and turn left. Drive west over the overpass for 1 mile to W.A. Barr Road. Turn left and drive 0.7 mile to North Shore Road, where you turn right.

Route Directions

0.0 Park in any of the pullouts on North Shore Road near its junction with W.A. Barr Road. Ride west on North Shore Road. *Supplies are available in Mount Shasta.*

1.5 Pavement turns to gravel.

2.5 Trail moves away from the lakeshore. Keep heading due west on the main road and ignore all turnoffs.

4.9 Crossing of Sacramento River.

5.0 LEFT on dirt road on far side of Sacramento River.

5.2 LEFT on paved W.A. Barr Road.

7.1 Siskiyou Lake Campground and Marina. *Water and supplies are available.*

10.3 Arrive at starting point.

SISKIYOU LAKE LOOP

3 WATERS GULCH AND FISH LOOP
Shasta Lake, north of Redding

DIRT SINGLE-TRACK

Difficulty: 3   **Total Distance:** 6.8 miles

Riding Time: 1-1.5 hours   **Elevation Gain:** 900 feet

Summary: Practice your bike handling skills on two short but sweet single-track loops.

When you're ready for a technical single-track challenge, but not ready for long mileage or steep uphills that climb halfway to the stars, you're ready to ride on the Waters Gulch and Fish Loop Trails at Shasta Lake. The trails roll along with only short ups and downs but offer multiple lessons in technical riding, with plenty of bridges to cross, rocks strewn along your path, exposed tree roots, tight turns, and steep drop-offs into Shasta Lake. Better keep your eyes on the road.

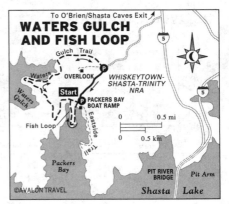

Aside from the all-in-good-fun single-track, the surrounding forest of pines and oaks and the views of the Sacramento River arm of Shasta Lake are quite pretty. If you stop to stare at the bright blue lake surface, you might get lucky and see a golden eagle or an osprey go fishing. As you ride, oak leaves frequently get caught in your spokes, making a great shuffling sound as your wheels spin.

Waters Gulch and Fish Loop are separate but connecting loops. What ties them together is a 0.6-mile stretch on Packers Bay Road, which you drive in on. You can ride out and back on the single-track in both directions for a 6.8-mile round-trip, or, if you decide after the first leg that you've had enough of this path's technical challenges, you can return downhill on pavement for a 4-mile round-trip.

Either way, start riding on Fish Loop, a short path around a small peninsula on Packers Bay. The trail gets narrower as manzanita bushes crowd in and brush your ankles. Fish Loop offers the best riding of the day and wonderful lake views, but it's over in only 0.7 mile. Too soon.

Go left where Fish Loop connects to Waters Gulch Trail. The trail undulates up and down through more manzanita and dense oak forest, then moves away from the lake as it crosses the strip of land separating Packers Bay from Waters

© ANN MARIE BROWN

a single-track challenge on Waters Gulch Trail at Shasta Lake

Gulch. As it nears the water again, the path becomes more technical and ascends more steeply. This is a good place to consider whether or not you will be comfortable returning downhill on this trail, or if you should loop back on pavement. Much of the upper part of Waters Gulch Trail has been heavily eroded and is quite rocky and narrow; the drop-off into a neighboring creek is nearly vertical. A couple of stairstep-style drops and an extremely tight, double switchback may give you pause. (I walked my bike here both uphill and downhill.) But shortly beyond the switchbacks, you're at the upper terminus of the trail, and probably feel disappointed (or perhaps lucky?) that it's over. Simply turn around and ride back or take the pavement downhill.

Remember that this is Shasta Lake, not Mount Shasta, so daytime temperatures in the summer months can be extreme. Plan your ride around the thermometer.

For more information, contact Shasta Lake Visitor Center, 530/275-1589; or Shasta–Trinity National Forest Headquarters, 530/226-2500, www.fs.fed.us/r5/shastatrinity.

Driving Directions

From I-5 at Redding, drive north for 15 miles and take the O'Brien/Shasta Caverns exit. Cross the freeway and get back on I-5 heading south. Drive 1 mile and take the Packers Bay exit. Drive 1.6 miles to the end of the road at the boat ramp.

Route Directions

0.0 Park at Packer's Bay boat ramp. Begin riding to the left at the Fish Loop Trailhead, which is 20 yards below a separate trailhead for Waters Gulch Trail. *Water is available at the trailhead.*

0.7 LEFT on Waters Gulch Trail.

3.1 Steep uphill with stairstep drops and tight switchbacks.

3.4 Upper trailhead parking area. TURN AROUND. *If you want to*

avoid the downhill single-track, follow the paved road downhill for a four-mile round-trip.

6.8 Arrive at starting point.

4 DRY FORK CREEK
Shasta Lake, north of Redding

DIRT SINGLE-TRACK

Difficulty: 3   **Total Distance:** 9.6 miles

Riding Time: 2 hours   **Elevation Gain:** 500 feet

Summary: One of the narrowest single-tracks around presents a challenge for riders at Shasta Lake.

The trail at Dry Fork Creek was built to assist anglers in accessing the good fishing areas near Shasta Dam, but it's become a favorite of mountain bikers. And no wonder—this is some sweet single-track. The only catch is that you can only ride it when the lake level is down about 15 feet or more at Shasta Dam, which isn't usually until mid-summer. If the lake isn't down, part of the trail is under water.

Due to the tragic events of September 11, 2001, vehicle access to Shasta Dam was restricted for nearly a decade, but as of 2010, you no longer need a permit to drive across the dam to access this trailhead. Now you simply need to produce your driver's license and vehicle registration and be willing to have your vehicle searched if the officers at the check station deem it should be. (For more information, contact the Bureau of Reclamation at 530/275-1554.)

Okay, so you can get to the trailhead without too much trouble. But before you hop on your saddle, consider this: Dry Fork Creek is not a trail for acrophobes. Almost five miles of single-track rise high above the lakeshore with some frighteningly steep drop-offs. Small rocks are abundant. The trail's width shrinks to less than 18 inches in places. If you're the kind of rider who gets psyched-out when you try to pick a line and follow it, you won't be happy here. In several places, this is one skinny trail.

On the other hand, if narrow trails don't bother you at all, you'll love the sweeping views of Shasta Lake from this pathway. If it's a hot summer day, it's easy enough to jump in the lake; the trail curves its way in and out of small coves. You might even want to bring along your fishing rod and drop a line in the water.

Located on the west side of Shasta Lake's massive dam, the Dry Fork Creek trail skirts the shore of the lake.

There are no trail junctions to worry about—just pure, unbridled riding. The first hill, right at the start of the ride, is the steepest of the day.

For more information, contact Shasta Dam Visitor Center, 530/275-4463; or Shasta Lake Visitor Center, 530/275-1589.

Options

The hottest "new" trail (built in 2005) in the Shasta Dam area is known as 76. If you're a single-track aficionado, you should give it a try. The best direction to ride it is downhill, not up, so pedal up the main road from the west end of Shasta Dam, then turn onto Road 1 (a dirt road). This will take you to Trail 76, and once on it, you will zoom downhill at lightning speed. It's pure adrenaline-pumping fun.

Driving Directions

From I-5 in Redding, drive north seven miles to the Shasta Dam/Highway 151 exit. Drive west for seven miles to the dam, cross it, and park.

Route Directions

0.0 Park on the west side of Shasta Dam. The trail begins about 150 yards down the dirt road to the lake. *Water is available at the trailhead.*

4.8 End of single-track at junction with dirt road. TURN AROUND.

9.6 Arrive at starting point.

5 CLIKAPUDI   BEST ☾
Shasta Lake, north of Redding

DIRT SINGLE-TRACK

Difficulty: 2   **Total Distance:** 9.7 miles

Riding Time: 2 hours   **Elevation Gain:** 400 feet

Summary: This popular single-track loop at Mount Shasta is manageable for riders of almost any ability.

You may have heard that the Clikapudi Trail, a longtime favorite of Redding-area fat-tire riders, burned to a crisp in a wildfire in 2004, and sadly, that's true. That's the bad news. The good news is that this type of landscape is well adapted to fire, and for the most part, the shrubs and trees have grown back even more lushly than before. The black oaks and pines are regenerating quickly and will soon form a shady canopy over much of the trail. For now, it's best to ride Clikapudi in spring or fall, or very early in the morning in summer. Lacking any tree cover, it's just too hot otherwise.

The name Clikapudi comes from the Wintu Native American word *kluku-puda,* which means "to kill." Fortunately it's a reference to a battle between the Wintu and local traders in the 1800s and does not reflect the difficulty of this trail's single-track.

In fact, this single-track is downright manageable, even for people who don't have a lot of technical riding experience. The surface is smooth more than rocky, curves are graceful and not tight, and the main obstacles are other trail users, not rocks and tree roots. With only two short but challenging hills, this is a good trail for building your confidence. At the few difficult spots, simply dismount and walk.

It's also a good trail for a swim on a hot day, of which there are plenty at Shasta Lake. Between miles 4.0 and 6.0, you'll find good places to drop your bike and splash into the water.

For more information, contact Shasta Lake Visitor Center, 530/275-1589; or Shasta–Trinity National Forest Headquarters, 530/226-2500, www.fs.fed.us/r5/shastatrinity.

Driving Directions
From I-5 in Redding, take Highway 299 east for 6 miles to Bella Vista. Just past the small town, turn left on Dry Creek Road and drive 5.5 miles to a fork. Go right on Bear Mountain Road. Drive 1 mile and turn right on Jones Valley Road. Look for the pullout on the left in 0.4 mile (before the campground).

Route Directions
0.0 Park at the trailhead on Jones Valley Road just before the campground. *Supplies are available at the store on Bear Mountain Road.*

1.3 STRAIGHT at junction with trail on right; this is your loop return.

2.9 Jones Valley parking area and boat ramp. *Water is available.*

3.7 LEFT at fork.

6.9 STRAIGHT on single-track at several junctions with jeep roads; watch for trail markers.

7.9 0.25-mile switchbacking descent to pavement.

8.2 RIGHT on Jones Valley Road.

8.3 LEFT back on trail.

8.5 LEFT at junction (this is the junction you visited at mile 1.3).

9.7 Arrive at starting point.

6 OAK BOTTOM CHANNEL/ GREAT WATER DITCH BEST **◖**
Whiskeytown Lake, west of Redding

DIRT SINGLE-TRACK AND PAVED ROAD WITH MINIMAL CAR TRAFFIC

Difficulty: 2   **Total Distance:** 6.6 miles (or 10.6-mile option)

Riding Time: 1.5 hours   **Elevation Gain:** 200 feet

Summary: Ride right along the shore of Whiskeytown Lake on an old water ditch that leads to Carr Powerhouse.

If you like riding on single-track and you like lakeside trails, the Oak Bottom Channel Trail is a perfect fit. It skirts the edge of Whiskeytown Lake, providing stunning blue-water views at almost every turn.

The trail is also known as the Great Water Ditch (and is called that on some park maps), but it is signed on both ends as Oak Bottom Channel Trail. It is built on one of the area's many water ditches, which were part of the original irrigation system that developer Levi Tower built in the gold rush days to supply his hotel, farm, and mining operations.

The trail starts at Oak Bottom Campground's access road and runs to the Carr Powerhouse, which is part of a huge water regulation system that is far more complicated than Levi Tower's: The powerhouse diverts water from the Trinity River, stores it in Trinity Lake, sends it by tunnel to Whiskeytown Lake, then sends it to Keswick Reservoir and into the Sacramento River. And it's all in an effort to keep the Central Valley from looking like a desert.

From the dirt pullout and trailhead along the Oak Bottom Campground access road, head downhill immediately for about 30 yards, then follow the single-track as it curves in and around the lakeshore. The trail runs between Whiskeytown Lake and Highway 299, so you are wowed by lake views the whole way. One section snakes through what may be the biggest manzanita bushes in all of Shasta–Trinity. The only minus is the road noise.

Where the trail ends at a paved road, follow the pavement to Carr Powerhouse Road, then cross Clear Creek and ride to the left to the Carr Powerhouse and picnic area.

For more information, contact Whiskeytown National Recreation Area, 530/246-1225, www.nps.gov/whis.

Options

To add four more miles to your ride, you can turn right after crossing Clear Creek (the road is pavement but soon turns to dirt, then single-track). After several steep uphill switchbacks, turn right, go straight at the next junction, then watch for a steep trail heading sharply downhill to the right. Now you're on Mill Creek Trail and will shortly reach the El Dorado Mine site. After examining the old mine buildings, continue on Mill Creek Trail past the ranger's house to the Tower Historic District and Tower Gravesite. Return the way you came.

Cruising along the edge of Whiskeytown Lake on the Oak Bottom Channel Trail.

© ANN MARIE BROWN

Driving Directions

From I-5 at Redding, take Highway 299 west for 13 miles (5 miles west of the Whiskeytown Lake Visitor Information Center). Turn left at the sign for Oak Bottom Campground and Marina. Drive 0.2 mile on the Oak Bottom access road and park in the pullout on the right.

Route Directions

0.0 Park at the trailhead pullout near the top of Oak Bottom access road.
Supplies are available at the camp store at the end of the road.

0.1 RIGHT at fork (hikers take trail on left).

0.3 Trail comes out just below Highway 299.

1.5 Stairsteps by pumphouse and gate. Go around the gate and turn LEFT on dirt road, then in 25 yards, turn RIGHT back on trail alongside lake.

2.1 End of Oak Bottom Trail. Continue on pavement.

2.7 LEFT on Carr Powerhouse Road.

2.8 Cross Clear Creek and turn LEFT. *You can also opt to turn right and follow the service road to a single-track trail that switchbacks uphill and cuts over to Mill Creek Trail and El Dorado Mine (see Options).*

3.3 Judge Francis Carr Powerhouse and picnic area. TURN AROUND.

6.6 Arrive at starting point.

7 BOULDER CREEK LOOP
Whiskeytown Lake, west of Redding

DIRT ROAD AND SINGLE-TRACK

Difficulty: 3

Riding Time: 2 hours

Total Distance: 8.6 miles

Elevation Gain: 1,200 feet

Summary: An epic ride at Whiskeytown that offers plenty of variety in terms of trail surface and scenery.

The Boulder Creek Loop is a classic Whiskeytown ride, with miles of technical single-track, a half-dozen creek crossings, and a couple of heartbreaking climbs. This is not a ride for beginners. The first 1.8 miles are the toughest aerobically (you gain 1,000 feet in this short stretch), but the next stint on Boulder Creek Trail's single-track is the toughest in terms of riding skills required.

Fortunately the first 1.8-mile hill climb is on a wide gravel and dirt road that is mostly shaded by oaks, pines, and madrones. After much grunting and huffing and puffing, you are rewarded with great views of Shasta Bally and Clear Creek Valley.

Next, single-track Boulder Creek Trail doles out a couple of small ups and downs before making its long drop into the Boulder Creek valley. This 3.7-mile stretch is what makes this loop so favored among local mountain bikers. It's just plain fun (and challenging) to negotiate your way across the numerous running creeks and to ride through dense, leafy, rocky woods. As the single-track progresses, it becomes increasingly more technical. The rocks seem to multiply exponentially.

Eventually the trail widens to a jeep road and meets up with South Shore Drive, where you cruise through a final three miles back to your car. Yes, you have one more big hill to face, but it's nothing like that first one. You may see a few cars on this last dirt road stretch.

For more information, contact Whiskeytown National Recreation Area, 530/246-1225, www.nps.gov/whis.

Options

Note that if you want to turn this into an overnight trip, two hiker/biker camps are located along the Boulder Creek single-track. A permit from the visitor center is required.

Driving Directions

From I-5 at Redding, take Highway 299 west for 15 miles (7 miles west of the Whiskeytown Lake Visitor Information Center). Turn left at the sign for Judge Francis Carr Powerhouse and drive 0.5 mile to the picnic area.

Route Directions

0.0 Park at the picnic area by Carr Powerhouse, then ride back out the way you came in and turn left on Crystal Springs Road (gravel jeep road). *Supplies are available in Redding or at the Oak Bottom camp store.*

0.1 RIGHT at fork.

1.8 End of climb.

1.9 LEFT at junction with Boulder Creek Trail (single-track).

5.5 LEFT on South Shore Drive.

8.6 Arrive at starting point.

8 SOUTH FORK MOUNTAIN LOOKOUT
Whiskeytown Lake, west of Redding

DIRT ROAD WITH MINIMAL CAR TRAFFIC

Difficulty: 3   **Total Distance:** 14 miles

Riding Time: 3 hours   **Elevation Gain:** 2,100 feet

Summary: Get your climbing legs on for this aerobic ride to South Fork Mountain's fire lookout tower.

Whiskeytown is best known among mountain bikers for its miles of single-track. But every now and then, you aren't in the mood for single-track; you just want to put your climbing legs to work and get an aerobic workout, preferably with some great destination at the top of the hill.

Enter the South Fork Mountain Lookout Road ride. The dirt road, which is open to cars but doesn't see many, winds its way uphill over seven miles with a consistent, moderate grade, allowing you to gain 2,100 feet before you know it. A few level stretches will even give you a breather. There are no technical challenges to worry about except controlling

your speed on the downhill return. Strong beginners can manage this ride, as long as they have the legs and lungs to grunt out a seven-mile, slow and sustained climb.

And the view from the top is worth it. From South Fork Mountain's fire lookout at 3,447 feet, you gaze down at Whiskeytown Lake directly south, the Trinity Mountains to the northwest, and the Sacramento River Valley and Mount Lassen to the east. Hang gliders are sometimes seen taking off near the summit.

The ride starts almost directly across Highway 299 from the Whiskeytown visitor center, on a road that starts out partially paved but soon turns to dirt. The few road junctions are obvious choices, so don't think at all—just head uphill. Don't forget to pack along a picnic lunch for the summit; you'll be hungry when you get there.

For more information, contact Whiskeytown National Recreation Area, 530/246-1225, www.nps.gov/whis.

Options

For an unusual adventure, try riding this road on a full moon night. Some bikers do so without even using a headlamp—the trail is that easy to follow.

Driving Directions

From I-5 at Redding, take Highway 299 west for eight miles. Turn left on John F. Kennedy Memorial Drive and park at the Whiskeytown Lake Visitor Information Center.

Route Directions

0.0 Park at the visitor center and ride your bike carefully across Highway 299 to the start of South Fork Mountain Lookout Road (slightly east/right of the visitor center and often not signed). *Supplies are available in Redding or at the Oak Bottom camp store.*

0.2 LEFT at junction (gate is usually open).

6.3 LEFT at junction.

7.0 South Fork Mountain Lookout and other buildings on summit. TURN AROUND.

14.0 Arrive at starting point.

SOUTH FORK MOUNTAIN LOOKOUT

9 MOUNT SHASTA MINE LOOP
Whiskeytown Lake, west of Redding

DIRT ROAD AND SINGLE-TRACK

Difficulty: 3

Riding Time: 1 hour

Total Distance: 3.1 miles

Elevation Gain: 500 feet

Summary: This mountain biking playground and practice site is a favorite for Redding locals and visitors.

It's hard to believe that a ride this brief could kick so many butts. The mileage is ridiculously short and the overall elevation gain is minimal. It's just that a few sections have what you might call grades from Hades—straight up or down and as rocky as Yosemite Valley. Still, this is a favorite ride at Whiskeytown, and you're sure to have plenty of company on it. Just know that if you aren't a strong rider or sure of your technical skills, you'll be walking some of the time. A key is to ride the loop clockwise, not counterclockwise. This makes the hills a lot more manageable.

The old Mount Shasta Mine itself is visible from the loop, but sadly, all there is to see is a hole in the ground surrounded by a chain-link fence and an interpretive sign. Gaze at the hole and consider that this mine, which operated 1897–1905, was the biggest gold producer in the entire Shasta mining district. It's strange to think of miners toiling away 100 years ago in a 465-foot-deep hole on land that is now our biking playground.

The loop begins with a steep 0.75-mile hill climb on a wide road to the top of Shasta Divide ridge, from which you'll gain high views of Whiskeytown Lake. Then it's a right turn on a menacing downhill single-track, which for many may be too steep to ride. Orofino Creek drops alongside the lower part of this stretch, high ridge overlooking Whiskeytown Lake on Mount Shasta Mine Loop

creating pretty pools and waterfalls early in the year. At the bottom of the trail, go right to reach the old mine site. Mountain bikers have made use of a large depression in the ground (probably an old slag pond) to create a spur trail for practicing a short but steep dip down, then up.

The last 1.2 miles from the mine back to the parking lot are the easiest—just fun, roller-coaster single-track through manzanita and pine forest. You'll pass by the Whiskeytown Cemetery, where you'll find some old gravesites worth viewing.

For more information, contact Whiskeytown National Recreation Area, 530/246-1225, www.nps.gov/whis.

Driving Directions
From I-5 at Redding, take Highway 299 west for 8 miles. Turn left on John F. Kennedy Memorial Drive (in front of the Whiskeytown Lake Visitor Information Center) and drive 1 mile, then turn left on Paige Bar Road and drive 1.2 miles to the dirt parking area on the left.

Route Directions
0.0 Park at the trailhead on Paige Bar Road. The trail (a dirt road) begins on the eastern end of the parking lot near the restrooms and between two big boulders. Go LEFT and uphill on the wide dirt road. *Supplies are available in Redding or at the Oak Bottom camp store.*

0.8 RIGHT on single-track trail (very steep downhill).

1.7 RIGHT on single-track at junction (it's a hard right turn).

1.9 Mount Shasta Mine on right.

2.6 RIGHT at junction, paralleling Paige Bar Road but not joining it, then immediately RIGHT again.

2.9 Pass by old Whiskeytown Cemetery.

3.1 LEFT to arrive at starting point.

10 SACRAMENTO RIVER TRAIL   BEST (

Redding

PAVED BIKE PATH

Difficulty: 1   **Total Distance:** 10 miles (or longer options)

Riding Time: 1 hour   **Elevation Gain:** 200 feet

Summary: Two architecturally outstanding bridges and the world-class Turtle Bay Museum can be visited on this easy ride in downtown Redding.

If ever there was a perfect, easy trail for teaching someone how to ride a bike, or for taking a casual Sunday afternoon ride with a friend, the Sacramento River Trail is it. It takes you away from the hustle and bustle of downtown and offers plenty of good places to sit on a bench and watch the water roll by.

Not surprisingly, the multiuse trail is popular with Redding locals, and you'll see plenty of dog walkers, anglers, baby strollers, and joggers in addition to dozens of squirrels and small flocks of quail. If you visit in midsummer, you can pick a few handfuls of blackberries along the trail (careful, they stain your cycling gloves). If you time your trip for fall, you'll witness one of Redding's finest displays of autumn color.

The first mile of trail west from Riverside Drive is so tame and suburban feeling that you'll be a little surprised when you suddenly enter wide-open foothill country. Here the paved trail seems out of place against the rugged landscape. At 2.5 miles, you reach a 418-foot-long, hiker and biker footbridge across the Sacramento River, just before Keswick Dam. A technological wonder, Ribbon Bridge is considered to be environmentally safe because it is a concrete stress-ribbon, meaning it is supported by 200-plus steel cables in its concrete deck instead of pilings or piers dug into the riverbed.

For the ride described here, you'll cross Ribbon Bridge to loop back on the river's opposite side, but for a longer ride (see *Options,*), you could continue straight ahead to connect to the Sacramento Rail Trail at Keswick Dam.

© JOHN KLEINFELTER

Sacramento River Trail

After crossing Ribbon Bridge and turning right, you'll find that this side of the paved trail is steeper and has more tight curves, making it less popular with walkers and joggers. At a junction with the Diestlehorst Bridge that would lead back to the starting point, continue straight on a trail extension that runs into downtown Redding. The trail continues through Caldwell Park, across Market Street, and to the Turtle Bay Exploration Park, a 250-acre complex that includes a 34,000-square-foot nature museum situated on the banks of the Sacramento River. The museum building itself is an architectural marvel, constructed mostly of recycled materials. In the summer months, don't miss a visit to the museum's Butterfly House, where hundreds of North American butterflies flit about a flower-filled garden (530/243-8850 or 800/887-8532, www.turtlebay.org). An outdoor patio at Turtle Bay Cafe (530/242-3181) lures museum visitors to lunch alongside the river.

The trail bridge by the museum, completed in 2004, is as architecturally interesting as the museum itself. Called Sundial Bridge, it looks like a boomerang with harp strings, and it functions as a real sundial. The floor of the span, built of frosted glass panels, is lit up at night. You and your bike can cross this beautiful bridge, but you are requested to dismount and walk your wheels.

For more information, contact City of Redding Community Services, 530/225-4512, www.reddingtrails.com. The best source for maps is www.healthyshasta.org, 530/229-8428.

Options

As of 2008, the Sacramento River Trail now connects with the Sacramento Rail Trail, which runs along the west side of Keswick Reservoir and then north to Lake Shasta's dam, 11.1 miles one-way. Riders on skinny tires can stick to these pleasant miles of riverside pavement, while mountain bikers can branch off onto a wealth of dirt trails, beginning on F.B. Trail on the far side of Ribbon Bridge. For more information and a trail map, go to www.healthyshasta.org.

Driving Directions

From I-5 at Redding, take Highway 299 west for two miles to its junction with Highway 273 heading north (North Market Street). Veer right on Highway 273, then turn left (west) on Riverside Drive. Don't cross over the river; go straight into the parking area at Riverside Park. Ride west on the bike trail from the parking area.

Route Directions

0.0 Park at Riverside Park and ride west on the bike trail. *Supplies are available in Redding; water is available at several points along the trail.*

2.5 Cross hiker and biker footbridge (Ribbon Bridge) across the Sacramento River.

5.2 STRAIGHT at junction with Diestlehorst Bridge on right.

7.4 Turtle Bay Exploration Park and Museum. *Supplies and a café are available.*

7.6 Sundial Bridge; TURN AROUND.

9.8 LEFT across Diestlehorst Bridge.

9.9 RIGHT on bike trail.

10.0 Arrive at starting point.

11 LASSEN PARK ROAD   BEST ◖

Lassen Volcanic National Park, east of Redding

PAVED ROAD WITH MODERATE CAR TRAFFIC

Difficulty: 5   **Total Distance:** 55.8 miles

Riding Time: 5 hours   **Elevation Gain:** 4,350 feet

Summary: Seeing Lassen Park from a bike is far better than seeing it from a car, but this out-and-back ride past volcanic wonders isn't for the aerobically challenged.

Lassen Volcanic National Park is California's best example of recent geothermal activity. Before the 1980 eruption of Mount St. Helens in Washington, Lassen Peak was the most recently erupted volcano in the contiguous United States. It first blew its top in 1914; major volcanic outbursts continued for seven years. The park exhibits many present-day examples of geothermal action, including steaming sulphur vents, mud pots, and boiling springs. This out-and-back ride on the main park road

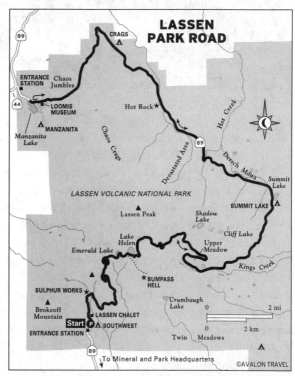

gives you a close look at this strange and beautiful volcanic terrain.

Because the ride follows the main park road, you will have to tolerate a great deal of car traffic, especially on summer weekends. The road has no shoulder and is quite narrow, so avoid riding at busy times. Weekday early mornings are best in summer. After Labor Day, when the park is largely deserted, is the ideal time to ride. The road is usually closed some time in October with the first snow and doesn't reopen until June. Although the season is short, the landscape of lakes,

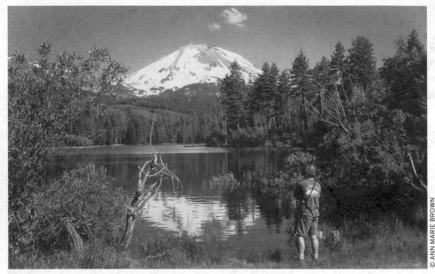

Mount Lassen rises above Manzanita Lake

volcanic peaks, and red and white fir forest is breathtaking. This is one of the greatest road rides in Northern California.

The grade is a simple up and down in both directions. The first 7 miles from Southwest Campground are a serious climb: You start at 6,800 feet in elevation and ascend to 8,500 feet at the Lassen Peak Trailhead area. Then you glide through the next 21 miles, dropping elevation to Manzanita Lake at 5,850 feet. After fueling up on snacks and drinks at the well-stocked Manzanita Camp Store and perhaps visiting the fascinating Loomis Museum, you turn around and head back. The climb is gentler on the return, but those last 7 miles drop like a rock back to Southwest Campground, with many extremely tight and narrow turns. Make sure you stop occasionally to give your brakes a rest; some of the drop-offs are severe, and there's no room for error.

For more information, contact Lassen Volcanic National Park, 530/595-4444, www.nps.gov/lavo.

Driving Directions

From I-5 in Red Bluff, drive east on Highway 36 for 45 miles. Turn north on Highway 89 and drive 4.5 miles to the park's southwest entrance station. Just beyond it is a large parking area on the right by Southwest Campground.

Route Directions

0.0 Park just past the entrance station near Southwest Campground.

Food is available at the chalet. Supplies are available in Mineral, 10 miles south.

0.1 Lassen Chalet. *Food and drinks are available.*

0.8 Sulphur Works on left. *Lock up your bike and take this 0.25-mile interpretive hike through the steaming fumaroles.*

5.7 Bumpass Hell Trailhead on right; Emerald Lake and Lake Helen on left. *Lock up your bike and take the three-mile Bumpass Hell hike to a larger and even more impressive geothermal area than Sulphur Works.*

6.8 Lassen Peak Trailhead on left.

16.4 Summit Lake Campground on right. *Water is available.*

27.9 Manzanita Lake area on left. TURN AROUND. *Supplies are available at the camp store 0.5 mile to the left; pay a visit to the nearby Loomis Museum to learn more about the park.*

55.8 Arrive at starting point.

12 LAKE ALMANOR RECREATION TRAIL

BEST ☾

south of Chester and Lassen Volcanic National Park

PAVED BIKE PATH

Difficulty: 1

Total Distance: 19 miles

Riding Time: 2 hours

Elevation Gain: 600 feet

Summary: Lake Almanor's paved bike trail makes an ideal family outing and provides a chance to spot ospreys and eagles.

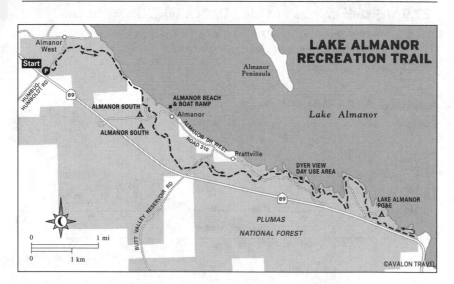

The Lake Almanor Recreation Trail is a popular paved path for campers staying at the lake's five campgrounds. The lake, set at 4,500 feet in elevation, is one of the largest artificially constructed lakes in California—13 miles long, 6 miles wide, and with 28,000 surface acres. It's well known among anglers, who ply its waters for rainbow trout, brown trout, and chinook salmon. It's also popular with water-skiers in summer.

The recreation trail makes a perfect family bike trip, and its 19-mile round-trip length is long enough to make you feel like you got some exercise. Unfortunately the path follows the lakeshore for only a small portion of its length, but still, it's quite pretty. Much of it runs through fragrant stands of pine, fir, and incense cedar and passes meadows covered in wildflowers in spring and early summer. Interpretive signs are posted at several points along the trail, explaining the local flora and fauna. Keep your eyes out for ospreys and bald eagles; they are frequently

© ANN MARIE BROWN

low water at Lake Almanor at the end of the summer

seen from the lake's west shore. Lake Almanor has the largest summer population of ospreys in California.

For more information, contact the Almanor Ranger District of Lassen National Forest, 530/258-2141, www.fs.fed.us/r5/lassen.

Driving Directions

From Chester, drive 3 miles west on Highway 36/89, then turn left (south) on Highway 89 and drive 4.3 miles. Turn left across from Humbug–Humboldt Road.

Route Directions

0.0 Park at the northern trail access across Highway 89 from Humbug–Humboldt Road. *Supplies are available in Chester.*

2.5 Almanor North and South Campground and boat ramp. *Water is available.*

4.2 Jake's Lake, an ephemeral wetland that dries up by July.

5.4 Cross Butt Valley Reservoir Road.

6.5 Dyer View day-use area.

9.5 End of trail at Lake Almanor PG&E Campground. TURN AROUND.

19.0 Arrive at starting point.

13 EAGLE LAKE TRAIL
north of Susanville

BEST ◖

PAVED BIKE PATH

Difficulty: 1

Total Distance: 10 miles

Riding Time: 1 hour

Elevation Gain: 100 feet

Summary: Pedal along the south shore of Eagle Lake, the second largest natural lake in California and one of the best spots in Northern California for bird-watching.

Was Eagle Lake named for our national bird? Yes, it was. From the shores of Eagle Lake, bald eagles and ospreys are commonly seen. On my bike ride, I spotted both of those remarkable birds, plus white pelicans, western grebes, Canada geese, a great blue heron, a beaver, mule deer, and golden-mantled ground squirrels by the dozens.

Eagle Lake is one of the best places to see wildlife in Northern California.

It's not surprising, considering a few facts: Eagle Lake is the second largest natural lake in California, after Lake Tahoe. Fed by natural, underwater springs, the lake is set in an enclosed basin with no natural outlets. As a result, its water is extremely alkaline. Only one species of trout can survive in it—the Eagle Lake rainbow trout. This fish is coveted for its size, fighting ability, and taste. Humans, as well as ospreys and eagles, find them quite delicious.

Eagle Lake's paved recreation trail starts at Christie Campground, near site number 12. The path stays right along the lake's south shore for the entire ride, curving in and out of pine forests and meadows, passing sandy beaches and offering nearly nonstop views of the water. Because the trail runs through several campgrounds, you have many chances for water breaks. At mile 4.0, you can stop at the marina store for snacks. Bike rentals are also available. A highlight along the trail is the wheelchair-accessible fishing area by the marina, which is also a prime bird-watching spot. Nearby Gallatin Beach is marked off for swimming.

Be on the lookout for eagles and ospreys on Eagle Lake Trail.

The lake is set at 5,100 feet in elevation, so it's often cool and comfortable up here when the Susanville area is much warmer.

For more information, contact the Eagle Lake Ranger District of Lassen National Forest, 530/257-4188, www.fs.fed.us/r5/lassen.

Driving Directions

From Susanville on Highway 36, drive west for 3 miles and then turn north on County Road A-1, Eagle Lake Road (next to the ranger station). Drive 14 miles to the lake, then follow the signs to Christie Campground.

Route Directions

0.0 Park outside Christie Campground at Eagle Lake and ride into the camp to site number 12 and the start of the trail. *Supplies are available in Susanville.*

4.0 Gallatin Beach, marina, and store. *Supplies are available.*

5.0 End of trail. TURN AROUND.

10.0 Arrive at starting point.

14 BIZZ JOHNSON TRAIL BEST ☾

Susanville, east of Red Bluff

DIRT ROAD

Difficulty: 2

Total Distance: 13.4 miles (or 51-mile option)

Riding Time: 2 hours

Elevation Gain: 500 feet

Summary: The initial miles of this 25-mile-long railroad grade are easy pedaling along the scenic Susan River canyon, perfect for any kind of rider.

The Bizz Johnson National Recreation Trail is one of the great success stories of the rails-to-trails movement in the United States. The longest rail trail in California, it follows the path of the Southern Pacific Railroad's Fernley and Lassen branch line between Susanville and Mason Station, 4 miles north of Westwood. Southern Pacific operated logging, freight, and passenger trains over the line in 1914–1955. Through the cooperative efforts of the Bureau of Land Management, U.S. Forest Service, and many community groups, the abandoned rail line is now a 25.4-mile-long trail for bikers, hikers, and horseback riders.

The wide dirt-and-gravel road is ideal for mountain biking, whether you want a short and easy cruise along the scenic Susan River, or a longer adventure riding the entire trail and then looping back on Highway 36 (see *Options*). The route has a very easy 2–3 percent grade except for one short section, so you can spin out the miles fairly quickly. If you opt for the loop, be forewarned that the 15-mile stretch on Highway 36 gets substantial car traffic. (Bus service is available on some days if you want to ride the entire trail one-way; call the contact numbers below for details.)

The trail begins at the Susanville Railroad Depot and Museum, which is open daily including holidays. The first 0.5 mile runs through Susanville's neighborhoods, then reaches the Millerton Road Trailhead and enters the scenic Susan River canyon. Both sides of the trail are lined with fascinating volcanic rocks; the pretty river flows mellifluously alongside. The trail passes through two old railroad tunnels (one 800 feet long and one 400 feet long and both extremely dark inside) and crosses nine scenic bridges. At the Devil's Corral Trailhead at mile 6.7, riders simply turn around and head back, enjoying the lovely river canyon all over again.

So who was Bizz Johnson, anyway? He was a former California congressman who worked on this project and many other public works.

one of two old railroad tunnels on the historic Bizz Johnson Trail

© ANN MARIE BROWN

For more information, contact the Bureau of Land Management's Eagle Lake Field Office, 530/257-0456, www.ca.blm.gov/eaglelake; or the Eagle Lake Ranger District of Lassen National Forest, 530/257-4188, www.fs.fed.us/r5/lassen.

Options

If you have all day to ride, you can complete a 51-mile loop by pedaling the entire length of the Bizz Johnson Trail, then looping back on Highway 36. Beyond the Devil's Corral Trailhead, the trail loses some of its scenic value, but fear not, it will get better soon. A detour takes you under Highway 36 with a short descent and climb. Then the trail moves farther from the river on a 6.2-mile stint to the Goumaz Trailhead. If you choose, you can pack your panniers and spend the night at Goumaz's primitive campground (bring your own water). From there, it's another 5.1 miles to Westwood Junction, the highest point on the trail at 5,500 feet, and then a final 7.4 miles to Mason Station. The higher elevations in this last stretch are a major departure from the initial arid miles of trail; Westwood Junction is ponderosa pine country (and snow country in winter).

To finish out the loop, ride four miles on county roads to Highway 36 and the small town of Westwood, where you'll find supplies and a 25-foot-tall carved statue of Paul Bunyan, symbol of the Paul Bunyan Lumber Company. Then take Highway 36 east to Susanville.

Driving Directions

From Highway 36 in Susanville, head east through town as the road becomes Main Street. At the first stoplight, turn right on South Weatherlow Street. Drive 0.4 mile to the railroad depot on the left.

Route Directions

0.0 Park at the Susanville Railroad Depot. *Supplies are available in Susanville.*

0.5 Millerton Road Trailhead.

6.7 Devil's Corral Trailhead. TURN AROUND.

13.4 Arrive at starting point.

MENDOCINO AND WINE COUNTRY

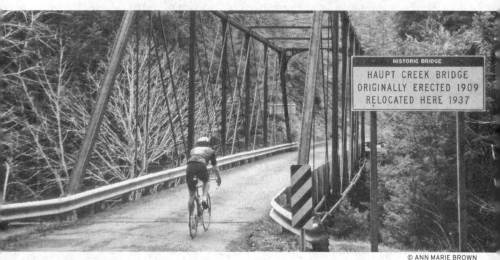

HISTORIC BRIDGE
HAUPT CREEK BRIDGE
ORIGINALLY ERECTED 1909
RELOCATED HERE 1937

© ANN MARIE BROWN

BEST BIKE RIDES

◖ **Butt-Kickers**
Boonville's Mountain View Road, **page 123.**

◖ **High Overlooks**
Mount St. Helena, **page 145.**

◖ **Oceanfront Rides**
Old Haul Road/Ten Mile Coastal Trail, **page 112.**

◖ **Waterfalls**
Fern Canyon Trail Bike and Hike, **page 115.**

◖ **Wildlife-Viewing**
Boggs Lake Loop, **page 136.**

◖ **Wine-Tasting**
Annapolis Road Loop, **page 130.**
Geyserville Winery Loop, **page 133.**
Healdsburg Westside and Eastside Loop, **page 142.**
Yountville and Silverado Trail, **page 160.**

The Mendocino and Wine Country region

encompasses a vast and diverse landscape from wave-swept beaches, rugged cliffs, and rolling sand dunes to vineyard-covered hills and valleys. Despite the technological advances of our modern 21st century, this area has retained its pastoral character more than perhaps anywhere else in California. Highway 1 winds up the rocky Pacific coast past seaside villages with population counts lower than their elevation, which is nearly at sea level. In much of the grassland hills east of the Sonoma and Mendocino coast, you're likely to see more sheep or cows than people. The talk in the towns is about the crab harvest, or how many head of cattle are grazing in what plot of land, or whether or not grapes can grow in the coastal hills.

This peaceful, rural countryside makes for marvelous bicycling on country roads with little car traffic. For something more exciting, you can pedal the coastal highway itself, where rocky promontories, stately lighthouses, and sandy coves offer breathtaking panoramas. If you're clamoring for a fine meal or a bed-and-breakfast to ease you out of the saddle at the end of the day, the town of Mendocino, with its charming shops and rugged headlands, always welcomes visitors.

Bicyclists heading to the Mendocino coast to experience nature will find plenty of it here. The area is blessed with an abundance of parks. Within a few miles of Mendocino's town limits are three state parks where bicycling is permitted – Van Damme, Russian Gulch, and MacKerricher. Mountain bikers looking to cover more distance can choose from hundreds of dirt roads and trails in nearby Jackson State Forest.

Unforgettable too are the inland valleys, where U.S. 101 runs north from Santa Rosa to the Wine Country. Most people think of the Sonoma and Napa Valleys as Wine Country, but the wine-growing regions expand into several other valleys as well: Alexander Valley east of Geyserville, Dry Creek Valley west of Geyserville, and the Russian River Valley between Guerneville and Healdsburg. Even Mendocino County is home to wineries in small towns like Boonville and Annapolis.

The Wine Country town of Healdsburg is worthy of special note as a haven for bicyclists. Its scenic, rural back roads are laced with tasting rooms. The local chamber of commerce happily supplies cyclists with area maps, and an annual Harvest Century Bicycle Tour is held each July. Fortunately, bicycling and wine-tasting go together like, well, a bold merlot and French bread spread with camembert. For a romantic date or even a relaxed family outing, the mostly level roads of the Wine Country valleys offer views of vineyards and picturesque farms, easy access to both world-famous and little-known tasting rooms, and celebrated cafés and gourmet grocery stores. If you like to eat, drink, and be merry, plus get a little exercise in the bargain, you'll enjoy this chapter's Wine Country bike rides.

For the best road riding in the more populated areas of Sonoma and Napa, avoid the wine tourist season, which is August–October. Instead, ride during the winter or in early spring, when the roads see much less traffic. One of the best bicycling months in Wine Country is February, when the mustard blooms beneath the grapevines and vineyards turn bright yellow.

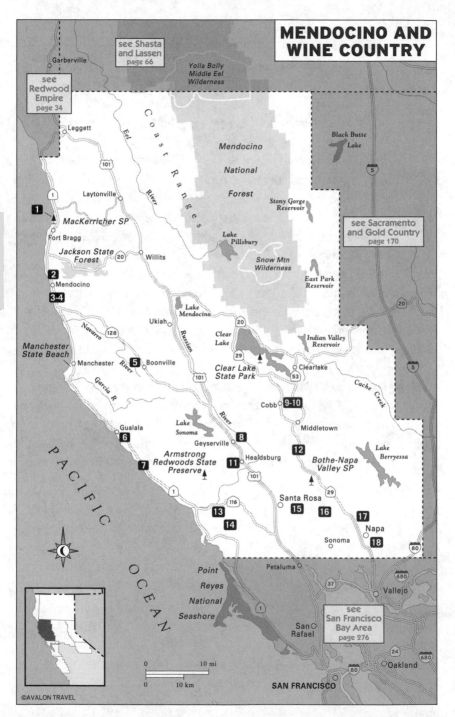

MENDOCINO AND WINE COUNTRY

see Shasta
and Lassen
page 66

Garberville

*Yolla Bolly
Middle Eel
Wilderness*

Black Butte
Lake

see
Redwood
Empire
page 34

Leggett

Coast Ranges

Mendocino

National

Forest

Eel River

Laytonville

1

MacKerricher SP

Fort Bragg

*Stony Gorge
Reservoir*

see Sacramento
and Gold Country
page 170

*Jackson State
Forest*

Willits

Lake
Pillsbury

*Snow Mtn
Wilderness*

2

Mendocino

3-4

Navarro

128

Ukiah

Lake
Mendocino

Russian River

Clear
Lake

20

*East Park
Reservoir*

*Indian Valley
Reservoir*

Manchester
State Beach

Manchester

5 Boonville

101

29

*Clear Lake
State Park*

Clearlake

53

Cache Creek

Garcia R

Gualala

6

Lake
Sonoma

River

Cobb **9-10**

Middletown

Lake
Berryessa

7

*Armstrong
Redwoods State
Preserve*

Geyserville

8

11 Healdsburg

12

*Bothe-Napa
Valley SP*

101

1

116

13

14

Santa Rosa

15

16

29

17

Napa

18

80

Sonoma

PACIFIC

*Point
Reyes
National
Seashore*

Petaluma

37

680

Vallejo

OCEAN

1

San
Rafael

see
San Francisco
Bay Area
page 276

24

Oakland

680

0   10 mi

0   10 km

80

SAN FRANCISCO

©AVALON TRAVEL

TRAIL NAME	LEVEL	DISTANCE	TIME	ELEVATION	PAGE
1 Old Haul Road/Ten Mile Coastal Trail	1	7.4 mi	1 hr	250 ft	112
2 Fern Canyon Trail Bike and Hike	1	3.2 mi	1.5 hr	200 ft	115
3 Fern Canyon Trail	1	5 mi	0.5-1.5 hr	250 ft	118
4 Comptche Loop	3	41.2 mi	3-4 hr	1,800 ft	120
5 Boonville's Mountain View Road	5	50 mi	5 hr	5,600 ft	123
6 Gualala Ridge and Point Arena Loop	3	40.3 mi	3-4 hr	1,600 ft	126
7 Annapolis Road Loop	4	24 mi	2-4 hr	2,300 ft	130
8 Geyserville Winery Loop	2	21.9 mi	1.5-2 hr	600 ft	133
9 Boggs Lake Loop	2	14.5 mi	1.5 hr	1,200 ft	136
10 Boggs Mountain Demonstration State Forest	3	12.2 mi	2 hr	1,800 ft	139
11 Healdsburg Westside and Eastside Loop	2	25.6 mi	1.5-2 hr	700 ft	142
12 Mount St. Helena	3	12 mi	2-3 hr	2,000 ft	145
13 Cazadero Loop	3	38.2 mi	3-4 hr	2,000 ft	148
14 Coleman Valley Loop	3	32.2 mi	2-3 hr	2,100 ft	151
15 Ledson Marsh and Lake Ilsanjo Loop	3	14.2 mi	2-3 hr	1,400 ft	154
16 Bald Mountain Loop	3	6.5 mi	1.5 hr	1,500 ft	157
17 Yountville and Silverado Trail	2	18 mi	1.5-2 hr	500 ft	160
18 Skyline Wilderness Park	3	6.8 mi	1.5 hr	1,200 ft	163

◼ OLD HAUL ROAD/ TEN MILE COASTAL TRAIL   BEST ◖

MacKerricher State Park near Fort Bragg

PAVED BIKE PATH

Difficulty: 1   **Total Distance:** 7.4 miles

Riding Time: 1 hour   **Elevation Gain:** 250 feet

Summary: Nonstop ocean views and a revamped historic railroad trestle await riders on this nearly level paved path.

First, the good news: Old Haul Road in MacKerricher State Park is one of the few trails near Mendocino where you can ride right alongside the ocean waves, enjoying miles of coastal scenery. It's a car-free, paved recreation trail, suitable for all kinds of riders and beach lovers. And as of 2008, the mid-trail Pudding Creek railroad trestle has been repaired and refashioned into a beautiful biking and pedestrian bridge, meaning that two sections of this trail have been linked in elegant fashion. Fort Bragg residents are rejoicing: No more riding on the highway.

Now the bad news: Old Haul Road, also called the Ten Mile Coastal Trail, has suffered serious storm damage over the years, and much of its north end is completely washed away, replaced by millions of grains of blowing sand. Park managers have been hoping for funds to repair or reroute it, but so far, they're just hoping.

But that hasn't stopped bikers from using Old Haul Road, a historic railroad grade built in 1915 for transporting redwood logs to the mill in Fort Bragg. Bicyclists arrive in great numbers every sunny day and share the trail with hikers, baby strollers, dogs on leashes, and even some equestrians. Everybody has a good time.

A 3.7-mile oceanside section from the western end of Ward Avenue south to the railroad trestle over Pudding Creek and into downtown Fort Bragg allows uninterrupted riding. For many years, this railroad trestle was closed off, but bikers and

© ANN MARIE BROWN

Riders enjoy non-stop ocean views from the Old Haul Road in MacKerricher State Park.

pedestrians cheered when state parks personnel managed to get the bridge fixed and reopened. It is now possible to ride all the way from MacKerricher State Park to Fort Bragg's Glass Beach along the historic Georgia-Pacific timber hauling road.

The first stretch of trail passes by wide-open beaches, dunes, and coastline, then enters the main camping and day-use area of MacKerricher State Park. Here you might want to get off your bike and do some exploring around Laguna Point, where harbor seals and tide pools are found along the rocky shore. South of the park, the trail becomes somewhat less scenic as it passes behind the backs of seaside motels, but still, to the west the open ocean is your constant companion—a symphony of white sand and wavy seas. The trail ends near Glass Beach, which was once the garbage dump for the city of Fort Bragg. Mother Nature had the last laugh, though, as the pounding of the waves transformed all those old beer and soda bottles into smooth, colorful sea glass, coveted by collectors. In the last few decades, Glass Beach has become such a popular scavenging spot that it's getting harder to find great glass specimens. Still, it's worth spending some time here searching for treasures.

Want more good news? The old Georgia-Pacific lumber mill, which was a closed-down eyesore along this southern stretch of trail, has been torn down, and by 2013 an extension of this recreation trail will be built across the mill's 400-acre property.

For more information, contact MacKerricher State Park, 707/964-9112 or 707/937-5804, www.parks.ca.gov.

Options

If you want to experience more of Old Haul Road, you can drive north on Highway 1 to just south of the Ten Mile River bridge, where the trail's north terminus is located. From here, you'll get a couple miles in the saddle before the pavement vanishes in the sand. This is the western edge of the 1,285-acre sand dune complex called Ten Mile Dunes, home to 12 threatened or endangered species, including the western snowy plover. If you wish to explore this area, head for the beach instead of walking on the fragile dunes. The Old Haul Road's entire length, including the unrideable sections, is seven miles one-way. Riding north from the Ward Avenue trailhead looks viable but isn't; the trail disappears into the sand in about 150 yards.

Driving Directions

From Mendocino, drive 13 miles north on Highway 1 to Ward Avenue (4 miles north of Fort Bragg and 1 mile north of MacKerricher State Park). Turn left and drive 0.7 mile to the road's end at a small parking area.

Route Directions

0.0 Park at the end of Ward Avenue at the sign for the recreation trail. Ride to your left (south). *Supplies are available in Fort Bragg.*

1.2 Gravel trail descends to main day-use area of MacKerricher State Park. *Lock up your bike and take a walk on the 0.5-mile Laguna Point Trail to see tide pools and sea lions, or walk the trail along the perimeter of Lake Cleone for bird-watching. Water is available at the campground.*

3.2 Pudding Creek railroad trestle; ride across.

3.7 Glass Beach. *Lock up your bike and explore this small city beach, which is littered with smooth sea glass.* TURN AROUND.

7.4 Arrive at starting point.

OLD HAUL ROAD/TEN MILE COASTAL TRAIL

2 FERN CANYON TRAIL
BIKE AND HIKE

BEST ◖

Russian Gulch State Park near Mendocino

PAVED BIKE PATH

Difficulty: 1

Total Distance: 3.2 miles (plus 3-mile hike)

Riding Time: 1.5 hours

Elevation Gain: 200 feet

Summary: Bring a bike lock along so you can park your wheels and enjoy this combination ride and hike to Russian Gulch Falls.

The Fern Canyon Trail at Russian Gulch State Park is hardly long enough to be considered a bike trail, yet it is always popular with riders. Why? Because cycling on the forested, fern-lined Fern Canyon Trail is only one part of the adventure; part two comes when you lock up your bike at the paved trail's terminus and take a hike to Russian Gulch Falls, a gushing 36-foot waterfall that drops into a rocky fern grotto. The falls are framed by toppled tree trunks and hundreds of ferns in a lush, picturesque setting. After a good rain, Russian Gulch Falls really pours, but it is lovely to see even in the dry summer months.

The trail directions are a breeze. Just get on your bike and ride from the trail-head at the edge of the campground, following the smooth paved path 1.6 miles to a junction, where you'll find a few picnic tables and a bike rack. Here you must lock up your bike and continue on foot to the waterfall. Two trail choices will get you there: a short, 0.7-mile route accessing it from the north, or a longer, 2.3-mile route accessing it from the south. After viewing the falls, you can either return the way you came or hike the alternate trail back (for a 3-mile round-trip hike). Then it's back on the saddle and a quick return ride to the trailhead.

Small riders may need some assistance on Russian Gulch State Park's Fern Canyon Trail.

If you're planning a romantic weekend in Mendocino, this makes a fine morning or afternoon outing. It's also a great trip for families.

For more information, contact Russian Gulch State Park, 707/937-5804 or 707/937-4296, www.parks.ca.gov.

Driving Directions

From Mendocino, drive two miles north on Highway 1 to the entrance to Russian Gulch State Park on the left. Turn left, then left again immediately to reach the entrance kiosk. Continue past the kiosk and turn left again to cross under the highway. Drive through the campground to the Fern Canyon Trail parking area. (If the camp is closed for the winter, you must park near the recreation hall and ride through the campground.)

Route Directions

0.0 Park at the Fern Canyon Trail parking area, past the campground.
Supplies are available in Mendocino. Water is available at the park campground.

1.6 Bike rack, picnic tables, and junction with Waterfall Loop Trail. TURN AROUND. *Lock up your bike and hike to Russian Gulch Falls from here, via either a 0.7-mile trail or a 2.3-mile trail.*

3.2 Arrive at starting point.

3 FERN CANYON TRAIL
Van Damme State Park near Mendocino

PAVED BIKE PATH

Difficulty: 1   **Total Distance:** 5 miles (or longer options)

Riding Time: 0.5-1.5 hours   **Elevation Gain:** 250 feet

Summary: This easy adventure gets riders up close and personal with the Little River, with an option to visit a pygmy forest of stunted trees.

It's a bit confusing: Within five miles of Mendocino are two Fern Canyon Trails. Both are paved bike trails, both were built on old logging roads, both are in state parks, and both carve their way through flora-rich canyons, paralleling streams.

Here's the difference: The Fern Canyon Trail in Russian Gulch State Park has an optional add-on hike to a waterfall (see ride 2, *Fern Canyon Trail Bike and Hike*). This Fern Canyon Trail, in Van Damme State Park, crosses the Little River dozens of times, revealing spawning salmon and steelhead in its clear pools in the winter months. The trail also has an option for an add-on mountain bike ride or hike to a pygmy forest of miniature cypress and pine trees.

Both trails are worth experiencing. The Fern Canyon Trail in Van Damme State Park has one big catch, though. During the rainy season, its multiple bridges are removed, so you can't travel past the first mile. Generally you can count on the entire trail being open April–October, but always phone the park before making a special trip. Storm damage during several winters in the last decade closed the trail completely for long periods, and if Mother Nature gets in the mood, it could happen again. A few brief, washed-out sections serve as a reminder of these stormy days; most riders carry their bikes over the breaks in the pavement.

The first 2.5 miles are nearly level, curving through the Little River's lush canyon lined with redwoods, firs, alders, berry bushes, and of course, ubiquitous ferns—10 different species are found here. Where the pavement ends, two optional trails continue onward (see *Options*).

For more information, contact Van Damme State Park, 707/937-5804 or 707/937-0851, www.parks.ca.gov.

Options

To continue your adventure beyond the pavement's end, you can choose from a 2.5-mile, hikers-only trail (skinny-tire riders can lock up their bikes at the bike rack and hike this path) or a 1.2-mile dirt road that is accessible to mountain bikes. Both trails lead to the pygmy forest, where sandy, highly acidic soil has produced miniaturized flora. Mountain bikers, be prepared for a small climb to get there. Although it's not a gut-thumping hill, it requires more of an effort than the paved path you've been following.

Driving Directions

From Mendocino, drive three miles south on Highway 1 to the entrance to Van Damme State Park on the left. Turn left and continue past the kiosk to the Fern Canyon Trail parking lot at the east end of the campground.

Route Directions

0.0 Park at the east end of the campground in the signed Fern Canyon Trail parking area. *Supplies are available in Mendocino. Water is available at the park campground.*

1.7 Pass the environmental campsites for hikers and bikers.

2.1 Fork in trail; take either route (they rejoin shortly).

2.5 Pavement ends. TURN AROUND. *Or, you can lock up your bike here and walk the hikers-only trail (on the left) 2.5 miles to the pygmy forest. If you have a mountain bike, you can continue riding on the dirt road to the right. It's 1.2 miles to the pygmy forest.*

5.0 Arrive at starting point.

4 COMPTCHE LOOP
south of Mendocino

PAVED ROADS WITH MINIMAL CAR TRAFFIC

Difficulty: 3

Riding Time: 3-4 hours

Total Distance: 41.2 miles

Elevation Gain: 1,800 feet

Summary: Visit the nearly forgotten lumber town of Comptche on this back-road ride in Mendocino County.

If you want to buy anything related to bikes in Mendocino, you have only one store to choose from: Catch-a-Canoe and Bicycles Too (707/937-0273, www.catchacanoe.com). The people that run the place are old hands at suggesting rides for Mendocino visitors, and this loop (or one of several shorter variations of it)

© ANN MARIE BROWN

Rocky sea stacks off the Mendocino coast provide picture-postcard scenery along the Comptche Loop.

is one of their standards. If you didn't bring your bike to Mendocino, fear not: These same nice folks will rent you one.

The ride starts at Van Damme State Park and heads up Little River Airport Road, with an optional stop at the park's pygmy forest at 3.2 miles. Here the pines and cypress trees grow only a few feet tall but are 50 to 100 years old. Their growth is stunted from the highly acidic, poorly drained soil.

After climbing some more, you gain a ridgeline 800 feet above the ocean, where Little River Road joins Comptche–Ukiah Road. A pleasant stretch of riding follows as you overlook inland canyons filled with miles of redwoods. The tiny town of Comptche, elevation 183 feet, is reached via two sustained descents punctuated by two level stretches. (One of the drops is almost four miles long; be glad you don't have to turn around and climb back up.) Here you and your wheels depart the dense forests and enter open pasturelands, dotted with herds of sheep and cows. Stop at the only store in Comptche, if it's open, to fuel up on snacks and drinks.

In the mid-19th century, Comptche was a bustling lumber center, like most of the other towns in Mendocino County. Things are quieter now. Today, besides the store, the local post office is the main center of Comptche town life.

A scenic stretch on Flynn Creek Road leads to Highway 128 and Navarro River Redwoods State Park, which borders both sides of the highway. You'll face more car traffic from here to the end of the ride, but the scenery is worth it: The nearly level road curves through shady redwoods, paralleling the Navarro River.

If it's a hot day, find yourself a cool pool to wade into (the best swimming holes are found in the two miles west of Dimmick Campground).

Before you know it, you're back at Highway 1, heading up the Navarro River grade to Navarro Point and then north through Albion and Little River to Van Damme State Park.

Driving Directions

From Mendocino, drive three miles south on Highway 1 to the entrance to Van Damme State Park on the left. Park in any of the park's day-use areas: either at the beach area on the west side of the highway or near the campground on the east side.

Route Directions

0.0 Park at one of the day-use areas at Van Damme State Park. Ride south on Highway 1. *Supplies are available in Mendocino.*

0.5 LEFT on Little River Airport Road.

3.2 Pygmy forest on left. *Walk the raised wooden walkway through stunted trees and flora.*

6.6 RIGHT on Comptche–Ukiah Road.

15.4 Comptche. *Supplies are available.*

15.5 RIGHT on Flynn Creek Road.

22.9 RIGHT on Highway 128.

26.5 Dimmick Campground on the left. *Water is available. Swimming holes are found west of the campground.*

34.5 RIGHT on Highway 1.

41.2 Arrive at starting point.

COMPTCHE LOOP

5 BOONVILLE'S MOUNTAIN VIEW ROAD

BEST (

Boonville to the Mendocino coast

PAVED ROADS WITH MINIMAL CAR TRAFFIC

Difficulty: 5

Total Distance: 50 miles

Riding Time: 5 hours

Elevation Gain: 5,600 feet

Summary: This challenging loop tests riders with one hill after another, but the scenic rewards make it all worthwhile.

There's more than one way to get to the Mendocino coast, and the best way is by bicycle from Boonville to Manchester on Mountain View Road. This is one of the great winding, twisting roads of Northern California—a former stagecoach route that is far too circuitous to encourage much car traffic. You will probably encounter deer instead, and quite possibly wild pigs.

The ride is an out-and-back, with nearly equal amounts of climbing and descending in both directions. You could just as well start this trip at the coast, if you desire, and ride to Boonville and back. The road has not one summit but several, the highest of which is about 2,200 feet in elevation.

Begin with a steep, 2-mile climb out of Boonville, passing the Boonville airport and redwood-filled Faulkner County Park, then prepare for a long, repeated series of descend, climb, descend, climb. This goes on for the duration of the trip, as you curve in and out of one forested mile after another, until at mile 19.5 you make a final 5.5-mile descent down to Highway 1 and the coast. During this last drop, you exit the woodland and enjoy wide views of open pastureland and the glimmering ocean surface—provided it's not foggy. You'll have plenty of sheep for companions along this last stretch.

The road deposits you about midway between Point Arena and Manchester, so take your pick: You can head south a couple of miles to see the Point Arena Lighthouse or eat at one of the town's cafés, or head north a couple of miles to visit Manchester State Beach (the nearby KOA store sells snacks and drinks). Both of these short add-ons are basically level, especially when compared to what you've just ridden.

The ride back to Boonville is a surprisingly different experience. This route serves as a great reminder that out-and-back rides are often as visually interesting as loops; everything looks different heading in the opposite direction. Even the climbs are different: The first 5 miles heading up from the coast are the hardest, but a few miles later you get to enjoy a three-mile-long downhill stretch. You'll face more ups and downs all the way back to Boonville.

Point Arena Lighthouse

© ANN MARIE BROWN

Understand that you need to be completely self-sufficient for this ride, because you won't find any 7-Elevens along Mountain View Road. Pack along a good repair kit and plenty of snacks. You can buy almost anything you need in Boonville, a small town best known for having its own language, called Boontling (it's one of only two recognized dialects of English in America). If you want a cup of coffee, ask for a "horn of zeese." The lingo was made up in the late 1880s, when outsiders started to infiltrate the remote town. It was a way for the old-timers to talk among themselves.

After your ride, be sure to stop in at the Buckhorn Boonville (707/895-3224, www.thebuckhornboonville.com), previously known as the Buckhorn Saloon, where you can partake in locally made beer from the Anderson Valley Brewing Company, Mendocino Brewing Company, and North Coast Brewery. Or, if you'd prefer to go straight to the source, you can visit Anderson Valley Brewing Company's tasting room and/or take a brewery tour (17700 Hwy. 253, Boonville, 707/895-2337, www.avbc.com). No matter which watering hole you choose, you deserve it, having just completed 50 miles in the saddle and more than 5,000 feet of climbing.

Driving Directions

From U.S.101 just south of Ukiah, take Highway 253/Boonville Road west for 19 miles to Highway 128. Turn right (north) and drive 1 mile to Boonville. (Or, from Cloverdale, take Highway 128 north for 27 miles.)

Route Directions

0.0 Park in Boonville near the intersection of Highway 128 and Mountain View Road. *Supplies are available in Boonville.*

2.3 Faulkner County Park on the left; end of first climb.

25.0 Arrive at Highway 1. TURN AROUND. *Ride south 3 miles to Point Arena for supplies or to visit its lighthouse, or ride north 2.1 miles to Kinney Road and turn left for supplies at the KOA store and a visit to Manchester Beach State Park.*

50.0 Arrive at starting point.

BOONVILLE'S MOUNTAIN VIEW ROAD

6 GUALALA RIDGE AND POINT ARENA LOOP
south of Mendocino

PAVED ROADS WITH MODERATE CAR TRAFFIC

Difficulty: 3   **Total Distance:** 40.3 miles (or 21.5-mile option)

Riding Time: 3–4 hours   **Elevation Gain:** 1,600 feet

Summary: This hilly loop ride passes one of the tallest operating lighthouses on the West Coast, and offers an abundance of coastal scenery to enjoy along the way.

© ANN MARIE BROWN

At very low tide, Bowling Ball Beach's sandstone "balls" are easily visible.

Today's suburban-looking Gualala Ridge used to be the stagecoach route from Gualala to Point Arena in the mid-1800s. Because this area is in Mendocino's well-known banana belt of warmer weather, much of the road is now lined with modern homes. They are a surprising sight on this still mostly remote coast.

Gualala Ridge is much drier than other ridges south of Mendocino; you won't find redwood forests here. The undeveloped areas are lined with madrones, manzanita, Douglas firs, and pines. Gaining the ridge requires a hefty 900-foot climb from Highway 1; the first mile will get your heart pumping. After that, the grade turns moderate and stays that way. Whether you choose the long loop or the short loop (see *Options*), the descent to Highway 1 is fast and furious.

The long loop offers two unusual highlights along its stretch: Bowling Ball Beach and Point Arena Lighthouse. Bowling Ball Beach is accessed by a 0.5-mile walk from Schooner Gulch State Beach, 4 miles south of Point Arena. Its unusual formation of large, rounded rocks gives Bowling Ball Beach its name. The "bowling balls" are most visible during extremely low tides; they are completely hidden at the highest tides.

Point Arena Lighthouse is tied with Pigeon Point Lighthouse in San Mateo County as the tallest operating lighthouse on the West Coast. It has been guiding ships since 1870, although the present structure was built after the original was destroyed in the 1906 earthquake. For a few bucks, you can climb the 145 steps to the top of the lighthouse tower, plus visit the adjacent visitor center to see a collection of fascinating old photos and maritime exhibits. And if you fall in love with the lighthouse and its surroundings, as most people do, a few neighboring cottages are available for overnight rental.

For more information, contact Point Arena Lighthouse and cottages, 707/882-2777, www.pointarenalighthouse.com.

Options

If you don't have the time or the stamina for this long loop, a shorter trip with less elevation gain can be made by turning left on Iverson Road at mile 8.0, then descending to Highway 1 over the next 4.5 miles. Another left on Highway 1 will put you in the village of Anchor Bay (supplies are available) in just 5.2 miles, and then it's only 3.8 miles back to your starting point. Total mileage is 21.5 miles with a 1,200-foot elevation gain. Although this shorter loop cuts off the lighthouse visit, you can always ride to it on another day by starting in downtown Point Arena. This makes an easy, pleasant, 10-mile round-trip excursion.

Driving Directions

From Jenner at the junction of Highways 1 and 116, drive north on Highway 1 for 36 miles to Gualala. Old State Highway (Road 501A) begins on the south side of town.

Route Directions

0.0 Park in downtown Gualala and ride to the south side of town and the junction of Highway 1 and Old State Highway (Road 501A). *Supplies are available in Gualala.*

0.3 LEFT on Old Stage Road.

6.0 Old Stage Road changes to Iverson Road at Fish Rock Road junction.

8.0 RIGHT on Ten Mile Cutoff Road (Road 503A).

13.5 STRAIGHT at stop sign and junction with Eureka Hill Road.

16.5 Eureka Hill Road becomes Riverside Drive in Point Arena. *Supplies are available in Point Arena.*

16.6 RIGHT on Highway 1 (heading north).

18.4 LEFT on Lighthouse Road at Rollerville Junction. *Supplies are available.*

20.7 Entrance kiosk for Point Arena Lighthouse; fee required to enter.

21.1 Point Arena Lighthouse; TURN AROUND.

23.8 RIGHT on Highway 1 (heading south).

29.6 Schooner Gulch State Beach and Bowling Ball Beach on the right.

35.4 Village of Anchor Bay. *Supplies are available.*
40.3 Arrive at starting point.

7 ANNAPOLIS ROAD LOOP

BEST ☾

Sonoma Coast near Sea Ranch

PAVED ROADS WITH MINIMAL CAR TRAFFIC

Difficulty: 4   **Total Distance:** 24 miles

Riding Time: 2-4 hours   **Elevation Gain:** 2,300 feet

Summary: A challenging hill climb leads to a high ridge on the Sonoma Coast, where cyclists can break for a little wine-tasting.

This pleasant but challenging road ride begins at the hamlet of Stewarts Point, once a thriving town located near the site of a busy shipping port at Fisherman's Bay. Today you won't find much in the neighborhood except a well-stocked general merchandise store and a post office.

You're on your own for most of this ride; there is little in the way of services for much of the route. Still, you're unlikely to need anything as long as you carry plenty of water to hydrate yourself through the long ascents. Yes, this is a route for those who enjoy climbing, but most of the grades are fairly gradual. Traffic is light along the entire loop, and the beautiful scenery is sure to fill your senses. A few historic bridges make good photo opportunities; you might want to bring along a camera.

The small town of Annapolis has two sights to its credit: its one-room schoolhouse, which has been restored by local volunteers, and the family-run Annapolis Winery (707/886-5460, www.annapoliswinery.com), which produces excellent sauvignon blanc, pinot noir, and gewürztraminer grapes. After many miles of no civilization, the Wine Tasting Today sign will take you by surprise. The tasting room is located just 50 feet off Annapolis Road and is open most days noon–5 P.M. If you visit in August, you can enjoy the fruits of their Gravenstein apple harvest, and perhaps even use their apple press to squeeze your own juice.

Beyond the winery, you'll start to see more homes of Annapolis residents, and as

© ANN MARIE BROWN

historic Haupt Creek Bridge on Stewarts Point-Skaggs Springs Road near Annapolis

the road drops down toward the coast, you'll enter the community of Sea Ranch. This residential development is well known for its woodsy architecture, which is a modern adaptation of the New England saltbox style. Designed to blend in with the coastal surroundings, this construction style was used to appease environmentalists who fought hard against the development of this stretch of coast. As part of the development agreement, the public is allowed access to four beaches in the Sea Ranch complex. You'll pass the signed turnoffs for Pebble Beach and Black Point Beach as you ride south back to Stewarts Point. Both are worth a look.

Driving Directions

From Jenner, at the junction of Highways 1 and 116, drive north on Highway 1 for 25 miles to Stewarts Point (2 miles south of Sea Ranch). Turn right on Stewarts Point–Skaggs Springs Road and park in the first available pullout.

Route Directions

0.0 Park at the pullout on the right side of Stewarts Point–Skaggs Springs Road, near its junction with Highway 1. *Supplies are available at Stewarts Point General Merchandise, or 11 miles north in Gualala.*

6.0 Historic Haupt Creek Bridge, originally erected in 1909 and moved here in 1937.

6.5 LEFT on Annapolis Road and cross bridge over Gualala River.

12.6 Pass Soda Springs Road on the right. Annapolis Winery is 50 feet down this road. *The winery is open most afternoons for tasting.*

13.4 Old Annapolis one-room schoolhouse.

14.5 Annapolis post office and a pay phone.

20.1 LEFT on Highway 1.

24.0 Arrive at starting point.

8 GEYSERVILLE WINERY LOOP   BEST ☾
north of Santa Rosa

PAVED ROADS WITH MODERATE CAR TRAFFIC

Difficulty: 2   **Total Distance:** 21.9 miles

Riding Time: 1.5-2 hours   **Elevation Gain:** 600 feet

Summary: Easy, mostly level riding through the Alexander Valley leads to multiple wineries and food stops.

This ride tours the wine region surrounding Geyserville and the Alexander Valley, one of the lesser visited of Northern California's grape-growing regions. The loop has a large number of junctions for its short mileage, so carry along a map and these suggested route directions. The abundant turns serve a purpose: They'll lead you past a half-dozen major wineries, plus a few interesting shops and sights.

One warning: Part of this ride follows Highway 128, where there is no shoulder, but thankfully not tons of traffic, either. Count on wide shoulders on the second half of the loop (west side of U.S.101) and narrow to nonexistent shoulders on the first half. If you don't like this arrangement, just ride out and back on the loop's west side.

The roads are quite level, and the scenery seems to encourage lingering more than intense pedaling. Stop in Jimtown for a cup of coffee and some discussion

The Geyserville Winery Loop is lined with grapevines.

about this year's grape crop, or at the Dry Creek General Store, established 1881, to find out about the history of this area. Do a little wine-tasting at one, or all, of the wineries along the route. Even teetotalers will want to stop on Dry Creek Road at Timber Crest Farms (4791 Dry Creek Rd., 707/433-8251), a farming and wine collective that sells a variety of gourmet treats, from olive oil to dried fruit to barbecue sauce.

Note that this area gets very hot in summer, so avoid midday riding then. Early spring is the loveliest season, when the air is cool and the mustard blooms amid the myriad grapevines.

For more information, contact the Healdsburg Chamber of Commerce, 707/433-6935 or 800/648-9922, www.healdsburg.org.

Driving Directions

From Santa Rosa, drive 25 miles north on U.S. 101 and take the Highway 128/Geyserville exit. Drive north on Geyserville Avenue for 1 mile and park in downtown Geyserville near the junction with Highway 128.

Route Directions

0.0 Park near junction of Geyserville Avenue and Highway 128 in downtown Geyserville. Ride east (right) on Highway 128. *Supplies are available in Geyserville.*

0.7 Cross bridge over Russian River.

0.9 RIGHT to stay on Highway 128.

1.9 De Lorimier Winery.

4.0 Murphy-Goode Winery.

4.5 LEFT on Geysers Road.

5.1 RIGHT on Red Winery Road.

7.4 RIGHT on Pine Flat Road.

7.8 STRAIGHT on Highway 128.

8.1 Pass through Jimtown. *Supplies are available.*

8.3 STRAIGHT on Alexander Valley Road. *Supplies are available at Alexander Valley Store and Bar.*

10.4 RIGHT on Lytton Station Road.

11.7 RIGHT on Lytton Springs Road.

11.9 Cross under U.S. 101.

12.6 Ridge and Lytton Springs Tasting Room.

13.2 Mazzocco Winery.

14.4 RIGHT on Dry Creek Road.

15.2 STRAIGHT at stop sign at Dry Creek General Store. *Supplies are available.*

15.3 Teldeschi Winery.

16.6 Timber Crest Farms (sells gourmet goodies).

18.0 Chateau Diana Winery.

18.8 RIGHT on Canyon Road.

19.7 J. Pedroncelli Winery.

20.9 Cross under U.S. 101.

21.0 RIGHT on Highway 128/Geyserville Avenue.

21.9 Arrive at starting point.

9 BOGGS LAKE LOOP   BEST ☾
south of Clear Lake

PAVED AND DIRT ROADS WITH MINIMAL CAR TRAFFIC

Difficulty: 2   **Total Distance:** 14.5 miles

Riding Time: 1.5 hours   **Elevation Gain:** 1,200 feet

Summary: Remote back roads lead past a geothermal power plant and an unusual nature preserve.

The rolling hills south of Clear Lake are the setting for this loop ride, which affords expansive views of the region from several high points. Along the route are two highlights of radically different ilk: the Calpine Geysers geothermal facility and Boggs Lake Ecological Reserve, a slice of land co-owned by The Nature Conservancy and the California Department of Fish and Game.

At Calpine Geysers, billed as "the hottest spot in Wine Country," Calpine operates a working geothermal power plant that is open for free public tours (Wed.–Sat. 10 A.M.–4 P.M.). The tour starts at the Calpine Geothermal Visitors Center in Middletown (866/439-7377, www.geysers.com). Visitors are then taken by bus to one of the 19 working power plants in the area.

At Boggs Lake, you'll find a nature preserve filled with wildflowers, several rare and endangered species of plants, and prime bird-watching. Over 150 species, including bald eagles, have been recorded in winter and spring.

When you reach the entrance to Boggs Lake at mile 7.2, lock up your bike and walk the 1-mile loop along the lakeshore. Look for two unusual plants: bladderwort, with yellow blossoms that cover the surface of the lake in spring; and water shield, which lives beneath the water year-round except for two successive springtime days, when it pushes its reddish purple blossoms above the water. On the first day, it opens its blooms to receive pollen from other plants, then it pulls back into the lake. On the second day, it protrudes from the lake once more, this time to disperse its own pollen before disappearing below the surface again, until the next year.

The ride has only one significant climb, on Bottle Rock Road, which lasts for 2 miles. Most of the route is suitable for a road bike except for a 1.5-mile stretch on Harrington Flat Road where the pavement turns to hard-packed dirt. If your road bike tires aren't too thin, you can probably get away with riding them. If you are pedaling your mountain bike, this loop heads past the entrance to Boggs Mountain Demonstration State Forest at mile 13.4, where you can easily add on some miles if you wish. The forest features a cornucopia of single-track trails for mountain bikers (see ride 10, *Boggs Mountain Demonstration State Forest*).

For more information, contact Boggs Lake Ecological Reserve, 707/944-5500.

Driving Directions
From Calistoga, take Highway 29 north for 17 miles to Middletown, then turn left on Highway 175 and drive 8 miles to Cobb.

Route Directions
0.0 Park in the lot by the post office and Cobb Village Inn on Highway 175. Ride north on Highway 175. *Supplies are available in Cobb.*

0.2 LEFT on Bottle Rock Road.

1.6 Calpine Geysers geothermal facility on left.

3.5 STRAIGHT at junction with Sulphur Creek Road.

6.7 RIGHT on Harrington Flat Road.

7.2 Boggs Lake Ecological Reserve on left. *Lock up your bike and take a walk on one of the preserve's trails.*

8.6 Pavement ends.

10.1 Pavement begins again.

10.9 STRAIGHT at junction with Sulphur Creek Road.

12.0 RIGHT on Highway 175.

13.4 Entrance road to Boggs Mountain State Forest. *Many mountain biking possibilities here* (see ride 10, *Boggs Mountain Demonstration State Forest*).

14.5 Arrive at starting point.

🔟 BOGGS MOUNTAIN DEMONSTRATION STATE FOREST
south of Clear Lake

DIRT ROAD AND SINGLE-TRACK

Difficulty: 3

Total Distance: 12.2 miles

Riding Time: 2 hours

Elevation Gain: 1,800 feet

Summary: The trails at Boggs Mountain are legendary among mountain bikers, but getting to this remote location takes some effort.

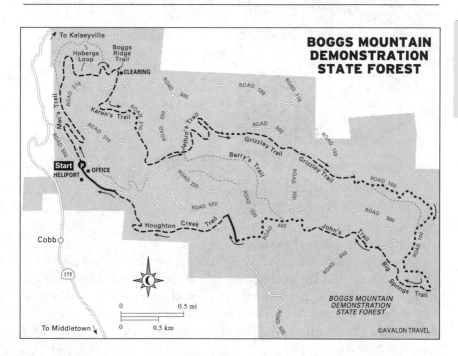

No Northern California biking guidebook would be complete without including Boggs Mountain Demonstration State Forest, a mecca of legal, fun, single-track trails for mountain bikers. And yet, most mountain bikers would be hard-pressed to say where exactly Boggs Mountain is, and what exactly a demonstration state forest is.

To set the record straight, Boggs Mountain is about midway between Calistoga and Clear Lake. If you're in the northern Napa Valley or the southern Lake County area, you're close. If not, you face a long drive from everywhere, but luckily the state forest has a campground. And a demonstration state forest is a place where

© ANN MARIE BROWN

riding through the autumn leaf litter at Boggs Mountain Demonstration State Forest

the California Department of Forestry experiments with forestry management techniques, including logging and fire-fighting, so expect to see some stumps and burned areas among the tall trees growing here. At Boggs Mountain, the land managers also allow many kinds of recreation, including hunting. Given this, it's best to avoid the area during deer season (usually late August and September).

The riding at Boggs Mountain is moderate, both in terms of technical and aerobic challenges. The terrain is mostly open woods and meadows at a 3,000-foot elevation; the hills are some-what steep but always short; and other trail users are generally few and far be-tween, although occasionally you will find groups of local bikers, or clubs from other areas, riding together. As mentioned previously, Boggs is a bit *out there,* so come prepared for near solitude. The delightful scenery will keep you company, from forests of ponderosa pines, black oaks, and Douglas firs to blooming wild-flowers and dogwoods in the spring.

Maps of the state forest are generally available at the kiosk in the parking lot at Forestry Road. Pick one up before you ride, as the 4,000-acre forest has a diz-zying number of trails, dirt roads, and junctions. If you get lost, just ride around as you please; every trail here has something to offer. One trail not to be missed is Houghton Creek Trail, the final leg of this loop; it's a fern- and flower-lined single-track dream.

For more information, contact Boggs Mountain Demonstration State Forest, 707/928-4378, www.boggsmountain.org.

Driving Directions

From Calistoga, take Highway 29 north for 17 miles to Middletown, then turn left on Highway 175 and drive 8 miles to Cobb. Continue 1 mile beyond Cobb and turn right on Road 500 (signed for State Fire Station). Drive 0.75 mile and park your car in the lot near the heliport and forestry office.

Route Directions

0.0 Park in the dirt lot by the forestry office and heliport. Follow Mac's Trail from the road alongside the parking lot. *Supplies are available in Cobb.*

0.8 LEFT on Hoberg's Loop Trail.

1.6 LEFT on Boggs Ridge Trail to clearing with vista point.

2.3 Junction with Road 210. Cross the road and pick up Karen's Trail.

3.0 RIGHT on Road 210, which soon narrows to single-track (trail becomes Scout Trail).

4.0 Junction with Road 200. Cross the road and pick up Jethro's Trail.

4.1 LEFT at junction with Berry's Trail (stay on Jethro's Trail).

4.8 RIGHT on Road 300.

5.3 LEFT on Grizzly Trail.

6.4 RIGHT on Road 100.

6.6 RIGHT on single-track Grizzly Trail.

7.1 RIGHT on Road 100.

7.2 Straight at junction of fire roads.

7.7 RIGHT (sharp) on Big Springs Trail.

8.4 Cross fire road and pick up John's Trail (a few yards to the left on the fire road).

9.2 LEFT on Road 400. Stay left at next three junctions.

9.7 RIGHT on Road 400.

10.1 RIGHT on Road 500.

10.5 LEFT on Houghton Creek Trail (also called simply Creek Trail) at junction with Road 200 and Calso Campground.

11.4 Cross creek.

11.9 LEFT on Road 500.

12.2 Arrive at starting point.

BOGGS MOUNTAIN DEMONSTRATION STATE FOREST

11 HEALDSBURG WESTSIDE AND EASTSIDE LOOP

west of Healdsburg

BEST ☾

PAVED ROADS WITH MODERATE CAR TRAFFIC

Difficulty: 2

Total Distance: 25.6 miles (or 20-mile option)

Riding Time: 1.5–2 hours

Elevation Gain: 700 feet

Summary: Prepare for multiple winery stops on this easy vineyard tour along the Russian River.

This is a classic winery road ride in the Russian River/Healdsburg area. Every day of the year you'll find cyclists on some part of this loop, which begins in downtown Healdsburg and passes dozens of wineries and tasting rooms. If you don't mind adding on a few miles on heavily trafficked River Road, you could easily start this ride in Guerneville as well.

To put this ride in perspective, in the first 6 miles you pass seven wineries and tasting rooms. Although each of the loop's wineries is worth a visit, a highlight is Hop Kiln Winery (707/433-6491, www.hopkilnwinery.com) at mile 6.1. Its much-photographed, three-towered hop barn is a designated historic site. Inside the barn is a well-stocked tasting room, with delicious mustards and other products for sale in addition to wines.

Another favorite is Foppiano Winery (707/433-7272, www.foppiano.com) at mile 23.7, where you can lock up your bike and take a self-guided tour that starts at the

© ANN MARIE BROWN

a stop at Hop Kiln Winery on Westside Road

tasting room and wends its way through vineyards to the Russian River. Foppiano's signature vintage is a petite sirah, which they have been making for 100 years.

If you want to learn about the history of California winemaking or see how wine is made, pay a visit to Rodney Strong Vineyard's Hospitality Center (707/431-1533, www.rodneystrong.com) at mile 22.6. This facility emphasizes visitor education along with its tasting and retail sales.

The loop begins and ends in the town of Healdsburg, a very bike-friendly town. The chamber of commerce at the junction of Healdsburg Avenue and Westside Road (707/433-6935 or 800/648-9922, www.healdsburg.org) will happily provide you with handouts on bike rides and wineries. Within walking distance are many cafés and shops, plus a few great bike stores.

Options

If in the course of riding this loop you have a few too many sips of wine (a forgivable error), you can cut the trip short by turning left on Wohler Road at 9.7 miles from the start. In 1 mile you'll cut over to Eastside Road, making a 20-mile round-trip. You will still get to see many of this ride's highlights.

Driving Directions

From Santa Rosa, drive 25 miles north on U.S. 101 and take the Westside Road/ Guerneville exit in Healdsburg. Turn east toward downtown Healdsburg and park in one of the public parking lots.

Route Directions

0.0 Park in downtown Healdsburg (near the junction of Healdsburg Avenue, Westside Road, and Redwood Highway) and ride west on Westside Road. *Supplies are available in Healdsburg.*

0.2 Cross under U.S. 101.

0.3 Alder Brook Tasting Room.

1.2 Mill Creek Tasting Room.

2.0 Armida Winery.

3.1 Rabbit Ridge Winery.

3.9 Belvedere Winery.

6.1 Hop Kiln Winery.

6.2 Rochioli Winery.

7.9 Davis Bynum Winery.

9.7 Wohler Road junction. *You could turn left here for a shortcut to Eastside Road and a 20-mile round-trip.*

10.7 Gary Farrell Vineyards.

12.5 LEFT to stay on Westside Road before bridge over Russian River.

12.6 LEFT on River Road (now looping back).

12.9 Berry's Market. *Supplies are available.*

14.7 Steelhead Beach Regional Park on left.

15.5 LEFT on Wohler Road.

16.1 RIGHT on Eastside Road.

17.3 LEFT at stop sign to stay on Eastside Road.

22.5 LEFT on Redwood Highway.

22.6 Rodney Strong Vineyards.

23.5 Limerick Lane Cellars on the left (0.5 mile off the road).

23.7 Foppiano Winery.

24.1 Cross under U.S. 101.

24.9 Bridge over Russian River.

25.6 Arrive at starting point.

12 MOUNT ST. HELENA

north of Calistoga

BEST ☾

DIRT ROAD

Difficulty: 3

Total Distance: 12 miles

Riding Time: 2–3 hours

Elevation Gain: 2,000 feet

Summary: A challenging climb leads to top-of-the-world views from the 4,343-foot summit of Mount St. Helena.

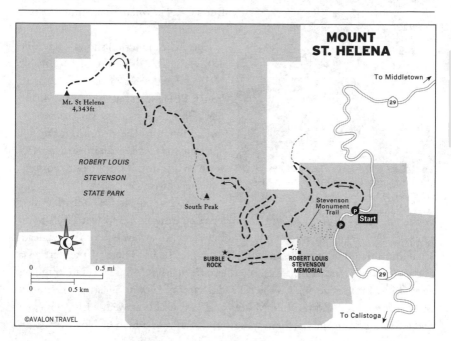

The spectacular view from the top of Mount St. Helena makes the protracted ascent on its wide, exposed road completely worth the effort. For the best possible trip, pick a cool, clear day in late autumn, winter, or spring—forget the hot days of summer. Then pack along a picnic lunch, fill your water bottles to the brim, drive to the trailhead, and start climbing.

You can turn off your brain for this ride, because it has only a few junctions along the entire route, and it's obvious which way to go. The dirt road's grade is fairly moderate, although unrelenting. You won't need your granny gear here, just some good aerobic endurance. And you don't have to wait until you reach the summit to reap visual rewards: You gain fine vistas of Napa Valley, the Vaca Mountains, Lake Berryessa, and the volcanic rock of the Palisades at several points along the road.

standing atop the summit of 4,343-foot Mount St. Helena

The ride starts out in a shady black oak forest, but all that changes after the first mile. Notice the terrain change as you climb: You're in big knobcone pines, manzanita, and madrones by 1.5 miles, enjoying the open sunshine and views of the Napa Valley. Keep climbing. At a tight switchback at 1.6 miles, you reach Bubble Rock, where rock climbers strut their stuff.

One major junction shows up at mile 4.0, along the ridgeline of Mount St. Helena. The road to the left leads to South Peak, a lesser summit at 4,003 feet. Continue straight for the mountain's higher northern summit, but not without first exclaiming over the vista from this point. This is your most expansive view so far.

Save your applause, because now you're only 2 miles from Mount St. Helena's summit at 4,343 feet. When you reach the top, pay no attention to the buildings and microwave equipment. Instead, stroll around and take in the amazing 360-degree scene. There's Lake Berryessa and the Sierra Nevada to the east. To the southeast lies Mount Diablo, 60 miles away. Most impressive of all is the clear-day view of Mount Shasta to the north, nearly 200 miles distant. Often Mount Lassen is visible as well, with 7,056-foot Snow Mountain in the northern foreground. Pull out a map of Northern California, a pair of binoculars, and your picnic lunch.

You may notice some odd-shaped rocks under your feet on the northwest side of the wide summit. If you've ever visited Devils Postpile National Monument in the eastern Sierra, you'll recognize them as the six-sided tops of lava columns. Although Mount St. Helena is composed of volcanic rock, it is not a volcano but part of a large, ancient lava flow.

For more information, contact Robert Louis Stevenson State Park, c/o Bothe–Napa Valley State Park, 707/942-4575 or 707/938-1519, www.parks.ca.gov.

Driving Directions

From Highway 29/128 in Calistoga, turn north on Highway 29 and drive eight miles to the gated Mount St. Helena Trailhead.

© ANN MARIE BROWN

Route Directions

0.0 Park in the pullouts alongside the gated road at the Mount St. Helena Trailhead. Start riding at the gate. *Supplies are available in Calistoga.*

0.7 LEFT at fork.

1.5 Pass the hikers-only Stevenson Monument Trail on left.

4.0 STRAIGHT at left turnoff for South Peak.

6.0 North Peak of Mount St. Helena, elevation 4,343 feet. TURN AROUND.

12.0 Arrive at starting point.

13 CAZADERO LOOP
west of Guerneville to the Sonoma Coast

PAVED ROADS WITH MODERATE CAR TRAFFIC

Difficulty: 3   **Total Distance:** 38.2 miles

Riding Time: 3-4 hours   **Elevation Gain:** 2,000 feet

Summary: This redwood-lined road ride leads to the small hamlet of Cazadero, then back out to the wide Pacific coastline.

Cazadero is not one of the more heavily visited towns in rural western Sonoma County, nor is it one of the more populated, yet three separate roads lead to it: Old Cazadero Road, the Cazadero Highway, and Austin Creek Road. This loop trip follows narrow, winding Austin Creek Road to Cazadero on an old railroad grade that was once used to haul redwood logs to the nearby mills. Because of its origins, the road has a very gradual grade and is only one lane wide in many stretches (these were narrow-gauge trains).

The road carves a path through dense groves of second- and third-growth redwoods, following picturesque Austin Creek the whole way. Enough homes line the road that you should be on the alert for auto traffic at all times, although you probably will encounter very little. If you tire of the somewhat rough paved surface of Austin Creek Road, you can cut over to much smoother Cazadero Highway, which parallels it, at mile 6.3. The two roads meet up again 3 miles later.

When you reach the not-so-bustling metropolis of Cazadero, you'll find a general store and a post office, and fairly often a couple of dogs sleeping in the street. At one time this was a busy logging community, but Cazadero is now better known for its dependably heavy rainfall each winter. This is one of the wettest places in all of California.

Beyond the town, you face a five-mile ascent on Fort Ross Road (1,300-foot climb), followed by a two-mile descent and another climb to a junction with Meyers Grade Road. The rest of the loop is a piece of cake, and if you are lucky enough to have clear weather, you'll enjoy ocean views as you descend to, and then ride alongside, Highway 1. From the top of Meyers Grade, the coastal view cruising the back roads from Cazadero to the Sonoma Coast

to the south expands to include Bodega Head, Tomales Bluff, and Point Reyes National Seashore—an awe-inspiring panorama.

When you reach the coast, take a short walk on the Vista Trail at the junction of Meyers Grade Road and Highway 1, or stop at one of the oceanview or riverview eateries in Jenner.

The final leg of this loop travels along busy Highway 116 back to Monte Rio, following the ever-scenic Russian River. Make a stop at Duncans Mills, which was once the site of a large lumber mill that processed the giant redwoods logged from these hills. Now it's a tiny village of shops and services.

Driving Directions

From Santa Rosa, take Highway 12 west for 5 miles to Sebastopol, then turn north on Highway 116 and drive 20 miles to Monte Rio (4 miles west of Guerneville).

Route Directions

0.0 Park in Monte Rio near the junction of Highway 116 (River Road) and Bohemian Highway. Ride west on Highway 116. *Supplies are available in Monte Rio.*

2.7 RIGHT on Austin Creek Road.

6.3 STRAIGHT on Austin Creek Road at junction with Cazadero Highway.

9.3 LEFT on Cazadero Highway into Cazadero. *Supplies are available.*

9.7 LEFT on Fort Ross Road at junction with Old Cazadero Road and King Ridge Road; begin five-mile climb.

15.3 Black Mountain Preserve on the left.

18.8 LEFT on Meyers Grade Road.

23.7 LEFT on Highway 1.

23.8 Vista Trail on the left. *Take a short walk on this Sonoma Coast State Beach overlook trail.*

28.5 Town of Jenner. *Supplies are available.*

30.0 LEFT on Highway 116.

33.8 Town of Duncans Mills. *Supplies are available.*

38.2 Arrive at starting point.

14 COLEMAN VALLEY LOOP
Occidental to Bodega Bay

PAVED ROADS WITH MINIMAL CAR TRAFFIC

Difficulty: 3

Riding Time: 2-3 hours

Total Distance: 32.2 miles

Elevation Gain: 2,100 feet

Summary: Let your wheels take you back a century or more on this road ride through rural western Sonoma County.

Western Sonoma County is a land psychologically so far removed from anything to the south and east of it that it seems a bit like Shangri-la. You see a lot of sheep out here, and they are happy-looking sheep. You'll see what I mean after you ride this loop.

The ride starts in the town of Occidental, a former railroad town now filled with quaint inns, good places to eat, and loads of charm. You can buy most anything you need here. From the center of town, take Coleman Valley Road west and uphill,

© ANN MARIE BROWN

bovine crossing on Coleman Valley Road

gaining 500 feet in the first two miles to the ridgeline. Watch for the old Coleman Valley schoolhouse, built in 1864 and one of the oldest still standing in California.

After a long and glorious ridgeline ramble through bucolic meadows, followed by a fast and furious 900-foot descent to the coast (prepare to brake for cows or sheep crossing the road), you find yourself at Highway 1 across from Coleman Beach. Pinch yourself a few times to be sure the idyllic landscape you just experienced wasn't a beautiful dream. What you're about to ride through is almost as dreamlike—a couple of miles of seaside cruising with the ocean waves breaking a few feet to your right.

When you reach the town of Bodega Bay, turn off on East Shore Road to cruise the perimeter of Bodega Harbor, a level, three-mile stretch that passes fishing boats and fish processing plants. Follow the road all the way to the tip of Bodega Head, then take the right fork to the west parking lot for a lovely ocean view, or climb up the Bodega Head Trail from there.

After enjoying the ocean air and salt spray, backtrack out of the harbor and take Bay Hill Road out of town. This peaceful eucalyptus-lined road climbs 600 feet from the coast, affording fine views of Bodega Bay over your right shoulder. Then it's downhill to Highway 1, and downhill some more to the town of Bodega. Of note: The town of Bodega, not Bodega Bay, was the setting for the Alfred Hitchcock movie *The Birds*. The old schoolhouse in the movie is located on Bodega Lane.

The last stretch follows Bodega Highway to Bohemian Highway and Freestone, where you might want to get a massage at Osmosis spa if your muscles are aching. If not, it's less than four miles back to your car in Occidental. Note that many riders opt to take Joy Road and Bittner Road back to Occidental (from just east of Bodega). Although these roads have less car traffic than the route suggested here, Joy Road demands a steep climb.

Driving Directions

From Santa Rosa, drive west on Highway 12 for 5 miles to Sebastopol. At the junction with Highway 116, continue straight on Bodega Highway for 5.7 miles, then turn right on Bohemian Highway. Drive 3.8 miles into the town of Occidental.

Route Directions

0.0 Park in downtown Occidental near the intersection of Bohemian Highway and Coleman Valley Road. Ride west on Coleman Valley Road. *Supplies are available in Occidental.*

1.8 RIGHT to stay on Coleman Valley Road.

10.1 LEFT on Highway 1 into Bodega Bay. *Supplies are available in Bodega Bay; water is available at campgrounds.*

12.4 RIGHT on East Shore Road.

12.5 RIGHT on West Shore Road. Ride out and back three miles along the edge of Bodega Harbor (road becomes Bay Flat Road). *Take the right fork to west parking lot for an ocean view and easy hike on Bodega Head Trail.*

15.5 Dead end at Bodega Head. TURN AROUND.

18.5 LEFT on East Shore Road.

18.6 LEFT on Highway 1.

18.7 RIGHT on Bay Hill Road (cross Highway 1 carefully).

22.6 LEFT on Highway 1.

23.5 LEFT on Bodega Highway.

24.0 Pass through town of Bodega. *Supplies are available.*

28.4 LEFT on Bohemian Highway.

28.7 Pass through town of Freestone. *Supplies are available.*

32.2 Arrive at starting point.

COLEMAN VALLEY LOOP

15 LEDSON MARSH AND LAKE ILSANJO LOOP

Annadel State Park, east of Santa Rosa

DIRT ROADS AND SINGLE-TRACK

Difficulty: 3

Total Distance: 14.2 miles

Riding Time: 2–3 hours

Elevation Gain: 1,400 feet

Summary: A must on every mountain biker's itinerary, Annadel State Park offers a variety of trails for all levels of riders.

Annadel State Park is a horsey kind of place. If you count the horse trailers in the parking lot, hoofprints all over the place, and horse manure along the trail, you might think more horses visit here than people.

But Annadel is also a mountain biker's place. Not just the ranch roads but also most of the single-track at Annadel is open to bikes. That's convenient, because you need to cover a lot of ground to see much of Annadel's 5,000 acres, which are filled with woodlands, meadows, creeks, wildflowers, and even a 26-acre lake.

This loop ride shows off two of Annadel's loveliest natural features: Ledson Marsh and Lake Ilsanjo. The riding is generally easy to moderate; the only difficulty is controlling your bike on some of the rocky trails and roads. Annadel is famous for its rocks. In the early 1900s, the area was extensively quarried to provide cobblestone for the city of San Francisco.

grasslands and oaks near Lake Ilsanjo in Annadel State Park

The trip starts at the trailhead at the end of Channel Drive. Take the wide ranch road uphill through a dense and shady Douglas fir forest, with a few redwoods and bay laurels for variety. At 2.1 miles, you'll head east on the single-track South Burma Trail, then connect with Marsh Trail and Ridge Trail to circle around Ledson Marsh. The marsh is popular with waterfowl and is a known habitat for the red-legged frog.

Next, you'll head west to loop back via Lake Ilsanjo. From the lake's earthen dam, you gain the best views of blue water, tules, and paddling water birds. Curious about the origin of the lake's moniker? Ilsanjo is a combination of Ilsa and Joe, the names of the land's former owners.

On the west side of Ilsanjo, head north on Rough Go, Live Oak, and North Burma Trails to connect to Channel Trail, which parallels the road you drove in on. Level Channel Trail heads back to the parking lot and your car.

For more information, contact Annadel State Park, 707/539-3911 or 707/938-1519, www.parks.ca.gov.

Driving Directions

From U.S. 101 in Santa Rosa, take the Fairgrounds/Highway 12 exit. Highway 12 becomes Farmers Lane as it heads through downtown Santa Rosa. Turn right on Montgomery Drive and drive 2.7 miles (veering to the right), then turn right on Channel Drive. It's 2.2 miles to the end of the road and the parking lot.

Route Directions

0.0 Park at the lot at the end of Channel Drive. Take wide Warren Richardson Trail uphill. *Supplies are available in Santa Rosa.*

0.8 RIGHT to stay on Warren Richardson Trail.

1.5 LEFT to stay on Warren Richardson Trail.

1.9 STRAIGHT to stay on Warren Richardson Trail.

2.1 LEFT on South Burma Trail (single-track).

4.1 LEFT on Marsh Trail.

5.0 RIGHT to stay on Marsh Trail.

5.4 Ledson Marsh; trail circles around it to the left.

6.4 RIGHT on Ridge Trail.

9.1 LEFT on Marsh Trail.

10.6 RIGHT on Canyon Trail to Lake Ilsanjo.

11.2 LEFT at Lake Ilsanjo.

11.4 STRAIGHT on Rough Go Trail.

11.9 STRAIGHT on Live Oak Trail.

12.7 LEFT on North Burma Trail.

13.4 RIGHT on Channel Trail.

14.2 Arrive at starting point.

LEDSON MARSH AND LAKE ILSANJO LOOP

16 BALD MOUNTAIN LOOP
Sugarloaf Ridge State Park, north of Sonoma

DIRT ROAD AND PAVED BIKE PATH

Difficulty: 3

Riding Time: 1.5 hours

Total Distance: 6.5 miles

Elevation Gain: 1,500 feet

Summary: This short but aerobically challenging loop provides plenty of scenery and a panoramic view from the 2,729-foot summit of Bald Mountain.

Although the grassy summit of Bald Mountain at 2,729 feet is the crowning glory of this loop trip in Sugarloaf Ridge State Park, each leg of the route presents its own rewards. This ride takes the most direct path to the summit, then loops back downhill on a roundabout tour of the park's varied terrain.

The short mileage might make this ride seem easy, but keep in mind that you must gain 1,500 feet in less than three miles. The climb is made easier because it mostly follows Bald Mountain Trail, a paved service road. Hooray for pavement when a steep ascent is on the menu.

The road begins in a hardwood forest but quickly climbs through slopes covered with ceanothus, manzanita, chemise, and toyon. The scented chaparral will take your attention away from the asphalt. At 2.4 miles, the pavement ends at a saddle and trail junction. The left fork leads to microwave-covered Red Mountain at 2,548 feet. You'll go right for Bald Mountain, now following a dirt fire road. The final 0.5 mile to the summit ascends grassy slopes with occasional outcrops of green serpentine. The dirt road curves around the north side of the mountain to meet Gray Pine Trail, the return of your loop. But first, take the short spur on the right to reach the 2,729-foot summit. It's bald indeed; not a single tree obstructs the sweeping view.

Two signs at the top identify all the neighboring landmarks, including Mount St. Helena, Mount Diablo, Bodega Bay, Mount Wittenberg in Point Reyes, Snow Mountain, Mount Tamalpais, the Golden Gate Bridge towers, Angel Island, and the Bay Bridge. Most impressive is the glimpse of the Sierra Nevada range, 130 miles away. A posted quote from author Robert Louis Stevenson sums it up: "There are days in a life when thus to climb out of the lowlands seems like scaling heaven."

From the summit, wide Gray Pine Trail descends swiftly along a ridge. You're likely to have much less company on this side of the park, which is good, because you'll need to concentrate on managing your downhill speed on the steep, rutted trail. A final stint on Meadow Trail is best ridden in springtime, when the trail's namesake meadow is littered with wildflowers: Douglas iris, California poppies, brodiaea, and blue-eyed grass. Often you'll spot deer grazing among them.

For more information, contact Sugarloaf Ridge State Park, 707/833-5712 or 707/938-1519, www.parks.ca.gov.

Options

To tack on a fun end-of-the-day activity to your mountain bike ride, plan your trip to Sugarloaf Ridge on one of the evenings when the Valley of the Moon Observatory Association is presenting an astronomy program at the park's Robert Ferguson Observatory (707/833-6979, www.rfo.org).

Driving Directions

From U.S. 101 in Santa Rosa, take the Fairgrounds/Highway 12 exit. Highway 12 becomes Farmers Lane as it heads through downtown Santa Rosa. Continue on Highway 12 for 11 miles to Adobe Canyon Road and turn left. (Or, from Highway 12 in Sonoma, drive 11 miles north to Adobe Canyon Road, then turn right.) Drive 3.5 miles to the park entrance kiosk. Park in the lot about 100 yards past the kiosk, on the left.

Route Directions

0.0 Park in the lot 100 yards past the entrance kiosk. Pick up Stern Trail, a wide paved road, by the kiosk. *Supplies are available in Kenwood.*

0.5 RIGHT on Bald Mountain Trail.

2.4 RIGHT at junction with trail to Red Mountain; pavement ends.

2.8 RIGHT on Gray Pine Trail, but first walk up short right spur to summit to check out all the landmarks.

3.9 RIGHT to stay on Gray Pine Trail.

5.3 RIGHT on Meadow Trail.

6.2 LEFT through parking lot. Follow paved road.

6.5 Arrive at starting point.

1 7 YOUNTVILLE AND SILVERADO TRAIL

BEST (

Napa Valley

PAVED ROADS WITH MODERATE CAR TRAFFIC

Difficulty: 2   **Total Distance:** 18 miles

Riding Time: 1.5–2 hours   **Elevation Gain:** 500 feet

Summary: On this easy Napa Valley road ride, you can fill up your panniers with purchases from multiple wineries and champagne vineyards.

This Wine Country ramble takes you past dozens of wineries and vineyards on a five-mile stretch of the famous Silverado Trail, plus gives you a tour of the restaurants, inns, and shops of Yountville, one of Napa County's charming towns. Take along a bike lock so you can stop at some of the wineries along the route. This is not a ride for hurrying.

The riding is mostly level, and although car traffic can be dense on weekends, the shoulders are wide on the more heavily traveled roads. Be forewarned that you do have to ride on busy Highway 29 for just under a mile, but the wide shoulder should give you confidence through this congested stretch.

In addition to the 10 major wineries you'll pass (Robert Sinskey, Silverado, Pine Ridge, Stagg's Leap, Regusci, Chimney Rock, Clos du Val, Christina, Trefethen, and Trio), you'll also have the chance to visit two champagne makers: small S. Anderson on Yountville Cross Road, and giant Domaine Chandon on California Drive. Technically their products must be called sparkling wine, not champagne, since their grapes are grown here in California, not in the Champagne region of France.

It's convenient to end your trip with a visit to Domaine Chandon (888/242-6366, www.chandon.com), located right across from where you parked your car. Nothing beats a little bubbly for celebrating a great ride in the Wine Country.

Driving Directions

From Napa, drive north on Highway 29 for nine miles to Yountville. Take the Yountville/Veterans Home exit, turn left on California Drive, and cross under the highway. Park in the large gravel pullout on the left, next to the railroad tracks and across from the Veterans Home sign.

Route Directions

0.0 Park at the junction of California Drive and Solano Avenue, in the gravel pullout by the railroad tracks. Ride back under the highway on California Drive. *Supplies are available in Yountville.*

0.1 LEFT on Washington.

0.8 LEFT at Y to stay on Washington.

1.8 RIGHT on Highway 29.

2.7 RIGHT on Yount Mill Road.

3.9 RIGHT to stay on Yount Mill.

5.0 LEFT on Yountville Cross Road.

6.0 Napa River Ecological Reserve on left.

6.6 S. Anderson Champagne.

6.9 RIGHT on Silverado Trail (wide bike lane). *Robert Sinskey, Silverado, Pine Ridge, Stagg's Leap, Regusci, Chimney Rock, and Clos du Val wineries are found in the next four miles. Stop for tours and tasting wherever you please.*

11.5 RIGHT on Oak Knoll Avenue.

12.4 LEFT on Big Ranch Road, then immediate RIGHT to get back on Oak Knoll.

12.7 Christina Vineyards.

13.1 Trefethen Winery.

13.6 Cross Highway 29.

13.7 RIGHT on Solano Avenue.

15.8 Trio Vineyards.

17.1 Ride past your parked car and under the gates of Domaine Chandon.

17.5 Domaine Chandon Visitor Center. TURN AROUND.

18.0 Arrive at starting point.

18 SKYLINE WILDERNESS PARK
Napa Valley

DIRT ROAD AND SINGLE-TRACK

Difficulty: 3 **Total Distance:** 6.8 miles

Riding Time: 1.5 hours **Elevation Gain:** 1,200 feet

Summary: A favorite haunt of local Napa mountain bikers, Skyline Wilderness Park provides plenty of single-track for intermediate and advanced riders.

The trailhead for Skyline "wilderness park" is located in an RV park packed with trailers, lawn chairs, and plastic flamingos. You can't access Skyline's fine trails without riding past the park's social hall and picnic areas, and through a corridor of chain-link fencing. (The latter passes by neighboring state hospital property.) It's an incongruous start to a nature-filled mountain bike ride.

Still, after a couple of minutes of this strange meandering, you leave it all behind and enter the quiet, steep-walled canyon of Marie Creek. The loop's first leg follows a wide fire road uphill alongside the creek for 2 miles to Lake Marie, a long, narrow reservoir that is popular with bass anglers. If you can look up while you're climbing, you'll notice striking cliff formations and caves among the dense forest of oaks, madrones, and bay laurel. Watch for the 100-year-old fig tree on the left at mile 1.3, near the junction with Bayleaf Trail. The enormous old tree still produces edible fruit.

At Lake Marie, cross over the lake's dam and turn right on Chaparral Trail. From here on out, the rest of your loop is single-track—and some of it is surprisingly tranquil Lake Marie at Napa's Skyline Wilderness Park

technical, earning this brief ride its #3 rating for difficulty. (This park was once the site of the World Cup mountain bike race. If you ride here, you're in good company.)

Chaparral Trail climbs up a slick, rocky, steep stretch (I walked my bike here) to join Skyline Trail, a part of the Bay Area Ridge Trail. Narrow Skyline Trail follows the park's southwest ridge for 3.5 miles, offering good views of Napa Valley and San Pablo Bay. Watch for stretches of old stone walls amid the oak grasslands, and some fine examples of buckeye, live oak, and bay. This is lovely country. You'll note that Skyline Trail is well named: From a high overlook at 3.8 miles, you can clearly make out the looming outline of Mount Tamalpais in Marin County. Looking north and west, you'll gain views of Mount Veeder and Sugarloaf Mountain.

Skyline Wilderness Park has other single-track trails open to mountain bikes, so when you finish this ride, you can do more exploring. Just make sure you ride only on legal trails; park rangers enforce the rules strictly here.

For more information, contact Skyline Wilderness Park, 707/252-0481, www. skylinepark.org.

Driving Directions

From Highway 29 in Napa, turn east on Imola Avenue. Follow Imola Avenue four miles to its end at 4th Avenue. Turn right into the park entrance.

Route Directions

0.0 Park at the signed parking area for Skyline Wilderness Park (there is an entrance fee). Follow the signs through the RV park to the actual trailhead. *Supplies are available in Napa.*

0.3 LEFT on Lake Marie Road.

2.3 LEFT across dam at Lake Marie.

2.4 RIGHT on Chaparral Trail (you may be walking and carrying your bike here).

2.9 RIGHT on Skyline Trail.

3.8 Indistinct trail to viewpoint leads right; take short trail to highest point on this ride.

4.4 Cross over Passini Road.

6.5 RIGHT to return to Lake Marie Road's start.

6.8 Arrive at starting point.

SACRAMENTO AND GOLD COUNTRY

© ANN MARIE BROWN

BEST BIKE RIDES

The Sierra Nevada foothills region surrounding

the north–south corridor of Highway 49 is known as the Gold Country or the Mother Lode. It's the place where James Marshall discovered gold in January 1848, sparking a huge and frenzied migration westward. When it became known that a rich vein of gold ran from Mariposa to Downieville, the history of California was forever changed. Although other areas of California experienced their own gold rush, it was the Mother Lode that ultimately produced the richest deposits of ore.

Evidence of the area's mining past is obvious, from historic brick and wooden buildings to old bridges, mines, water ditches, and an abundance of antiques shops. Many of the region's towns have barely changed since their heydays: Streets are just wide enough for two stagecoaches to pass, sidewalks are made of wood planks, buildings are constructed of stones from local rivers and streams, and storefronts look like they're right out of a movie set. You can travel for many miles in the Gold Country without ever seeing a traffic light.

Roaring river canyons bounded by rolling, low-elevation foothills studded with oaks, pines, manzanita, and chamise make up the landscape of the Gold Country. Above the steep-sloped canyons are volcanic tablelands and miles of open grasslands, which make fine grazing land for cattle and horses. Golden California poppies, blue lupine, and white mariposa lilies carpet the hillsides and meadows from March to May. Hot weather is to be expected in summer, which means the roads and trails in this region are best for riding in the autumn, winter, and spring months.

Although the gold rush is long over, many of the area's towns have discovered there's gold to be found in the outdoor recreation industry, specifically mountain biking. The towns of Downieville and Nevada City have developed a tourism business focused on the sport. Bed-and-breakfasts, cafés, and outfitters cater to visiting mountain bikers, who test their suspensions on miles of rutted dirt roads and rock-studded trails bordered by steep drop-offs into rugged stream and river canyons. Road bikers aren't left out of the action; they can travel quiet back roads leading to gold boomtowns that have long since gone bust, or spin past some of the Gold Country's most intriguing attractions, including California Caverns and Daffodil Hill. There's a whole lot of California here waiting to be rediscovered, and the best way to do it is on two wheels, rolling along wildflower-covered hills in springtime.

Also included in this region is the Central Valley, with its seemingly endless acres of cotton, orchards, and grazing lands, which are watered by its famous rivers: the Sacramento, American, and Feather, among others. Extending for hundreds of miles from these rivers are marshy wetlands that attract ducks and waterfowl. The Central Valley, which may seem like an empty wasteland to drivers on I-5 or Highway 99, is a place of critical refuge for millions of birds on the Pacific Flyway. From the seat of a bike, you can develop a new appreciation for this vast patchwork of farmland interspersed by labyrinthine waterways. The region's relatively level roads offer fast and fun spinning for road cyclists, with much to see along the way.

SACRAMENTO AND GOLD COUNTRY

see Shasta
and Lassen
page 66

Lassen
National
Forest

Susanville

Honey
Lake

Chester

Red Bluff

Tehama State
Wildlife Area

Lake
Almanor

Mtn Meadows
Reservoir

Antelope
Lake

Bucks Lake
Wilderness

Quincy

Lake
Davis

Black Butte
Lake

Plumas
National
Forest

Little Grass
Valley Reservoir

see Tahoe and
Northern Sierra
page 220

1-2

Chico

Lake
Oroville

3

Downieville

4

Tahoe

Truckee

Oroville

Sacramento River

99
70

Nevada
City

5

National Forest

Lake
Tahoe

Marysville

Yuba
City

Feather River

Colfax

6

Auburn

7-8

Folsom
Lake

9

Placerville

10

Cache Creek

Lake
Berryessa

SACRAMENTO

11

13

Calaveras
Big Trees
State Park

see Mendocino
and Wine Country
page 110

12

14

15

Stanislaus
NF

see
San Francisco
Bay Area
page 276

San Joaquin
Delta

Camanche
Reservoir

New
Hogan
Lake

Sonora

New Melones
Lake

Stockton

Walnut Creek

Modesto

Don Pedro
Reservoir

0   10 mi

0   10 km

©AVALON TRAVEL

TRAIL NAME	LEVEL	DISTANCE	TIME	ELEVATION	PAGE
1 Chico to Paradise Loop	3	34 mi	3 hr	1,400 ft	172
2 Lower and Upper Bidwell Park	2	17.6 mi	2 hr	700 ft	174
3 Feather Falls	3	9.6 mi	2 hr	1,300 ft	177
4 Downieville Downhill	3	13.7 mi	2 hr	250 ft	180
5 Pioneer Trail	2	10 mi	2 hr	600 ft	183
6 Foresthill Divide Loop	3	11.4 mi	1-2 hr	1,800 ft	186
7 Lake Clementine Loop	3	11.2 mi	2 hr	1,700 ft	189
8 Quarry Road Trail	2	10.8 mi	2 hr	1,200 ft	192
9 Salmon Falls/Darrington Trail	3	18.8 mi	3-4 hr	2,000 ft	195
10 Sly Park's Jenkinson Lake	2	7.4 mi	2 hr	600 ft	198
11 American River Parkway	2	65.6 mi	5 hr	450 ft	201
12 Sacramento River Delta	2	48.5 mi	3 hr	150 ft	204
13 Sutter Creek and Volcano Loop	3	28.2 mi	2.5-3 hr	1,800 ft	208
14 Cavern to Cavern Loop	5	39.7 mi	3-4 hr	3,800 ft	211
15 Sugar Pine Railway	2	8.6 mi	1 hr	500 ft	214

1 CHICO TO PARADISE LOOP
Chico to Paradise

PAVED ROADS WITH MODERATE CAR TRAFFIC

Difficulty: 3   **Total Distance:** 34 miles

Riding Time: 3 hours   **Elevation Gain:** 1,400 feet

Summary: This loop is a challenging training ride that follows a stretch of the Wildflower Century route.

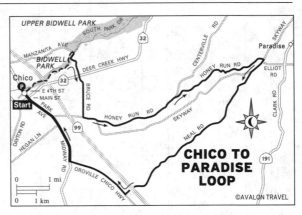

Every April, more than 3,000 bicyclists climb up Honey Run Road from Chico to Paradise. It's part of the annual Wildflower Century, a rite of passage for Chico-area cyclists.

Local riders use this as a regular workout ride, starting from a multitude of locations in downtown Chico. For simplicity, I describe the route starting from Main and East 4th Streets heading into Bidwell Park. A huge and well-managed city park, Bidwell has plenty of water fountains, picnic tables, benches, and children's play areas. It is well protected by shade trees: Oaks, maples, and sumacs line the route.

You'll follow Manzanita Avenue out of the park. Manzanita Avenue becomes traffic-intensive Bruce Road, which soon intersects the Skyway. The Skyway is your ticket to Honey Run Road, which is what you're here for. A twisting, winding snake of a road, Honey Run gets steeper and narrower as you climb (it gains 1,600 feet in six miles). As you ascend, you'll pass by a historic covered bridge over Butte Creek, known as America's only three-level covered bridge. You don't ride through it—the road crosses the creek on a more modern bridge just upstream. The ascent is the steepest in its final four miles above Honey Run Covered Bridge, where the pavement narrows to one lane.

When you finally top out at the town of Paradise, you're on the Skyway again. Turn right and then shortly left on Neal Road at the stoplight. Neal Road is mostly downhill all the way to Highway 99. Cross the highway and turn right on Chico–Oroville Highway, then turn right on Midway and ride back into Chico.

One caveat: If you feel uncomfortable riding around car traffic, avoid this loop during commute hours.

For more information, contact the Chico Chamber of Commerce and Visitor Center, 530/891-5556, www.chicochamber.com.

Driving Directions

From Highway 32 heading east into Chico, stay on Highway 32 as it becomes Nord Avenue, Walnut Street, and finally West 9th Street; turn left onto West 9th Street. Drive about 10 blocks on West 9th Street until you reach Main Street, then turn left. Turn right on East 4th Street and park.

Route Directions

0.0 Park near East 4th and Main Streets in Chico. Ride east on East 4th Street into Bidwell Park. *Supplies are available in Chico. Water is available in Bidwell Park.*

0.3 Enter Bidwell Park and ride on South Park Drive (closed to cars).

3.3 RIGHT on Manzanita Avenue; the road becomes Bruce Road.

6.7 LEFT on the Skyway.

7.5 LEFT on Honey Run Road.

11.9 Covered bridge (veer RIGHT to stay on Honey Run Road). *Water is available.*

14.0 Road narrows to one lane.

17.5 RIGHT on the Skyway at end of Honey Run Road. *Supplies are available in Paradise.*

18.4 LEFT on Neal Road at the stoplight.

28.0 Cross Highway 99.

28.4 RIGHT on Chico–Oroville Highway.

31.4 RIGHT on Midway; Midway becomes Park Avenue (bike path parallels Midway for most of its length).

33.8 RIGHT on Main Street.

34.0 Arrive at starting point.

CHICO TO PARADISE LOOP

Elevation in Feet

Distance in Miles

2 LOWER AND UPPER BIDWELL PARK
Chico

DIRT AND PAVED ROADS WITH MINIMAL CAR TRAFFIC

Difficulty: 2

Riding Time: 2 hours

Total Distance: 17.6 miles

Elevation Gain: 700 feet

Summary: Enjoy an easy ride that travels along a stretch of Big Chico Creek in Bidwell Park.

The third largest city park in the United States includes a wilderness area that Chico locals call a miniature Grand Canyon. Grand it is. The 3,670-acre park encompasses both sides of Big Chico Creek canyon for five miles heading up into the foothills. This ride travels its length, providing an introduction to the area. If you like what you see, Bidwell Park has several other mountain biking trails, including a good amount of single-track. One of the many bike shops in town can point you on your way.

© ANN MARIE BROWN

Lower Bidwell Park offers easy riding through plentiful shade trees, while Upper Bidwell Park presents more challenges.

This ride starts in Lower Bidwell Park with an easy cruise on pavement past tree-lined picnic areas, play areas, and water fountains. Shortly past Five Mile Recreation Area, you enter Upper Bidwell Park, which is a somewhat wilder version of the tame Lower Park. Note that dirt Upper Park Road is open to cars except for Sunday and Monday (your best choice for a ride). It's also closed to cars but open to bikes in the days following a rain. Single-track trails in the upper park, however, are closed to bikes during wet conditions.

Upper Park Road passes by tempting swimming holes at Alligator Hole, Bear Hole, Salmon Hole, and Brown's Hole. On warm days, bring a bike lock so you can access these Chico Creek pools. The road also travels past a series of basalt cliffs at Devil's Kitchen, which were formed over millions of years by the eroding action of the creek.

For more information, contact the City of Chico Parks Division, 530/896-7800, www.chico.ca.us.

Driving Directions

From Highway 32 heading east into Chico, stay on Highway 32 as it becomes Nord Avenue, Walnut Street, and finally West 9th Street. Turn left on West 9th Street and drive about 10 blocks until you reach Main Street, then turn left. Turn right on East 4th Street and park.

Route Directions

0.0 Park at East 4th and Main Streets in Chico. Ride east on East 4th Street into Bidwell Park. *Supplies are available in Chico. Water is available in Bidwell Park.*

0.3 Enter Bidwell Park and ride on South Park Drive (closed to cars).

3.3 Cross Manzanita Avenue; stay on paved path.

3.5 Five Mile Recreation Area; bear RIGHT.

3.9 RIGHT on Wildwood Avenue. Cross the street and pick up bike path. Ride past Horseshoe Lake and Chico Rod and Gun Club.

4.7 Bike path ends at paved road and gate.

4.9 Road changes from pavement to gravel and dirt.

7.3 Devil's Kitchen parking area.

8.8 End of park road. TURN AROUND.

17.6 Arrive at starting point.

3 FEATHER FALLS   BEST **☾**
Plumas National Forest near Oroville

DIRT SINGLE-TRACK

Difficulty: 3   **Total Distance:** 9.6 miles

Riding Time: 2 hours   **Elevation Gain:** 1,300 feet

Summary: Visit continental America's sixth highest freefalling waterfall on this wonderfully scenic ride near Oroville.

It's hard to believe the Feather Falls National Recreation Trail is open to mountain bikes. This loop trail is one of the finest hiking trails in Northern California, leading to a destination that is unsurpassed: Feather Falls, the sixth highest freefalling waterfall in the continental United States and the fourth highest in California.

The 640-foot waterfall is spectacular, and so is the trail that accesses it. Built as a loop, one side is shorter and steeper; the other side is longer and more level. Because it's a designated National Recreation Trail, the Feather Falls route is well maintained and has posted trail markers every 0.5 mile.

Bikes should take the longer side of the loop in both directions. It makes both the ascent and descent more manageable, and it will minimize your contact with hikers, who are the main trail users. Bikes are restricted to a 10-mph speed limit, which can be tough to maintain since the trail surface is smooth and has few technical challenges except for in its last 0.5 mile.

This is not a trail for hurrying. The northern Sierra foothills terrain shows off an incredible variety of plant life, including 17 species of trees: ponderosa pine, incense cedar, Douglas fir, black oak, canyon oak, madrone, bigleaf maple, white alder, bay, dogwood, digger pine, and more. They are joined by 20 kinds of shrubs, 11 types of vines, and 10 different ferns. Wildflower lovers should visit March–May, when more than 180 species been identified. That's also when the waterfall is usually at its peak flow.

From the trailhead, you reach the start of the loop in an easy 0.25 mile. Take the right fork (the longer way), and descend for the next 1.5 miles to a bridge crossing over Frey Creek. Then, parallel the creek and come out to a wide view of the Middle Fork Feather River canyon and Bald Rock Dome, a granite dome that rises 2,000 feet above the river.

At 4.3 miles, you come to a wooden bench and trail junction where the two legs of the loop connect. They become one for the final 0.5-mile ascent to the Feather Falls overlook. Be prepared to walk or stash your bike over the next stretch; some areas are quite treacherous. A couple of switchbacks bring you to a fenced viewpoint above the Middle Fork Feather River; in a few more pedal strokes, you're at the left turnoff for the falls overlook. Walk your bike along an elaborate series of short walkways that lead to a granite outcrop jutting into the middle of the canyon. From here, you have a straight-on view of Feather Falls and the Fall River canyon—guaranteed to take your breath away.

the magnificent 640-foot Feather Falls flooded with spring snowmelt

© ANN MARIE BROWN

For more information, contact the Feather River Ranger District of Plumas National Forest, 530/534-6500, www.fs.fed.us/r5/plumas.

Driving Directions

From Highway 70 in Oroville, take the Oroville Dam Boulevard exit (Highway 162) and drive east 1.6 miles to Olive Highway/Highway 162. Turn right and drive 6.5 miles on Highway 162. Turn right on Forbestown Road and drive 6 miles. Turn left on Lumpkin Road and drive 11 miles. Turn left at the sign for Feather Falls and drive 1.6 miles to the trailhead.

Route Directions

0.0 Park at the Feather Falls Trailhead. *Supplies are available in the town of Feather Falls, four miles away. Water is available at the trailhead.*

0.2 RIGHT at fork at start of loop.

1.7 Bridge over Frey Creek.

4.3 RIGHT where two legs of the loop join.

4.6 LEFT at overlook turnoff.

4.8 Feather Falls overlook. TURN AROUND.

9.6 Arrive at starting point.

4 DOWNIEVILLE DOWNHILL   BEST 🌑
Gold Lakes Basin to Downieville

DIRT ROAD AND SINGLE-TRACK

Difficulty: 3   **Total Distance:** 13.7 miles

Riding Time: 2 hours   **Elevation Gain:** 250 feet (4,200-foot loss)

Summary: One of Northern California's most famous one-way mountain bike rides traces a steep descent from the high mountains to the foothills.

The little gold rush town of Downieville is now a mountain biker's town. Every shop, restaurant, and inn caters to the mountain biking tourist. And every weekend, downtown Downieville is filled with bikers milling around, usually splattered with mud or covered with dust, drinking cool drinks, and reviewing the day's adventures with their friends.

Ninety-nine percent of them have just completed the Downieville Downhill, a world-famous one-way ride from Packer Saddle in the Gold Lakes Basin, elevation 7,100 feet, to Downieville, elevation 2,800 feet. You do the math.

There are several possible routes for the ride, but they all begin and end at the same spots. The route directions below follow the relatively new Sunshine Trail, completed in 2005, to Bucher Ranch Trail, then Third Divide Trail, and then First Divide Trail, since those trails are least vulnerable to erosion. (The Forest Service is greatly concerned about trail damage because so many thousands of people ride the Downieville Downhill each summer.) Even though the route is all downhill except for one short climb around mile 5.9, it is not by any means easy. The multiple miles of single-track will present plenty of challenges for intermediate to advanced riders: sharp turns, loose trail surfaces, steep drop-offs, jagged rocks, and the like. Most

© ANN MARIE BROWN

The town of Downieville is friendly to mountain bikers.

riders are quite exhausted after this ride, although intrepid types will do it twice in one day. Beginners should count themselves out altogether, sip a cappuccino back in Downieville, and wait patiently for their friends. Bucher Ranch Trail, which was used by the miners in the mid-19th century, is the most technical of the trail segments.

Besides the downhill single-track, the biggest draw of this ride is the incredible variety it provides. The scenery is spectacular: The trail passes meadows, crosses streams with waterfalls and swimming holes, and winds through wildflowers. At 7,100 feet, the trail runs through old-growth red fir forests, but as the elevation drops the trees change to ponderosa pines and incense cedars. Try to go slow enough so you can enjoy this place, not just barrel through it.

The driving directions below are to Downieville, since most people leave their cars there. Several tour operators in town will drop you off at the Packer Saddle trailhead, approximately 25 miles (45 minutes) from Downieville off Gold Lake Highway.

For more information, contact the Downieville Ranger District of Tahoe National Forest, 530/288-3231, www.fs.fed.us/r5/tahoe. For shuttle service to the trailhead, contact Yuba Expeditions, 530/289-3010, www.yubaexpeditions.com; or Downieville Outfitters, 530/289-0155, www.downievilleoutfitters.com.

Options

Although it is far and away the most famous, the Downieville Downhill is not the only trail to ride in this area. The tour operators in Downieville can supply you with a shuttle ride for several other gnarly single-track rides, including Chimney

Rock and Empire Creek, which was once rated by *Bike* magazine as having "the best downhill in California." Other popular rides include Halls Ranch and the North Yuba Trail.

Driving Directions

From Nevada City, drive 45 miles northeast on Highway 49 to Downieville. (Or, from Truckee, drive 25 miles north on Highway 89, then turn west at Sierraville on Highway 49 and drive 35 miles to Downieville.) Numerous tour operators offer shuttle services from Downieville to the Packer Saddle trailhead.

Route Directions

0.0 Your shuttle driver will drop you off at Packer Saddle. Start riding on the single-track Sunshine Trail. *Supplies are available in Downieville or at Bassetts Station, five miles from Packer Saddle.*

1.3 LEFT on Bucher Ranch OHV Trail.

2.0 LEFT on Bucher Ranch single-track (where the road curves to the right).

3.8 LEFT at junction with Pauley Creek Trail on right.

5.7 Bridge crossing.

6.0 RIGHT on Third Divide Trail; begin smooth and fast section.

8.3 LEFT on Lavezzola Road. *If you are tired of single-track, you can ride this dirt road all the way back to Downieville instead of taking the single-track at mile 9.4.*

9.4 Cross bridge, then turn RIGHT to enter the primitive campground. Pick up the dirt road, which soon turns to single-track (the single-track goes left; this is First Divide Trail).

11.2 Cross Lavezzola Road and take the dirt road, which changes to single-track and then widens again (this is still First Divide Trail).

12.7 LEFT on paved road. Cross bridge into Downieville.

13.7 Arrive at shuttle staging point in Downieville.

5 PIONEER TRAIL

BEST ◖

off Highway 20, east of Nevada City

DIRT SINGLE-TRACK

Difficulty: 2   **Total Distance:** 10 miles (or 20.6- or 30.2-mile options)

Riding Time: 2 hours   **Elevation Gain:** 600 feet

Summary: Single-track aficionados gather east of Nevada City for the chance to ride all or part of this fun, forested ride.

Pioneer Trail is the standard ride for mountain bikers seeking single-track in the Nevada City area. Like the gold rush town of Downieville, Nevada City has become a mecca for bikers, with enough trails in the area to keep us riding on new territory for a long time. The word around town is that while mountain biking may have been born in Marin County, it has matured in Nevada County. A number of professional bike racers live and train in the area.

Pioneer Trail is a perfect pathway for an introduction to the region. Because this trail starts at 3,500 feet in elevation and slowly cruises up to 5,000 feet, its first several miles are snow free most of the year. Pioneer Trail sees a lot of use, especially on weekends, and especially in summer, when people are attracted to the multiple cool and shady campgrounds along Highway 20.

Another reason for this trail's popularity is that it can be as easy or as difficult as you want it to be, depending on how far you go. Most riders with some single-track experience can handle the first 5 miles of the trail. More advanced riders can enjoy up to 15 miles of single-track (one-way). Some bikers choose to leave cars at various points along Highway 20 and ride a one-way downhill shuttle trip, but the elevation gain is so gradual that you might as well ride out and back and get some exercise. Some hardcore types even ride this trail on their single-speeds.

Pioneer Trail's single-track weaves through the trees as it parallels Highway 20.

Pioneer Trail is divided into a lower and upper section. Both follow close to Highway 20, often in sight of the road, for their entire length. Lower Pioneer is less technical and easier to ride, so start there and test your skills before moving on to Upper Pioneer (see *Options*). The lower section runs from Harmony Ridge Market to White Cloud Picnic Area and Campground, a 10-mile round-trip with an extremely gradual 600-foot elevation change. The trail dips and rolls through the trees, crossing numerous driveways and dirt roads. Diamond-shaped markers on the trees keep you on the right path. Although the black oak and ponderosa pine forest is so dense that you don't gain any views, the beauty is in the journey here. This smooth, rolling trail is just plain fun to ride, with few technical challenges.

For more information, contact the Nevada City Ranger District of Tahoe National Forest, 530/265-4531, www.fs.fed.us/r5/tahoe.

Options

At White Cloud Picnic Area, the trail crosses the highway, enters White Cloud Campground, and becomes the more advanced upper trail. The tread gets rockier and narrower until you reach Skillman Group Campground at mile 10.3. Some riders turn around here for a 20.6-mile round-trip; the intrepid continue onward to Omega Overlook and Rest Stop, another 5 miles east. Complete the whole thing and you're looking at a 30.2-mile round-trip and 1,800-foot elevation gain.

Driving Directions

From Nevada City, at the junction of Highways 49 and 20, take Highway 20 east for five miles. Look for Harmony Ridge Market on the left (across from Scotts Flat Road); park in the rear area of the lot, where it's signed for mountain bikers.

Route Directions

0.0 Park at Harmony Ridge Market. Trail is on the right side of the store (signed). *Supplies are available at the market.*

5.0 White Cloud Picnic Area. TURN AROUND. *Water is available across the street at the campground.*

10.0 Arrive at starting point.

6 FORESTHILL DIVIDE LOOP
Auburn State Recreation Area

DIRT ROAD AND SINGLE-TRACK

Difficulty: 3	**Total Distance:** 11.4 miles (or 22.6-mile option)
Riding Time: 1-2 hours	**Elevation Gain:** 1,800 feet

Summary: The fast and fun single-track here is on a trail designed specifically for mountain biking.

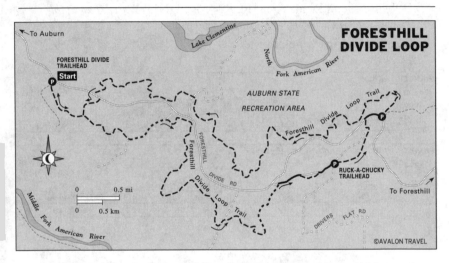

At the trailhead for the Foresthill Divide Loop, I met a 20-something male on two wheels, who was trying to jump over a foot-high barricade from a standstill position. He kept bouncing along on his bike, getting more and more air each time, trying to get high enough to clear that barricade. Then, using the same pogo-stick technique, he flipped his bike around a full 180 degrees. His feet never left the pedals.

I'm a 40-something female. If this guy was the type of rider who frequented the Foresthill Divide Loop, I didn't want any part of it. But even though this ride is often discussed in hushed tones around the bike shops of Auburn, it turns out that the trail is mostly smooth, smartly constructed single-track. Compared to the rocky dirt roads in the area that are so popular for mountain biking, this trail is downright easy to ride. Built by mountain bikers for mountain bikers, it was constructed so that the trail wouldn't erode easily. The path is single-track but not too narrow, its ups and downs are reasonably gradual, and its multiple swoops, turns, and curves are just plain fun. It's easy to get going pretty fast, but that's a mistake: You have a good chance of running into equestrians or hikers, who also use this path.

© ANN MARIE BROWN

Foresthill Divide Loop offers some shade in Auburn's hot summer climate.

Much of the trail runs through manzanita and black oak forest. In summer, this is by far the most comfortable trail in Auburn State Recreation Area because of its abundant shade. Look forward to canyon views and hilltop panoramas from the tops of several short climbs.

Although it crosses paths with some dirt roads and busy Foresthill Road, the route is well signed all the way. Foresthill Divide Loop can be ridden in either direction, and it makes little difference which way you choose. I've described a counterclockwise loop.

For more information, contact Auburn State Recreation Area, 530/885-4527, www.parks.ca.gov.

Options
A connector trail links the Foresthill Divide Loop with the Lake Clementine Loop (see ride 7, *Lake Clementine Loop*), so you can ride them both together (22.6 miles).

Driving Directions
From Sacramento, take I-80 east to Auburn and exit at Foresthill Road. Go right (east) on Foresthill Road. From its junction with Lincoln Way in Auburn, continue 4.6 miles on Foresthill Road to the trailhead on the right.

Route Directions

0.0 Park at the Foresthill Divide Trailhead. Take the left fork to start. *Supplies are available in Auburn.*

0.6 RIGHT at sign for Foresthill Divide Loop Trail.

1.0 LEFT on a dirt road.

1.5 Trail runs close to Foresthill Road.

3.3 LEFT on a dirt road, then immediate RIGHT on single-track.

3.8 LEFT on a dirt road.

4.4 RIGHT on paved road, then immediate RIGHT on single-track.

4.9 Ruck-a-Chucky Trailhead parking area (Drivers Flat Road); ride across it and pick up trail.

5.6 Cross busy Foresthill Road carefully. Trail continues 70 yards to the right at parking area; veer left on trail.

9.0 Cross dirt road to Lake Clementine.

10.4 Cross busy Foresthill Road again. Trail continues 25 yards to the left.

10.8 RIGHT at junction (same junction you visited at mile 0.6).

11.4 Arrive at starting point.

FORESTHILL DIVIDE LOOP

7 LAKE CLEMENTINE LOOP
Auburn State Recreation Area

DIRT ROAD AND SINGLE-TRACK

Difficulty: 3   **Total Distance:** 11.2 miles (or 7.3-mile option)

Riding Time: 2 hours   **Elevation Gain:** 1,700 feet

Summary: If you like steep ups and downs and gnarly drop-offs, you'll love this ride in the Auburn foothills.

The Lake Clementine Loop strings together five different trails to form a classic Auburn ride, one that is a favorite among locals and visitors alike. You're either climbing or descending for every pedal stroke of this ride, which runs between two different forks of the American River: the Middle Fork and the North Fork. Prepare to get a quadriceps workout.

The first leg of the route is Stagecoach Trail, an old 1880s stagecoach route, which drops from Russell Road in Auburn down to the confluence of the North and Middle Forks of the American River at the Old Foresthill Bridge. It's a fast

One leg of the Lake Clementine Loop drops below the Old Foresthill Bridge.

descent on a well-worn dirt road—keep your speed below the posted 15 mph and enjoy the expansive views of the river canyon. At the bottom, cross the old bridge to connect with Lake Clementine Trail on the left. You'll climb upward toward the fancy "new" bridge, a marvel of mechanical engineering that looms 750 feet above this canyon.

The trail closely follows the edge of the North Fork, with some steep and scary drop-offs, until it reaches paved Lake Clementine Road. Next comes another nasty uphill (the pavement should help the ascent, but it doesn't feel like it on a hot day) to Fuel Break Trail and finally Culvert Trail. Here the real fun, and a long-awaited downhill, begins. You ride through an extremely dark and cool tunnel under Foresthill Road, then connect to Confluence Trail at Mammoth Bar OHV Area. Confluence Trail is the most technically challenging trail of the day; it is extremely narrow and features exposed drop-offs, tree roots, and rocks galore. The path doesn't allow much room for error; a fall here means a 30-foot drop into the river.

If you make it through Confluence Trail, you're back at the Old Foresthill Bridge, and now all you have to do is climb back up Stagecoach to your car. Remember how fun it was to fly down? Now you'll experience it from the opposite (climbing) perspective. Fortunately, after an initial technical stretch, the going gets easier, and more scenic, as you head uphill.

For more information, contact Auburn State Recreation Area, 530/885-4527, www.parks.ca.gov.

Options

If you aren't sure of your ability to handle this ride, you can cut it shorter by starting from the trailhead at the junction of Highway 49 and Old Foresthill Road by the American River (drive 3 miles southeast on Highway 49 from Auburn). This will cut off the first steep descent from Russell Road and the ensuing climb back uphill at the end, dropping your mileage to 7.3 miles.

Driving Directions

From Sacramento, take I-80 east to Auburn and exit at Russell Road. Drive southeast to the junction of Russell Road and Lincoln Way, then continue on Russell Road for 0.5 mile to a dirt parking area on the left (where Russell Road becomes Foresthill Road).

Route Directions

0.0 Park at the Stagecoach Trail parking area on Russell Road. *Supplies are available in Auburn.*

1.8 RIGHT at fork.

2.0 LEFT on Old Foresthill Road/Bridge where Stagecoach Trail ends.

2.1 LEFT on Lake Clementine Trail.

2.3 LEFT to stay alongside river.

3.9 RIGHT at gate at paved Lake Clementine Road.

5.3 RIGHT at gate, then follow trail on the right (Fuel Break Trail).

6.0 LEFT on Culvert Trail.

6.5 Go through culvert under Foresthill Road.

7.1 Cross Old Foresthill Road and enter Mammoth Bar OHV Area; follow gravel road.

7.3 RIGHT at gate onto Confluence Trail.

9.2 LEFT at Old Foresthill Road/Bridge.

9.3 RIGHT on Stagecoach Trail.

11.2 Arrive at starting point.

LAKE CLEMENTINE LOOP

8 QUARRY ROAD TRAIL

BEST **(**

Auburn State Recreation Area

DIRT ROAD

Difficulty: 2

Total Distance: 10.8 miles

Riding Time: 2 hours

Elevation Gain: 1,200 feet

Summary: One of the easiest mountain biking trails to be found in the Auburn foothills, this route has opportunities for swimming in the Middle Fork of the American River.

Beginning mountain bikers can become easily discouraged at Auburn State Recreation Area. From the novice's standpoint, the local trails climb with the average grade of a skyscraper. Their surfaces are rutted and rocky. The sun beats down upon them year-round. But still, the recreation area is wildly popular with mountain bikers. Every trailhead is filled with cars, and every car sports a bike rack. What's a wannabe to do?

Head for Quarry Road Trail, which follows the south side of the canyon of the

© ANN MARIE BROWN

easy riding on Quarry Road Trail along the Middle Fork of the American River

Middle Fork of the American River. The trail, really a wide road, starts near the confluence of the North and Middle Forks and runs for 5.4 miles to Maine Bar (spelled Main Bar on some maps). It's mostly level and smooth, with only three steep but short climbs over its entire distance. Quarry Road presents few technical challenges, except for the discipline it requires to keep your eyes on the trail instead of the beautiful American River flowing by. Do keep watch, however: Sections of the trail have washed out in winter storms and the drop-offs are severe.

One of Quarry Road's great charms is that it's a breeze to follow. It sticks to the river's edge for its entire distance and is frequently marked with small WST signs, which stand for Western States Trail (although technically this is the "alternate" Western States Trail, a lengthy equestrian trail). The few spur trails that intersect are all clearly signed No Bikes.

If it's a warm day, you'll have plenty of company in the first 0.5 mile, as sunbathers wander with their inner tubes in search of a good swimming hole. The level of solitude increases as you progress into the canyon. An old quarry, the trail's namesake, is the first notable landmark. The path gets slightly more technical (read: rocky) beyond the quarry.

Quarry Road continues, rolling up and down tiny hills, for several miles of uninterrupted riding and great vistas of the steep river canyon. The canyon's slopes are punctuated by a few foothill pines—scraggly-looking conifers with gray-green needles—and some interesting rock outcrops. Occasional side trails lead down to the river; take any of them if you wish to cool off.

After about 4 miles, you'll leave the sunshine and the river views and head into dense oak and pine forest, where the trail narrows. You reach Maine Bar at 5.4 miles, where Maine Bar Trail takes off on the right and bikes are prohibited. Relax at the picnic table for a few minutes, then turn around and ride westward, enjoying the river canyon all over again.

For more information, contact Auburn State Recreation Area, 530/885-4527, www.parks.ca.gov.

Driving Directions

From Sacramento, take I-80 east to Auburn and exit at Highway 49 south. Head southeast through Auburn on Highway 49 for 3 miles. At the bottom of the canyon, where Highway 49 turns right and crosses a bridge over the river, set your odometer. In 0.4 mile, turn left on a dirt road (it's easy to miss). Quarry Road Trail is the gated dirt road by the parking area.

Route Directions

0.0 Park at the Quarry Road trailhead off Highway 49, just beyond the highway bridge over the river. *Supplies are available in Auburn.*

2.0 Mammoth Bar OHV Area across the river.

3.3 Browns Bar Trail intersects on the right.

5.4 Maine Bar. TURN AROUND.

10.8 Arrive at starting point.

9 SALMON FALLS/ DARRINGTON TRAIL

BEST **☾**

South Fork of the American River near Folsom Lake

DIRT ROAD AND SINGLE-TRACK

Difficulty: 3   **Total Distance:** 18.8 miles (or shorter/longer options)

Riding Time: 3-4 hours   **Elevation Gain:** 2,000 feet

Summary: Sweet single-track set in the red clay of the foothills above the South Fork of the American River is suitable for most mountain bikers.

This is a classic Sierra foothills mountain bike ride with two names: Salmon Falls and Darrington Trail. Most people call it the former, after a nearby waterfall on the South Fork of the American River, but its official, mapped name is the latter. If you live anywhere near Sacramento and you own a mountain bike, you've probably ridden this trail. If you haven't, you should. Strong, adventurous beginners can probably manage it as long as they are willing to walk some of the more technical sections, most of which happen to be in the first mile of trail. Salmon Falls Trail starts out treacherous, but gets easier as it goes. It's a good place to practice your bike handling skills, and to watch yourself improve.

The trail meanders high above the South Fork of the American River just before the river empties into Folsom Lake. This is manzanita and rattlesnake

© ANN MARIE BROWN

chaparral on the single-track Salmon Falls/ Darrington Trail

country—too hot and dry in the summer, but just right the rest of the year. The mostly wide single-track rolls along, offering expansive river canyon views. Name your pine trees as you ride: ponderosa, foothill, and Jeffrey. Name your oak trees as you ride: valley, black, and Oregon. If it's summer, you'll wish there were a whole lot more of them—the reddish-colored earth lining the trail seems to reflect the heat of the sun.

Since Salmon Falls is an out-and-back, you can customize the route any way you wish. The best of the ride is over at about mile 7.5; this makes a good turnaround point if you don't need to refill your water bottles. If you do, continue to popular Peninsula Campground at mile 9.4 and slake your thirst, or cool off in the lake. Some people opt to ride this trail as a one-way route with a car shuttle, leaving a second car at the camp area.

For more information, contact Folsom Lake State Recreation Area, 916/988-0205, www.parks.ca.gov.

Options

If you had so much fun on Salmon Falls/Darrington Trail that you're still hungering for more, try the nearby Sweetwater Trail, a similarly technical, out-and-back single-track. The trailhead is 0.25 mile farther west on Salmon Falls Road (cross over the bridge), at the river access area on the right. The signed trail begins by the restrooms at the far west end of the parking lot.

During the fall and winter when the water level is at its lowest, an old bridge across the river gets exposed and allows riders to loop together the Salmon Falls and Sweetwater Trails, instead of riding out and back on one or both.

Driving Directions

From Sacramento, take I-80 east to Auburn and exit at Highway 49 south. Head southeast through Auburn on Highway 49, then continue 6 miles through the town of Cool. Drive 3.3 miles past Cool on Highway 49, then turn right on Rattlesnake Bar Road. Turn left immediately on Salmon Falls Road and drive 6.1

miles to the trailhead on the right. There is additional parking 100 yards farther, across the highway bridge, in the pullouts on the right side of the road.

Route Directions

0.0 Park at the Darrington Trailhead. Take the lower, more obvious trail from the edge of the parking lot. *Supplies are available in Cool.*

1.0 LEFT on old road.

1.5 Road becomes single-track (veer RIGHT).

3.3 LEFT on jeep trail.

7.5 Optional turnaround point before climb begins (if you don't need water from Peninsula Campground).

8.0 STRAIGHT at four-way intersection of dirt roads.

8.9 Gate and paved road; follow the pavement to Peninsula Campground.

9.4 Peninsula Campground. TURN AROUND. *Water is available.*

18.8 Arrive at starting point.

SALMON FALLS/DARRINGTON TRAIL

10 SLY PARK'S JENKINSON LAKE
Pollock Pines, east of Placerville

DIRT SINGLE-TRACK

Difficulty: 2

Riding Time: 2 hours

Total Distance: 7.4 miles

Elevation Gain: 600 feet

Summary: Leave the heat of the foothills behind on this forested ride at Jenkinson Lake.

Sly Park Recreation Area is best known for family camping in its conifer-filled woods and fishing, swimming, and waterskiing in its blue waterway, Jenkinson Lake, which happens to be a major drinking water supply for El Dorado County. It's the kind of place where Boy and Girl Scout troops go for a weekend, and memories are made. It's also very popular with equestrians, who have access to a horse camp and a riding trail encircling the lake.

All this means it's surprising that mountain bikes are allowed here. But they are, and so far, conflicts have been rare. Make sure you pay attention to trail signs; in many spots, bikers and hikers take one fork and equestrians take another. Pay close attention or Mr. Ed may give you a swift kick in the rear (tire or otherwise).

The entire trail is a loop around the lake and a mix of single-track, double-track, and pavement. However, the best part of the trail is the first 3.7 miles (all single-track) on the lake's south shore. The rest of the loop has many confusing junctions amid a maze of campgrounds and picnic areas. I recommend riding out-and-back on the first 3.7 miles and not bothering with the whole loop, unless you enjoy riding through parking lots jammed with restrooms, barbecue grills, RVs, and campers.

From the lake's dam, the well-signed single-track snakes and rolls through a wonderfully scented pine and fir forest. Watch out for narrow, twisting spots and some scary drop-offs. Lake views are quite pretty, especially early in the season when the lake is full.

© ANN MARIE BROWN

Pines and firs line Sly Park's Jenkinson Lake trail.

An interesting highlight is the 0.5-mile-long tunnel near the Hazel Creek Bridge, which was part of the original water system that formed Jenkinson Lake. Check out the museum in the main part of the park to learn more about it.

For more information, contact Sly Park Recreation Area, 530/295-6824, www. eid.org.

Options
Watch for a junction right after you cross a bridge over Park Creek. If you turn right here for a short distance, you'll find a lovely waterfall and cool creek pool to dip your feet in.

Driving Directions
From Placerville, drive 15 miles east on U.S. 50 to Pollock Pines. Exit on Sly Park Road and head south. In 4.4 miles, you will pass the main entrance to Sly Park; continue beyond it for 0.5 mile to the left turnoff for Mormon Emigrant Trail. Turn left, cross the first dam, and park off the road near the second dam. The trailhead is signed Southshore Hiking Trail on the southeast side of the second dam.

Route Directions
0.0 Park alongside the road near second dam and start riding on Southshore Hiking Trail. *Supplies are available at store across Sly Park Road from main park entrance.*

3.5 RIGHT just before the Hazel Creek Bridge. Follow the trail uphill to see the long tunnel.

3.6 Backtrack to main trail and cross Hazel Creek Bridge.

3.7 Arrive at Hazel Creek Campground. TURN AROUND. *Water is available.*

7.4 Arrive at starting point.

11 AMERICAN RIVER PARKWAY   BEST C
Sacramento to Folsom Lake

PAVED BIKE PATH

Difficulty: 2   **Total Distance:** 65.6 miles (or shorter options)

Riding Time: 5 hours   **Elevation Gain:** 450 feet

Summary: More than 500,000 people each year ride this remarkable bike path alongside the American River.

The American River Parkway is one of the oldest and longest paved bike paths in the United States, a 32.8-mile trail leading all the way from Discovery Park in Sacramento to Folsom Lake. If you're in the mood, you can pedal the whole thing for 65.6 miles of paved recreation trail riding, with only a few slight rises for hills. Most of the 450 feet of elevation gain comes in the last 2 miles to Folsom Lake.

Some sections are more scenic than others, however, so if it's your first trip, you might want to go straight to one of the best parts and ride west from Beals Point at Folsom Lake. To do so, start at the trail's eastern terminus. After leaving the Beals Point parking area (which can be an absolute zoo on summer weekends because of the lake's sandy beach and swimming areas), pick up the bike trail and ride to your left (west). Numbers painted on the trail's surface mark your mileage. You are starting at 32.8; the numbers drop as you ride west—31, 30, 29, etc.

Your first vistas are of Folsom Lake as you ride around its northwest edge on a wing of the huge, 340-foot Folsom Dam. The 18,000-acre reservoir was created in 1955 by building a main concrete dam on the American River, as well as several wing dams and dikes. Next, you'll ride by a place you've heard about but never thought you'd visit: Folsom State Prison. Fortunately your surroundings quickly become less foreboding as you pedal through acres of grasslands with the American River at your side.

At 3 miles out, the river is dammed once again, this time by Nimbus Dam. You ride past Lake Natoma, which is smaller and quieter than Lake Folsom. Just beyond the highway bridge before Negro Bar is a high overlook looking down at the lake, with small boats floating by and people wading near the shore. A turnaround here, near mileage marker 29, will give you a 7-mile round-trip, perfect for families with small children. Or continue onward for another 6.5 miles to the Nimbus Fish Hatchery; a turnaround here makes a 20-mile round-trip. You will have a slight uphill on the way back to Folsom Lake, but it doesn't amount to much.

If you choose to start riding from downtown Sacramento instead, note that the trail's western terminus at Discovery Park isn't in the safest neighborhood. However, a one-mile spur trail runs from Discovery Park to touristy yet picturesque

Old Sacramento, a much nicer area with shops, amenities, and parking. You could begin riding from there, or from two dozen other trailheads, including Sacramento State University, Goethe Park, and Nimbus Fish Hatchery. Restrooms, picnic tables, and water are available at numerous spots along the trail. Free maps of the American River Parkway and Sacramento's other paved bike trails are available at any bike shop in town, or on the web from the agencies noted below.

Although the trail does cross a few major streets, this is remarkably peaceful pedaling in an extremely urban area. Bird-watching and berry picking are popular activities along the trail.

For more information, contact the County of Sacramento Department of Regional Parks, 916/875-6961, www.sacparks.net; or the American River Parkway Foundation, 916/486-2773, www.arpf.org.

Driving Directions

To reach the western terminus of the trail at Discovery Park: From I-5 in Sacramento, take the Richards Boulevard exit (or Garden Highway exit) and follow the signs to Discovery Park on the west side of I-5. The bikeway begins at the park (underneath I-5).

To reach the eastern terminus of the trail at Folsom Lake: From I-80 in Sacramento, drive east for 15 miles and take the Douglas Road exit near Roseville. Drive east 5.3 miles on Douglas Road, then turn right on Auburn–Folsom Road and drive 1.7 miles. Turn left at the sign for Beals Point; you'll cross the bike path as you drive to the parking area.

Route Directions

0.0 Park at the Discovery Park trailhead in Sacramento. The following are route directions for riding the entire trail west to east, although you could easily reverse the route or ride only a part of it. Supplies are available in Sacramento; water is available at many points along the trail.

2.8 STRAIGHT at junction (don't cross the river).

6.5 Cal Expo.

7.9 LEFT at junction (path crossing the river leads to Cal State Sacramento).

14.0 Goethe Park. Cross the river to the south side.

23.0 Nimbus Fish Hatchery and Hazel Avenue Bridge. Cross the river and pick up trail on the north side.

28.0 Jedediah Smith Bridge/Rainbow Bridge.

32.8 End of trail at Beals Point at Folsom Lake. TURN AROUND.

65.6 Arrive at starting point.

12 SACRAMENTO RIVER DELTA   BEST ☾
southwest of Sacramento

PAVED ROADS WITH MODERATE CAR TRAFFIC

Difficulty: 2   **Total Distance:** 48.5 miles

Riding Time: 3 hours   **Elevation Gain:** 150 feet

Summary: Brave the Delta breezes and go for a spin along the waterways and sloughs of the Sacramento River, passing by an opulent mansion and the historic town of Locke.

It's flat out here. Flat as a pancake. Flat as a desktop. Flat as the fertile Sacramento River plains.

If you just want to spin out some fast miles, there may be no better place to do it than around the Sacramento River Delta, where the pavement is smooth and hills are nonexistent. Only one element can slow you down and that's the wind, which comes up fairly consistently every afternoon. Those infamous Delta breezes that bring joy to the lives of local windsurfers can mean drudgery for cyclists. It's wise to avoid summer days when the Central Valley heats up; that's when the great wind machine along the waterways starts working hardest.

The Delta ride starts in the small town of Franklin and heads south along the Sacramento River, then circles back via four islands: Randall, Sutter, Grand, and Andrus. The islands, like dozens of others in the area, were created in the early 20th century by dredging the Delta wetlands and constructing the levees that we

© ANN MARIE BROWN

the historic Chinese town of Locke

ride on today. Enterprising pioneers realized that if they could keep this swampy land high and dry, it would make rich soil for planting crops. And they were right. If you can time it right, ride through this fertile region in the spring, when the area's walnut, apple, and pear orchards are in bloom.

Other highlights of the trip include good bird-watching opportunities at the Stone Lakes National Wildlife Refuge in the first stretch out of Franklin. Although the public can enter the refuge only on a few Saturdays each month, a wealth of bird life fills the surrounding skies year-round.

It's also a pleasure to ride past numerous old bridges and drawbridges across the Sacramento River and its sloughs. When automobiles became a common form of transportation in the early 20th century, more and more roads were constructed around the Delta. But with so many waterways to cross, the only options were building bridges or providing ferry service. In many places, standard bridges could not be built, as they would make it impossible for tall boats to pass through the shallow Delta waters. Drawbridges were the solution, and even today boaters in the Delta must pay careful attention to the schedule of openings and closings. If the bridge tender has gone home for the day, a tall boat may have to wait to pass through until the next day.

On Grand Island Road, you'll get a look at the historic Grand Island Mansion, an Italian Renaissance–style villa (tours are available on most Sundays with advance reservations, 916/775-1705, www.grandislandmansion.com). The 58-room villa, built in 1917, is the largest private estate in Northern

California. It is available for rent for weddings and corporate events, and has been featured as a backdrop in many furniture and clothing catalogs. If you can find a place to change out of your biking clothes, make reservations for their famous Sunday brunch.

The ride also passes through the historic Chinese town of Locke, which was founded in 1915 after a fire broke out in the Chinese section of nearby Walnut Grove. Locke is listed on the National Register of Historic Places as the only town in the United States built exclusively by the Chinese for the Chinese. At its peak, Locke was home to about 1,000 Chinese people. It's worth spending some time on Main Street and visiting the Dai Loy Museum (916/776-1661, www.locketown.com), which was a former Chinese gambling den, and the Boarding House Visitors Center (916/776-1661, www.locketown.com), with its exhibits interpreting the history of Chinese immigrants in the area.

The ride follows narrow levee roads for almost its entire distance. Traffic can be heavy on Highway 160, but the rest of the roads should be fairly quiet. As you pedal alongside the blue, flat-water estuaries, it's fun to think of the days when a few hundred paddle wheelers plied these waters, carrying passengers and goods from Sacramento to San Francisco and announcing their arrival with steam-driven calliopes. One of these old ships, the five-story *Delta King,* now serves as a luxury hotel in Sacramento. It's an elegant relic of an almost forgotten time in California's history.

Options

North of Locke off Highway 160 lies the town of Clarksburg, a small riverside community that makes an ideal hub for a mostly level road-biking trip. Clarksburg has become a popular wine-growing region; start and end your ride at the Old Sugar Mill (35265 Willow Ave., 916/744-1615, www.oldsugarmill.com), and you can sample a selection of the local varietals at this converted sugar mill. Also within riding distance are Bogle Winery, Wilson Vineyards, and Scribner's Bend.

Driving Directions

From Sacramento, take I-5 south for 15 miles to the Hood–Franklin Road exit. Turn left (east) on Hood–Franklin Road and drive 1.2 miles to Franklin School, on the left.

Route Directions

0.0 Park near the Franklin School and ride west on Hood–Franklin Road. *Supplies are available in Sacramento or in towns along this ride.*

3.3 Town of Hood. *Supplies are available.*

3.6 LEFT on River Road (Highway 160).

5.5 RIGHT on Randall Island Road.

7.4 RIGHT on River Road (Highway 160).

7.6 Town of Courtland. *Supplies are available.*

8.9 LEFT on Sutter Slough Bridge Road (Highway 160) after bridge.

10.0 RIGHT on Grand Island Road after bridge.

16.0 STRAIGHT to stay on Grand Island Road.

24.5 RIGHT on Highway 160.

24.7 LEFT on Isleton Road.

28.0 RIGHT on Andrus Island Road.

32.7 RIGHT on bridge across slough; road becomes River Road.

33.0 Town of Walnut Grove. *Supplies are available.*

33.7 Town of Locke. *Supplies are available.*

40.0 STRAIGHT on Highway 160.

41.2 Town of Courtland. *Supplies are available.*

41.4 LEFT on Randall Island Road.

43.3 LEFT on Highway 160.

45.2 RIGHT on Hood–Franklin Road.

48.5 Arrive at starting point.

SACRAMENTO RIVER DELTA

13 SUTTER CREEK AND VOLCANO LOOP
north of Jackson

PAVED ROAD WITH MODERATE CAR TRAFFIC

Difficulty: 3   **Total Distance:** 28.2 miles (or 34.2-mile option)

Riding Time: 2.5-3 hours   **Elevation Gain:** 1,800 feet

Summary: Quaint gold rush towns and springtime daffodils await on this ride through the Sierra foothills.

Sutter Creek's main thoroughfare is lined with antiques shops, bed-and-breakfast inns, and restaurants. It's not quite what the gold miners must have imagined for the town back in the 1850s, but it's a charming place to spend a weekend and/or to use as a starting point for this loop ride in the Gold Country. The ride travels to the town of Volcano, which enjoyed a four-year stint as a gold boomtown from 1848 until 1852. The party ended when it was determined that the area was actually outside of the rich gold quartz belt. Today Volcano is a friendly town with a brewery and shops.

From Sutter Creek's post office, ride east on Gopher Flat Road, which becomes Shake Ridge Road. After 12.7 pleasant miles, turn right on Rams Horn Grade. If you time your trip carefully and show up between mid-March and mid-April, you're in for a visual treat. On your left is Daffodil Hill, where you can feast your eyes on the spectacle of more than 400,000 daffodils and tulips blooming on the hillside. This extravaganza is the work of several generations of the McLaughlin family, who have been planting and caring for the bulbs for more than 100 years.

© ANN MARIE BROWN

When the flowers are blooming in early spring, Daffodil Hill is an unforgettable sight.

Visitors are allowed to wander the planted hillsides. As many as 4,000 people show up per day on sunny weekends (to find out the exact timing of the bloom, during March and April phone 209/296-7048).

From Daffodil Hill, it's a steep downhill through pine and oak forest into Volcano, elevation 2,053 feet. Spend some time enjoying the town, then head west on Sutter Creek Road. You'll have a fun, 12-mile descent alongside pretty Sutter Creek back to your starting point.

For more information, contact the Amador County Chamber of Commerce, 209/223-0350, www.amadorcountychamber.com.

Options

If you'd like to add on a few more miles, Indian Grinding Rock State Historic Park (209/296-7488) is three steep miles from Volcano. (Take Pine Grove–Volcano Road south from town.) This is California's only state park dedicated primarily to Native American culture. The surface of the eponymous limestone outcrop features more than 1,200 mortar holes (made by Miwok Indians grinding acorn meal) as well as petroglyphs. A campground is available if you wish to turn this trip into an overnighter.

Driving Directions

From Stockton, take Highway 88/104 east for 45 miles to Highway 49, then turn north and drive 1.5 miles to Sutter Creek.

Route Directions

0.0 Park near the post office in Sutter Creek. Ride east on Gopher Flat Road, which becomes Shake Ridge Road. *Supplies are available in Sutter Creek.*

12.7 RIGHT on Rams Horn Grade; Daffodil Hill is on the left.

15.7 Town of Volcano. *Supplies are available. If you wish to add on six miles to your round-trip, ride out and back to Indian Grinding Rock State Park on Pine Grove–Volcano Road. Note that this is a steep descent to the park and a steep climb back out.*

15.8 STRAIGHT on Sutter Creek Road.

27.8 RIGHT on Highway 49.

28.2 Arrive at starting point.

SUTTER CREEK AND VOLCANO LOOP

14 CAVERN TO CAVERN LOOP   BEST ☾
Murphys, northeast of Angels Camp

PAVED ROADS WITH MODERATE CAR TRAFFIC

Difficulty: 5   **Total Distance:** 39.7 miles

Riding Time: 3-4 hours   **Elevation Gain:** 3,800 feet

Summary: Try something really unusual on your next bike trip – a demanding loop ride that visits two limestone caves in '49er Gold Country.

The Cavern to Cavern Loop tours the rugged Sierra foothills and visits a few famous and forgotten gold rush towns, including Murphys, Calaveritas, and Sheep Ranch. Along the way, you can opt to visit two unusual Gold Country attractions: California Caverns (209/736-2708, www.caverntours.com) and Mercer Caverns (209/728-2101, www.mercercaverns.com), limestone caves that were first explored during the gold rush years. If it's a warm day, you'll be grateful for their cool, dark interiors.

Begin your ride in Murphys, elevation 2,171 feet, named for the Murphy Brothers, who struck gold here in 1848. Many historic stone structures stand in its

The historic Murphys Hotel is the start and finish of the Cavern to Cavern Loop through the Gold Country hills.

tree-shaded downtown, including the Murphys Hotel, which bears bullet scars from 150 years ago. North of Murphys, off Sheep Ranch Road, is Mercer Caverns. You can pay a few bucks for a 45-minute walking tour of the caves.

Next, follow San Domingo Road west to Dogtown Road through lovely oak forest and continue into the one-horse town of Calaveritas, elevation 1,040 feet, where you ride underneath an old railroad trestle. This is remote country compared to the busier Gold Country towns along Highways 4 and 49. Head east on Old Gulch Road and climb 1,000 feet to Michel Road and Mountain Ranch. A right turn takes you to California Caverns, a state historic landmark. Cave tours of varying lengths are available. (Skip this four-mile out-and-back if you're getting weary; there's more work ahead to finish out the loop.)

After your cavern tour, take Mountain Ranch Road east to Sheep Ranch Road and then head south to the hamlet of Sheep Ranch, which was once the site of gold mines operated by the Hearst family. It's now all but abandoned. The final southward run on Sheep Ranch Road back to Murphys can be murder if you're already tired; Sheep Ranch Road doles out four steep climbs and descents. Good thing there is an ample supply of tall, cool drinks waiting for you in Murphys.

Driving Directions

From Stockton, take Highway 4 east for 50 miles to Angels Camp. Continue east on Highway 4 for 9.5 more miles and take the Murphys Business District exit, which becomes Main Street.

Route Directions

0.0 Park in Murphys near the junction of Main Street and Sheep Ranch Road. Ride north on Sheep Ranch Road. *Supplies are available in Murphys.*

1.5 Road to Mercer Caverns on left. *Tour of the caverns available for a fee.*

2.1 LEFT on San Domingo Road.

7.2 RIGHT on Dogtown Road.

7.5 LEFT on Dogtown Road.

10.5 RIGHT on Calaveritas Road.

10.6 LEFT on Calaveritas Road.

12.5 RIGHT on Old Gulch Road.

16.6 RIGHT on Michel Road.

19.4 RIGHT on Cave City Road.

21.2 California Caverns. TURN AROUND. *Tour of the caverns available for a fee.*

23.0 RIGHT on Michel Road.

23.3 RIGHT on Mountain Ranch Road. *Supplies are available in Mountain Ranch.*

26.2 RIGHT on Sheep Ranch Road.

30.7 Sheep Ranch.

39.7 Arrive at starting point.

CAVERN TO CAVERN LOOP

15 SUGAR PINE RAILWAY   BEST ☾
west of Strawberry

DIRT ROAD AND SINGLE-TRACK; PAVED ROAD WITH MINIMAL CAR TRAFFIC

Difficulty: 2   **Total Distance:** 8.6 miles (or 18.6-mile option)

Riding Time: 1 hour   **Elevation Gain:** 500 feet

Summary: This peaceful riverside ramble follows the Stanislaus River on a historic railroad grade.

The Sugar Pine Railway was named for the very large sugar pines that were harvested in this area and shipped along the railroad line from 1906 to 1965. A portion of that rail route, called the Strawberry Branch, is the basis for this trail along the sun-dappled Stanislaus River.

The trail starts at the river bridge near Fraser Flat Campground. Heading to your right (east), the dirt path starts out wide but eventually narrows to single-track. It's simple to follow; the path hugs the river and there are no turnoffs. Watch for an old wooden flume on the river's far side, known as the Philadelphia Ditch. Built in 1899 to supply gold miners with water to work their diggings, the flume is currently used by Pacific Gas and Electric Company to carry water and generate power from the Stanislaus River.

At 2.2 miles, the trail narrows considerably, turns away from the river, and heads uphill through meadows and forest. At 2.8 miles, the single-track ends at a paved road, Old Strawberry Road. You can turn around here or ride into the town of Strawberry for lunch. To do so, turn left on the pavement. Ride 1 mile on Old Strawberry Road, then turn right on Strawberry Drive and ride to the Strawberry Inn. If you're not in the mood for a sit-down lunch, there's a grocery store across the street.

For more information, contact the Summit Ranger District of Stanislaus National Forest, 209/965-3434, www.fs.fed.us/r5/stanislaus.

Options

If you enjoyed this stretch of trail, head over to Lyons Reservoir to pedal another piece of the old railroad grade. Drive 7 miles west on Highway 108 to Lyons Reservoir Road, 2 miles east of Mi-Wuk Village. Turn right on Lyons Reservoir Road (open only May–Oct.) and drive 2.1 miles to the day-use area. Park and ride to your left on the gated dirt road. This trail is even easier, wider, and smoother than the Fraser Flat section of the rail trail. The path runs for 5 level miles to its end at a neighborhood on Middle Camp Road. A turnaround here will add 10 miles to your day.

The old Sugar Pine Railway tunnels through dense forest alongside the Stanislaus River.

Driving Directions

From Sonora, drive east on Highway 108 for 30 miles to the Fraser Flat turnoff, 9 miles east of Mi-Wuk Village and 2 miles west of Strawberry. (If you reach the Cold Springs Store, you've gone too far east.) Turn left on Forest Service Road 4N01, signed for Fraser Flat and Spring Gap. Drive 2.5 miles to the Fraser Flat Bridge.

Route Directions

0.0 Park in the dirt pullout on the right, just before crossing the Fraser Flat Bridge. Ride on the trail heading upstream. *Supplies are available in Strawberry or Mi-Wuk Village.*

2.8 LEFT on Old Strawberry Road (paved).

3.7 RIGHT on Strawberry Drive.

4.3 Strawberry Inn. TURN AROUND.

8.6 Arrive at starting point. Follow the route description above (*see Options*) to drive to another trailhead for the rail trail at Lyons Reservoir, adding on another 10 miles round-trip.

SUGAR PINE RAILWAY

TAHOE AND NORTHERN SIERRA

© ANN MARIE BROWN

BEST BIKE RIDES

❰ Butt-Kickers
Sonora Pass Road Ride, **page 265.**

❰ High Overlooks
Martis Peak Lookout and Watson Lake, **page 231.**

❰ Historic Rides
Masonic Mountain/Chemung Mine, **page 271.**

❰ Paved Bike Paths
Truckee River Recreation Trail, **page 234.**

❰ Single-Track Rides
Emigrant Trail, **page 225.**
Hole-in-the-Ground Trail, **page 228.**

For most visitors, the Tahoe region is clearly

defined by its 22-mile-long, azure blue lake – "a noble sheet of blue water lifted six thousand three hundred feet above the level of the sea, and walled in by a rim of snow-clad mountain peaks," in the eloquent words of Mark Twain. The 10th deepest lake in the world (1,645 feet at its deepest point), and one with remarkable water clarity, it is among the most notable features in the landscape of North America.

Bicycling visitors to the Tahoe region will note two other outstanding features (besides the mammoth lake): rocks and hills. Whereas road cyclists will have to tackle only the latter, mountain bikers will frequently encounter both elements when riding through Tahoe's spectacular High Sierra scenery. In conjunction with the heart-pumping, high-elevation air, these obstacles make Tahoe well suited to riders seeking a challenge.

But that's not to say there aren't opportunities for the more casual rider. Tahoe is laced with paved bike paths, from the scenic Truckee River Trail, which closely follows the rushing waters of the Truckee, to the more pedestrian West Shore Trail, which parallels busy Highway 89 from Tahoe City to Sugar Pine Point. Novice to intermediate mountain bike riders will find dirt trails to suit their abilities in the canyons of the lake's west shore. And for those who just want to coast downhill, not crank uphill, a few Tahoe ski resorts operate their lifts in the summer so mountain bikers can be whisked to high summits, then cruise downhill on two wheels.

The rides detailed in this chapter also encompass somewhat lesser-traveled regions surrounding Lake Tahoe, including Plumas County and the Gold Lakes Basin (north of Tahoe) and the Bridgeport area (southeast of Tahoe). Also within this mountainous region are four High Sierra passes between Tahoe and Yosemite; from north to south they are Echo Pass (U.S. 50), Carson Pass (Highway 88), Ebbetts Pass (Highway 4), and Sonora Pass (Highway 108). Carson and Ebbetts are two of the passes featured in the annual Markleeville Death Ride, one of California's premier cycling events, which brings even expert riders to their knees with its staggering 15,000 feet of elevation change and 129-mile distance. Even if you'd never consider riding in a bike tour of this magnitude, it's worth showing up in July just to watch the spectacle.

The only disappointing fact about biking around Tahoe is that the season is so short. Snow can fall as early as mid-October, and some years the spring melt can hold off until late June. Mountain bikers may find that even though trails may be snow free as early as Memorial Day, they may be too wet to ride until mid- or late July.

Because of the brief season, thousands of riders take to the roads and trails of Tahoe each year in only a few months' time period. To avoid the crowds, the best time is usually September and October, when most of the summer visitors have gone home. And how fortunate, because that's when Tahoe's famous fall color show occurs. It's worth the wait.

TAHOE AND NORTHERN SIERRA

see Shasta
and Lassen
page 66

see Sacramento
and Gold Country
page 170

see Yosemite and
Mammoth Lakes
page 524

©AVALON TRAVEL

TRAIL NAME	LEVEL	DISTANCE	TIME	ELEVATION	PAGE
1 Mills Peak Lookout	2	6.6 mi	1-2 hr	800 ft	222
2 Emigrant Trail	3	31.8 mi	4 hr	2,000 ft	225
3 Hole-in-the-Ground Trail	4	16.7 mi	3-4 hr	2,100 ft	228
4 Martis Peak Lookout and Watson Lake	3	22.2 mi	2 hr	2,500 ft (or 1,200 ft)	231
5 Truckee River Recreation Trail	2	11.2 mi	1 hr	150 ft	234
6 Ward Creek and Alpine Meadows Loop	2	15.7 mi	2-3 hr	1,000 ft	237
7 Twin Peaks and Stanford Rock Loop	4	16.4 mi	3-4 hr	2,500 ft	239
8 Barker Pass and Blackwood Canyon	2	10 mi	1-2 hr	1,300 ft	242
9 General Creek Campground to Lost Lake	3	13.8 mi	2.5-3 hr	1,400 ft	245
10 Fallen Leaf Lake Road	1	11 mi	1 hr	600 ft	248
11 Angora Ridge Lookout and Lakes	2	12 mi	1.5 hr	1,100 ft	251
12 Big Hill Lookout and Wrights Lake	3	27 mi	3 hr	2,700 ft	254
13 Big Meadow to Dardanelles and Round Lakes	3	8.4 mi	2 hr	1,200 ft	257
14 Burnside Lake Road	2	11.4 mi	2 hr	1,100 ft	259
15 Bear Valley to Alpine Lake	2	7 mi	1.5 hr	900 ft	262
16 Sonora Pass Road Ride	5	29 mi	3-4 hr	3,900 ft	265
17 Buckeye Hot Springs	2	9.2 mi	2-3 hr	600 ft	268
18 Masonic Mountain/Chemung Mine	3	10.4 mi	2-3 hr	1,600 ft	271

1 MILLS PEAK LOOKOUT
Gold Lakes Basin near Graeagle

DIRT ROAD WITH MINIMAL CAR TRAFFIC

Difficulty: 2   **Total Distance:** 6.6 miles (or 11.2-mile option)

Riding Time: 1-2 hours   **Elevation Gain:** 800 feet

Summary: Attain a view-filled mountain summit topped with a fire lookout tower – without a hefty climb.

The reward of any fire lookout ride is always an impressive summit vista with a wide scope on the surrounding terrain. Although many fire lookouts are top-notch mountain biking destinations, by their nature they are rarely attained without a steep climb.

Mills Peak Lookout in the Gold Lakes Basin is the exception. Perched on a rocky escarpment at 7,310 feet in elevation, the lookout offers an all-encompassing view of the Mohawk Valley and the Sierra Buttes to the south, but with a total climb of only 800 feet from the trailhead.

The well-graded dirt lookout road is open to cars and gets some traffic on summer weekends, so a weekday ride is preferable. It's virtually impossible to get lost, as the road is marked with black arrows on orange signs nailed to trees (snowmobile markers). The surface is only a little rocky and not technical at all, and although it's uphill all the way, the grade is quite moderate. This is a ride that strong beginners could accomplish.

And what a feeling of accomplishment when they reach the summit. The lookout tower itself is a square white cabin that was built in 1932. It is staffed somewhat inconsistently July 4–October 1 each year. Even if the tower is closed,

© ANN MARIE BROWN

The historic Mills Peak Lookout sits at 7,310 feet in the Gold Lakes Basin.

you can check out the marvelous view from its base, which is almost as good as from the top.

On the ride back downhill, be sure to stop at the Red Fir Nature Trail located 1.1 miles from the lookout (or 2.2 miles from Gold Lake Highway). Lock up your bike and take a short walk through the marvelous red fir forest, where the staghorn moss on the trees' large trunks gives an indication of the previous winter's snow level.

For more information, contact the Beckwourth Ranger District of Plumas National Forest, 530/836-2575, www.fs.fed.us/r5/plumas.

Options

If when you return to your car you are still bounding with energy, ride north 0.5 mile on Gold Lake Highway and turn right at the sign for Frazier Falls. Ride 1.8 miles to the signed trailhead, then lock up your bike and take the 0.5-mile walk to the plunging 250-foot cataract. The round-trip ride to the Frazier Falls Trailhead will add 4.6 nearly level miles to your ride, making an 11.2-mile day.

Driving Directions

From Graeagle, head south on Highway 89 for 1.5 miles, then turn right (west) on Gold Lake Highway, also signed as Lakes Basin Recreation Area. Drive 7 miles to the sign for Mills Peak Lookout (0.5 mile south of Gold Lake Campground). The lookout road is on the left; park in the gravel pullout on the right side of Gold Lake Highway, then ride across the highway to the start of the lookout road.

Route Directions

0.0 Park in the pullout across Gold Lake Highway from the start of Mills Peak Lookout Road. *Water is available at Gold Lake Campground, 0.5 mile north on Gold Lake Highway.*

1.1 LEFT at fork.

2.2 Red Fir Nature Trail on the right. *Visit the big trees now or on your way back.*

3.3 Summit and lookout tower. TURN AROUND.

6.6 Arrive at starting point. Add on an optional ride to Frazier Falls Trailhead and walk to the falls; see *Options.*

2 EMIGRANT TRAIL

BEST C

north of Truckee near Stampede Reservoir

DIRT SINGLE-TRACK

Difficulty: 3

Total Distance: 31.8 miles (or shorter options)

Riding Time: 4 hours

Elevation Gain: 2,000 feet

Summary: If other trails in Tahoe are still snow covered, this mellow rolling single-track will give you the chance to get your bike out of storage and on the trail.

The Commemorative Overland Emigrant Trail is a 15-mile stretch of single-track that runs from Stampede Reservoir (the largest lake in the Tahoe area after Lake Tahoe itself) to Prosser Creek Reservoir (about one-fifth the size of Stampede). Both lakes are popular for fishing, boating, and camping, and now this trail has made them famous among the mountain biking crowd.

This is *the* ride to do around Lake Tahoe in the early summer because the area between Stampede and Prosser Reservoirs is typically snow free a month before everywhere else near Tahoe. On a June weekend, the Emigrant Trail can be packed with riders who have been waiting all winter to get back on their bikes. Early summer is also the best time to visit the two reservoirs, because they are subject to severe drawdowns later in the year. By July and August, it gets quite dry and hot out here, and most of the bikers have moved on to somewhere cooler.

You can start the ride on either end; the elevation change is almost the same in both directions. Although the mileage is long for single-track, the grade consists of lots of gentle, rolling ups and downs through open pine and fir forests and meadows. Sage and mule's ears are common foliage.

If you've had some experience on single-track, you can ride pretty fast here; the only technical skill needed is the ability to balance on a narrow trail—the surface is generally smooth and hard packed. Novices can enjoy this trail, although they probably won't want to ride the entire length of it. The main difficulty is that the trail is bisected by what seems like dozens of dirt roads and creekbeds. Fortunately there are signs everywhere, so it's hard to go wrong. You must ford a few streams on this ride; most of the creeks are too high and wide early in the summer to ride through. If the water is high in Prosser Creek at 8.2 miles, you will have to ride over to Highway 89 to cross it. This adds about a mile to your ride (included in the ride mileage).

Note that this is called the "Commemorative" Overland Emigrant Trail because it's not exactly the real thing. Most of the actual trail taken by emigrants in the 1850s has been wiped out by roads and reservoirs; this trail parallels the original route.

For more information, contact the Truckee Ranger District of Tahoe National Forest, 530/587-3558, www.fs.fed.us/r5/tahoe.

Options

Many people ride this route as a shuttle, leaving one car at each end. That's one way to shrink the total mileage, but the easier way is just to cut the ride short anywhere you please and turn around. Take your pick. Besides its two end points near Stampede and Prosser Reservoirs, the trail can also be accessed at Donner Camp Picnic Area on Highway 89, or along Old Reno Road out of Hobart Mills.

Driving Directions

From Truckee, take I-80 east for 7 miles and exit at Hirschdale/Stampede Reservoir. Cross under the freeway, then drive 8 miles north on Stampede Road to Dog Valley Road. Turn left and drive 2.5 miles to the end of the pavement (past the turnoff for the boat ramp). A small parking area is on the left, and the Emigrant Trail begins here.

Route Directions

0.0 Park at the Emigrant Trailhead at Stampede Reservoir. *Supplies are available in Truckee.*

0.2 LEFT (straight) toward Old Reno Road.

4.1 Cross paved road.

7.0 Cross old paved road.

7.4 Cross wooden bridge.

7.9 Cross paved road; view of Prosser Reservoir far off on the left.

8.1 RIGHT on dirt road, then immediate LEFT back on Emigrant Trail.

8.2 Prosser Creek Crossing on left (to be used only in low water late in the summer). If high water, go straight to Highway 89, where you can cross the creek on the highway.

8.8 LEFT on Highway 89 and across the bridge (walk your bike on left side of road).

8.9 LEFT on trail just past the guardrail.

9.6 Back on Emigrant Trail, which comes in from the left.

10.5 Cross paved road.

11.6 Donner Camp Parking area. Go RIGHT on pavement and cross Highway 89. *A short interpretive trail about the Donner Party is found here, plus picnic tables and restrooms.*

11.7 LEFT on trail before the dirt road.

12.5 Cross Alder Creek Road.

13.6 Cross Schussing Road; prepare to cross Alder Creek three times in the next mile.

15.9 Trail ends at a dirt road. TURN AROUND.

31.8 Arrive at starting point.

EMIGRANT TRAIL

3 HOLE-IN-THE-GROUND TRAIL BEST ◖
Donner Pass, west of Truckee

DIRT ROAD AND SINGLE-TRACK; PAVED ROAD WITH MINIMAL CAR TRAFFIC

Difficulty: 4 **Total Distance:** 16.7 miles

Riding Time: 3-4 hours **Elevation Gain:** 2,100 feet

Summary: This spectacular mountain biking loop covers more than 10 miles of single-track and passes by two swimming lakes and some dramatic geology.

In 1998, Hole-in-the-Ground Trail was Tahoe's newly built, "secret" mountain biking loop. Today every summer weekend hundreds of riders spin their wheels on this loop. It just goes to show that you can't keep a good trail secret.

The trail's popularity is warranted. It visits two granite-bound swimming lakes (Sand Ridge and Lower Lola Montez) and doles out 10-plus miles of exciting single-track. Although you may see hikers and equestrians on sections of the loop, the main traffic will be other bikers. The ride is not for novices, and even intermediate riders will face technical challenges along the route. Plan for a long day unless you are very skilled at single-track riding.

Note that the loop can be ridden in either direction, and can also be started near the Soda Springs fire station. The trail signs are easier to discern if you ride it the way it's described here. (Because of the amount of riders who congregate here, the trail is exceptionally well signed and well maintained.) Riding in this direction, you'll start with a steep climb up a dirt road and end with a couple of miles

Awe-inspiring vistas abound along Hole-in-the-Ground Trail.

of road riding. In between, you have lots of fun, technical single-track.

Starting at the Castle Peak Trailhead, 1 mile of rocky jeep road leads you to the Hole-in-the-Ground Trail. Nine miles of single-track follow. The first stretch includes a heart-pumping climb up Andesite Ridge, with awe-inspiring views of Castle Peak and Squaw Valley. Next comes a 2.5-mile descent on a knife-thin ridge; try to keep your eye on your front wheel and not the stunning Sierra scenery. After more ups and downs, plus the two possible side trips to the lakes, the route joins Lower Lola Montez Lake Trail and cruises downhill to the Soda Springs fire station, then loops back on pavement. On the downhill Lola Montez section, please walk your bike through the steepest areas to prevent erosion.

So what's the hole in the ground? Nothing too exciting, just a grassy depression in the earth that fills up with snowmelt in early summer. You'll see it north of the spur to Lower Lola Montez Lake.

For more information, contact the Truckee Ranger District of Tahoe National Forest, 530/587-3558, www.fs.fed.us/r5/tahoe.

Driving Directions

From Soda Springs, drive three miles east on I-80 and take the Castle Peak/Boreal Ridge Road exit. Cross under the freeway and follow the pavement to its end at a metal gate, about 100 yards from I-80. Park alongside the road near the gate, but do not block it.

Route Directions

0.0 Park at the end of the pavement on Castle Peak Road. *Supplies are available in Soda Springs.*

0.1 RIGHT at unsigned fork in the jeep road.

0.5 LEFT at unsigned fork in the jeep road.

1.0 LEFT at junction with Hole-in-the-Ground Trail.

2.4 Top of the ridge and great views.

4.3 LEFT at trail junction.

5.4 0.25-mile trail to Sand Ridge Lake on the left. *This lake is a great spot for a swim or a break.*

7.6 Dirt road crosses the trail. Stay straight on single-track.

9.7 0.25-mile trail to Lower Lola Montez Lake on the right. *This lake is an even better spot for a swim or a break.*

10.1 Single-track becomes a wide jeep road, Lower Lola Montez Lake Trail. *Watch for signs to stay on the trail, which alternates as single-track and wide road and passes through private property.*

12.8 Trail reaches pavement. Ride downhill past the fire station.

13.1 LEFT on Donner Pass Road and cross over I-80.

13.8 Soda Springs store. *Supplies are available.*

14.6 LEFT on dirt road signed for Central Sierra Snow Laboratories.

14.8 LEFT at fork.

15.8 Boreal Ridge Ski Resort parking lot. Ride across the lot and pick up Castle Peak/Boreal Ridge Road.

16.2 Take Castle Peak Road under I-80.

16.7 Arrive at starting point.

HOLE-IN-THE-GROUND TRAIL

4 MARTIS PEAK LOOKOUT AND WATSON LAKE

BEST ◖

north of Lake Tahoe near Brockway Summit

PAVED ROADS WITH MINIMAL CAR TRAFFIC

Difficulty: 3

Total Distance: 22.2 miles (or 13.2-mile option)

Riding Time: 2 hours

Elevation Gain: 2,500 feet (or 1,200 feet)

Summary: A visit to tranquil Watson Lake and view-filled Martis Peak Fire Lookout are the rewards for this moderate road ride.

This paved road ride to two wonderful Tahoe destinations can be split into two rides for those with less time or energy. The first leg is a 7.8-mile out-and-back ride to Martis Peak Fire Lookout, elevation 8,656 feet, one of the best overlook points in the Tahoe area. The second leg is a 13.2-mile out-and-back to Watson Lake, a shallow and popular swimming lake. The two legs of the ride are joined by a 0.6-mile stretch on Highway 267. If you ride the whole thing, you get a 22.2-mile day of fun and scenery. If you want to take it easy, skip the lookout tower ascent and just ride to Watson Lake, which has longer mileage but much less climbing.

On the Martis Peak ride, the route is easy to follow. You simply stay on the paved road and ignore the numerous junctions with dirt roads. You climb, climb, and climb some more, and after you've gained 1,500 feet in 3.9 miles, you're at the fire lookout. The tower is staffed by a Forest Service worker in summer and fall, who will be happy to interpret for you the great view of Lake Tahoe and Carnelian Bay to the south, Boca and Stampede Reservoirs to the north, Donner Lake, Mount Tallac, the airport in Truckee, Twin Peaks, and so on. On clear days you can even see Mount Lassen, far, far away. The actual summit of Martis Peak is about 200 yards away (accessible via a dirt trail), but the view is best from the fire lookout.

After you've taken in the spectacle from up high, a speedy descent brings you back to the junction of the lookout road and Highway 267. Cross the highway carefully, then ride south for 0.6 mile and turn west on Road 73, Mount Watson Road. A 500-foot elevation gain occurs in the first 1.5 miles from Highway 267,

© ANN MARIE BROWN

Martis Peak Fire Lookout is one of the best overlook points in the Tahoe area.

followed by a dip and another climb. Once you're on the ridgeline, the riding is easier and you gain some good views of Lake Tahoe through the trees. Continue straight until you are 5.9 miles from Highway 267, where you turn left at the orange spray-painted rock (Road 16N50). The lake is less than a mile away. Hope you brought your swimsuit.

For more information, contact Lake Tahoe Basin Management Unit, 530/543-2600, www.fs.fed.us/r5/ltbmu.

Driving Directions

From Tahoe City, drive northeast on Highway 28 to Highway 267. Turn left on Highway 267 and drive 3.7 miles north. Just beyond Brockway Summit, turn right on Martis Peak Lookout Road.

Route Directions

0.0 Park in any available pullout at the start of Martis Peak Lookout Road. *Supplies are available in Kings Beach or Tahoe Vista at Highway 28 and Highway 267.*

3.9 Martis Peak Lookout, elevation 8,656. TURN AROUND.

7.8 Cross Highway 267 and ride LEFT (south).

8.4 RIGHT on Road 73, Mount Watson Road.

14.3 LEFT at orange spray-painted rock (Road 16N50).

15.0 Watson Lake. TURN AROUND.

15.7 RIGHT back onto Road 73, Mount Watson Road.

21.6 Cross Highway 267 and ride LEFT (north).

22.2 RIGHT on Martis Peak Lookout Road. Arrive at starting point.

MARTIS PEAK LOOKOUT AND WATSON LAKE

5 TRUCKEE RIVER RECREATION TRAIL

BEST ☾

Tahoe City to Squaw Valley ski resort

PAVED BIKE PATH

Difficulty: 2 **Total Distance:** 11.2 miles (or longer options)

Riding Time: 1 hour **Elevation Gain:** 150 feet

Summary: Bikers of all abilities will enjoy this scenic, easy pedal alongside the Truckee River.

Of the many paved bike paths in the Tahoe area, the Truckee River Trail is far and away the most scenic and well loved. On summer weekends, it can be difficult negotiating your way amidst all the other bikers, in-line skaters, walkers, and baby strollers on the trail. Nonetheless, whether you're a novice rider or Lance Armstrong, you shouldn't miss this fun cruise. During peak vacation

season, your best bet is to ride at the edges of the day—early in the morning or just before sunset—to avoid most of the trail traffic. On one beautiful September evening, the trail was peaceful enough that I was able to spot a beaver swimming in the Truckee River, as well as dozens of Canada geese.

The route parallels Highway 89 north of Tahoe City, but it was ingeniously built so that much of its path is 15–20 feet below the highway embankment and within a few feet of the river. Because of this, the sight and sound of cars are no distraction and the river takes center stage.

The trail travels past the entrance to Alpine Meadows ski area, then continues for another mile to the entrance to Squaw Valley, crossing picturesque Midway Bridge along the way. Food and shops are available at both ski resorts. A common

© ANN MARIE BROWN

Truckee River Recreation Trail is one of Lake Tahoe's most scenic pathways.

practice is to ride to the River Ranch Inn at the Alpine Meadows turnoff and have lunch on its riverside deck. Or, if you like, you can extend your trip into Squaw Valley. A two-mile-long paved trail runs beside Squaw Valley Road, with views of the meadow and surrounding peaks.

For more information, contact Tahoe City Public Utility District, Parks and Recreation Department, 530/583-5544, www.tahoecitypud.com.

Options

After you return to the 64 Acres Park trailhead in Tahoe City, you can check out the other paved trails that start there. The Lakeside Trail runs a short distance east to Fanny Bridge and Commons Beach, and then after a short stretch on the road, riders can connect to the 2.5-mile Dollar Point Trail, which travels from Tahoe State Recreation Area to Dollar Point. Also starting at 64 Acres, the West Shore Trail heads south for 9 miles to Sugar Pine Point State Park. Be forewarned, however: Despite its terrific lakeshore views, West Shore Trail has one major drawback—it crosses Highway 89 dozens of times. Use caution if you ride it.

Driving Directions

From Tahoe City at the Y-junction of Highways 89 and 28, drive 0.25 mile south on Highway 89 to the sign for the recreation trail parking area on the right (at 64 Acres Park). Turn right (west) and park.

Route Directions

0.0 Park at trailhead and ride across the wooden bridge, then turn LEFT. *Water is available at the trailhead; supplies are available in Tahoe City.*

4.5 Alpine Meadows ski area and River Ranch Inn. *Supplies are available.*

5.0 Cross scenic Midway Bridge.

5.6 Trail's end across from the entrance to Squaw Valley ski resort. TURN AROUND. *Supplies are available.*

11.2 Arrive at starting point.

6 WARD CREEK AND ALPINE MEADOWS LOOP
southwest of Tahoe City

DIRT ROAD, PAVED ROADS WITH MINIMAL CAR TRAFFIC, AND PAVED BIKE PATH

Difficulty: 2

Riding Time: 2-3 hours

Total Distance: 15.7 miles

Elevation Gain: 1,000 feet

Summary: This is a great exercise ride without a lot of technical challenges on the west shore of Lake Tahoe.

This is a great ride for when you want an aerobic workout without all the steep hills and rocky trails that Tahoe usually throws at mountain bikers. On this loop, you ride enough miles to get away for a few hours and achieve an exercise high, but your nerves aren't jangled from trying to negotiate narrow single-track saddled with rocks, ruts, and steep drop-offs on both sides. This is a ride for stress-free spinning, perfect for a summer evening after work. Even strong beginners can handle the Ward Creek and Alpine Meadows Loop, as long as they have the fitness level to last for 15.7 miles. Completing this ride can be a real confidence builder.

Much of the trail travels through neighborhoods and the ski areas near Alpine Meadows, so the scenery isn't as spectacular as some other rides at Tahoe. You do gain some views of Lake Tahoe, the Truckee River, and the Paige Meadows area. If it's scenery you're after, hold out for the final six miles on the bike path alongside the Truckee River and heading south along Lake Tahoe's shore—those last miles will not disappoint. Note that this ride passes by the Tahoe Rim Trail's Twin Peaks Trailhead on Ward Creek Boulevard. For details on that trail, see ride 7, *Twin Peaks and Stanford Rock Loop.*

For more information, contact Lake Tahoe Basin Management Unit, 530/543-2600, www.fs.fed.us/r5/ltbmu.

Driving Directions

From Tahoe City, drive three miles south on Highway 89 to William Kent Campground, north of Pineland Drive.

Route Directions

0.0 Park near William Kent Campground and ride south on the Highway 89 bike trail. *Supplies are available in Tahoe City.*

0.2 RIGHT on Pineland Drive.

0.6 LEFT on Twin Peaks Drive at sign for Ward Valley; road becomes Ward Creek Boulevard and then Courchevel Road.

3.3 RIGHT on Chamonix Street; pavement soon turns to dirt road.

3.6 RIGHT on Road 16N48 (dirt).

4.7 Cross creek and pass road on right (stay left).

7.8 Steep descent and sharp turn to right.

8.2 Forest Service gate. Continue on paved road.

8.6 RIGHT on Alpine Meadows Road.

9.6 RIGHT on Highway 89. Ride the bike path alongside the highway.

13.3 RIGHT across bridge and into main parking area for Tahoe City bike paths. Head south on paved path that parallels Highway 89.

15.7 Arrive at starting point.

WARD CREEK AND ALPINE MEADOWS LOOP

7 TWIN PEAKS AND STANFORD ROCK LOOP
southwest of Tahoe City

DIRT ROAD AND SINGLE-TRACK; PAVED ROADS
WITH MINIMAL CAR TRAFFIC

Difficulty: 4   **Total Distance:** 16.4 miles

Riding Time: 3-4 hours   **Elevation Gain:** 2,500 feet

Summary: More of a bike-hike than a ride, this strenuous loop doles out
some of the best of what Tahoe has to offer.

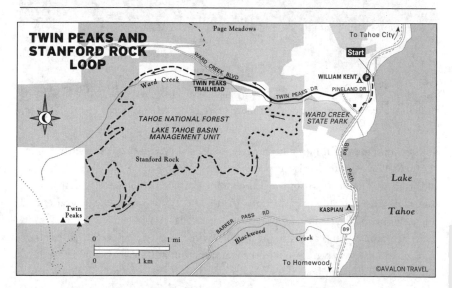

You'll want to have the lightest bike possible for this ride, because you may have
to carry it—a lot. This is not a trail for bikers who are unhappy when pushing or
carrying their wheels. Everyone does it on this loop. Most simply give up, stash
their bikes, and hike, particularly in the last mile to the Twin Peaks summit.

The adventure begins at William Kent Campground, a mere 3 miles south of
Tahoe City. The first 2.3 miles are a warm-up on paved roads as you head out to
the old Ward Creek Trailhead, now called the Twin Peaks Trailhead, an official
part of the Tahoe Rim Trail. The next 3 miles are a gentle streamside ride on a
smooth dirt road, which then narrows into the kind of single-track that provides
fodder for sweet mountain biking dreams. In addition to the enjoyable riding,
the July wildflower display alongside Ward Creek is often one of the best in the
Tahoe region.

But at mile 5.8, where the trail moves away from Ward Creek, your dreamlike

© ANN MARIE BROWN

Twin Peaks and Stanford Rock Loop is much more difficult than it looks on this first easy leg along Ward Creek.

biking state may turn into a nightmare. Over the next 2.6 miles, the trail gains 1,800 feet on a grade that is steeper than many hiking trails. Consider this: Since this trail was made a part of the Tahoe Rim Trail, it is much easier than it used to be. Extensive trail work was done in the late 1990s to lessen the grades and increase the mileage on this route. Thank heavens.

When at last you reach the summit of Twin Peaks, elevation 8,878 feet (*sans* mountain bike; you can stash it at the trail junction at mile 7.4 before continuing on foot for the last mile to the summit), you'll understand why you put yourself through this: The views of Lake Tahoe and the Granite Chief Wilderness are stupendous. Congratulate yourself on a fine achievement.

You must backtrack one mile from Twin Peaks' summit before looping back via Stanford Rock. Although you might expect the way home to be all downhill, you have one more climb and a ridgeline ramble to reach Stanford Rock. Then before you know it you're back on paved Ward Creek Boulevard, nonchalantly riding through the suburban neighborhood as if nothing extraordinary just happened in your life. But you know that it did.

For more information, contact Lake Tahoe Basin Management Unit, 530/543-2600, www.fs.fed.us/r5/ltbmu.

Driving Directions
From Tahoe City, drive three miles south on Highway 89 to William Kent Campground, north of Pineland Drive.

Route Directions

0.0 Park near William Kent Campground and ride south on the Highway 89 bike trail. *Supplies are available in Tahoe City.*

0.2 RIGHT on Pineland Drive.

0.6 LEFT on Twin Peaks Drive at sign for Ward Valley; road becomes Ward Creek Boulevard.

2.3 LEFT at Twin Peaks Trailhead (gated dirt road). Follow the main road and ignore all turnoffs.

5.1 Dirt road ends and single-track begins at Ward Creek.

5.8 Steep climb begins.

7.4 RIGHT at road to Twin Peaks (stash your bike here; there's an 800-foot climb ahead over the next mile).

8.4 Summit of Twin Peaks, elevation 8,878 feet. TURN AROUND.

9.4 RIGHT to loop back via Stanford Rock.

14.8 RIGHT at Ward Creek Boulevard (paved).

16.4 Arrive at starting point.

TWIN PEAKS AND STANFORD ROCK LOOP

8 BARKER PASS AND BLACKWOOD CANYON
southwest of Tahoe City

PAVED ROADS WITH MINIMAL CAR TRAFFIC

Difficulty: 2   **Total Distance:** 10 miles (or 14.1-mile option)

Riding Time: 1-2 hours   **Elevation Gain:** 1,300 feet

Summary: This route offers a paved ride through Blackwood Canyon and up Barker Pass for skinny-tire riders, and a longer loop partially on dirt for fat-tire riders.

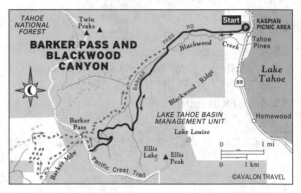

For the lucky locals who live along the shores of Lake Tahoe, Barker Pass Road is a favored exercise ride. The road is used by cross-country skiers, cyclists, in-line skaters, skateboarders, and yes, cars. But cars are secondary. The sign at the road's junction with Highway 89 says, "This is a multipurpose road: keep your speed down for driving." For the most part, people do. The scenery is lovely on the way to Barker Pass: aspen groves in the canyons and old-growth firs as you rise up the pass. There's plenty to look at as you ride.

The road is smooth pavement for the 5 miles from the off-highway vehicle area, allowing road cyclists a 10-mile out-and-back spin with a healthy 1,300-foot climb. For the locals, it's a fast, convenient workout. Mountain bikers can continue on a loop, using the dirt road of Blackwood Canyon for the downhill (see *Options*). Some choose to ride the dirt road uphill and descend on pavement, but this is a much more challenging ride: The dirt road packs 1,300 feet of elevation gain into only 3 miles, while the pavement spreads it out over 5 miles. Plus there's the added difficulty of a rough, rocky surface versus smooth asphalt. It all depends on what kind of a workout you want.

The ride described here goes uphill on paved Barker Pass Road to where the road surface turns to gravel at the popular Ellis Peak Trailhead. Riders on skinny tires who wish to add a hike to their day can do so by walking steeply uphill to Ellis Peak, 3.5 miles away. Even if you only climb 1 mile to the top of the ridge,

© ANN MARIE BROWN

Barker Pass is a multipurpose road, with both dirt and paved roads.

the views are terrific. (Some mountain bikers attempt to ride this trail, but they always wind up pushing their bikes. You'll see why in the first 0.5 mile.)

For more information, contact Lake Tahoe Basin Management Unit, 530/543-2600, www.fs.fed.us/r5/ltbmu.

Options

Mountain bikers can keep riding where the pavement ends, following the now-dirt Barker Pass Road for another 0.5 mile. A left turn on a dirt road near the Pacific Crest Trail junction takes you downhill to Barker Meadow and along Barker Creek. Two miles farther, turn right and climb steeply through two major switchbacks (ignore the numerous side roads and stay on the main road) until you return to the dirt Barker Pass Road. Turn right, heading back toward Barker Pass, and then left on Blackwood Canyon Road 1.3 miles farther. You'll make a fast descent back downhill. Total mileage is 14.1 miles, with about 1,600 feet of elevation gain. Note that much of Blackwood Canyon Road is rough, steep, and loose, so watch your speed. And be cautious of off-highway vehicle users, who frequent this area, especially on weekends.

Driving Directions

From Tahoe City, drive 4.2 miles south on Highway 89 to Forest Service Road 03, Barker Pass Road, at Kaspian Picnic Area. Turn right (west) and drive 2 miles to Blackwood Canyon OHV area. Turn right on the dirt road to the parking area.

Route Directions

0.0 Park at the Blackwood Canyon OHV parking area. Ride back out to paved Barker Pass Road and head right (west). *Supplies are available in Tahoe City.*

5.0 Pavement ends. TURN AROUND. *Add on an optional hike to Ellis Peak.*

10.0 Arrive at starting point.

9 GENERAL CREEK CAMPGROUND TO LOST LAKE

Sugar Pine Point State Park, south of Tahoe City

DIRT ROAD AND SINGLE-TRACK

Difficulty: 3   **Total Distance:** 13.8 miles (or 4.7-mile option)

Riding Time: 2.5-3 hours   **Elevation Gain:** 1,400 feet

Summary: A technical single-track trail and jeep road leads to swimmable Lost Lake.

If you want to get the kids started on mountain biking, Sugar Pine Point State Park is a great place to do it. By the same token, if you want to gain 1,400 feet on a challenging ride to a pretty alpine lake, Sugar Pine Point State Park is a great place to do that, too.

Two different rides, one trailhead—and it happens to be situated at one of Lake Tahoe's nicest state park campgrounds in woods filled with sugar pines. On a family camping trip, the kids can beg an adult to take them on the short loop while

General Creek Loop offers easy riding through the sugar pines.

others saddle up for the bigger adventure to Lost Lake. Everyone will return to their campsite smiling.

All riders begin at the same place: campsite 149 in General Creek Campground. Head straight past the first bridge, following the wide, smooth, dirt-and-sand track. The trail runs between a dense forest of assorted pines and firs on the north side of General Creek and open meadows on the south side. One of the prettiest stretches is where the trail crosses a wooden bridge over a marsh at mile 2.4; look for blooming corn lilies and wildflowers in the spring.

This is the spot where "easy riders" turn left to start looping back to the start (see *Options*), while intrepid riders continue straight ahead for Lost Lake. The trail starts out easy but soon narrows to single-track, running over and around tree roots and boulders. Soon you will probably have to push or carry your bike, if not because of the obstacles then because of the loose, marble-like rock surface. (Think bike-hike and enjoy the upper-body workout.) After crossing General Creek, the single-track climbs mercilessly and then dead-ends into a jeep trail. Head left and climb (or push your bike through the rocks) to a high ridge, passing Duck Lake on your left on your way to Lost Lake, elevation 7,700 feet. Swimming, anyone? You deserve it.

For more information, contact Sugar Pine Point State Park, 530/525-7982 or 530/525-3345, www.parks.ca.gov.

Options

Families and beginning riders will enjoy riding the General Creek Loop, which follows the same route as the trail described above for the first 2.4 miles. Near the marsh, you'll turn left where Lost Lake riders go straight. Enjoy another 1.3 miles of mellow riding on the opposite side of General Creek, then turn left to cross a bridge over the creek. On the far side of the bridge, go right to return to campsite 149 and your starting point. This makes a pleasant 4.7-mile round-trip.

If after completing this short loop you want to do more easy riding, it's simple to connect to Lake Tahoe's West Shore bike path, which is paved. Just follow the park road out to Highway 89 and pick up the trail heading north. It crosses busy Highway 89 a few times, but it is almost completely level and leads to some interesting locations along the lakeshore. The trail extends all the way to Tahoe City, 10 miles north.

Driving Directions

From Tahoe City, drive nine miles south on Highway 89 to the General Creek Campground entrance on the right.

Route Directions

0.0 Park in the day-use parking area near the kiosk, then ride your bike on the park road. Stay to the right in the campground loop to access site 149 and the trail. (Ride mileage begins at the day-use parking.) *Water is available in the campground; supplies are available on Highway 89.*

0.7 RIGHT onto trail at campsite 149.

0.9 STRAIGHT at junction with road on left (return of General Creek Loop).

2.4 STRAIGHT at junction.

2.9 LEFT at Lost Lake/Lily Pond junction; sections of this trail are not rideable, so prepare to push your bike.

4.4 Cross General Creek; on far side, trail goes uphill next to the creek.

4.8 LEFT on jeep road to Lost Lake. Walk your bike through the boulders.

6.6 Duck Lake on the left. Continue past it.

6.9 Lost Lake. TURN AROUND.

13.8 Arrive at starting point.

GENERAL CREEK CAMPGROUND TO LOST LAKE

GENERAL CREEK LOOP (Option)

10 FALLEN LEAF LAKE ROAD
south of Lake Tahoe on Fallen Leaf Lake

PAVED ROAD WITH MODERATE CAR TRAFFIC

Difficulty: 1   **Total Distance:** 11 miles

Riding Time: 1 hour   **Elevation Gain:** 600 feet

Summary: One of South Lake Tahoe's most popular paved rides leads along the shoreline of aspen-lined Fallen Leaf Lake.

Fallen Leaf Lake Road is an honest-to-goodness road, complete with car traffic and speed limit signs, but it's as much like a paved recreation trail as any road could be. On summer days, you'll find as many bikers and hikers on this lakeside route as automobiles. Due to the number of recreationists, plus the narrowness of the road, cars are forced to go slow, which makes the route safer for bikes than it would otherwise be. Still, I wouldn't recommend it for young children, or for bikers who are prone to attention deficits.

The road is an easy, level cruise that provides close-up views of large, 400-foot-deep Fallen Leaf Lake. In its final 2 miles, Fallen Leaf Lake Road is only 20 feet from the water's edge. Aside from the lake views, the ride's payoff is 5 miles out at a 100-foot cascade on Glen Alpine Creek, which roars with snow-melt into July. In another 0.5 mile, the road dead-ends at the Glen Alpine Trail-head for the Desolation Wilderness, a trailhead so popular that often there isn't enough parking.

The first three miles pass by Fallen Leaf Campground and through a long stretch of forest. This may be the most peaceful part of the ride, before the road narrows to the width of one car and skirts the lakeshore, passing by a large number of summer homes. You must watch for traffic entering and exiting driveways as you ride.

The final two lakeside miles bustle with activity from the houses, the Fallen Leaf Lake Store and Marina, the roadside waterfall, and the trailhead at Glen Alpine. But even with all the people sharing the narrow road, you still have plenty of chances to admire pretty Fallen Leaf Lake. Fortunately, on a bike you can travel at just the right speed to enjoy it.

For more information, contact Lake Tahoe Basin Management Unit, 530/543-2600, www.fs.fed.us/r5/ltbmu.

Options

Pedalers looking for level, paved, family-style riding in the South Shore area that is completely free of car traffic should try out the Pope-Baldwin Bike Path, a 3.4-mile trail that runs from the junction of Emerald Bay Road/Highway 89 and 15th Street in South Lake Tahoe (1.3 miles north of the Y) to 0.5 mile north of Baldwin Beach. Along the way, the trail passes by Camp Richardson Resort, the Tallac Historic Site, the Taylor Creek Visitor Center, and Pope, Baldwin, and Kiva Beaches. If you wish, you can connect to Fallen Leaf Lake Road from this trail by crossing Emerald Bay Road/ Highway 89.

A mellow ride on Fallen Leaf Lake Road leads to a turnaround at the Glen Alpine Creek Bridge.

© ANN MARIE BROWN

Driving Directions

From South Lake Tahoe at the northern junction of U.S. 50 and Highway 89, drive northwest on Highway 89 for three miles to the left turnoff for Fallen Leaf Lake (one mile past Camp Richardson Resort). Turn left on Fallen Leaf Lake Road and park in one of the dirt pullouts along the road.

Route Directions

0.0 Park in the pullout at the start of Fallen Leaf Lake Road (near its junction with Highway 89) and start riding on the paved road. *Supplies are available one mile east at Camp Richardson, or farther east in South Lake Tahoe.*

0.5 Stay straight at right fork for Fallen Leaf Campground. *Water is available.*

4.4 Fallen Leaf Lake Store and Marina. *Supplies are available.*

4.8 LEFT at fork for Stanford High Sierra Camp.

5.0 Glen Alpine Creek waterfall.
5.5 End of the road at Glen Alpine Trailhead. TURN AROUND.
11.0 Arrive at starting point.

11 ANGORA RIDGE LOOKOUT AND LAKES
south of Lake Tahoe near Fallen Leaf Lake

DIRT AND PAVED ROADS WITH MINIMAL CAR TRAFFIC

Difficulty: 2   **Total Distance:** 12 miles

Riding Time: 1.5 hours   **Elevation Gain:** 1,100 feet

Summary: Enjoy a view-filled climb from Fallen Leaf Lake up to Angora Ridge, where you'll access two granite-lined lakes and a historic resort.

This route to Angora Ridge Lookout and Angora Lakes is a fairly easy cruise on both paved and dirt roads to a high overlook of Lake Tahoe and two granite-bound lakes. You'll share much of the ride with some car traffic, but it's quite manageable because most drivers are going slow and enjoying the scenery (this isn't a through road). If you're in the mood for an aerobic workout and some stellar scenery with no technical challenges, this is your ride.

The road starts out paved and then alternates as paved and dirt as it climbs gently to the top of Angora Ridge, elevation 7,290 feet. Views are good from the road, but walk a few feet to the fire lookout buildings to get the best perspective on Fallen Leaf Lake, 1,000 feet below you.

From the lookout, the road descends slightly to the parking area for Angora Lakes. The last mile to the lakes is on a car-free dirt trail, but the route is shared with a lot of hikers and dog walkers. You'll ride uphill to Lower Angora Lake, which has a few private homes on its shore, then proceed on level ground to more beautiful Upper Angora Lake, home to Angora Lakes Resort and its handful of picturesque cabins. (You must lock up your bike at the bike rack before entering the resort area.)

The upper lake at 7,280 feet is a perfectly bowl-shaped, glacial cirque lake, set in a pine and fir forest with lots of rounded-rock boulders sprinkled around. Although it's nearly impossible to get a reservation to stay at one of Angora Lake's cabins, the resort owners encourage day-use visitors. They rent rowboats by the

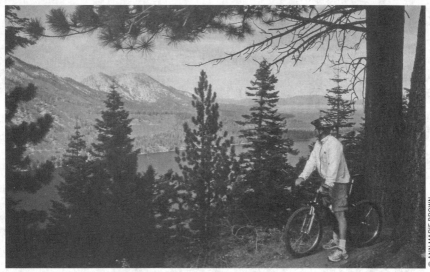

Angora Ridge Lookout provides great views of Fallen Leaf Lake through the trees.

hour and run a small refreshment stand, pumping out lemonade by the gallon to thirsty bikers and hikers. A small sandy beach is popular for swimming and wading in summer.

For more information, contact Lake Tahoe Basin Management Unit, 530/543-2600, www.fs.fed.us/r5/ltbmu.

Driving Directions

From South Lake Tahoe at the northern junction of U.S. 50 and Highway 89, drive northwest on Highway 89 for three miles to the left turnoff for Fallen Leaf Lake (one mile past Camp Richardson Resort). Turn left on Fallen Leaf Lake Road and park in the dirt pullouts along the road.

Route Directions

0.0 Park in the pullout at the start of Fallen Leaf Lake Road (near its junction with Highway 89) and start riding on the paved road. *Supplies are available one mile east at Camp Richardson, or farther east in South Lake Tahoe.*

0.5 Stay straight at right fork for Fallen Leaf Campground. *Water is available.*

2.0 LEFT on paved Tahoe Mountain Road and head uphill.

2.4 RIGHT on Road 1214 (dirt Angora Ridge Road).

4.3 Angora Ridge Fire Lookout on right; great view of Fallen Leaf Lake.

5.4 Parking lot for lakes; ride across the lot.

5.5 Go past wooden markers and continue uphill on wide dirt trail.

5.8 Lower Angora Lake on left.

6.0 Upper Angora Lake; lock up your bike and walk the final steps to the lake. TURN AROUND.

12.0 Arrive at starting point.

ANGORA RIDGE LOOKOUT AND LAKES

12 BIG HILL LOOKOUT AND WRIGHTS LAKE
Crystal Basin Recreation Area off U.S. 50

PAVED ROAD WITH MINIMAL CAR TRAFFIC

Difficulty: 3   **Total Distance:** 27 miles (or 7-mile option)

Riding Time: 3 hours   **Elevation Gain:** 2,700 feet

Summary: The back roads of the Crystal Basin Recreation Area lead to the historic Big Hill Lookout and idyllic Wrights Lake.

Few fire lookout towers have access roads that are paved all the way to the top, but the Big Hill Lookout does. This makes this road ride perfect for skinny tires or fat tires—an ideal trip that both kinds of riders can enjoy. In addition, the short climb to the lookout tower provides a healthy leg-and-lung workout in very little time and mileage. (It's like taking a Spinning class at the gym, but without all the yelling and loud music.)

Because this ride goes out and back in two directions from Ice House Campground, less hearty riders can climb to the lookout tower and call it a day (see *Options*), while more ambitious types continue on to Wrights Lake, adding another 20 miles to their day.

From the start of Big Hill Lookout Road, 1 mile from the campground, the pavement ascends 700 feet over 2.5 miles. You'll be panting when you arrive at the summit, elevation 6,130 feet. The modern lookout, built in 1994 to replace the original 1933 building that burned down, has a neighboring heliport used for fast attacks on forest fires. (If the firefighters aren't busy, they might let you admire their shiny red helicopter.)

Oddly, the views from the top of Big Hill are of Union Valley Reservoir to the north and much smaller Wrights Lake to the east, but not of Ice House Reservoir directly below. One interesting bit of history: Big Hill Lookout was utilized during World War II for the protection of hot air balloons carrying fire bombs.

After admiring the view, enjoy the fast downhill coast back to Ice House Road,

The short climb to Big Hill Lookout leads to a fire lookout tower and a view of the Crystal Basin.

then cross it again and return to the fork just before the campground. Prepare to gain another 1,500 feet in elevation over the next 10 miles. The pavement rolls through mostly forested terrain to Wrights Lake Campground and the pretty lake itself, which is ideal for swimming and fishing. The large, busy campground has a small visitor center that is staffed in summer.

For more information, contact the Pacific Ranger District of Eldorado National Forest, 530/644-6048 or 530/644-2349, www.fs.fed.us/r5/eldorado.

Options

For a much easier ride, just make a quick climb up and back from the campground to the lookout tower and call it a day. Total distance is seven miles and elevation gain is only 700 feet.

Driving Directions

From Pollock Pines, drive 9 miles east on U.S. 50 and turn north on Ice House Road (Forest Service Road 3). Drive 10.5 miles to the right turnoff for Ice House Campground. Turn right, drive 1 mile and park in or near the campground (if you are not camping, do not park in designated campsites).

Route Directions

0.0 Park at Ice House Campground and ride back out to Ice House

Road. *Water is available at the campground; supplies are available at nearby Ice House Resort.*

1.0 Cross Ice House Road to the start of Road 11N58, Big Hill Lookout Road.

3.5 Big Hill Lookout. TURN AROUND.

7.0 LEFT at junction just before Ice House Campground (signed for Wrights Lake, Road 11N52).

8.7 LEFT on Forest Service Road 32.

14.9 LEFT on Wrights Lake Road.

17.0 Wrights Lake Campground and the lake. TURN AROUND. *Water is available at the campground.*

27.0 Arrive at starting point.

13 BIG MEADOW TO DARDANELLES AND ROUND LAKES

south of South Lake Tahoe

DIRT SINGLE-TRACK

Difficulty: 3   **Total Distance:** 8.4 miles

Riding Time: 2 hours   **Elevation Gain:** 1,200 feet

Summary: One of South Lake Tahoe's most popular mountain biking trails leads to two remarkably different lakes.

In case you've been living in a cave for the past decade and don't know about it, the Tahoe Rim Trail is a 165-mile-long trail that runs along the mountain ridges surrounding Lake Tahoe, passing through two states and six counties. After years of hard work and political wrangling, it was completed in 2000. The entire trail is open to hikers and equestrians, with somewhat more limited stretches open to mountain bikes.

One of the main access points for bikers is the Big Meadow Trailhead on Highway 89 south of South Lake Tahoe. From this major trailhead, riders can head north to Freel Meadows or Armstrong Pass, or south to Round Lake and Dardanelles Lake—all on single-track trails. This ride follows the latter route to both lakes for an 8.4-mile out-and-back. The mileage may be low, but the riding is fairly technical and challenging, and the visual rewards are great. Don't forget your bathing suit for a dip in the two beautiful, but extremely different, lakes.

Their difference lies in their geologic origins. Round Lake, which you'll visit first, is surrounded by stark-looking volcanic cliffs. Dardanelles Lake is a classic, glacially sculpted water body, surrounded by granite cliffs and boulders. As the crow flies, these two lakes are only about a mile apart, but they couldn't be more disparate—a clear example of the contrasting forces of fire and ice that have shaped the Sierra Nevada.

Don't be discouraged by the extremely rocky stretch of trail that takes off from Highway 89 right at the start. Walk your bike if you need to—many riders do. After the first 0.5 mile, the surface and grade improves markedly. Much of the trail is forested with giant red firs and sweet-smelling Jeffrey pines, except for a 0.25-mile stint through sunny Big Meadow. Both Round and Dardanelles Lakes are shallow enough so that the water warms up for swimming. I recommend a backstroke to the far shore of Dardanelles, where you'll find many small boulder islands.

For more information, contact Lake Tahoe Basin Management Unit, 530/543-2600, www.fs.fed.us/r5/ltbmu.

Driving Directions

From Meyers, drive south on Highway 89 for 6.5 miles to the Big Meadow Trailhead on the left side of the road.

Route Directions

0.0 Park at the Big Meadow Trailhead near the restrooms (bear left). The trail begins on the southwest side of the parking lot loop. *Supplies are available in Meyers or South Lake Tahoe.*

0.2 Cross Highway 89 and pick up the single-track by the signboard.

0.5 RIGHT at fork for Big Meadow.

1.9 Steep downhill stretch.

2.2 LEFT for Round Lake at Christmas Valley junction.

2.8 Round Lake. TURN AROUND.

3.4 LEFT at junction for Christmas Valley.

3.6 LEFT at trail to Dardanelles Lake.

4.8 Arrive at Dardanelles Lake. TURN AROUND.

6.0 RIGHT at junction.

6.2 LEFT at junction.

8.2 Cross Highway 89.

8.4 Arrive at starting point.

BIG MEADOW TO DARDANELLES AND ROUND LAKES

14 BURNSIDE LAKE ROAD
Hope Valley, south of South Lake Tahoe

DIRT ROAD WITH MINIMAL CAR TRAFFIC

Difficulty: 2   **Total Distance:** 11.4 miles

Riding Time: 2 hours   **Elevation Gain:** 1,100 feet

Summary: This wintertime cross-country ski trail makes a great summer mountain biking route for those who just want to spin their wheels without a lot of technical challenges.

For strong beginners, or intermediates looking for a moderate workout coupled with a fun destination, Burnside Lake Road offers a scenic and not-too-strenuous cruise through conifers and aspens to wide, shallow Burnside Lake, elevation 8,100 feet. The lake is good for trout fishing and better for swimming. On a hot day, you won't complain about the grasses and tules rimming its edges; you'll just drop your bike on the ground and wade in. Save some energy to take the short hike from the lake's edge to a high overlook of the Hot Springs Valley area.

The wide dirt road is open to cars, but because its only destination is the lake, it doesn't get much traffic. (On a beautiful September Saturday, we saw about 10 cars total; most were parked for firewood cutting.) The road has some washboard and is mildly rocky in places, but riding it doesn't require any technical skills. A gradual grade takes you uphill to the lake—it's just relentless enough to get you sweating. One short, steep stretch is covered in broken pavement, which produces better traction for the climb. As you ride, ignore the numerous possible side roads and stay on Burnside Lake Road.

If possible, time your trip for October, when the aspens lining much of the route turn bright gold. Or take a ride in spring when the snow has melted but the road is not yet open to cars.

For more information, contact the Carson Ranger District of Humboldt–Toiyabe National Forest, 775/882-2766, www.fs.fed.us/r4/htnf.

Burnside Lake is a fine spot for a swim or to try your luck at fishing.

Driving Directions

From Meyers, drive south on Highway 89 for 11 miles to its junction with Highway 88. Immediately across Highway 88 is the start of a dirt road, with a large parking area and Hope Valley Wildlife Area information sign.

Route Directions

0.0 Park at junction of Burnside Lake Road and Highway 88 (across from Highway 89), by Hope Valley Wildlife Area signboard. Ride south on Burnside Lake Road (Forest Service Road 019). *Supplies are available at Sorenson's Resort, 1.2 miles east on Highway 88.*

2.6 Beautiful aspen grove.

2.9 RIGHT at fork to stay on Road 019.

5.5 LEFT at fork to stay on Road 019.

5.7 Burnside Lake. TURN AROUND. *Lock up your bike and take a 0.7-mile hike to an overlook 1,000-plus feet above Markleeville and Hot Springs Valley. The trail starts from the southeast end of the lake. Beyond a series of meadows and forest, you'll come out to the granite-lined overlook.*

11.4 Arrive at starting point.

15 BEAR VALLEY TO ALPINE LAKE

off Highway 4, east of Arnold

DIRT SINGLE-TRACK AND PAVED BIKE PATH

Difficulty: 2   **Total Distance:** 7 miles

Riding Time: 1.5 hours   **Elevation Gain:** 900 feet

Summary: A short, easy single-track makes a fun connector path between Bear Valley and Alpine Lake.

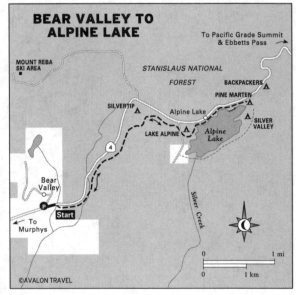

Beautiful Alpine Lake on Highway 4 is the centerpiece of the Bear Valley Recreation Area. The granite-bound lake at elevation 7,300 feet is popular for trout fishing and has three Forest Service campgrounds near its lakeshore.

This single-track trail is the non-highway route to Alpine Lake from Bear Valley, the latter being the big "town" in these parts. Although short, the trail includes a one-mile, heart-pumping climb. The trickiest part is finding the start, which is just a few hundred feet east of Bear Valley on the south side of Highway 4. I had to ride up and down the highway a few times before I spotted it (I'm told that it is sometimes signed, sometimes not).

The trail parallels Highway 4 at first, then heads away from the road and continues uphill. It meanders through the forest, then meets up with a portion of the historic Emigrant Trail pioneer route. After skirting the south side of Silvertip Campground, the trail turns into a wide gravel path that leads downhill toward Alpine Lake. A dirt road connects you to Lakeshore Trail, a paved bike trail that parallels the north shore of Alpine Lake. Lakeshore Trail runs smack in between Highway 4 and the lake, but the latter is so pretty with its rocky shoreline and shady pine forest that you won't even notice the nearby cars.

This paved trail runs between Alpine Lake and Highway 4.

The riding is so pleasant on this trail that I recommend an out-and-back, although you could easily turn this into a loop by heading back on Highway 4. Summer vacation traffic, especially on weekends, makes the loop option less appealing.

For more information, contact the Calaveras Ranger District of Stanislaus National Forest, 209/795-1381, www.fs.fed.us/r5/stanislaus.

Options

You can turn this ride into a semi-loop by following the dirt trail and road on the back side of Alpine Lake (look for the trail at Pine Marten Campground), then returning on the single-track to Bear Valley.

Driving Directions

From Arnold, drive 29 miles east on Highway 4 to Bear Valley. Turn left on Bear Valley Road and park in any of the public parking areas near the shops.

Route Directions

0.0 Park at Bear Valley. Ride back out Bear Valley Road, turn left on Highway 4, and pick up the single-track on the right side of the road in about 75 yards. *Supplies are available in Bear Valley.*

1.8 Junction with Emigrant Trail.

2.1 Silvertip Campground.

2.3 LEFT on dirt road.

2.5 RIGHT on paved bike path.

3.5 East end of Alpine Lake. TURN AROUND. *Or take one of possible loop options described above.*

7.0 Arrive at starting point.

16 SONORA PASS ROAD RIDE   BEST C
Highway 108 from Dardanelle to Sonora Pass summit

PAVED ROAD WITH MODERATE CAR TRAFFIC

Difficulty: 5   **Total Distance:** 29 miles (or 58-mile option)

Riding Time: 3-4 hours   **Elevation Gain:** 3,900 feet

Summary: If you're looking for a true hill challenge to test your mettle, Sonora Pass provides that, and more.

Some hard-core cyclists ride Tioga Pass, the mighty 9,945-foot pass in northern Yosemite with breathtaking glacial scenery and even more breathtaking high-elevation air. Equally hard-core cyclists ride 8,730-foot Ebbetts Pass, the impossibly narrow, winding, and steep mountain road that is part of the epic Markleeville Death Ride bike tour each July. But hard-core cyclists who qualify as true "cyclopaths" ride Sonora Pass—Highway 108, the steepest grade and most strenuous highway route across the Sierra Nevada.

The ride isn't for the faint of heart, or weak of quadriceps. From the traditional starting point at Dardanelle Resort, elevation 5,765 feet, to Sonora Pass, a mere 14.5 miles east, the route gains almost 4,000 feet, with grades as high as 26 percent. You'd think most cyclists would kiss the ground when they finally attain the Sonora Pass summit at 9,624 feet, but no... a few who have completely lost their minds just keep riding—all the way downhill to U.S. 395, doubling their distance (see *Options*). Having lost another 2,700 feet in elevation, riders have two choices: Turn around and ride back up the pass, or call their mommies to come pick them up.

Mere mortals are overwhelmed just driving Sonora Pass. The scenery is beyond spectacular—the granite and volcanic landscape is the sort of thing you'd hope to find after a week of backpacking in the far reaches of the Sierra. Since there's little or no shoulder on most of Highway 108, be wary of cars. Chances are good the drivers will be gawking at the scenery.

One of the most challenging road rides in the Sierra is the trail through the 9,624-foot Sonora Pass.

Options

Double your distance and your self-inflicted pain by continuing from Sonora Pass summit downhill to U.S. 395. You'll pass Leavitt Falls Vista (great view of the West Walker River Valley and a waterfall in a box canyon on Leavitt Creek) at mile 20.8, Leavitt Meadows Campground at mile 22.5 (stop here for a drink of water and to check your brakes), and Sonora Bridge Campground at mile 27.0 (ditto on the water and brakes). Finally, at 29 miles you reach U.S. 395, and then, yes, you turn around and ride back uphill. Total distance is 58 miles; total elevation gain is 6,600 feet. This makes the Death Ride look like mere child's play.

Driving Directions

From Sonora, drive 50 miles east on Highway 108 to Dardanelle Resort on the right side of the road (18 miles east of Strawberry).

Route Directions

0.0 Park at or near Dardanelle Resort. *Supplies and lodging are available.*

2.0 Pidgeon Flat Campground and The Columns of the Giants Trailhead. *You'll be too tired to hike this short path on your way back, so go see this volcanic rock formation now. It's a mere 0.25-mile walk.*

3.0 Eureka Valley Campground. *Water is available.*

5.8 Baker Campground and turnoff for Kennedy Meadow. *Water is available.*

8.4 Vista point followed by more brutal climbing.
14.5 Sonora Pass summit, elevation 9,624 feet. TURN AROUND.
29.0 Arrive at starting point.

17 BUCKEYE HOT SPRINGS
west of Bridgeport

DIRT ROAD WITH MINIMAL CAR TRAFFIC

Difficulty: 2   **Total Distance:** 9.2 miles (or 18.8-mile option)

Riding Time: 2-3 hours   **Elevation Gain:** 600 feet

Summary: This gravel road ride leads to a hot springs pool in remote Buckeye Creek.

A dip in a cold stream with hot springs bubbling up from its depths is the reward for this ride from U.S. 395 in Bridgeport. Even if you don't partake in the soothing waters, the view from Buckeye Road as it ascends out of Bridgeport Valley is ample reward on its own.

The gravel surface of Buckeye Road provides good traction, and the grade alternates between climbing and leveling out, giving you several chances to catch your breath. On the down side, the road is very narrow and has some frightening drop-offs. It is open to cars, although most drivers prefer to access the hot springs and neighboring Buckeye Campground via the paved Twin

The ride to Buckeye Hot Springs provides expansive views of Bridgeport Valley.

Lakes Road. Still, get far to the side if you hear a car coming on one of the tight, narrow curves.

The path is simple to follow—a straight course with no turnoffs. Initially the road climbs for 1 mile, then it levels as it travels through a piñon pine forest. Where the trees open up, you have stunning views of wide Bridgeport Valley and the jagged peaks of the Sawtooth Range to the northeast. At 4.6 miles, you reach the parking area for the hot springs. (There is no sign, but this spot is easy to identify by the cars parked there.) If you wish, lock up your bike or carry it downhill a few hundred feet to the stream, then take a dip in the undeveloped springs. Those possessing a modest disposition might want to look around before they head to the stream: Occasional Buckeye Creek bathers have been spotted wearing only their birthday suits. Know before you go.

For more information, contact the Bridgeport Ranger District of Humboldt–Toiyabe National Forest, 760/932-7070, www.fs.fed.us/r4/htnf.

Options

To turn this out-and-back ride into a longer loop, continue on the dirt-and-gravel road past the hot springs for 0.2 mile to a right fork leading to Buckeye Campground (you can get water here if you need some). Stay left at the fork, and in 3 more miles the road surface turns to pavement. Shortly you'll reach Doc and Al's Resort, where you can buy a candy bar if you're hungry, then continue on to Twin Lakes Road. Go left on paved Twin Lakes Road and enjoy an easy 7-mile cruise back down to U.S. 395. Next comes the only unpleasant part of the loop: a 3.8-mile stint on the busy highway back to your car. Fortunately there's a wide shoulder. Total loop mileage is 18.8 miles, with 800 feet of elevation gain, almost all of it in the first stretch to the hot springs.

Driving Directions

From Bridgeport, drive north on U.S. 395 for 3.8 miles. Turn left on gravel

Buckeye Road, which is also signed for Buckeye Campground. Park in the large parking pullout alongside the start of the road.

Route Directions

0.0 Park at the start of Buckeye Road near its junction with U.S. 395. *Supplies are available in Bridgeport.*

1.0 First mile of climbing ends and road levels out.

1.4 Stay straight at two consecutive junctions.

2.2 Pass through a burned forest area; road climbs again.

2.8 Pass a Toiyabe National Forest sign.

3.0 Road levels out.

4.6 Buckeye Hot Springs parking area (an unsigned dirt parking area on the left side of the road). TURN AROUND. *A hiking trail leads a few hundred feet down to the river and the hot springs. Buckeye Campground is 0.5 mile farther; water is available.*

9.2 Arrive at starting point.

18 MASONIC MOUNTAIN/ CHEMUNG MINE

BEST C

northeast of Bridgeport near Bridgeport Reservoir

DIRT ROAD WITH MINIMAL CAR TRAFFIC

Difficulty: 3

Total Distance: 10.4 miles

Riding Time: 2-3 hours

Elevation Gain: 1,600 feet

Summary: This ride takes you back through time to a piece of Bridgeport's mining history.

The Chemung Mine was one of a half-dozen profitable gold mines on the slopes of Masonic Mountain, a remote area northeast of Bridgeport. Chemung Mine kept producing gold right up until the 1950s, when it was closed down. Many of its buildings still stand. Allow some time in your ride to walk around the mine site, letting your imagination relive the excitement of the gold rush days.

The route is simple to follow, as there are no turnoffs. Occasional cars traverse this dirt road; stay alert for them as they usually aren't expecting cyclists. The road makes a moderate uphill climb through a somewhat desolate forest of piñon pines and western junipers, so don't expect any shade. When you reach the mine and stamp mill ruins, you'll find a lovely grove of aspens, and a marvelous vista to the west of the Sawtooth Range. Views of the Sweetwater Mountains to the north are also good.

Take some time to poke around the six mine buildings and the machinery and debris left outside them. Don't be tempted to enter the buildings, though; they are gradually decaying and falling down. Be especially cautious around the mine shafts themselves.

For more information, contact the Bridgeport Ranger District of Humboldt–Toiyabe National Forest, 760/932-7070, www.fs.fed.us/r4/htnf.

Early 20th century mine buildings still stand along the slopes of Masonic Mountain.

Driving Directions

From Bridgeport on U.S. 395, turn north on Highway 182 and drive 3.7 miles alongside Bridgeport Reservoir. Turn right on Forest Service Road 046, Masonic Road, which is just east of the reservoir's fishing access area. Park off the road in any available pullout.

Route Directions

0.0 Park alongside Masonic Road near its junction with Highway 182. *Supplies are available in Bridgeport.*

1.3 Cattle guard; walk your bike.

1.6 Hairpin turn and a Toiyabe National Forest sign.

4.2 Road begins to level out; pass an old mine shaft from the neighboring Success Mine.

5.2 RIGHT to visit Chemung Mine buildings. TURN AROUND.

10.4 Arrive at starting point.

SAN FRANCISCO BAY AREA

© ANN MARIE BROWN

BEST BIKE RIDES

❰ **Butt-Kickers**
Woodside to Coast Long Loop, **page 424.**

❰ **Families**
Bear Valley Trail Bike and Hike, **page 289.**

❰ **High Overlooks**
Mount Diablo Summit Ride, **page 380.**

❰ **Historic Rides**
Old Stage Road and Old Railroad Grade to East
    Peak, **page 327.**
Stewartville and Ridge Trails Loop, **page 367.**

❰ **Oceanfront Rides**
Golden Gate Bridge and Marin Headlands Loop,
    page 345.
Pescadero and San Gregorio Loop, **page 434.**

❰ **Paved Bike Paths**
Nimitz Way and Wildcat Canyon, **page 349.**
Sawyer Camp Recreation Trail, **page 409.**

❰ **Single-Track Rides**
Middle Ridge Loop, **page 459.**

❰ **Waterfalls**
Berry Creek Falls Bike and Hike, **page 462.**

❰ **Wildlife-Viewing**
Point Reyes Lighthouse, **page 292.**
Stinson Beach and Mount Tamalpais Loop, **page 324.**

❰ **Wine-Tasting**
Monte Bello Loop, **page 447.**

Whether your tastes run to fat tires or skinny

tires, Campagnolo or Rockshox, the San Francisco Bay Area is an undisputed mecca for cyclists. Home to thousands of pairs of well-toned legs, closets full of black Lycra shorts, more than 100 bike shops, dozens of cycling clubs, and countless miles of dirt and paved trails, the City by the Bay and its surrounding landscape afford a world of opportunities for mountain bikers, road cyclists, and recreational riders of all types, including those pulling Burley trailers or sporting training wheels.

The Bay Area has all the right ingredients for cycling nirvana: hilly back roads, narrow and winding coastal Highway 1, world-famous landmarks like the Golden Gate Bridge and Pigeon Point Lighthouse, and even Mount Tamalpais, the self-proclaimed birthplace of mountain biking. It was on Mount Tam's steep slopes that Gary Fisher, Joe Breeze, and others held the first formal off-road bike races in the late 1970s. Those first bikes were heavy, clunky, and downright dangerous, but a few years and a few modifications later, mountain bike fever caught on and an industry was born.

Several park agencies around the Bay Area are particularly friendly to mountain bikers. We're fortunate to have the East Bay Regional Park District, Golden Gate National Recreation Area, and Midpeninsula Regional Open Space District on our side. Even Point Reyes National Seashore allows mountain bikes on many of its trails – a rarity in the national park system. Several state parks do, too: Mount Diablo, Mount Tamalpais, Big

Basin Redwoods, Angel Island, McNee Ranch, Portola, Henry Coe, and China Camp. A handful of these parks even allow bikers on some of their single-track trails, not just the wide fire roads.

For a tamer ride, the San Francisco Bay Area is nationally recognized for its wealth of paved bike paths, most of which began as railroad right-of-ways. Seven of these trails are described in this chapter, varying in length from 6 to 30 miles. If you want to commute by bike to work, or spin your wheels on an easy Sunday afternoon outing, or teach a kid how to ride a bike without training wheels, there is no better place to do so than on a paved, car-free recreation trail.

Then there are the miles of back roads that travel the lesser known regions between the Bay Area's traffic-clogged interstates and highways. For the road cyclist, there are more routes to ride here than one could complete in a lifetime, and there is much to do besides just pedal. From the seat of your bike, you can visit historic sites, quaint villages, wineries, waterfalls, astronomy observatories, and so much more. Or, you can just coast by and enjoy the scenery. Set among natural features such as towering redwood forests, teeming bay wetlands, and the rugged coastline south to Waddell Creek and north to the outer reaches of west Marin County, the San Francisco Bay Area is the most wild metropolitan area in the United States. Whether you choose to ride on road or trail, you'll be witness to an urban wilderness like no other.

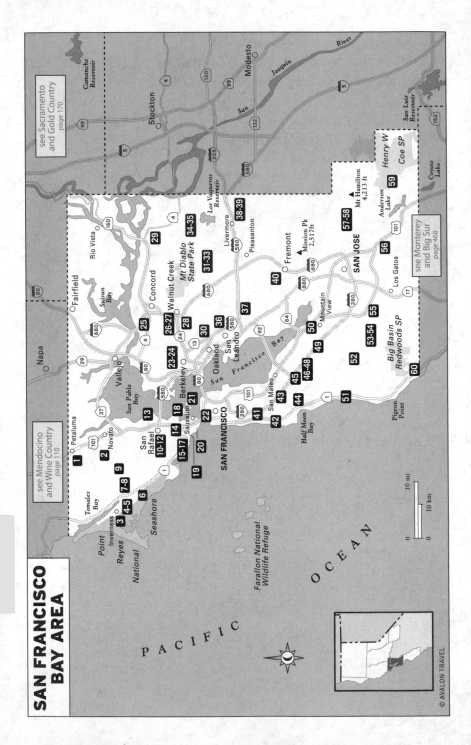

TRAIL NAME	LEVEL	DISTANCE	TIME	ELEVATION	PAGE
1 Petaluma and Dillon Beach Ramble	3	55.3 mi	4 hr	1,800 ft	280
2 Cheese Company and Tomales Bay Loop	3	46 mi	3–4 hr	1,800 ft	283
3 Estero Trail	2	12 mi	3 hr	1,200 ft	286
4 Bear Valley Trail Bike and Hike	1	6.2 mi (plus 1.8-mile hike)	2 hr	500 ft	289
5 Point Reyes Lighthouse	3–4	45 mi	3.5–4.5 hr	1,900 ft	292
6 Stewart Trail	4	13 mi	2–3 hr	2,500 ft	296
7 Bolinas Ridge and Olema Valley Loop	2	15 mi	2 hr	1,000 ft	299
8 Cross Marin Trail and Bolinas Ridge Loop	3	13.4 mi	2.5 hr	1,250 ft	302
9 Nicasio Reservoir Loop	2	24.5 mi	2 hr	900 ft	306
10 Pine Mountain Loop	3	13.2 mi	2.5 hr	2,000 ft	309
11 Tamarancho Loop	3	11.7 mi	2 hr	1,000 ft	312
12 Fairfax and Mount Tamalpais Loop	3	31.8 mi	3–4 hr	2,200 ft	315
13 China Camp Bay View Loop	3	11.6 mi	2 hr	600 ft	318
14 Three Lakes Loop	2	11.2 mi	1.5 hr	900 ft	321
15 Stinson Beach and Mount Tamalpais Loop	4	23.9 mi	3 hr	2,700 ft	324
16 Old Stage Road and Old Railroad Grade to East Peak	2	8 mi	1.5 hr	1,100 ft	327
17 Old Railroad Grade to West Point Inn	3	13.8 mi	2 hr	1,700 ft	330
18 Tiburon and Belvedere Loop	2	10.5 mi	1 hr	700 ft	333
19 Tennessee Valley and Coyote Ridge Loop	3	6.5 mi	1.5 hr	1,200 ft	336
20 Marin Headlands Miwok and Bobcat Loop	4	14 mi	2 hr	2,100 ft	339

TRAIL NAME	LEVEL	DISTANCE	TIME	ELEVATION	PAGE
21 Perimeter Trail and Fire Road Loops	2	9.6 mi	2 hr	900 ft	342
22 Golden Gate Bridge and Marin Headlands Loop	3	15 mi	1.5-2 hr	1,500 ft	345
23 Nimitz Way and Wildcat Canyon	2	11.3 mi	2 hr	800 ft	349
24 Skyline Loop	3	28.5 mi (or 23-mile option)	2 hr	2,000 ft	352
25 Carquinez Strait Loop	2	18.5 mi	1.5-2 hr	1,200 ft	356
26 Briones Crest Loop	2	8 mi	1.5 hr	1,200 ft	359
27 Three Bears Loop	3	19.5 mi	1.5 hr	1,600 ft	362
28 Lafayette–Moraga Regional Trail	1	15.4 mi	1.5 hr	550 ft	364
29 Stewartville and Ridge Trails Loop	3	10.8 mi	2 hr	1,900 ft	367
30 East and West Ridge Loop	2	9.4 mi	2 hr	1,100 ft	371
31 Wall Point and Barbeque Terrace Loop	3	9.4 mi	2 hr	1,600 ft	374
32 Mitchell and Donner Canyons Loop	4	13.1 mi	2.5 hr	2,900 ft	377
33 Mount Diablo Summit Ride	4	29.6 mi	4-5 hr	3,200 ft	380
34 Round Valley Ramble	1	10.8 mi	1.5 hr	600 ft	383
35 Volvon and Valley View Loop	3	8.4 mi	2 hr	1,200 ft	386
36 Lake Chabot Loop	3	13.3 mi	2 hr	1,200 ft	389
37 Palomares Road	3	20.2 mi	1-2 hr	1,900 ft	392
38 Morgan Territory Road	4	46.4 mi	3-4 hr	3,500 ft	394
39 Livermore Winery Ride	2	19.5 mi	2 hr	800 ft	397
40 Alameda Creek Trail	1	24 mi	2 hr	200 ft	400

TRAIL NAME	LEVEL	DISTANCE	TIME	ELEVATION	PAGE
41 Sweeney Ridge Loop	3	7.3 mi	2 hr	1,100 ft	403
42 Montara Mountain	3	9.6 mi	2 hr	2,000 ft	406
43 Sawyer Camp Recreation Trail	1	12 mi	1 hr	250 ft	409
44 Half Moon Bay Back Roads	3	24.1 mi	2 hr	1,500 ft	412
45 Purisima Redwoods Loop	3	10 mi	2-3 hr	1,600 ft	414
46 El Corte de Madera Creek Loop	3	10.5 mi	2 hr	1,400 ft	417
47 Woodside to Skyline Short Loop	4	20 mi	1.5-2 hr	2,200 ft	421
48 Woodside to Coast Long Loop	5	57.1 mi	5-7 hr	5,800 ft	424
49 Russian Ridge and Coal Creek Loop	2	7.3 mi	1.5 hr	800 ft	428
50 Stanford and Portola Valley Loop	2	18 mi	1.5 hr	750 ft	431
51 Pescadero and San Gregorio Loop	3	28.7 mi	2 hr	1,200 ft	434
52 Old Haul Road Loop	3	17.6 mi	3 hr	2,100 ft	437
53 Big Basin and Boulder Creek Loop	4	43 mi	3-4 hr	3,300 ft	440
54 Saratoga Gap Loop	3	12.9 mi	2-3 hr	1,600 ft	444
55 Monte Bello Loop	4	27 mi	3 hr	2,300 ft	447
56 Coyote Creek Trail	2	29.4 mi	2-3 hr	400 ft	450
57 Mount Hamilton	4	23 mi	2 hr	2,700 ft	453
58 Grant Ranch Loop	3	10.9 or 12 mi	2 hr	1,600 ft	456
59 Middle Ridge Loop	4	10.8 mi	2 hr	2,100 ft	459
60 Berry Creek Falls Bike and Hike	2	11.6 mi	2.5 hr	550 ft	462

1 PETALUMA AND DILLON BEACH RAMBLE

Petaluma to Dillon Beach, northwest Marin County

PAVED ROADS WITH MINIMAL CAR TRAFFIC

Difficulty: 3   **Total Distance:** 55.3 miles (or 25-mile option)

Riding Time: 4 hours   **Elevation Gain:** 1,800 feet

Summary: Sheep, cows, and llamas are your companions on this Petaluma countryside ride.

Chileno Valley Road is the long, rambling way to get to the coast from Petaluma, but for bicyclists, it's the obvious choice. The road is filled with small ups and downs, multiple curves and twists, and a whole lot of cows standing beside it and sometimes in it. Few motorists bother with this road; they use the more direct Bodega Avenue instead.

After a 12.6-mile stint on Chileno Valley's bucolic, pasture-lined thorough-fare, this rambling 55-mile ride makes a loop through the small towns of Valley Ford, Dillon Beach, and Tomales. This results in a perfect half-day ride with no killer climbs, but with plenty of great scenery, both in the inland hills and on the windswept coast.

Each of these three towns has an interesting history. Valley Ford was a potato-farming community in the 19th century, but in the 1920s the residents took up sheep farming. Little has changed since then; you'll still see plenty of woolly sheep, plus an abundance of cows and a smattering of llamas. Dillon Beach has been a seaside resort since 1888, when George Dillon constructed a hotel at the end of

Pasture-lined Chileno Valley Road is the rambler's way from Petaluma to the coast.

the West Marin railroad line, hoping to attract city folk to the local beaches and clamming beds. Tomales was a railroad stop in the late 1880s. Today its short main street boasts the revered Tomales Bakery (707/878-2429, www.tomalesbakery.com), which is always worth a calorie-replenishing stop, a general store, and a café and restaurant.

Options

If the mileage on this ride seems intimidating, it is easy enough to cut it into two rides for two separate days: a 25-mile out-and-back on Chileno Valley Road starting from Helen Putnam Regional Park, and a 27-mile loop through Tomales, Dillon Beach, and Valley Ford, starting from any of those towns.

Driving Directions

From U.S. 101 in Petaluma, take the Petaluma Boulevard South exit and drive north 2 miles. Turn left (west) on Western Avenue and drive 2.2 miles, then turn left on Chileno Valley Road and drive 0.8 mile to Helen Putnam Regional Park on the left.

Route Directions

0.0 Park at Helen Putnam Regional Park and ride west on Chileno Valley Road. (Parking is available inside the park or in pullouts along the road.) *Supplies are available in Petaluma.*

3.0 RIGHT to stay on Chileno Valley Road.

12.6 LEFT on Tomales–Petaluma Road.

13.8 RIGHT on Alexander Road.

14.8 RIGHT on Fallon–Two Rock Road.

17.2 LEFT on Petaluma–Valley Ford Road (hamlet of Two Rock).

26.0 LEFT on Valley Ford Estero Road (town of Valley Ford). *Supplies are available.*

31.8 RIGHT on Dillon Beach Road. Ride out and back through Dillon Beach, then TURN AROUND and return to junction with Valley Ford Road. *Supplies are available in Dillon Beach.*

34.6 RIGHT on Dillon Beach Road.

37.2 RIGHT on Shoreline Highway (Highway 1) in town of Tomales. *Supplies are available.*

37.5 LEFT on Tomales–Petaluma Road.

42.7 RIGHT on Chileno Valley Road.

52.3 LEFT to stay on Chileno Valley Road.

55.3 Arrive at starting point.

2 CHEESE COMPANY AND TOMALES BAY LOOP

Novato to Marshall, northwest Marin County

PAVED ROADS WITH MINIMAL CAR TRAFFIC

Difficulty: 3

Riding Time: 3-4 hours

Total Distance: 46 miles

Elevation Gain: 1,800 feet

Summary: This cycling and snacking tour of western Marin County is perfect for road riders.

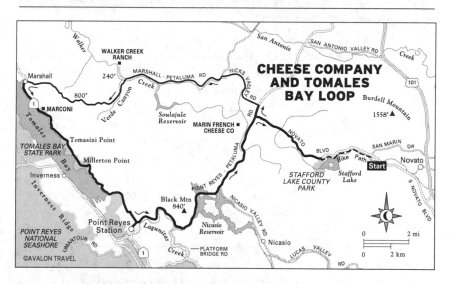

This is a ride for the gourmet cyclist. You'll work up an appetite on this 46-mile ride, then satisfy it with barbecued oysters from Tomales Bay and brie and camembert from the Marin French Cheese Company.

Although Marin County has many scenic road rides, this is one of the loveliest. It offers a mix of pastoral hills and green, fertile valleys, plus level riding along the edge of Tomales Bay. The bucolic charms of this excursion will make you forget you are in the same county (perhaps even in the same country) as the busy corridor of U.S. 101 north of the Golden Gate.

Plus, the loop visits two of west Marin's most charming towns: Marshall and Point Reyes Station. Marshall is known for two things: tranquil bay views and shellfish. More than half of California's oyster and shellfish growers lease acreage on the floor of Tomales Bay. To sample the local mollusks, head for the Hog Island Oyster Company (415/663-9218, www.hogislandoysters.com), Tomales Bay the start of Marshall–Petaluma Road's demanding two-mile climb

Oyster Company (415/663-1242, tomalesbayoysters.com), or the Marshall Store (415/663-1339, www.themarshallstore.com), all which are located right alongside Highway 1. Don't like oysters? Order the clam chowder.

The quaint town of Point Reyes Station is 0.3 mile off the loop and worth a side trip. The old railroad town features an eclectic mix of shops and cafés, including the ever-popular Bovine Bakery (415/663-9420), purveyor of organic, handmade pastries, which has a crowd of road bikers thronging at its doors every weekend morning.

The ride has two major hills that are worthy of a warning. The first is a two-mile brutal stint on Marshall–Petaluma Road. Although the seldom-traveled road is a beauty, with lots of ups, downs, and winding curves, its one major hill is infamous for bringing cyclists to their knees. Know in advance that the hardest climbing takes place from mile 15.9 to 17.5, in an area called Three Peaks.

With that ascent accomplished, your reward is a euphoric descent to the coast at Marshall, where after snacking on a dozen or more oysters, you'll enjoy nine miles of gentle pedaling along the edge of Tomales Bay. To best enjoy the exquisite water's-edge scenery, plan this ride for a weekday, when you'll contend with a lot fewer cars on Highway 1. Weekends can be very busy here.

After your bayside stint, you can opt for a brief side trip into Point Reyes Station, or just head inland for the final leg to the Marin French Cheese Company (7500 Red Hill Rd., 707/762-6001, www.marinfrenchcheese.com). Tours of the cheese factory are available at 10 A.M., 11 A.M., 12 P.M., and 3 P.M. daily; cheese and other picnic supplies are for sale. On this stretch, you'll face the second big hill, about a mile past Nicasio Reservoir. The ascent is sustained over 1.5 miles, but it's not as bad as the Marshall–Petaluma hill because you know a big round of brie is waiting on the other side. Be sure to take the Cheese Company's factory tour so you can learn how the yummy stuff is made. *Bon appétit.*

Driving Directions

From San Rafael, drive north for 10 miles on U.S. 101 and take the San Marin Drive exit. Drive northwest for 2.7 miles to the intersection of San Marin Drive and Novato Boulevard, where the bike path begins.

Route Directions

0.0 Park at the intersection of San Marin Drive and Novato Boulevard in Novato, then ride west on the bike path that parallels Novato Boulevard. *Supplies are available in Novato.*

2.5 Pass Stafford Lake County Park on the left; bike trail ends and you ride on Novato Boulevard. *Water is available.*

6.2 RIGHT on Petaluma–Point Reyes Road.

6.7 LEFT on Hicks Valley Road.

9.4 LEFT on Marshall–Petaluma Road.

15.9 Start of steepest climb.

17.5 Summit.

20.3 LEFT on Highway 1 in Marshall. *Supplies are available at various restaurants in town, including the Hog Island Oyster Company, Tomales Bay Oyster Company, and the Marshall Store.*

24.3 Tomales Bay Oyster Company on right.

25.1 Tomales Bay State Park/Millerton Point beach and picnic area.

29.2 LEFT on Petaluma–Point Reyes Road. *Or go right to head into town of Point Reyes Station in 0.3 mile.*

33.1 LEFT at junction with Platform Bridge Road.

33.9 Pass Nicasio Reservoir.

39.3 LEFT into Marin French Cheese Company parking lot. *Supplies are available.*

39.7 RIGHT on Novato Boulevard.

43.5 Pick up bike trail at Stafford Lake County Park.

46.0 Arrive at starting point.

CHEESE COMPANY AND TOMALES BAY LOOP

3 ESTERO TRAIL
Point Reyes National Seashore

DIRT ROAD AND SINGLE-TRACK

Difficulty: 2

Riding Time: 3 hours

Total Distance: 12 miles

Elevation Gain: 1,200 feet

Summary: Enjoy water-view riding alongside Home Bay and Drakes Estero in the cow pasturelands of Point Reyes.

The Estero Trail is quintessential Point Reyes. It's full of good surprises, including an exemplary display of Douglas iris in spring; a dense Monterey pine forest; ample bird-watching opportunities; nonstop views of estuary, bay, and ocean; and access to a pristine beach and high bluff-top overlook. To fully enjoy this excursion, pack a lunch and binoculars and plan on an unhurried ride. The only downside? The route is in cow territory, and the chubby bovines' hooves can make a rutted mess of the old ranch roads, especially in the wet season. It's best to save this ride for summer and fall, after the trails have dried and hardened.

From the parking lot, Estero Trail laterals across a grassy hillside, then rounds a corner and descends into a dense stand of Monterey pines, the tall and aged remains of an old Christmas tree farm and the nesting site of owls and egrets. Shortly the trail opens out to blue, serene Home Bay. A bridge crossing leads you to the first of several short climbs, this one rewarding you with high views of Home Bay's junction with Drakes Estero.

The ride continues parallel to, and mostly high above, the estuary, offering nonstop water views. If the tide is out, mudflats and the oyster beds of nearby

Estero Trail crosses a bridge over Home Bay, then parallels the edge of Drakes Estero.

Drakes Bay Oyster Farm will be revealed. If the tide is in, you'll see miles of azure water. You'll climb and descend a total of three hills on this trail; the third one has a lone eucalyptus tree growing on its summit.

At 2.5 miles, a sign marks Drakes Head to the left and Sunset Beach straight ahead. Turn left and climb through grasslands and chaparral to a confusing maze of cattle gates and fences (watch for arrow signs along the fence). Drakes Head Trail continues southward; the path crosses a coastal prairie and ends on a high bluff overlooking the ocean and Limantour Spit, a long, narrow stretch of sand and grass-covered dunes.

After a pause to enjoy the view, return to the previous junction, then go left on Sunset Beach Trail. The path levels and in 1.5 miles you are within reach of Sunset Beach, where Drakes Estero meets up with Estero de Limantour. A large, quiet pond separates you from the coast, and as the trail continues along the edge of Drakes Estero it soon becomes mucky and impassable for bike tires. Stash your bike and explore beautiful Sunset Beach on foot (best at low tide; consult a tide table for optimal timing).

For more information, contact Point Reyes National Seashore, 415/464-5100, www.nps.gov/pore.

Driving Directions

From San Francisco, cross the Golden Gate Bridge and drive north on U.S. 101 for 7.5 miles. Take the Sir Francis Drake Boulevard exit west toward San Anselmo and drive 20 miles to the town of Olema. At Olema, turn right (north) on Highway 1 for about 150 yards, then turn left on Bear Valley Road. Drive 2.2 miles on Bear Valley Road until it joins with Sir Francis Drake Highway. Bear left on Sir Francis Drake and drive 7.6 miles to the left turnoff for the Estero Trailhead. Turn left and drive 1 mile to the trailhead parking on the right.

Route Directions

0.0 Park at Estero Trailhead. *Supplies are available in the town of Inverness on Sir Francis Drake Highway.*

1.1 Bridge across Home Bay.

2.5 LEFT at junction with Drakes Head Trail (Sunset Beach Trail continues straight).

2.8 Maze of cattle gates, fences, and hiker gates; follow the fence-line path signed with arrows.

3.2 RIGHT on Drakes Head Trail; trail becomes indistinct in places—keep heading south toward the bluff's edge.

4.5 Drakes Head overlook. TURN AROUND.

6.5 LEFT on Sunset Beach Trail at previous junction.

8.0 Arrive at edge of pond with Sunset Beach beyond; stash your bike and explore on foot. TURN AROUND.

12.0 Arrive at starting point.

4 BEAR VALLEY TRAIL BIKE AND HIKE

BEST ◖

Point Reyes National Seashore

DIRT ROAD

Difficulty: 1 **Total Distance:** 6.2 miles (plus 1.8-mile hike)

Riding Time: 2 hours **Elevation Gain:** 500 feet

Summary: This easy, scenic trip on two wheels and two feet is suitable for the whole family.

Don't forget your bike lock for this short, scenic ride in Point Reyes National Seashore. You'll pedal for 3.1 miles, then hike almost a mile to the top of Arch Rock, a spectacular coastal overlook. Because of this trail's well-deserved popularity, you should time your trip for a weekday or an early morning on the weekend. It's more fun to ride if you aren't dodging a crowd of bikers and hikers.

Beginning just past the Bear Valley Visitor Center and Morgan Horse Ranch, the wide dirt trail is simple to follow. Several side trails intersect Bear Valley Trail but none are open to bikes. Just stay on the main path and cruise beneath the shady forest canopy, comprised of a mix of alders, bay laurel, and fir. At the midway point, after the only noticeable climb of the ride, you'll reach grassy Divide Meadow, a popular picnic spot. Deer are commonly seen here.

At 3.1 miles, the trail reaches a bike rack and several trail junctions. Lock up your bike and continue on foot to Arch Rock. The trail continues the final steps to Arch Rock on the Bear Valley Trail Bike and Hike

through the woods for 0.5 mile, following Coast Creek, then suddenly opens out to coastal marshlands. The final steps of the hike are extremely dramatic as you walk along the top of Arch Rock's jagged, jade-green bluff, which juts out over the sea. The wind can howl with tremendous fury here, which may come as a surprise after your stint on the sheltered forest trail.

A spur trail leads down the cliffs to the beach; it's worth hiking during low tide when you can crawl through the tunnel of Arch Rock and explore the beach. Many visitors are content to stay on top of Arch Rock and enjoy the view of the surging waters below. If luck is with you, you'll catch sight of a passing gray whale, or at least a couple of sea lions.

For more information, contact Point Reyes National Seashore, 415/464-5100, www.nps.gov/pore.

Options

Although there is no way to extend the biking part of this bike-and-hike trip, you can extend the hike by backtracking 0.25 mile from Arch Rock to a junction with Coast Trail. Turn left (north) on Coast Trail and follow it for 1 mile to the left turnoff for Kelham Beach, which is unsigned but marked by a single massive eucalyptus tree. Or, you can hike a 4-mile loop and return to the bike rack by following Coast Trail north for 0.5 mile, turning right on Sky Trail, then right again on Baldy Trail.

Driving Directions

From San Francisco, cross the Golden Gate Bridge and drive north on U.S. 101 for 7.5 miles. Take the Sir Francis Drake Boulevard exit west toward San Anselmo and drive 20 miles to the town of Olema. At Olema, turn right (north) on Highway 1 for about 150 yards, then turn left on Bear Valley Road. Drive 0.5 mile, then turn left at the sign for Seashore Headquarters Information. Drive 0.25 mile and park in the large lot on the left, past the visitor center. Start riding along the park road, heading for the signed Bear Valley Trail.

Route Directions

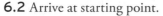

0.0 Park at Bear Valley Trailhead just past the visitor center. Ride west on the continuation of the park road, which turns to dirt at a wide gate. *Supplies are available less than a mile away in Olema; water is available at the visitor center.*

1.6 Divide Meadow.

3.1 Bike rack and junction with Glen, Baldy, and Bear Valley Trails; TURN AROUND. *Lock up your bike and hike 0.9 mile on Bear Valley Trail to Arch Rock (straight ahead).*

6.2 Arrive at starting point.

BEAR VALLEY TRAIL BIKE AND HIKE

5 POINT REYES LIGHTHOUSE

BEST ☾

Point Reyes National Seashore

PAVED ROADS WITH MODERATE CAR TRAFFIC

Difficulty: 3 (4 if windy) **Total Distance:** 45 miles (or 20-mile option)

Riding Time: 3.5-4.5 hours **Elevation Gain:** 1,900 feet

Summary: An often windswept cruise through the rural Point Reyes countryside, this route offers optional stops at a few of the park's highlights.

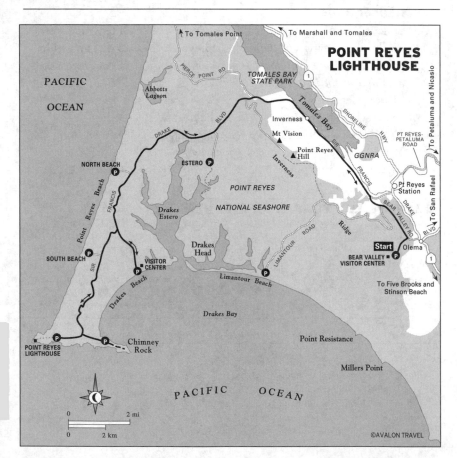

Road cycling in Point Reyes National Seashore can be heavenly if the weather gods are on your side. If they aren't, you could face headwinds of 40-plus miles per hour, or fog so dense you miss all the scenery the park has to offer. Remember this: Autumn and spring days are the surest bets for clear weather. Winter isn't bad

© ANN MARIE BROWN

A visit to the lighthouse is one highlight of a road ride in Point Reyes.

either, and that's when you have the best chance of spotting migrating whales from the park's shores. This road tour travels to two of the park's best whale-watching spots—the Point Reyes Lighthouse and Chimney Rock—and detours to gastronomic delights at Drakes Beach Café (a lunch of seasonal greens and barbecued oysters) and Drakes Bay Family Farms (fresh oysters straight from the shell).

From the Bear Valley Visitor Center, the route follows Bear Valley Road to Sir Francis Drake Highway and the bayside town of Inverness. Then Sir Francis Drake heads northwest into the park, leaving most of civilization behind with a short but steep ascent up and over Inverness Ridge. The ride continues on Sir Francis Drake as it threads through fields of colorful wild mustard and acres of cow pastures to the western tip of Point Reyes National Seashore.

At Chimney Rock Trailhead, you can walk a 1.5-mile stretch where more than 60 species of wildflowers bloom in springtime on a narrow, windswept headland jutting into Drakes Bay, or look for elephant seals and gray whales in winter or spring. The ride finishes at Point Reyes Lighthouse, where 300-plus steps descend to this breathtaking coastal promontory. To tour the lighthouse, plan your trip for Thursday through Monday; it's closed year-round on Tuesday and Wednesday.

For more information, contact Point Reyes National Seashore, 415/464-5100, www.nps.gov/pore. Drakes Beach Café (415/669-1297, www.drakescafe.com) is located at 1 Drakes Beach Road. Drakes Bay Family Farms (415/669-1149, www.drakesbayoyster.com) is located at 17171 Sir Francis Drake Boulevard. Hours vary seasonally.

Options

If the wind is too stiff to make this ride enjoyable, try this more protected option: Begin your ride as described, then bear right at mile 7.4 on Pierce Point Road. Pedal 1.2 miles and then turn right on Tomales Bay State Park Road. One mile down the park road is lovely Heart's Desire Beach. An out-and-back ride to this mostly wind-sheltered beach is about 20 miles.

Driving Directions

From San Francisco, cross the Golden Gate Bridge and drive north on U.S. 101 for 7.5 miles. Take the Sir Francis Drake Boulevard exit west toward San Anselmo and drive 20 miles to the town of Olema. At Olema, turn right (north) on Highway 1 for about 150 yards, then turn left on Bear Valley Road. Drive 0.5 mile, then turn left at the sign for Seashore Headquarters Information. Drive 0.25 mile and park by the visitor center.

Route Directions

0.0 Park at Bear Valley Visitor Center, then ride back out the park road the way you came in. *Water is available at the visitor center.*

0.2 LEFT on Bear Valley Road.

1.8 LEFT on Sir Francis Drake Highway.

5.9 Town of Inverness. *Supplies are available.*

7.4 LEFT at Y-junction with Pierce Point Road.

8.7 STRAIGHT at junction with Mount Vision Road.

9.4 STRAIGHT at junction with Estero Trailhead Road.

10.4 Drakes Bay Family Farms entrance on left. *If the oyster company is open, stop in for a grown-in-Point Reyes snack.*

13.2 STRAIGHT at junction for North Beach.

15.1 RIGHT at junction with Kenneth C. Patrick Visitor Center and Drakes Beach (save the left fork for your return trip).

19.4 LEFT at access road for Chimney Rock Trailhead.

20.3 Chimney Rock Trailhead. TURN AROUND. *Hike or mountain bike the 1.5-mile Chimney Rock Trail in winter for whale-watching and in spring for wildflowers. From December to April, walk a few hundred yards to the Elephant Seal Overlook to see the seals hauled out on Drakes Beach.*

21.2 LEFT on Sir Francis Drake Highway.

21.8 Point Reyes Lighthouse parking lot. TURN AROUND. *Tour the lighthouse and neighboring visitor center.*

26.7 RIGHT for Kenneth C. Patrick Visitor Center and Drakes Beach.

28.3 Drake's Beach parking lot. TURN AROUND. *The visitor center features fascinating exhibits on local history, flora, and fauna (open weekends only). Drakes Beach Café serves lunch Friday–Monday in winter, Thursday–Monday in spring and summer, and Saturday–Sunday in autumn.*

29.9 RIGHT on Sir Francis Drake Highway.

45.0 Arrive at starting point.

POINT REYES LIGHTHOUSE

6 STEWART TRAIL
Point Reyes National Seashore

DIRT ROAD

Difficulty: 4   **Total Distance:** 13 miles

Riding Time: 2-3 hours   **Elevation Gain:** 2,500 feet

Summary: An up-and-down ride on a conifer-lined dirt road leads from the inland valley to the Point Reyes coast.

Few national parks permit bikes on their trails, and even fewer allow bike-in camping at remote campgrounds. Point Reyes National Seashore is a rare exception, and Stewart Trail from Five Brooks Trailhead is your ticket to two backcountry camps in Point Reyes: Glen and Wildcat. Those wishing to bike-backpack can make a reservation and get a permit for one of the camps. Riders looking for a challenging day-time sojourn will also enjoy pedaling Stewart Trail.

Be prepared for some climbing; this is an aerobically strenuous ride with a long ascent in both directions of the out-and-back. The initial climb begins 0.25 mile from the parking lot and makes a steady 1,200-foot ascent over 3.5 miles to a ridge called Fir Top. The name is apt; the area is completely shaded by Douglas firs. Then Stewart Trail drops steeply toward the ocean, losing all that hard-won elevation, plus another 100 feet. At 5.2 miles is the turnoff for forest-sheltered Glen Camp, where some riders spend the night. Stewart Trail continues downhill to the coast and Wildcat Camp. As you descend, be sure to give your brakes a rest now and then by stopping to enjoy occasional peeks at the ocean through the trees. And keep in mind that you'll face this slope in the uphill direction on your way home. Stewart Trail ends 6.5 miles out at Wildcat Camp. Day visitors and campers alike will want to lock up their wheels and head to the neighboring beach to explore.

For more information and/or camping permits, contact Point Reyes National Seashore, 415/464-5100, www.nps.gov/pore.

© ANN MARIE BROWN

Stewart Trail provides a challenging day trip or the chance for an overnight camping experience in one of two backcountry camps in Point Reyes.

Options

If you're burning with energy, an option from Wildcat Camp is to hike two miles south on Coast Trail (bikes are not allowed) to visit Alamere Falls, one of the Bay Area's loveliest waterfalls. The falls drop 50 feet over a coastal bluff to the sea.

Driving Directions

From San Francisco, cross the Golden Gate Bridge and drive north on U.S. 101 for 7.5 miles. Take the Sir Francis Drake Boulevard exit west toward San Anselmo and drive 20 miles to the town of Olema. At Olema, turn left (south) on Highway 1 for 3.5 miles to Five Brooks Trailhead on the right.

Route Directions

0.0 Park at Five Brooks Trailhead. Ride out the paved road past a large pond. *Supplies are available in Olema; water is available at the trailhead.*

0.2 RIGHT on wide Stewart Trail.

3.0 RIGHT to stay on Stewart Trail at junction with Ridge Trail.

3.8 Arrive at Fir Top summit at 1,324 feet.

5.2 LEFT to stay on Stewart Trail at junction with Glen Trail (campers staying at Glen Camp turn right here).

6.5 Arrive at Wildcat Camp; TURN AROUND. *Lock up your bike and*

visit neighboring Wildcat Beach, or take a two-mile hike south on the
Coast Trail to Alamere Falls.

13.0 Arrive at starting point.

7 BOLINAS RIDGE AND OLEMA VALLEY LOOP

Golden Gate National Recreation Area near Olema

DIRT ROAD

Difficulty: 2

Total Distance: 15 miles (or 26-mile option)

Riding Time: 2 hours

Elevation Gain: 1,000 feet

Summary: Pedal uphill past the bovines and through the grasslands of Bolinas Ridge, then choose from a variety of fast and fun descents.

The first time you ride Bolinas Ridge, you wonder how a trail could go up and down so much without ever leveling out. The path seems to have no pedal-and-cruise sections; you are either climbing up or coasting down the whole way (more of the latter than the former). The ridge's roller-coaster grassland terrain is just

Open pasturelands line the northern edge of Bolinas Ridge near Olema.

plain fun, and scenic to boot: Its high points afford expansive views of Bolinas Lagoon to the south and Tomales Bay to the north. The trail is well suited for all levels of riders; beginners can go out and back for a few miles while the more advanced can choose from a variety of loops.

The key is to start on the Olema side of Bolinas Ridge at the Sir Francis Drake Boulevard trailhead, rather than on the Mount Tamalpais side at the Bolinas–Fairfax Road trailhead. From the Olema side, less ambitious riders can pedal southward for a handful of miles as the trail climbs moderately. Much of Bolinas Ridge is cattle country, so you'll have to lift your bike over several livestock gates in the first couple miles of trail. Be sure to leave every gate the way you found it, either open or closed. The route carves through open pasturelands until the 5.4-mile mark, where it suddenly enters a thick of Douglas fir and redwood forest. Say good-bye to the sun and the views and hello to the refreshing woods. When you've had enough and are ready to turn around and head home, a fun descent awaits.

Meanwhile, those with more energy can continue southeast on Bolinas Ridge and then loop around to Highway 1 on Randall Trail, a steep downhill track. The second half of the loop is an easy cruise northward on mostly level Highway 1 back to Olema. Your car awaits one mile up Sir Francis Drake Boulevard. If the idea of riding on pavement insults your mountain biking sensibilities, you can omit a few road miles by riding the dirt Olema Valley Trail, which parallels Highway 1 all the way from Dogtown to the Five Brooks Trailhead. This is a dry-season option only, however; marshy Olema Valley is notorious for flooding with even the slightest rain.

For more information, contact Golden Gate National Recreation Area, 415/331-1540, www.nps.gov/goga.

Options

If you're enjoying Bolinas Ridge Trail so much that you are not ready to loop back when you reach Randall Trail at 6.2 miles out, you can sign up for a much longer and harder day by continuing an additional 3.2 miles to the high point of Bolinas Ridge at 1,700 feet, then pedaling 1.7 miles farther to a junction with paved Bolinas–Fairfax Road. A right turn here will provide you with a fast and furious descent over 4.5 miles to Highway 1, where you turn right and ride 10 miles back to your car on Sir Francis Drake Boulevard just outside of Olema. This is a ride worthy of bragging rights, totaling 26 miles and 2,200 feet of elevation gain.

Driving Directions

From San Francisco, cross the Golden Gate Bridge on U.S. 101 and travel north toward San Rafael. Take the Sir Francis Drake Boulevard exit west toward San Anselmo and drive 19.5 miles to the trailhead for the Bolinas Ridge Trail on the left side of the road. If you reach the town of Olema and Highway 1, you've gone 1 mile too far.

Route Directions

0.0 Park at the Bolinas Ridge trailhead pullout alongside Sir Francis Drake Boulevard, one mile northeast of Olema. Ride uphill and veer left onto the wide dirt road. *Supplies are available in Olema.*

1.4 RIGHT at junction with Jewell Trail to stay on Bolinas Ridge.

5.2 STRAIGHT at junction with Shafter Trail.

6.2 RIGHT at junction with Randall Trail.

7.9 RIGHT at junction with Highway 1.

14.0 RIGHT at junction with Sir Francis Drake Boulevard in Olema.

15.0 Arrive at starting point.

8 CROSS MARIN TRAIL AND BOLINAS RIDGE LOOP

Samuel P. Taylor State Park near Olema

DIRT ROAD/TRAIL AND PAVED BIKE PATH

Difficulty: 3	**Total Distance:** 13.4 miles
Riding Time: 2.5 hours	**Elevation Gain:** 1,250 feet

Summary: An old railroad trail leads into the redwoods for an easy ride, but ambitious mountain bikers can follow a strenuous loop back to their starting point.

© ANN MARIE BROWN

A cyclist and his dog enjoy the redwood-shaded Cross Marin Trail.

The Cross Marin Trail/Sir Francis Drake Bikeway is one trail with two names, under two different park jurisdictions. It's called the Cross Marin Trail when it's on Golden Gate National Recreation Area land, and the Sir Francis Drake Bikeway when it's on Samuel P. Taylor State Park land. The trail with two names is an old rail trail, built in 1874 by the North Pacific Coast Railroad. It offers something for skinny tires and fat tires alike, with three miles of smooth pavement and another two miles of gravel and dirt suitable for mountain bikes. While plenty of people ride out and back on the bike path only, a more strenuous loop can be made by connecting to Bolinas Ridge Trail.

The route begins in dense woods as it travels parallel to Lagunitas Creek, also called Papermill Creek. This is mellow pedaling on smooth pavement; the first few miles are suitable even for young children. There's plenty of time to look around and admire the thick second-growth redwood stands, which are cushioned by an undergrowth of sorrel, ferns, and flowering blue milkmaids in spring. Too soon, your primeval redwood fantasy gets rudely interrupted by campgrounds, restrooms, and other indicators of civilization. Just beyond Redwood Grove Picnic Area, the paved surface erodes to gravel and dirt, and skinny tires must turn around. Mountain bikers continue riding, crossing a footbridge (an old railroad trestle) over Sir Francis Drake Boulevard. Two miles later the trail reaches the park boundary, where Shafter Bridge arches over Lagunitas Creek. Here, novice riders should turn around and head back the way they came; more energetic bikers should continue onward. In years past, riders had to ford the stream here to access the trails on the other side, but in 2004 the Marie Dhority Bridge was built to accommodate bikers and pedestrians, and to protect the spawning steelhead trout that make their way up this stream in the rainy season. As you ride over this sturdy bridge, note the rock-lined pools in the creek below; in summer this is a popular swimming area known as The Inkwells.

Now comes the only treacherous part of this ride: You must cross Sir Francis Drake Boulevard with great caution (it's best to walk your bike) and then make your way to the parking lot to your right, on the far (northwest) side of the creek. At the parking lot, pick up Shafter Fire Road and prepare for a gnarly, 1.8-mile winding climb that slays even the best of 'em (1,100-foot gain). At the top, a heavenly, mostly downhill cruise on Bolinas Ridge Trail awaits. Where the trail ends at Sir Francis Drake Highway, cruise down the paved road back to your car.

For more information, contact Golden Gate National Recreation Area, 415/331-1540, www.nps.gov/goga; or Samuel P. Taylor State Park, 415/488-9897, www. parks.ca.gov.

Driving Directions

From San Francisco, cross the Golden Gate Bridge on U.S. 101 and drive north for 7.5 miles. Take the Sir Francis Drake Boulevard exit west toward San Anselmo and drive 18.7 miles to the right turnoff for Platform Bridge Road, located 3.4 miles past the main entrance to Samuel P. Taylor State Park. (If you reach the town of Olema and Highway 1, you have gone 1.8 miles too far.) Turn right on Platform Bridge Road and park in the pullout on the left.

Route Directions

0.0 Park at the Platform Bridge Road trailhead. Ride on the paved path leading from the pullout, cross a concrete bridge, go about 50 feet, then turn left on the signed Cross Marin Trail. *Supplies are available in Olema, two miles west.*

1.5 STRAIGHT at junction with Jewell Trail.

2.7 State park camping and picnic areas. *Water is available.*

3.0 Pavement ends; skinny tires must turn around.

3.4 Cross bridge over Sir Francis Drake Highway.

5.0 Trail reaches Marie Dhority Bridge over Lagunitas Creek's Inkwells. Cross the bridge and then walk your bike across Sir Francis Drake Boulevard and 30 yards northwest, to the parking area on the far (northwest) side of the creek.

5.2 Take Shafter Fire Road uphill.

7.0 RIGHT on Bolinas Ridge Trail at end of climb.

12.2 RIGHT on paved Sir Francis Drake Highway at end of Bolinas
    Ridge Trail.

13.3 LEFT on Platform Bridge Road.

13.4 Arrive at starting point.

9 NICASIO RESERVOIR LOOP
western Marin County

PAVED ROADS WITH MODERATE CAR TRAFFIC

Difficulty: 2   **Total Distance:** 24.5 miles (or 44-mile option)

Riding Time: 2 hours   **Elevation Gain:** 900 feet

Summary: The country roads of western Marin County make up the backbone of this gentle, scenic ride.

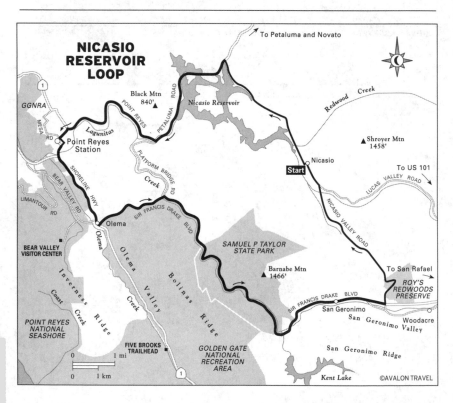

A favorite of Marin County cyclists, this 24.5-mile road ride is an easy-to-moderate loop on mostly level back roads surrounding the small town of Nicasio and its large reservoir. Although these roads see some traffic, especially on nice-weather weekends, most drivers in the area are accustomed to sharing the road with bikes.

The loop begins in Nicasio, a gentrified country town—the kind of place where almost everybody owns at least one horse. The first 10 miles on Nicasio Valley Road and Point Reyes–Petaluma Road provide nearly perfect cycling, with a wide shoulder, smooth paved surface, and relatively few cars. The two roads skirt the

The scenic back roads of the Nicasio Reservoir Loop are favored by Marin County cyclists.

edge of Nicasio Reservoir, a surprisingly large and pretty lake that is popular year-round for shoreline bass fishing.

Upon reaching Highway 1, you'll ride through Point Reyes Station and Olema—both good stops for coffee, food, and camaraderie with other bikers. Then Sir Francis Drake Boulevard climbs and curves through Samuel P. Taylor State Park and continues gently uphill through a succession of small towns: Lagunitas, Forest Knolls, and San Geronimo. There's more traffic on this second half of the loop, but it's still manageable. By the golf course in San Geronimo, you'll turn north on Nicasio Valley Road, where there's a lovely grove of redwoods known as Roy's Redwoods, a perfect place to get off the saddle for a short walk. All in all, this is an easy, low-pressure ride, with plenty of places to stop and enjoy the countryside.

Options

You could easily add on up to 10 miles each way by parking near the junction of Lucas Valley Road and U.S. 101, then riding your bike to Nicasio. (To do so, leave your car on one of the side streets that intersects Lucas Valley Road. The road has a wide shoulder for the first 4 miles, then no shoulder at all for the next 6, but not a lot of traffic, either.)

Driving Directions

From San Rafael, drive 3 miles north on U.S. 101 and take the Lucas Valley Road exit. Drive 10.4 miles west on Lucas Valley Road, then turn right on Nicasio Valley Road. Drive 0.5 mile and park in the town of Nicasio.

Route Directions

0.0 Park in the town of Nicasio and ride north on Nicasio Valley Road. *Supplies are available in Nicasio or San Rafael.*

3.2 LEFT on Point Reyes–Petaluma Road.

6.3 RIGHT to stay on Point Reyes–Petaluma Road.

9.4 LEFT on Shoreline Highway (Highway 1).

9.8 LEFT on Shoreline Highway through town of Point Reyes Station. *Supplies are available in Point Reyes Station.*

10.0 RIGHT to get back on Highway 1.

10.2 STRAIGHT to stay on Highway 1.

12.2 LEFT on Sir Francis Drake Boulevard in Olema. *Supplies are available in Olema.*

17.0 Pass through Samuel P. Taylor State Park.

20.0 LEFT on Nicasio Valley Road by San Geronimo golf course. *Roy's Redwoods Open Space Preserve makes a nice place for a short walk.*

24.5 Arrive at starting point.

10 PINE MOUNTAIN LOOP
Marin Municipal Water District near Fairfax

DIRT ROAD

Difficulty: 3   **Total Distance:** 13.2 miles

Riding Time: 2.5 hours   **Elevation Gain:** 2,000 feet

Summary: Pedal a challenging mountain-biking loop that travels through the wild landscape of the Marin Watershed.

The heart and soul of Marin mountain biking lies in the lands west of Fairfax, where the crowded county suburbs give way to grasslands, open ridges, and mixed woodlands of oak, bay, and Douglas fir. The first mile of the Pine Mountain Loop gives you long looks over your right shoulder of the civilization you are leaving behind—much of Marin County, San Pablo Bay, the Richmond Bridge, and Mount Diablo are in plain view—but soon you will see only chaparral-lined hillsides and rolling ridgetops.

The summit of Pine Mountain, elevation 1,762, forms the first challenge in this loop's advanced aerobic workout. You'll climb 700 feet to the top, often on a rutted and rocky surface, in this loop's first 2.3 miles. The next 4 miles are much easier; most of your energy will be spent controlling your speed on swift descents.

© ANN MARIE BROWN

A few healthy climbs provide an aerobic workout on the Pine Mountain Loop near Fairfax.

A short but lovely section meanders along the edge of Kent Lake. Then at 7.2 miles you'll start to climb again, this time gaining 1,100 feet spaced out over 4 miles. Gear down and suck in as much oxygen as you can.

An unusual sight worth noting is a stand of dwarf Sargent cypress trees off San Geronimo Ridge Fire Road. The Sargent cypress is a rare evergreen that grows in scattered groves in the region surrounding Mount Tamalpais. It is usually stunted in size when rooted in serpentine soil, as is the case here. Cypress trees that are more than 100 years old may be only a few feet tall. Watch for the miniature Sargent cypress forest between miles 10.5 and 11.

For more information on Marin Municipal Water District lands, phone Sky Oaks Ranger Station at 415/945-1181 or visit www.marinwater.org.

Options

If you are riding in the winter or spring months, you could add a short bike-and-hike adventure to this ride. After the initial 1.1-mile climb on Pine Mountain Road, turn left on Oat Hill Road and ride downhill. In 0.3 mile, you'll see a large trail signboard on the right. Bikes aren't allowed on this lovely path, so lock up and/or stash your bike, then hike downhill for 0.7 mile to the top of Carson Falls, one of Marin County's prettiest waterfalls. It's a long chain of four pool-and-drop cataracts that pour into rock-lined pools. Carson Falls' green-gray rock looks like serpentine, but it's actually a type of greenstone basalt. Tread carefully near the water's edge; not only is the wet rock slippery, but the pools are also home to threatened amphibians, including the foothill yellow-legged frog.

Driving Directions

From San Francisco, cross the Golden Gate Bridge and drive north on U.S. 101 for 7.5 miles. Take the Sir Francis Drake Boulevard exit west toward San Anselmo, then drive 6 miles to the town of Fairfax. Turn left by the Fairfax sign (on Pacheco Road), then turn right immediately on Broadway. In one block, turn left on Bolinas Road. Drive 3.8 miles on Bolinas Road, past the golf course, to the dirt parking area on the left side of the road.

Route Directions

0.0 Park in the dirt parking area on the left side of Bolinas–Fairfax Road. The fire road begins across the road. *Supplies are available in Fairfax.*

1.1 STRAIGHT at junction with Oat Hill Road. *Or turn left for a bike-and-hike trip to Carson Falls; see* Options.

1.5 LEFT to stay on Pine Mountain Road.

2.3 Summit of Pine Mountain at 1,762 feet.

5.6 RIGHT at junction near Kent Lake.

8.8 RIGHT at four-way intersection.

9.8 RIGHT on San Geronimo Ridge Fire Road.

11.2 RIGHT at junction with Repack Trail (also called Cascade Canyon) on left.

11.7 STRAIGHT to rejoin Pine Mountain Road.

12.1 STRAIGHT at junction with Oat Hill Road.

13.2 Arrive at starting point.

PINE MOUNTAIN LOOP

11 TAMARANCHO LOOP

Tamarancho Boy Scout Camp near Fairfax

DIRT SINGLE-TRACK

Difficulty: 3

Total Distance: 11.7 miles

Riding Time: 2 hours

Elevation Gain: 1,000 feet

Summary: Mountain bikers find single-track nirvana on this loop near the town of Fairfax.

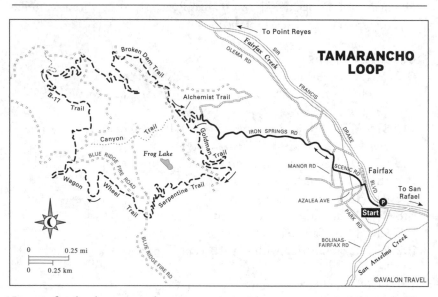

It costs five bucks to get a day-use permit to ride your mountain bike at the Boy Scouts' Camp Tamarancho, but think of it as a pass to the best mountain bike park around. If you live near Fairfax, invest in the annual pass (about $50) and you'll have long-term access to gorgeous single-track that was built by mountain bikers for mountain bikers. Whether you come here repeatedly or only one day, with your first glimpse of the sign that says "Bicycles MUST stay on single-track," you will think you have died and gone to mountain biking heaven.

Tamarancho is deservedly popular, so the trails can be crowded on weekends. Your best bet is to ride here on a weekday, and preferably not at midafternoon in summer, when it can be hot as Hades. There are no trail choices to make, just a single loop set up for mountain bikers. Yes, it's almost exclusively single-track, and yes again, the loop presents plenty of technical challenges. Beginning riders probably would not be happy here. Some hikers also use the trail, although most pedestrians stick to the camp's dirt roads on the inside of this loop, where bikes are not permitted.

The Tamarancho Loop rolls and dips, curving in and out of dense oak and bay woodland and open, grassy areas. Several short climbs of less than a mile in length give you a moderate workout, but without the drudgery of a long, sustained ascent. You'll snake through more than three dozen switchbacks along the route. It's all fun, but make sure your eyes and ears are alert for other riders, because otherwise you may not see them until you're right on top of them.

One leg of the loop, Wagon Wheel Trail, leaves the Boy Scouts' property and travels through Marin County Open Space land. The entire route is well signed (always watch for the arrow signs where the single-track crosses fire roads). Although the loop itself is just over 7 miles, the entire ride length is 11.7 miles because there is no parking permitted anywhere near Tamarancho. You leave your car in downtown Fairfax and ride 1.6 miles to a connecting trail off pothole-ridden Iron Springs Road, which deposits you on the loop. The loop itself can be ridden in either direction; a clockwise loop is described here.

For more information, contact the Boy Scouts' Camp Tamarancho, 415/454-1081, www.boyscouts-marin.org.

Driving Directions

From San Francisco, cross the Golden Gate Bridge and drive north on U.S. 101 for 7.5 miles. Take the Sir Francis Drake Boulevard exit west toward San Anselmo, then drive 6 miles to the town of Fairfax. Turn left by the Fairfax sign on Pacheco Road, then turn right on Broadway and park in downtown Fairfax. The public parking lot on your right (bordered by Pacheco Road, Sir Francis Drake Boulevard, and Broadway) allows free four-hour parking.

Route Directions

0.0 Park in downtown Fairfax in the four-hour parking lot between Sir Francis Drake Boulevard and Broadway. Exit the parking lot and ride west on Broadway. *Supplies are available in downtown Fairfax.*

0.3 LEFT on Azalea (west of Fairfax Lumber), then immediate RIGHT on Scenic.

0.5 RIGHT on Manor.

0.6 LEFT on Rockridge.

0.7 STRAIGHT on Iron Springs Road (Rockridge veers to the right). Watch for large potholes on Iron Springs Road.

1.6 LEFT on single-track connector trail to Tamarancho (Alchemist Trail).

2.2 LEFT on Goldman Trail.

2.9 Cross fire road to join Serpentine Trail.

4.0 Cross fire road to join Wagon Wheel Trail.

5.5 STRAIGHT on fire road to connect to B-17 Trail on left; steep hill.

6.9 RIGHT on Broken Dam Trail at junction with B-17 Extension Trail.

9.1 Cross Iron Springs Road to join Goldman Trail.

9.5 LEFT on single-track leading back to Iron Springs Road.

10.1 RIGHT on Iron Springs Road.

11.7 Retrace route through Fairfax to arrive at starting point.

12 FAIRFAX AND MOUNT TAMALPAIS LOOP

Bolinas-Fairfax Road to Mount Tamalpais

PAVED ROADS WITH MODERATE CAR TRAFFIC

Difficulty: 3

Riding Time: 3-4 hours

Total Distance: 31.8 miles

Elevation Gain: 2,200 feet

Summary: A classic tour of Mount Tamalpais and the Marin Watershed, this route is suitable for experienced road cyclists.

If you like country back roads with few cars and a variety of scenic terrain, you'll love riding Bolinas–Fairfax Road. This 32-mile loop travels the rolling upper portion of the old stage road from the town of Fairfax to the top of Bolinas Ridge. (The steeper lower stretch of Bolinas–Fairfax Road is ridden in the *Stinson Beach and Mount Tamalpais Loop,* ride 15.) The winding pavement curves through miles of open space in the protected lands of the Marin Watershed, where deer and raptors are more common than people, and cyclists are more common than automobiles. Most of the route travels through open grasslands and can be quite warm in the summer months, but the scenery changes dramatically at about 7 miles, when you reach the western lakeshore of large Alpine Lake, then cross its dam and enter dense redwood forest for a heart-pumping, 2.5-mile climb to Bolinas Ridge (850-foot gain).

At the road's high point, you'll turn left and pedal along one of the Bay Area's most filmed and photographed roads—West Ridgecrest Boulevard, site of dozens of car commercials and calendar shots. Ocean views are dazzling from this high ridge, which is surrounded by the grassy hillsides of Mount Tamalpais State Park. You'll gain another 500 feet as you traverse the ridge, then make a fast descent down Pantoll Road to Panoramic Highway. A left turn here brings you to Four Corners (exercise caution on this no-shoulder stretch of narrow pavement), where you make a transitional descent from the open ridgeline roads of Mount Tamalpais to the narrow hillside streets of Mill Valley. It's down, down, down for a solid eight miles from the top of Pantoll Road on Mount Tam to Miller Avenue in Mill Valley. Your brakes will get plenty of work.

The final nine miles of the loop are a northward run through the Marin County towns of Corte Madera, Larkspur, Kentfield, Ross, and San Anselmo. A lunch stop at one of the cafés in downtown Larkspur is highly recommended.

Driving Directions

From San Francisco, cross the Golden Gate Bridge and drive north on U.S. 101 for 7.5 miles. Take the Sir Francis Drake Boulevard exit west toward San Anselmo, then drive 6 miles to the town of Fairfax. Turn left by the Fairfax sign on Pacheco Road, then turn right on Broadway and park in downtown Fairfax. The public parking lot on your right (bordered by Pacheco Road, Sir Francis Drake Boulevard, and Broadway) allows free four-hour parking.

Route Directions

0.0 Park in downtown Fairfax in the four-hour parking lot between Sir Francis Drake Boulevard and Broadway. Exit the parking lot and ride west on Broadway for one block to the start of Bolinas–Fairfax Road. *Supplies are available in downtown Fairfax.*

0.1 LEFT on Bolinas–Fairfax Road (note that this road is sometimes signed as Bolinas Road or Fairfax–Bolinas Road).

7.9 Cross Alpine Dam and begin steep climb through shady redwood forest.

10.4 LEFT on West Ridgecrest Boulevard at top of Bolinas Ridge.

14.3 RIGHT on Pantoll Road; begin fast descent.

15.7 LEFT on Panoramic Highway.

20.2 LEFT on Sequoia Valley Road at Four Corners junction (Sequoia Valley Road changes names to Edgewood Road and then Molino Avenue).

22.0 LEFT on Montford Avenue.

22.1 LEFT to stay on Montford Avenue.

22.3 RIGHT on Miller Avenue. *Supplies are available on Miller Avenue.*

22.7 LEFT on Camino Alto by Tamalpais High School.

23.2 Cross East Blithedale Avenue to stay on Camino Alto (Camino Alto changes names to Corte Madera Avenue and then Magnolia Avenue). *Cafés, restaurants, and supplies are available on Magnolia Avenue in Larkspur.*

26.7 Larkspur bike path runs alongside road; follow path or road.

27.1 Cross Bon Air Road; bike path ends; follow bike lane.

27.9 LEFT on Kent Avenue, which becomes Poplar Avenue.

28.8 LEFT on Lagunitas Road at Ross Commons Park.

28.9 RIGHT on Shady Lane.

29.6 RIGHT on Bolinas Avenue, then immediate LEFT on San Anselmo Avenue.

30.2 Follow Bridge Avenue, then LEFT on Sycamore Avenue (Sycamore changes names to Center Boulevard, Lansdale Avenue, then back to Center Boulevard).

31.8 Arrive at starting point.

FAIRFAX AND MOUNT TAMALPAIS LOOP

13 CHINA CAMP BAY VIEW LOOP

China Camp State Park near San Rafael

DIRT ROAD AND SINGLE-TRACK

Difficulty: 3

Riding Time: 2 hours

Total Distance: 11.6 miles

Elevation Gain: 600 feet

Summary: Enjoy fun single-track riding in one of Marin County's most popular biking parks, and a glimpse at San Pablo Bay's shrimp-fishing history.

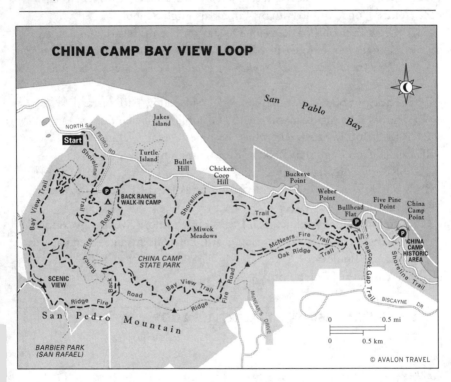

China Camp State Park is a rare bird in the California State Park system. One of only a handful of state parks that allows mountain bikes on single-track trails, China Camp also holds a scenic location on San Pablo Bay, with blue-water vistas from more than 1,500 shoreline acres. Bikers and hikers generally mind their manners and get along just fine here, although in recent years the park has seen a lot more of the former and fewer of the latter, especially on weekends. Over time, China Camp has metamorphosed into a biker's park.

It's also a historic preserve, showcasing the remains of a Chinese shrimp-fishing

ANN MARIE BROWN

Views of San Pablo Bay can be seen from China Camp's trails.

village from the 19th century, where immigrants netted shrimp from the bay. Don't neglect visiting the historic buildings and experiencing the unique history of this area.

Several rides are possible at China Camp. Beginners should stick to the smooth single-track Shoreline Trail (see *Options*), while more advanced riders will want to tackle the rutted, steep hills in the backcountry of the park. The route described here is a good workout that supplies plenty of short but steep grades for practicing your ascending and descending skills. Highlights include a visit to one of Marin County's best viewpoints, a Nike radar site at 900 feet above the bay; and pedaling on Oak Ridge Trail, a lovely pathway through grasslands and oak woodlands.

For more information, contact China Camp State Park, 415/456-0766, www. parks.ca.gov.

Options

Novices should begin their love affair with China Camp State Park's trails with an easy cruise on Shoreline Trail. Pick up the single-track by the park entrance kiosk and stay on it all the way to Miwok Meadows Group Camp (2.6 miles), where you follow a dirt road for a short distance before getting back on Shoreline Trail. At 5.2 miles, go left on Village Trail, then cross San Pedro Road and follow the pavement to China Camp Village. Here you can lock up your bike and explore the historic buildings and museum. A snack bar is open on weekends and holidays. An out-and-back ride to the old fishing village covers 11.2 miles, but you can shorten your trip to 8 miles by returning on North San Pedro Road.

Driving Directions

From San Francisco, cross the Golden Gate Bridge and drive north on U.S. 101

for 11 miles to San Rafael. Take the North San Pedro exit and drive east for 3.5 miles to China Camp State Park.

Route Directions

0.0 Park along the road near Back Ranch Meadows Campground. Follow Shoreline Trail from the right side of the kiosk. *Supplies are available in San Rafael. Water is available at the campground.*

0.1 RIGHT on Bay View Trail.

0.5 RIGHT on fire road, then immediate LEFT back on Bay View Trail.

1.1 LEFT to stay on Bay View Trail.

2.0 RIGHT (hairpin) on trail to Bay Hills Drive.

2.6 LEFT on paved Bay Hills Drive; steep uphill.

3.0 Nike radar base; great views of Marin County and San Francisco Bay.

3.3 LEFT on Ridge Fire Road.

3.6 LEFT at junction; steep downhill.

3.9 RIGHT on fire road at power line junction; stay RIGHT on Bay View Trail.

5.2 LEFT at junction with Ridge Fire Road.

5.5 LEFT on Miwok Fire Road for 30 yards, then RIGHT on Oak Ridge Trail.

5.8 Cross fire road to stay on Oak Ridge.

6.2 Cross fire road to stay on Oak Ridge.

6.8 STRAIGHT on Peacock Gap Trail.

6.9 STRAIGHT on Shoreline Trail.

8.7 STRAIGHT on fire road, then RIGHT at restrooms by picnic area to get back on Shoreline Trail.

9.6 LEFT at V-junction.

9.9 LEFT on Shoreline Trail.

10.1 LEFT on Shoreline Trail.

11.6 Arrive at starting point.

14 THREE LAKES LOOP
Marin Municipal Water District near Ross

DIRT ROAD

Difficulty: 2

Riding Time: 1.5 hours

Total Distance: 11.2 miles

Elevation Gain: 900 feet

Summary: This lake-filled ride in the Marin Watershed is bound to get beginning and intermediate mountain bikers hooked on the sport.

Phoenix Lake is the most popular of the five lakes in the Mount Tamalpais Watershed, but due to a cruel twist of fate it also has the smallest parking lot, with space for only about 15 cars. That means that the hundreds of anglers, hikers, equestrians, baby stroller–pushers, and mountain bikers who want access to Phoenix Lake on summer weekends have to fight it out for a parking space. No street parking is available anywhere near the lake on weekends and holidays (the well-to-do residents of Ross have made sure that their streets are clearly signed and the No Parking rule is strictly enforced), so it's a good thing you're on two wheels. Unless it's a weekday, you must ride a short stretch on the street to gain access to this terrific lake-filled loop.

It's best to leave your car at the large parking lot at Ross Commons Park and pedal from there. A 1.1-mile ride brings you to the jam-packed parking lot at Natalie Coffin Greene Park. Go around the gate and uphill to Phoenix Lake's dam. You've arrived at the first lake of the Three Lakes Loop. Ride around the

Lagunitas Lake is the oldest and loveliest of the watershed reservoirs on the Three Lakes Loop.

right side of the lake, passing a log cabin built in 1893, then climb uphill on Shaver Grade through dense redwoods to join the paved access road to Bon Tempe and Lagunitas Lakes. After briefly skirting the edge of Bon Tempe Lake, you'll face the best scenery of the day as you circle Lagunitas Lake, crossing three small bridges. Make sure you utilize the bridges and don't take shortcuts across the streams. These waterways are important habitat for newts and other amphibians. Lagunitas is the oldest of the Marin lakes; its dam was built in 1873. Both Lagunitas and Bon Tempe Lakes are great spots for bird-watching and fishing.

Too soon, you leave the water behind and face a climb up Lakeview Fire Road. Don't forget to turn around and check out the trail's promised "lake view." The final stretch of the loop follows Eldridge Grade, one of the first wagon routes to the summit of Mount Tamalpais, built in 1889. Be cautious on the steep descent on this old, well-worn trail, which has been reduced to single-track in some stretches.

For more information on Marin Municipal Water District lands, phone Sky Oaks Ranger Station at 415/945-1181 or visit www.marinwater.org.

Driving Directions

From San Francisco, cross the Golden Gate Bridge and drive north on U.S. 101 for 7.5 miles. Take the Sir Francis Drake Boulevard exit west toward San Anselmo, then drive 3 miles to Lagunitas Road on the left, across from the Marin Art and Garden Center. Turn left on Lagunitas Road and park at Ross Commons (junction of Lagunitas and Kent Roads).

Route Directions

0.0 Park at Ross Commons. Ride west on Lagunitas Road. *Supplies are available in Ross.*

1.1 Natalie Coffin Greene Park parking lot; go around the gate and across the bridge, climbing up to Phoenix Lake's dam.

1.4 RIGHT to head around the lake.

1.6 LEFT at junction with Worn Springs Road on the right. *Water is available.*

2.0 RIGHT on Shaver Grade at four-way Phoenix Junction.

3.2 LEFT to stay on Shaver Grade at Five Corners Junction.

3.8 LEFT at gate on paved Sky Oaks Road.

4.3 Ride along edge of Bon Tempe Lake on paved road.

5.1 Lake Lagunitas parking lot. Stay on right side of parking lot to pick up the dirt road leading up to the right side of the dam.

5.7 LEFT at junction with Rock Springs/Lagunitas Fire Road; stay along the lakeshore.

6.5 RIGHT on Lakeview Fire Road.

7.1 LEFT on Eldridge Grade.

8.4 RIGHT to stay on Eldridge Grade (trail narrows considerably).

9.2 RIGHT at Phoenix Junction; backtrack alongside Phoenix Lake and back to Lagunitas Road.

11.2 Arrive at starting point.

THREE LAKES LOOP

15 STINSON BEACH AND MOUNT TAMALPAIS LOOP

Mount Tamalpais State Park

BEST ◖

PAVED ROADS WITH MODERATE CAR TRAFFIC

Difficulty: 4

Total Distance: 23.9 miles

Riding Time: 3 hours

Elevation Gain: 2,700 feet

Summary: A day on less-traveled roads showcases the wonders of Mount Tamalpais, from coast to mountaintop.

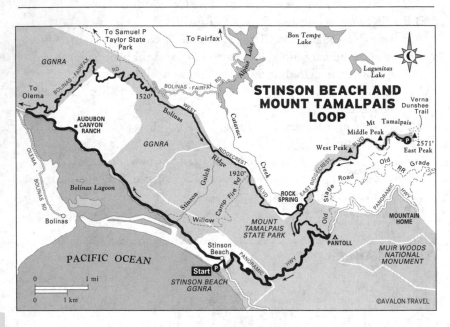

This ride is a workout, but it's well worth it, considering the film-burning quality of the Marin landscape you'll traverse. A level, four-mile warm-up alongside Bolinas Lagoon on Highway 1 is followed by a circuitous and unrelenting 1,500-foot climb up the historic Bolinas–Fairfax stage road. When at last you reach the top, prepare yourself for one of the Bay Area's most filmed and photographed roads—West Ridgecrest Boulevard on Mount Tamalpais, site of dozens of car commercials and calendar shots. The trees give way to open grassy hillsides, where deer graze and hang gliders take off for a breezy, graceful descent to the ocean below. You'll keep climbing as you travel the ridge, but much more gradually from here onward.

At Rock Springs parking lot and road junction, continue straight for another 2.9 miles to Mount Tamalpais's East Peak at elevation 2,571 feet. The vistas are even

© ANN MARIE BROWN

As you get closer to the summit of 2,571-foot Mount Tamalpais, take a break and enjoy the panoramic view of Marin County.

better from this summit than what you've seen so far. In addition to the bird's-eye view out to sea, much of Marin County and San Francisco comes into full perspective. East Peak's snack stand is open on weekends to refuel hungry bikers. When you've had your fill of snacks and views, backtrack to the Rock Springs parking lot.

Now it's time for a steep, fast, memorable descent. The traffic will pick up as you drop to Pantoll Ranger Station, and it will continue racing downhill to the ocean, but you'll be rolling along just as fast, or maybe faster, than the cars. Since you are riding on aptly named Panoramic Highway, take a break now and then to admire the views of the coast ahead and Mount Tamalpais behind.

With a final screech of brakes, you come to a stop sign at Highway 1. A right turn and you're back at your car in less than 0.5 mile. Hope you brought your swimsuit for a dip in the ocean at Stinson Beach, or your wallet for a well-deserved meal at the beachside hamburger stand.

For more information, contact Mount Tamalpais State Park, 415/388-2070, www.parks.ca.gov.

Driving Directions

From San Francisco, cross the Golden Gate Bridge and drive north on U.S. 101 for 4 miles. Take the Mill Valley/Stinson Beach/Highway 1 exit and continue straight for 1 mile to a stoplight at Shoreline Highway (Highway 1). Turn left on Shoreline Highway and drive 12 miles to Stinson Beach. Turn left at the sign for Stinson Beach parking (Golden Gate National Recreation Area).

Route Directions

0.0 Park at Stinson Beach parking lot, ride out to Highway 1, and turn left (north). *Supplies are available in the town of Stinson Beach.*

1.0 Edge of Bolinas Lagoon; look for hauled-out seals and a wide variety of birds.

3.3 Audubon Canyon Ranch. *The ranch, a major great egret nesting site, is open to the public on weekends and holidays mid-March–mid-July. Walk a 0.5-mile trail to a viewing platform, then look through sighting scopes into the nests of baby egrets.*

4.3 RIGHT on Bolinas–Fairfax Road (unsigned paved road with open metal gate). Begin 4.4-mile climb.

8.7 RIGHT on West Ridgecrest Boulevard.

12.5 STRAIGHT at Rock Springs parking lot.

15.4 East Peak parking lot; TURN AROUND. *Water and snacks are available. Lock your bike and walk the one-mile Verna Dunshee Trail that circumnavigates the peak.*

18.3 LEFT at Rock Springs parking lot.

19.8 RIGHT on Panoramic Highway at Pantoll junction. *Water is available across the road by the ranger station.*

23.5 RIGHT on Highway 1.

23.9 LEFT into Stinson Beach parking lot; arrive at starting point.

STINSON BEACH AND MOUNT TAMALPAIS LOOP

16 OLD STAGE ROAD AND OLD RAILROAD GRADE TO EAST PEAK   BEST ☾
Mount Tamalpais State Park

DIRT ROAD

Difficulty: 2   **Total Distance:** 8 miles

Riding Time: 1.5 hours   **Elevation Gain:** 1,100 feet

Summary: Take a ride through Mount Tamalpais history on this out-and-back trip to its 2,571-foot East Peak.

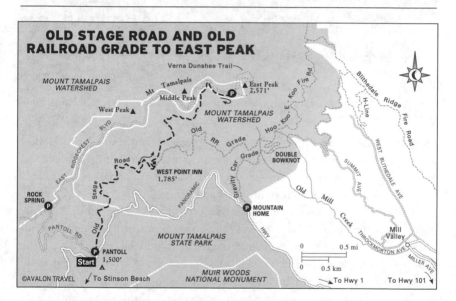

Although you could just drive your car on paved roads to Mount Tam's famous summit, this ride on a stretch of the old Mount Tamalpais Scenic Railway is a much more enjoyable way to get there.

The railway, known in the early 1900s as the "Crookedest Railroad in the World," carried passengers through 281 turns and curves up the slopes of Mount Tamalpais. The last two miles of this ride trace the train's exact route to the mountain summit, while the first two miles follow the route used by passengers who rode the stagecoach to Stinson Beach and Bolinas. (See ride 17, *Old Railroad Grade to West Point Inn*, for more riding on Old Railroad Grade.) The two halves of this ride converge at West Point Inn, as much a popular stopover for cyclists and hikers today as it was for train and stage passengers 100 years ago.

Begin your ride at the large parking area by Pantoll Ranger Station. After a

The historic Old Stage Road provides views of Angel Island, southern Marin County, and the San Francisco skyline.

hasty and cautious crossing of Panoramic Highway, mount your bike and follow the paved Old Stage Road. The pavement soon turns to dirt, and the views of San Francisco and Marin start to amaze you. Old Stage Road's grade is remarkably gradual as it winds through myriad twists and turns.

At West Point Inn, fill up your water bottle at their old stone fountain, or buy a glass of lemonade and have a seat on the outside deck, then pick up Old Railroad Grade on the inn's west side and continue uphill to East Peak. This dirt road is steeper, and much rockier, than Old Stage Road. At the trail's end you'll find yourself at the paved East Peak parking lot, enjoying far-reaching views of Marin County, the East Bay, and San Francisco and its bridges. Be sure to walk up the stairs to the Gardner Fire Lookout so you can say you went to the tip-top of the mountain.

For more information, contact Mount Tamalpais State Park, 415/388-2070, www.parks.ca.gov. Contact the West Point Inn at 415/388-9955 or 415/646-0702, www.westpointinn.com (closed on Monday; summer hours 11 A.M.–6 P.M., winter hours 11 A.M.–5 P.M.).

Options

If you don't want to ride back the way you came, you can always follow the paved route back to Pantoll: Take West Ridgecrest Boulevard 2.9 miles to Rock Springs, then turn left on Pantoll Road and ride 1.5 miles downhill, for an 8.4-mile loop. This is a fun loop if you don't mind competing with car traffic.

Driving Directions

From San Francisco, cross the Golden Gate Bridge and drive north on U.S. 101 for 4 miles. Take the Mill Valley/Stinson Beach/Highway 1 exit and continue straight for 1 mile to a stoplight at Shoreline Highway (Highway 1). Turn left on Shoreline Highway and drive 2.5 miles, then turn right on Panoramic Highway. Drive 0.9 mile to a junction of roads. Continue straight 4.3 miles farther to Pantoll Ranger Station and the parking lot on the left.

Route Directions

0.0 Park by Pantoll Ranger Station, then cross Panoramic Highway to the start of Pantoll Road. On the right is a paved road signed Old Stage Road to East Peak. *Supplies are available in Mill Valley.*

0.1 Begin riding on Old Stage Road.

0.4 Pavement turns to dirt.

2.0 West Point Inn. After enjoying the view, pick up Old Railroad Grade on the left (west) side of the inn. *Water and snacks are available.*

4.0 RIGHT on pavement at East Peak parking lot; TURN AROUND. *A small visitor center, overlook area, and the Gardner Fire Lookout are located here. Walk the Verna Dunshee Trail or climb the stairs to the lookout for the best view of the day.*

8.0 Arrive at starting point.

OLD STAGE ROAD AND OLD RAILROAD GRADE TO EAST PEAK

17 OLD RAILROAD GRADE TO WEST POINT INN
Mill Valley to Mount Tamalpais

DIRT ROAD

Difficulty: 3

Total Distance: 13.8 miles (or 17.8-mile option)

Riding Time: 2 hours

Elevation Gain: 1,700 feet

Summary: One of Marin County's most popular mountain bike routes follows the trail of a historic railroad up the slopes of Mount Tamalpais.

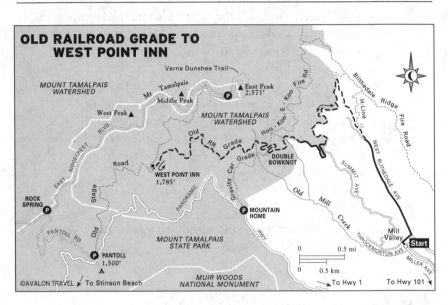

Beginning in Mill Valley, this popular ride on the slopes of Mount Tamalpais follows the lower route of the "Crookedest Railroad in the World," a major tourist attraction that carried passengers up the mountain in the early 1900s. Your destination is historic West Point Inn, built in 1904 to serve railway passengers and still serving cyclists and hikers today. The inn has small cabins for rent and sells drinks and snacks. Its water fountain will come in handy after you ride these 6.9 ascending (and dusty in summer) miles.

Downtown Mill Valley is Cyclist Central on fair-weather weekends. You'll have to park a mile or so from the start of Old Railroad Grade; there is almost no parking at the trailhead. From downtown, follow West Blithedale Road to the Marin Open Space District gate at the start of the railroad grade. This is your level warm-up; soon you start to climb on a remarkably consistent grade. The lower

Mountain bikers use historic West Point Inn as a rest stop on the ascent up Mount Tamalpais.

portion of the trail is heavily shaded by redwoods and Douglas firs; you won't start to feel the summer heat until you ascend above the tree canopy. A highlight of the ride is the double bowknot, where the railroad curved through a series of tight, gradual switchbacks. You'll know it when you ride it.

This trail is an excellent choice for mountain bikers who have progressed past the beginner stage but aren't interested (or ready for) very technical riding. It offers a solid aerobic and leg workout with only minor challenges from rocks and ruts. And the big carrot is that West Point Inn provides a scenic and relaxing destination.

For more information, contact Mount Tamalpais State Park, 415/388-2070, www.parks.ca.gov; or Marin Municipal Water District, 415/945-1195. The West Point Inn can be reached at 415/388-9955 or 415/646-0702, www.westpointinn.com (closed on Monday; summer hours 11 A.M.–6 P.M., winter hours 11 A.M.–5 P.M.).

Options

If you wish to add a few more miles, Old Railroad Grade continues another two miles from West Point Inn to East Peak (see ride 16, *Old Stage Road and Old Railroad Grade to East Peak*). From there, you could retrace your tire treads or loop back on Eldridge Grade, Indian Fire Road, and Hoo Koo E Koo Road. Check the Mount Tamalpais State Park map, available at Pantoll Ranger Station, for details.

Driving Directions

From San Francisco, cross the Golden Gate Bridge and drive north on U.S. 101 for six miles. Take the Tiburon/Highway 131/East Blithedale Avenue exit, then turn left and drive two miles west on East Blithedale. Turn left on Throckmorton Avenue and drive one block to Miller Avenue in downtown Mill Valley.

Route Directions

0.0 Park near the junction of Miller and Throckmorton Avenues in Mill Valley. Ride north on Throckmorton for one block to its junction with East and West Blithedale Avenues. *Supplies are available in the surrounding blocks.*

0.1 LEFT on West Blithedale.

1.4 RIGHT at gate on dirt Old Railroad Grade.

2.1 LEFT at junction.

3.3 RIGHT on pavement (uphill) where dirt road ends.

3.7 Back on dirt road.

4.4 RIGHT at junction; start of double bowknot.

6.9 West Point Inn. TURN AROUND or continue two miles to East Peak. *Water and snacks are usually available.*

13.8 Arrive at starting point.

18 TIBURON AND BELVEDERE LOOP

Tiburon Peninsula

BIKE PATH AND PAVED ROADS WITH MODERATE CAR TRAFFIC

Difficulty: 2   **Total Distance:** 10.5 miles (or longer options)

Riding Time: 1 hour   **Elevation Gain:** 700 feet

Summary: For easy riding with stunning bay views, you can't do much better than the Tiburon and Belvedere Loop.

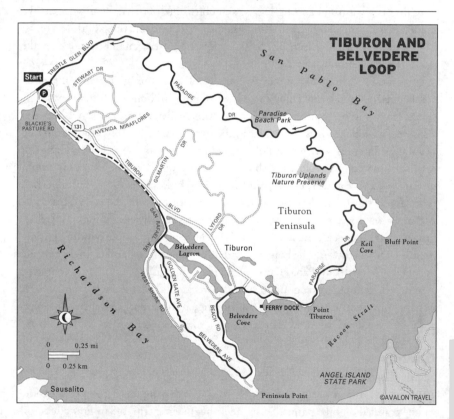

This combined bike path and paved road ride provides the chance to pedal around some prime real estate along scenic San Francisco Bay—the type of property that 99.9 percent of us would never be able to afford in our wildest dreams.

The first part of the ride follows the Tiburon Bike Path from Blackie's Pasture, just outside of the town of Tiburon. The popular trailhead is well known for its large statue of a horse, which was built to commemorate Blackie, who grazed in this pasture until his salad days ended at the ripe old age of 33, in

1966. Local admirers put up a gravestone, and later this handsome statue, in his memory.

The bike path travels east for 2.3 miles into downtown Tiburon, although the ride described here leaves the path after the first mile. This converted rail trail was once the track of the Northwestern Pacific Railroad, which provided passenger and freight service from Corte Madera to Tiburon. The trail provides close-up bay views—the water laps within 20 feet of the trail at high tide—and glimpses of Sausalito, the Golden Gate Bridge, and Mount Tamalpais. At low tide, bird-watching is rewarding, as long-legged shorebirds are perpetually digging in the mudflats for a meal. The trail also passes the Richardson Bay Wildlife Ponds. Managed by the Richardson Bay Sanitary District, these small bird ponds make good use of Tiburon's sewage.

After a right turn on San Rafael Avenue, you'll ride through ultra-wealthy Belvedere neighborhoods and enjoy a free show of multimillion-dollar bay views. The streets narrow to one lane wide; it's a wonder there aren't more collisions between Bentleys and Rolls Royces. Stay as far to the right as you can. Next you'll drop into downtown Tiburon, which is usually packed with tourists on weekends. Hang out with the crowds and explore the shops, or make a quick escape by turning right on Paradise Drive and climbing your first serious hill, which lasts for nearly a half mile. You'll stay on well-named Paradise Drive for most of the rest of this ride. Although the road is extremely narrow and has virtually no shoulder, traffic is generally light and cars must drive slowly because of its multiple winding curves. As you wind northward, the houses eventually become fewer and farther between, and views of north San Pablo Bay open wide. You'll pass the entrance to Paradise Beach Park, a popular hangout on summer weekends. People come from all over Marin County for swimming and sunning here. Too soon, you reach a junction with Trestle Glen Drive and must turn back to Blackie's Pasture.

Options

Multiple options for extending this ride are possible. Many cyclists start in Mill Valley or Sausalito and ride to Blackie's instead of driving there (most of the route can be traveled on bike paths). Some riders begin their trip in San Francisco, follow the Sausalito and Mill Valley bike paths to Tiburon, cruise around this loop, have lunch at a local restaurant, then take the easy way home—by riding the ferry back to San Francisco. Those who are more ambitious simply ride back. No matter how you do it, it's a fine way to spend a day.

Driving Directions

From San Francisco, cross the Golden Gate Bridge and drive north on U.S. 101

for 6 miles. Take the Tiburon/Highway 131/East Blithedale Avenue exit and drive east for 1.5 miles, then turn right at Blackie's Pasture Road and park in the large parking lot.

Route Directions

0.0 Park at Blackie's Pasture parking lot. Ride east on the paved bike trail. *Supplies are available in Mill Valley or Tiburon.*

1.2 RIGHT on San Rafael Avenue (leave bike path).

1.6 LEFT to stay on San Rafael Avenue.

1.7 RIGHT on Golden Gate Avenue and up the hill.

1.9 STRAIGHT at stop sign.

2.0 Cross intersection and continue on Belvedere Avenue (straight and slightly to the right).

3.2 RIGHT on Beach Road.

3.5 RIGHT to stay on Beach Road.

3.8 STRAIGHT at stop sign (stay on Beach Road).

4.0 RIGHT on Main Street. *Supplies are available in downtown Tiburon.*

4.3 RIGHT on Paradise Drive.

6.6 Trailhead for Tiburon Uplands Nature Preserve on left (hiking trail only).

7.6 Paradise Beach Park on right. *Water is available.*

9.7 LEFT on Trestle Glen Drive.

10.2 Cross Tiburon Boulevard at stoplight and crosswalk; pick up bike path on far side and ride west (to your right).

10.4 LEFT into Blackie's Pasture parking lot.

10.5 Arrive at starting point.

TIBURON AND BELVEDERE LOOP

19 TENNESSEE VALLEY AND COYOTE RIDGE LOOP

Golden Gate National Recreation Area near Mill Valley

DIRT ROAD AND SINGLE-TRACK

Difficulty: 3   **Total Distance:** 6.5 miles

Riding Time: 1.5 hours   **Elevation Gain:** 1,200 feet

Summary: While training wheels and Burley trailers ride an easy out-and-back to Tennessee Beach, those seeking more of a workout explore the high ridges above.

On weekends, the Tennessee Valley Trailhead in Mill Valley is busier than a shopping mall at Christmas. The parking lot is filled with a mix of bikers, walkers, and runners, all wanting to get a piece of the scenery at Tennessee Valley Beach and/or its surrounding ridges and hillsides.

And no wonder: There's something for everyone here. Biking families and novice riders enjoy the easy, wide dirt road that rolls gently out to Tennessee Beach, a black-gravel pocket beach framed by jagged bluffs on both sides. Mountain bikers seeking more of a challenge choose from two possible loops: Tennessee Valley and Coyote Ridge to the west or Miwok and Bobcat to the east. (The latter loop can also be accessed from the Marin Headlands and is described in ride 20, *Marin Headlands Miwok and Bobcat Loop*.)

Those simply following Tennessee Valley Trail to the beach will find the path amazingly easy and scenic. Bring a bike lock (a bike rack is provided) and a picnic for the picturesque beach, and be sure to hike up the short trail on the north bluff for a memorable view of the coast.

The longer loop described here takes off 0.6 mile before the beach (might as well ride over and check it out first, since you're here), then makes a short but

Lock up your bike, take off your cycling shoes, and explore the black sands of Tennessee Beach.

hellacious climb up Coastal Trail. At the summit, catch your breath and enjoy the views, because there's more climbing ahead on Coyote Ridge Trail. A final downhill stint on Miwok Trail will bring you back to Tennessee Valley Trailhead with some exciting—and surprisingly technical—single-track. (Don't let the railroad-tie stairs 0.5 mile from the end catch you by surprise.) This loop's total mileage is short, but the steep uphills and rutted dirt trails dole out a solid workout. And it goes without saying that the Marin Headlands scenery never disappoints.

For more information, contact Golden Gate National Recreation Area, 415/331-1540, www.nps.gov/goga.

Driving Directions

From San Francisco, cross the Golden Gate Bridge and drive north on U.S. 101 for 4 miles. Take the Mill Valley/Stinson Beach/Highway 1 exit and continue straight for 0.6 mile to Tennessee Valley Road on the left. Turn left and drive 2 miles to the trailhead.

Route Directions

0.0 Park at Tennessee Valley Trailhead and follow the main, wide road southwest. *Supplies are available in Mill Valley, two miles north.*

1.3 STRAIGHT at junction with Coastal Trail.

1.9 Tennessee Beach bike rack. TURN AROUND.

2.5 LEFT at junction with Coastal Trail; hill climb.

3.1 RIGHT at junction.

3.8 LEFT then immediate RIGHT on Coyote Ridge Trail.

4.3 STRAIGHT at two Green Gulch junctions.

4.4 High point and end of climb.

4.6 STRAIGHT on Miwok Trail.

5.4 RIGHT to stay on Miwok Trail.

5.6 STRAIGHT on Miwok at junction with Countryview Road Trail on left.

6.5 Arrive at starting point.

20 MARIN HEADLANDS MIWOK AND BOBCAT LOOP

Golden Gate National Recreation Area near Sausalito

DIRT ROAD AND SINGLE-TRACK; PAVED ROADS WITH MODERATE CAR TRAFFIC

Difficulty: 4   **Total Distance:** 14 miles

Riding Time: 2 hours   **Elevation Gain:** 2,100 feet

Summary: Just across from the Golden Gate Bridge, this scenic ride takes you far from city life into the wonders of the Marin Headlands.

Riders can choose from many possible starting points for this loop: the San Francisco or Marin sides of the Golden Gate Bridge, the Tennessee Valley Trailhead in Mill Valley, the Rodeo Avenue exit off U.S. 101 near Sausalito, or Rodeo Beach at the Marin Headlands. The ride described here starts from the Conzelman parking lot on the northwest side of the Golden Gate Bridge because that allows for the most off-road miles. (Three of the total 14 miles

The long climb on the Miwok Trail to the top of Wolf Ridge in the Marin Headlands will get your heart and lungs pumping.

are paved; the rest are wide fire roads and single-track.) Ride this loop any way you like; it's all good.

Like the other Marin Headlands loop described in this book (see ride 19, *Tennessee Valley and Coyote Ridge Loop*), this route offers ocean views, grasslands, wildflowers, and coastal hills. Two significant climbs will get your heart and lungs pumping. One is a 1.5-mile stretch on Miwok Trail from Rodeo Valley up to the top of Wolf Ridge. The other is the 1.5-mile Marincello Trail heading uphill from Tennessee Valley. At least the ascents are memorable: You'll gain some wide blue-water views. One other potential problem is the encroaching poison oak on Coastal Trail. Sometimes the Park Service maintains this trail; sometimes not. Better carry some Tecnu (a lotion used to treat poison oak) just in case.

A highlight is Bobcat Trail, which drops through one of the Bay Area's most special places, the Gerbode Valley. This beautiful valley was just barely saved from development in the 1960s, when a community for 20,000 people was planned for the area. With your first glimpse of Gerbode Valley, you'll grimace at the thought of developers paving over its pristine grasslands. Chalk up a victory for the hawks, butterflies, and bobcats. And yes, the latter are often seen on Bobcat Trail.

For more information, contact Golden Gate National Recreation Area, 415/331-1540, www.nps.gov/goga.

Options

A backpacking camp is found 0.5 mile off Bobcat Trail, so you could turn this ride into an overnight adventure. Don't overload your mountain bike's panniers, however, or these hills will be very unforgiving.

Driving Directions

From San Francisco, cross the Golden Gate Bridge on U.S. 101 and take the first exit north of the bridge, Alexander Avenue. Turn left and loop back under the freeway, then turn right on Conzelman Road (signed for Marin Headlands). Park in the lot on the left, 100 feet up the road.

Route Directions

0.0 Park at lot at start of Conzelman Road, on the northwest side of the Golden Gate Bridge. Ride out of the parking lot and turn left and uphill on Conzelman. *Supplies are available in Sausalito, two miles away.*

1.3 RIGHT at junction with McCullough Road (paved); then LEFT on signed, dirt Coastal Trail (beware of poison oak).

2.9 STRAIGHT at junction to cross paved Bunker Road.

3.0 LEFT on Rodeo Valley Trail.

3.4 LEFT on Bobcat Trail at Y-junction.

3.5 RIGHT on Miwok Trail; now you're on the loop; steep climb ahead.

4.6 RIGHT to stay on Miwok at junction with Wolf Ridge Trail.

4.9 LEFT on Old Springs Trail (single-track; can be very rutted).

6.2 Stables at Tennessee Valley Trailhead. Walk your bike through stables and parking lot and pick up Marincello Trail on right (northeast) edge of lot; prepare to climb.

7.7 LEFT on Bobcat Trail.

8.5 RIGHT to stay on Bobcat at junction with Rodeo and Alta Trails; steep descent into Gerbode Valley begins.

10.5 LEFT on Rodeo Valley Trail at end of loop; backtrack on Rodeo Valley Trail, Coastal Trail, and Conzelman Road to parking lot.

14.0 Arrive at starting point.

MARIN HEADLANDS MIWOK AND BOBCAT LOOP

21 PERIMETER TRAIL AND FIRE ROAD LOOPS

Angel Island State Park

BEST ☾

DIRT ROAD AND DETERIORATING PAVEMENT

Difficulty: 2

Total Distance: 9.6 miles

Riding Time: 2 hours

Elevation Gain: 900 feet

Summary: The most desirable real estate in the Bay Area is yours for the day on this view-filled ride on Angel Island.

view of the Bay Bridge and San Francisco from Angel Island's Perimeter Trail

The Perimeter Trail at Angel Island State Park provides 360-degree views from its setting in the middle of the bay, making it arguably the most scenic bike trail in the entire Bay Area. Views change constantly as you pedal, allowing you to see the cities and towns surrounding the bay in an entirely new perspective. One of the best vistas lies on the southeast side of the island, where an open stretch captures the Bay and Golden Gate Bridges, plus Alcatraz Island. The 180-degree scene encompasses the whole sweep of urban skylines from Berkeley to San Francisco to Sausalito.

And the island doles out more than just views. Bikers can also enjoy two sandy beaches just off the trail, a wealth of historic sites, and the simple joy of a boat trip—a half-hour ferry cruise from various cities around the bay.

Perimeter Trail is a partially paved road, with the pavement deteriorating to gravel and dirt in places. True to its name, the trail loops around the island's perimeter, so you can ride your bike in either direction (the route suggested here goes counterclockwise). History lessons are readily available because Angel Island has had a long and varied past as a military outpost, a Russian sea otter hunters' site, and an immigrant detention center. Be sure to read the interpretive signs around the island or stop in at the visitor center near Ayala Cove to get more information.

Many island visitors are satisfied to ride only the 5.5-mile Perimeter Trail, but if you'd like to get away from the crowds and enjoy some more exercise, you can connect to a loop-within-the-loop, a dirt fire road on the island's interior. The route suggested here connects the two loops at the fire station on the north side of the island, but you can also connect them via the cutoff for Mount Livermore on the southeast side. Because the upper fire road is higher in elevation, it offers even more expansive views than Perimeter Trail.

One note of caution: The wind can blow at Angel Island, and the fog can come in on a moment's notice, so come prepared with an extra jacket, even on sunny days.

For more information, contact Angel Island State Park, 415/435-1915, www. angelisland.org.

Driving Directions

Ferry service to Angel Island is available from Tiburon, San Francisco, and Oakland/Alameda. For Tiburon departures, contact the Tiburon Ferry at 415/435-2131, www.angelislandferry.com. For Oakland or Alameda departures, contact East Bay Ferry at 510/522-3300, www.eastbayferry.com. For San Francisco departures, contact Blue and Gold Fleet at 415/773-1188, www.blueandgoldfleet.com.

Route Directions

0.0 Arrive at ferry landing at Ayala Cove. Retrieve your bike from the ferry and ride to your right, past the café and toward the picnic area. *Water, pay phones, restrooms, and rental lockers are available at the ferry landing; food is available at the landing café.*

0.2 LEFT on gravel bike trail by picnic area.

0.5 RIGHT on Perimeter Trail.

1.3 West Garrison and Camp Reynolds.

1.7 Cutoff for road to Perle's Beach; views of San Francisco and Alcatraz from the beach.

2.9 STRAIGHT on Perimeter Trail at junction with upper Fire Road.

3.5 East Garrison and old military hospital.

3.9 LEFT at junction with upper Fire Road at Fire Station.

4.3 RIGHT on Fire Road.

7.7 RIGHT on connecting road back to Perimeter Trail.

8.0 LEFT on Perimeter Trail.

9.1 RIGHT at junction with trail to Ayala Cove.

9.6 Arrive at starting point.

22 GOLDEN GATE BRIDGE AND MARIN HEADLANDS LOOP   BEST 【

Golden Gate National Recreation Area near Sausalito

PAVED ROADS WITH MODERATE CAR TRAFFIC

Difficulty: 3

Riding Time: 1.5-2 hours

Total Distance: 15 miles

Elevation Gain: 1,500 feet

Summary: A favorite training ride for city cyclists, this loop is also ideal for visitors seeking a true taste of the City by the Bay and its environs.

This ride is classic San Francisco, with vista after vista of world-class scenery. Beginning at Fort Point in San Francisco's Presidio, the route crosses the Golden Gate Bridge, then follows Conzelman Road through the Marin Headlands, with frequent jaw-dropping views back toward the mouth of the Golden Gate. A challenging climb up to Hawk Hill (920 feet) is followed by a dizzying descent on cliffside Conzelman Road, which thankfully is one-way in this stretch. Make sure your brakes are working well before you begin the precipitous drop.

At the edge of the headlands, a narrow strip of land curves out to I nita Lighthouse, which can be visited via a one-mile round-trip walk. T___ your trip carefully: The 1855-built lighthouse is open only on Saturday, Sunday, and

Rodeo Beach is an excellent spot to take a break on the Golden Gate Bridge and Marin Headlands Loop.

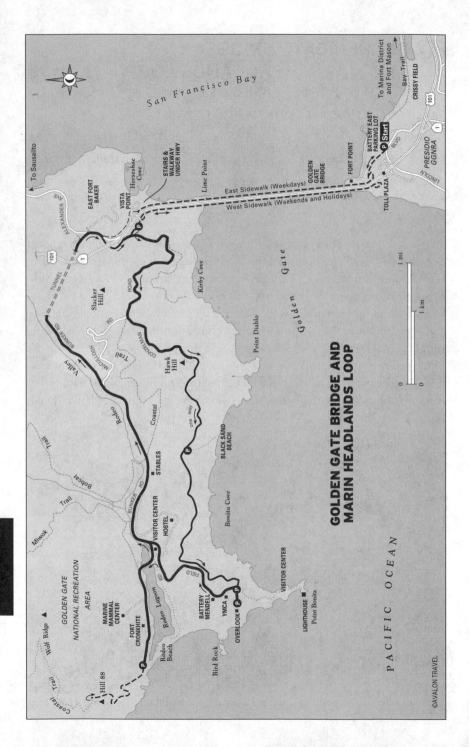

GOLDEN GATE BRIDGE AND MARIN HEADLANDS LOOP

©AVALON TRAVEL

Monday 12:30–3:30 p.m., and is accessed via a 50-foot-long tunnel and 40-yard-long suspension footbridge. Its location is the most dramatic of any lighthouse on the California coast; don't miss seeing it.

Other highlights along the loop include Black Sand Beach, the Marin Headlands Visitor Center, and beautiful Rodeo Beach and Rodeo Lagoon. With all these places to visit, a bike lock is more than a good idea. The trip back includes a ride through a long, lighted tunnel with bike lanes, and then another jaunt across the magnificent Golden Gate Bridge.

Use some caution in crossing the bridge, especially if you ride on a weekday, when you must use the east sidewalk (shared with oblivious pedestrians toting video cameras). On weekends, cyclists ride on the west sidewalk while pedestrians use the east sidewalk, so there's less congestion. Either way, keep your speed down and take time to enjoy the view from 225 feet above San Francisco Bay.

For more information, contact Golden Gate National Recreation Area, 415/331-1540, www.nps.gov/goga.

Driving Directions

From the Crissy Field and marina area of San Francisco, take Lincoln Boulevard west toward the Golden Gate Bridge. Turn right just before the bridge entrance into the Battery East parking lot at Fort Point.

Route Directions

0.0 Park at the Battery East parking lot at Fort Point on Lincoln Boulevard (east side of the Golden Gate Bridge). At the entrance to the parking lot is a gated, paved road that is signed as a bike route (#202) to get on the bridge. *Water and snacks are available at Bridge Cafe at the bridge entrance (Bridge View Area).*

0.2 Start across the Golden Gate Bridge (ride on west side on weekends and holidays and east side on weekdays; obey all posted instruction signs for cyclists).

1.8 LEFT up hill on Conzelman Road at north (Marin County) side of Golden Gate Bridge. *If you're on the east sidewalk, exit at the Vista Point area and take the stairway underpass under the highway to the start of Conzelman Road. If you're on the west sidewalk, follow the signs for cyclists to the start of Conzelman Road.*

3.5 LEFT at junction with McCullough Road.

4.1 Summit of Hawk Hill; two-way road turns to one-way and descent begins.

5.0 Parking lot for Black Sand Beach on left. *Lock up your bike and hike 0.5 mile to one of Marin County's most spectacular beaches.*

6.0 STRAIGHT for Point Bonita Lighthouse.

6.5 Lighthouse trailhead. *Lock up your bike and hike 0.5 mile to the lighthouse.*

6.7 Road ends at Battery Mendell and overlook. TURN AROUND.

7.8 Marin Headlands Visitor Center on left.

8.0 LEFT at junction with Bunker Road.

8.5 LEFT at junction; Marin Mammal Center above to the right.

8.9 Road ends at Rodeo Beach parking lot. TURN AROUND. *Lock up your bike and explore the beach and lagoon trail. Mountain bikers can continue up Coastal Trail (gated road) 1.6 miles from parking lot to the top of Hill 88 and a spectacular view; a turnaround is required at the top.*

10.0 LEFT at junction of Field Road and Bunker Road.

12.2 Entrance to one-way tunnel. Push the button to alert motorists that a cyclist is in the tunnel.

12.7 Exit tunnel and ride uphill.

12.9 RIGHT at stop sign.

13.2 Start of Conzelman Road. Return to proper side of the bridge according to day of the week.

15.0 Arrive at starting point.

GOLDEN GATE BRIDGE AND MARIN HEADLANDS LOOP

23 NIMITZ WAY AND WILDCAT CANYON

BEST ☾

Tilden and Wildcat Canyon Regional Parks, Berkeley hills

DIRT ROAD AND PAVED BIKE PATH

Difficulty: 2

Total Distance: 11.3 miles

Riding Time: 2 hours

Elevation Gain: 800 feet

Summary: The East Bay's most scenic paved trail forms one leg of this fun mountain biking loop.

© ANN MARIE BROWN

In contrast to the high ridgeline ride on Nimitz Way, Wildcat Creek Trail rolls along the base of Wildcat Canyon, paralleling its stream.

Of all the paved recreation trails in the East Bay, Nimitz Way wins the prize for best views. Perched on the tip of San Pablo Ridge in Tilden Park, the trail serves up nonstop scenery variations. Near its start, cyclists survey San Pablo Reservoir, with Briones Reservoir behind, plus looming Mount Diablo. A few pedal cranks later, San Francisco Bay, the Golden Gate Bridge, and Angel Island come into view. At every turn in the trail, over every hill, you gain a different perspective. First the Richmond Bridge appears, next the Gold Coast shows up, soon San Francisco's skyline emerges, and finally the Brothers Islands steal the scene. On a clear day, the ever-changing panorama will amaze you.

Paved Nimitz Way is mostly level with only one short hill right before the pavement ends at 3.9 miles. It is well loved by every kind of rider, including those on tricycles and training wheels, and with good reason. Mountain bikers use Nimitz Way to connect to dirt trails in Tilden and Wildcat Canyon parks. The ride described here is an easy-to-moderate loop through Wildcat Canyon that affords a good workout, memorable views, and the chance to spot hawks, bunnies, and even a bobcat in the grassy hills of Wildcat Canyon. Be forewarned that the loop has two very steep downhills, where I've seen riders walking their bikes while simultaneously biting their nails. Hey, at least you don't have to ride *up* those hills.

If you're planning on riding in this area on the weekend, get to the Inspiration Point parking lot early. The place is Bike City every Saturday and Sunday, and parking spots are at a premium.

For more information, contact East Bay Regional Park District, 510/562-7275 or 510/635-0135, www.ebparks.org.

Driving Directions

From I-580 in Oakland, take Highway 24 east. Go through the Caldecott Tunnel and exit at Orinda. Turn left on Camino Pablo. Drive north for 2 miles, then turn left on Wildcat Canyon Road. Drive 2.4 miles to the Inspiration Point parking lot.

Route Directions

0.0 Park at Inspiration Point parking lot and take the well-signed Nimitz Way Trail. *Supplies are available in Berkeley or Orinda.*

3.9 End of paved Nimitz Way Trail. Go through gate to join dirt San Pablo Ridge Trail; ignore trails branching right and left.

5.2 LEFT on Belgum Trail; steep descent.

6.1 LEFT on Wildcat Creek Trail. *Water is available 0.5 mile to the right on Wildcat Creek Trail (Alvarado Staging Area).*

7.7 STRAIGHT at junction with Mezue Trail on left.

7.9 LEFT at junction with Havey Canyon Trail, then immediate RIGHT on Conlon Trail.

9.9 RIGHT on paved Nimitz Way.

11.3 Arrive at starting point.

24 SKYLINE LOOP
Berkeley and Oakland hills

PAVED ROADS WITH MODERATE CAR TRAFFIC

Difficulty: 3   **Total Distance:** 28.5 miles (or 23-mile option)

Riding Time: 2 hours   **Elevation Gain:** 2,000 feet

Summary: This road ride travels past three of the East Bay hills' most popular parks, offering an abundance of San Francisco Bay views.

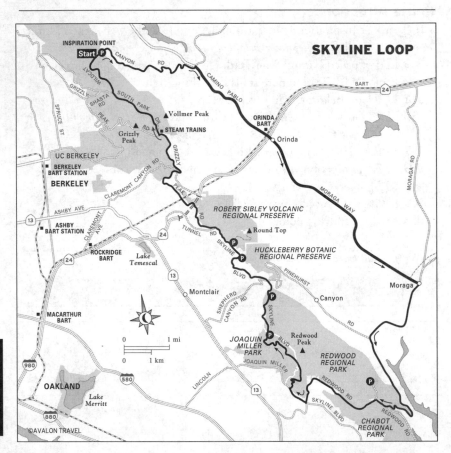

You can't call yourself a road cyclist in the San Francisco Bay Area until you've ridden the Skyline Loop in the East Bay hills. On a clear day, the loop's far-reaching views of San Francisco Bay, the cities of the East Bay, and Mount Diablo will knock your socks off. The route has just enough hills to provide a workout, but none are so steep that they are out of the range of possibility for most riders.

Far-reaching views of San Francisco Bay and the East Bay are seen from the Skyline Loop.

Plus, the roads have surprisingly little traffic, except for Moraga Way, which has a wide shoulder. All this and you can easily start the ride from Orinda, Moraga, Berkeley, or at one of several parks on Skyline Boulevard.

This route describes the loop starting from the Inspiration Point parking lot at Tilden Regional Park, a popular gathering place for cyclists on weekends and a great place to find a riding partner. (Get there early to procure a parking spot.) This trailhead choice means you begin your ride with a twisty descent and end with a twisty climb on Wildcat Canyon Road. But the ride has a multitude of climbs and descents, so you might as well get in the swing of things from the start.

The major hills are on Pinehurst Road, Skyline Boulevard, and Grizzly Peak Road. (The latter two roads are where you gain most of your bay.views.) You also face a steep descent on South Park Drive, just after you pass the miniature steam train at Tilden Park, where families pay a few bucks to go for a 12-minute, open-air train tour. Keep your speed down as you descend on this moderately busy park road—not just to avoid cars, but also to avoid California newts: The cute brown and orange salamanders cross the road by the thousands each year during the rainy season. During the peak newt migration, South Park Drive is closed to cars, but open to cyclists.

Besides Tilden, this loop passes by two other East Bay regional parks: Redwood and Robert Sibley. Redwood is a popular spot for mountain biking and hiking. Sibley's main feature is Round Top Peak, the remains of an ancient volcano.

For more information about Tilden, Redwood, and Sibley Regional Parks,

contact East Bay Regional Park District, 510/635-0135 or 510/562-7275, www.
ebparks.org.

Options

For riders short on time, note the shortcut in the route directions at mile 10.9 on
Pinehurst Road. Turning right instead of left on Pinehurst will cut 5.5 miles off
the loop, but you'll face a steep climb up to Skyline Boulevard. The Pinehurst
shortcut does have its charms, however: The road sees almost no car traffic, is
lined with redwoods, and passes by the tiny hamlet of Canyon, with its one-room
schoolhouse and post office.

Driving Directions

From I-580 in Oakland, take Highway 24 east. Go through the Caldecott Tunnel
and exit at Orinda. Turn left on Camino Pablo. Drive north for 2 miles, then turn
left on Wildcat Canyon Road. Drive 2.4 miles to the Inspiration Point parking lot.

Route Directions

0.0 Park at Inspiration Point parking lot. Turn left out of the lot and
head downhill on Wildcat Canyon Road. *Supplies are available in
Berkeley or Orinda.*

2.4 RIGHT on Camino Pablo Road.

4.5 Cross under Highway 24; Camino Pablo becomes Moraga Way.

4.6 Arrive in Orinda. *Supplies are available.*

9.1 RIGHT on Canyon Road. *Supplies are available at the shopping center.*

10.9 LEFT on Pinehurst Road. *You can cut 5.5 miles off the loop by turning
right on Pinehurst Road here. After a steep climb, you'll rejoin the route
at mile 20.4, below, where you'll go straight onto Skyline.*

13.8 RIGHT on Redwood Road.

16.2 RIGHT on Skyline Boulevard.

16.8 RIGHT to stay on Skyline Boulevard at Joaquin Miller Road.

19.9 Redwood Regional Park Skyline gate. *Water is available.*

20.4 LEFT to stay on Skyline Boulevard at Pinehurst Road.

21.9 Robert Sibley Regional Preserve. *Water is available.*

22.0 RIGHT on Grizzly Peak Road.

24.4 STRAIGHT to stay on Grizzly Peak Road.

25.6 Tilden Regional Park's miniature steam train. *Water is available.*

25.8 RIGHT on South Park Drive.

27.3 RIGHT on Wildcat Canyon Road.

28.5 Arrive at starting point.

25 CARQUINEZ STRAIT LOOP
Martinez to Crockett

PAVED ROADS WITH MINIMAL CAR TRAFFIC

Difficulty: 2   **Total Distance:** 18.5 miles (or longer options)

Riding Time: 1.5-2 hours   **Elevation Gain:** 1,200 feet

Summary: One of the most interesting features of the San Francisco Bay waterway system, Carquinez Strait is the showpiece of this ride.

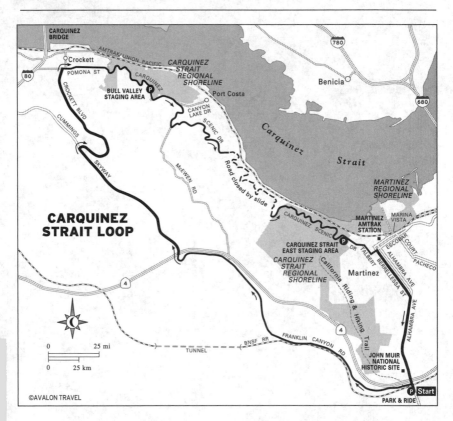

The northeastern arm of the conglomeration of waterways that constitute the bay and river delta, Carquinez Strait forms the narrow passageway between San Pablo and Suisun Bays. It's the meeting place of the Sacramento and San Joaquin Rivers, where they join together to flow to the Pacific Ocean through the Golden Gate.

Hundreds of thousands of king salmon once passed through here on their way to the Sacramento and San Joaquin Rivers to spawn. Native Americans lived off their abundance for centuries. In the 1800s, white settlers set up commercial fishing

Grasses and weeds push up through the broken pavement on this stretch of Carquinez Scenic Drive, which has been closed to cars since 1982.

operations and canneries along the strait; king salmon ruled the economy of this area. Today the only salmon you'll find in the towns of Martinez and Crockett are on dinner plates in homes and restaurants, but it is fascinating to recall the area's history as you ride this road tour between the two towns.

Due to events in more recent history, one portion of this road loop is closed to cars. A landslide in 1982 washed out a 1.7-mile-long section of Carquinez Scenic Drive. There's still enough road left for cyclists, but watch for broken pavement, gravel, and rocks. (You might want to ride your fat-tire bike here, or make sure you have a pair of Kevlar tire liners in your skinny tires.) It's easy to get distracted by the views overlooking Carquinez Strait, a wide expanse of blue waterway punctuated by the journeying of ships, large and small. As Carquinez Scenic Drive twists and turns, you gain ever-changing views of the Carquinez Bridge and the towns of Benecia and Vallejo.

Most of the climbing is accomplished in the first five miles of this ride (600-foot gain). The rest of the loop's ups are short, 200-foot-or-less climbs. There's also an exhilarating downhill on Crockett Boulevard into Crockett.

Options

For more views of the waterway, stop at Carquinez Strait Regional Shoreline just outside of Crockett and hike the one-mile Carquinez Overlook Loop Trail. Mountain bikers can also access the dirt California Riding and Hiking Trail from this ride's trailhead (the Park and Ride lot). Pedaling east, the trail connects to the paved Contra Costa Canal Trail in just under four miles. The Canal Trail then connects to the Iron Horse Regional Trail.

Driving Directions

From Walnut Creek, take I-680 north for six miles to Highway 4. Turn west on Highway 4 and drive three miles; take the Alhambra Avenue exit and drive south to the Park and Ride lot on the right.

Route Directions

0.0 Park at the Park and Ride lot at the junction of Alhambra Avenue and Franklin Canyon Road. Ride west on Franklin Canyon Road. *Supplies are available in Walnut Creek, Concord, or Martinez.*

4.4 RIGHT on Cummings Skyway.

6.5 RIGHT on Crockett Boulevard.

8.5 RIGHT on Pomona Street into downtown Crockett; Pomona Street becomes Carquinez Scenic Drive just outside of town. *Supplies are available in downtown Crockett.*

10.3 Carquinez Regional Strait Shoreline on the left (Bull Valley Staging Area). *You can lock up your bike and hike the one-mile Carquinez Overlook Loop Trail.*

12.5 Road closure; ride around the gate.

14.2 Road is open to cars again.

16.4 RIGHT on Talbart Street.

16.5 LEFT on Escobar Street.

16.6 RIGHT on Berrellessa Street (becomes Alhambra Avenue).

18.5 Arrive at starting point.

CARQUINEZ STRAIT LOOP

26 BRIONES CREST LOOP
Briones Regional Park near Orinda

DIRT ROAD AND SINGLE-TRACK

Difficulty: 2   **Total Distance:** 8 miles (or 13.5-mile option)

Riding Time: 1.5 hours   **Elevation Gain:** 1,200 feet

Summary: Ride through the grasslands and alongside the cows in an old Spanish land grant couched between three freeways.

Briones Regional Park is nearly 6,000 acres of grasslands and oaks that was once part of Rancho San Felipe, a Spanish land grant. In the mid-1800s, it was an important fruit-growing region. Today it's the grassy home of grazing cows and is frequently visited by mountain bikers, dog walkers, hikers, and horseback riders.

The park is well known for its sunny exposure, numerous dirt roads, and large expanse of open grasslands. Bordered on three sides by freeways—Highway 4, I-680, and Highway 2—it's an oasis of open space in a heavily urbanized area.

Briones Regional Park contains nearly 6,000 acres of rolling grassland hills.

Because of an absence of shade in the park, summer is not the best time for a ride here. It can be as hot as Hades on July and August afternoons, although quite pleasant in winter, spring, and fall. Note that cows roam the Briones pasturelands, so as you ride you must pass through a number of cattle gates. And those same cows are notorious for rutting the heck out of the ranch roads, so expect a lot of bumps, especially noticeable on the downhills. Dual-suspension comes in handy here.

The first 0.5 mile of the Briones Crest Loop is on wide single-track and constitutes a grunt of a climb (three short hills with a total 400-foot elevation gain). But beyond that, the remaining hills are more moderate. Most of the ride is on wide ranch roads, which lend themselves to some fun downhills.

Don't forget to pause for a moment at mile 4.3, where you pass Briones Peak, the highest point in the park at 1,483 feet. The hilltop affords great views of mighty Mount Diablo.

For more information, contact East Bay Regional Park District, 510/635-0135 or 510/562-7275, www.ebparks.org.

Options

To extend your mileage and increase your workout, you can turn this ride into a double loop. Follow the route directions below to mile 7.7, then turn right on Old Briones Road. Travel 1.6 miles, then turn right on Briones Crest Trail (you'll pass Briones Peak again). Then, less than a mile later, go straight on Table Top Trail, heading for the radio antennas. In 0.8 mile, you'll be back on Briones Crest Trail. In another 0.5 mile, go right on Crescent Ridge Trail, pedaling past the archery range. You'll face a memorably steep descent. At 12.7 miles, go right on Homestead Valley Trail, then left on Old Briones Road 0.5 mile farther. This will take you back to the parking lot where you started your ride.

Driving Directions

From I-580 in Oakland, take Highway 24 east. Go through the Caldecott Tunnel and continue another 1.5 miles. Take the Orinda exit, then turn left on Camino Pablo and drive north for 2 miles. Turn right on Bear Creek Road and drive 4.4 miles, then turn right into the Briones Regional Park/Bear Creek Staging Area entrance. Turn left just past the kiosk and park in the lower parking lot.

Route Directions

0.0 Park in the lower parking lot at the Bear Creek Staging Area. The trailhead is at the end of the parking lot on the left. Follow Briones Crest Trail. *Water is available at the trailhead. Supplies are available in Orinda.*

0.1 RIGHT at Y-junction onto Briones Crest Trail.

0.5 End of the climb; trail widens and levels out.

1.1 STRAIGHT on Briones Crest Trail at junction with Deer Creek Trail. Stay straight on Briones Crest Trail at next four junctions.

3.3 Pass by Sindicich Lagoons (ranch ponds).

3.5 RIGHT on Old Briones Road.

3.6 LEFT on Briones Crest Trail.

4.3 Briones Peak, elevation 1,483 feet.

4.4 RIGHT to stay on Briones Crest Trail.

4.8 STRAIGHT on Briones Crest Trail.

5.7 STRAIGHT on Briones Crest Trail.

6.2 RIGHT on Homestead Valley Trail.

7.7 LEFT on Old Briones Road.

7.8 Go around gate and pass upper parking lot.

7.9 RIGHT at kiosk into lower parking lot.

8.0 Arrive at starting point.

27 THREE BEARS LOOP
near San Pablo Reservoir and Orinda

PAVED ROADS WITH MODERATE CAR TRAFFIC

Difficulty: 3   **Total Distance:** 19.5 miles

Riding Time: 1.5 hours   **Elevation Gain:** 1,600 feet

Summary: A classic East Bay road ride, this loop cruises along bike lanes and wide road shoulders past San Pablo and Briones Reservoirs.

Every serious East Bay cyclist has his or her own version of the Three Bears ride, with a variety of starting points and mileage totals. But what all those rides have in common is a heart-pumping, aerobic "crank" up the triumvirate of hills on Bear Valley Road, affectionately known as Papa Bear, Mama Bear, and Baby Bear.

This is one of the shorter versions of that classic ride, perfect for after work or any time you want a workout on the bike without taking up a whole day. By starting and ending near downtown Orinda, you can complete the Three Bears Loop in just under 20 miles. The loop can be ridden in either direction. As it is described here, you face Mama Bear first (450-foot climb), Papa Bear second (500-foot climb), and save the easiest hill for last (only 100 feet for the Baby). In between, there is a rest stop at Briones Regional Park, where you can fill up your water bottles or have a seat at a shady picnic table.

Except for the first leg on busy San Pablo Dam Road and a short stretch through a cluster of red-tile-roofed subdivisions, most of the loop is on quiet back roads surrounded by open space. Bike lanes and wide shoulders make riding here stress-free. A highlight of this ride is its lovely views of two of the East Bay Municipal Utility District's reservoirs: San Pablo and Briones. In June, the roadside buckeye trees are in full bloom, wafting their sweet aroma through the air. The grasslands and chaparral plants emit their own pungent smell as they dry in the summer heat. You're far more likely to see quail and deer crossing the road than a parade of cars. This is the kind of pleasant ride you can do again and again, any time you're in the mood for a little exercise.

Driving Directions

From I-580 in Oakland, take Highway 24 east. Go through the Caldecott Tunnel and continue another 1.5 miles. Take the Orinda exit, then turn left on Camino Pablo and drive north for 2 miles. Turn right on Bear Creek Road and park in the pullout immediately on the left. (If this pullout is full, you can park in downtown Orinda, 1.6 miles south on Camino Pablo Road, then ride to this point.)

Route Directions

0.0 Park at the top of Bear Creek Road, near its junction with Camino Pablo/San Pablo Dam Road. Ride out to Camino Pablo/San Pablo Dam Road. *Supplies are available in Orinda.*

0.1 RIGHT on San Pablo Dam Road.

5.4 RIGHT on Castro Ranch Road.

7.6 RIGHT on Alhambra Valley Road.

10.4 RIGHT on Bear Creek Road.

11.9 Start up Mama Bear.

13.0 Top of Mama Bear.

14.3 LEFT at Briones Regional Park Bear Creek Staging Area. *Water is available.* TURN AROUND.

14.9 LEFT on Bear Creek Road.

15.2 Start up Papa Bear.

17.4 Top of Papa Bear.

18.9 Start up Baby Bear.

19.5 Arrive at starting point (top of Baby Bear).

28 LAFAYETTE-MORAGA REGIONAL TRAIL
near Lafayette and Moraga

PAVED BIKE PATH

Difficulty: 1

Total Distance: 15.4 miles

Riding Time: 1.5 hours

Elevation Gain: 550 feet

Summary: This is a paved bike trail for every kind of rider, from first-timers on training wheels to East Bay bike commuters.

When suburbs grow so large that they connect town to town without any buffer of open land between them, one of the smartest things city planners can do is create spaces where people can get a little fresh air and sunshine—places protected from cars, traffic, and urban noise. The Lafayette–Moraga Trail is such a place, and it is used by more than half a million people per year.

It's not exactly a trip to the wilderness, but you will see plenty of squirrels along the trail—not plain old Bay Area gray squirrels, but cute and chubby red squirrels with shiny, rust-colored coats. I spotted some busily burying nuts in flower beds, their genetic instinct preparing them for the long, hard, snowbound winter that will never come to sunny Moraga.

Also in the cute category, it's not uncommon to see an entire pack of Cub Scouts ride by, dressed in their smart navy blue uniforms and tiny bicycle helmets. That's the kind of trail this is. A stretch of the old San Francisco–Sacramento Railroad, the path retains some of its railroad history with white crossing signs proudly displayed at junctions around Lafayette.

On the negative side, Lafayette–Moraga Trail is intersected by several roads.

The Lafayette–Moraga Regional Trail was opened in 1976 as one of the first 500 converted rail trails in the United States.

Only one, St. Mary's Road, is likely to have much traffic. Beyond this crossing, you leave most of the neighborhoods behind and see less of St. Mary's Road (which parallels the trail up to this crossing). The trail passes St. Mary's College, which has a pretty white church tower set in the hillside and is surrounded by green playing fields. Shortly thereafter is Moraga Commons, a town park with a play area, restrooms, par course, and the like. A waterfall sculpture is located near a sign noting that the Lafayette–Moraga Trail was opened in 1976 as one of America's first 500 rail trails. The trail's final stretch leads out to the country, ending at the Valle Vista Staging Area on Canyon Road, where you simply turn around and head back.

For more information, contact East Bay Regional Park District, 510/635-0135 or 510/562-7275, www.ebparks.org.

Options

If you're a fan of paved recreation trails in the East Bay, you must take a ride on the Iron Horse Regional Trail, which runs between the cities of Concord and Dublin, following the Southern Pacific Railroad right-of-way established in 1891. When completed, the Iron Horse Trail will stretch 55 miles from Livermore in Alameda County to Suisun Bay in Contra Costa County, connecting 12 cities. Currently about 30 miles of trail are accessible. For more information and a trail map, go to www.ebparks.org.

Driving Directions

From I-580 in Oakland, take Highway 24 east toward Walnut Creek. Go through the Caldecott Tunnel and take the Pleasant Hill Road exit south. Drive 0.7 mile to Olympic Boulevard and turn right. The parking lot is on the right in about 50 yards.

Route Directions

0.0 Park at Olympic Staging Area. *Water is available along the trail.*

1.1 STRAIGHT at junction with Briones-to-Mount Diablo Trail.

3.3 Cross St. Mary's Road.

3.4 Lafayette Community Center. *Water is available.*

5.2 St. Mary's College campus.

6.0 Moraga Commons park. *Water is available.*

7.7 Valle Vista Staging Area. TURN AROUND.

15.4 Arrive at starting point.

29 STEWARTVILLE AND RIDGE TRAILS LOOP

BEST (

Black Diamond Mines Regional Preserve near Antioch

DIRT ROAD

Difficulty: 3

Total Distance: 10.8 miles

Riding Time: 2 hours

Elevation Gain: 1,900 feet

Summary: A little-known slice of East Bay history is revealed at this mountain bike–friendly East Bay regional park.

From 1860 to 1906, the Mount Diablo Coal Field was the largest coal mining district in California. Located in what is now Black Diamond Mines Regional Preserve, this productive coal field on the northern side of Mount Diablo prompted the digging of 12 major mines and the growth of five townships. Much of this mining history, and a large acreage of rolling grassland hills and chaparral-clad slopes, is preserved at Black Diamond Mines.

This loop ride reveals some of the park's highlights and adds some heart-pumping, leg-burning exercise to the bargain. Start with a mind-expanding trip to the park's Greathouse Visitor Center, which has been closed for many years for structural improvements but is scheduled to reopen in summer 2012, then pedal the level Railroad Bed Trail to Stewartville Trail. A 0.5-mile ascent brings you to

Ride through grassy valleys and steep hills on the Stewartville and Ridge Trails Loop.

a cattle gate at a high point. Pass through the gate and admire the deep, grassy valley below you. The good news is that you're going to ride into that pretty valley; the bad news is that you'll have to climb back out of it.

Don't miss two spurs off the loop: Upper Oil Canyon Trail, which leads steeply uphill to an overlook of the valley, and Tunnel Trail to Prospect Tunnel, an obvious gaping hole in the hillside. You can explore about 150 feet into the dark, cool mine shaft before you reach a steel gate. The shaft was driven in the 1860s by miners in search of coal, or "black diamonds."

A mile past Tunnel Trail, make a sharp left turn on Ridge Trail, leaving the valley and beginning a steep, two-mile-long ascent. Ridge Trail rollercoasters along, dipping down occasionally but more often rising on very steep grades (steep enough that you may be forced to walk your bike). The painful climb is eased by the sudden appearance of views to the north of Carquinez Strait, Suisun Bay, Pittsburg, and Antioch. Pause to enjoy the vistas while you catch your breath.

When at last Ridge Trail returns you to the gate at Stewartville Trail, consider a rest on the bench by the gate, where you can admire the rolling terrain you just explored. Then it's an easy 1.4 miles back to your car.

Because there is no technical single-track on this ride, it may be tempting to bring beginning mountain bikers here. But unless they are very fit and ambitious, the many short but steep ascents may break their spirit. All riders should stay away from this park's trails when they are wet; the place is famous for its clay-like mud, which can bring your wheels to a dead standstill, even on the downhills.

For more information, contact East Bay Regional Park District, 510/635-0135 or 510/562-7275, www.ebparks.org. Black Diamond Mines Regional Preserve (510/544-2750) is located at 5175 Somersville Road in Antioch.

Options

If a ride around this park whets your appetite for more information on this area's mining history, consider taking a tour of the silica-producing Hazel-Atlas Mine at Black Diamond Mines Regional Preserve. The guided one-hour tour travels 400 feet back into the mine tunnel so participants can see the office of the mine boss, ore chutes, and other features. Tickets for the tour ($5 per person) can be purchased at the park visitor center. Tours are offered on weekends only, March–November, at noon and 3 P.M.

Driving Directions

From Highway 4 in Antioch, take the Somersville Road exit south. Drive three miles south on Somersville Road to the parking lot by the visitor center.

Route Directions

0.0 Park by the visitor center on Somersville Road. Take Railroad Bed Trail from the southern end of the parking lot. *Water is available at the visitor center; supplies are available in Antioch.*

0.7 LEFT on Stewartville Trail.

1.4 Cattle gate and viewpoint. Go through gate, then RIGHT to stay on Stewartville Trail; steep descent.

1.8 RIGHT at junction with Miners Trail to stay on Stewartville Trail.

3.2 RIGHT on Upper Oil Canyon Trail.

4.4 Arrive at overlook. TURN AROUND.

5.6 RIGHT to continue on Stewartville Trail.

6.1 LEFT on Tunnel Trail. Park your bike and walk into the dark tunnel, then TURN AROUND.

6.4 LEFT to continue on Stewartville Trail.

7.3 LEFT (very sharp turn) on Ridge Trail; steep climb begins.

9.4 RIGHT on Stewartville Trail at cattle gate.

10.1 RIGHT on Railroad Bed Trail.

10.8 Arrive at starting point.

30 EAST AND WEST RIDGE LOOP

Redwood Regional Park near Oakland

DIRT ROAD

Difficulty: 2

Total Distance: 9.4 miles

Riding Time: 2 hours

Elevation Gain: 1,100 feet

Summary: Just a few minutes from downtown Oakland lie dense groves of redwood trees, an observatory and planetarium, and one of the East Bay's most popular mountain biking trails.

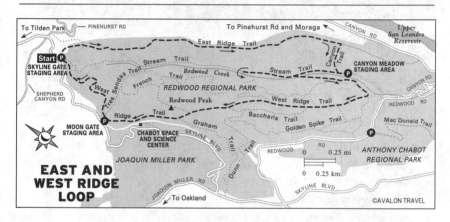

They don't call this place Redwood Regional Park for nothing. The dark, shaggy-barked trees grow more than 100 feet tall, and their shady canopy covers a vast expanse of the park. The redwoods are the second-generation offspring of the original trees that once towered over this canyon. Between 1840 and 1860, loggers felled these ancient giants to provide lumber for the growing cities of San Francisco and San Jose.

The redwoods aren't the only prizes of Redwood Regional Park. The park is bordered by two high ridges to the east and west, both of which offer expansive views. This loop ride, a standard for East Bay mountain bikers, travels outward on East Ridge and back on West Ridge. Although the ride is entirely on wide dirt roads, it still presents some technical challenges, particularly on a steep, rutted downhill on Canyon Trail and a steep uphill on West Ridge Trail. Strong beginners should be able to handle it, or at least walk their bikes if they can't.

From the Skyline Gate Staging Area, follow East Ridge Trail generally downhill for 3 miles in a two-steps-down, one-step-up fashion, rolling along small hills. Watch for long-distance views of the reservoirs to the east. Turn right on Canyon Trail, drop steeply, then follow Stream Trail into the canyon for an up close look

West Ridge Trail at Redwood Regional Park offers views of Oakland and San Francisco Bay to the west and Mount Diablo to the east.

at some of the park's redwood stands. After a brief, level out-and-back on Stream Trail, you'll face a hardy climb on West Ridge Trail. The first 0.75 mile is the worst (400-foot gain), but the trail continues to ascend moderately for almost 3 miles.

West Ridge Trail's final stretch passes by the observatory at the Chabot Space and Science Center (worth a visit; see *Options*). You'll catch fine glimpses of Oakland and San Francisco Bay to the west; equally good is the view to the east of looming Mount Diablo at 3,849 feet. The last mile is a delightfully easy cruise back to Skyline Gate through a shady forest of bay laurel, madrone, and Monterey pine.

For more information, contact East Bay Regional Park District, 510/635-0135 or 510/562-7275, www.ebparks.org.

Options

Combine this ride with a visit to the Chabot Space and Science Center. The center keeps a watch on the stars, including 9,100 of a simulated variety, which appear daily on the planetarium's 70-foot domed ceiling. Peer through massive telescopes, admire a moon rock, sit in a replica of the Mercury space capsule, or ponder the Milky Way while you nosh at the Celestial Cafe. Visit www.chabotspace.org for more information. Hours are 10 A.M.–5 P.M. Wednesday–Thursday, 10 A.M.–10 P.M. Friday–Saturday, and 10 A.M.–5 P.M. Sunday.

Driving Directions

From I-580 in Oakland, take the 35th Avenue exit and turn north. Drive 2.4 miles

(35th Avenue will become Redwood Road). Turn left on Skyline Boulevard and drive 3.7 miles to the Skyline Gate Staging Area, located at the intersection of Skyline and Pine Hills Drive. (Skyline Boulevard makes a sharp right turn after the first 0.5 mile.)

Route Directions

0.0 Park at Skyline Gate Staging Area and take East Ridge Trail, the northernmost of three possible trails. *Water is available at the trailhead.*

2.9 RIGHT on Canyon Trail.

3.3 RIGHT on Stream Trail at Canyon Meadow Staging Area.

3.6 STRAIGHT at junction with Bridle Trail; you'll return to this intersection shortly.

4.2 End of bikes-allowed section of Stream Trail. TURN AROUND. *Stop at one of five picnic areas under the redwoods. Water is available.*

4.8 RIGHT on Bridle Trail upon return to previous junction.

5.0 RIGHT on West Ridge Trail; begin ascent to ridge.

6.3 RIGHT to stay on West Ridge Trail.

7.7 Chabot Space and Science Center.

9.4 Arrive at starting point.

31 WALL POINT AND BARBEQUE TERRACE LOOP

Mount Diablo State Park near Danville

DIRT ROADS

Difficulty: 3	**Total Distance:** 9.4 miles
Riding Time: 2 hours	**Elevation Gain:** 1,600 feet

Summary: This challenging dirt loop on the Devil's Mountain, 3,849-foot Mount Diablo includes a visit to *Flintstones*-inspired Rock City.

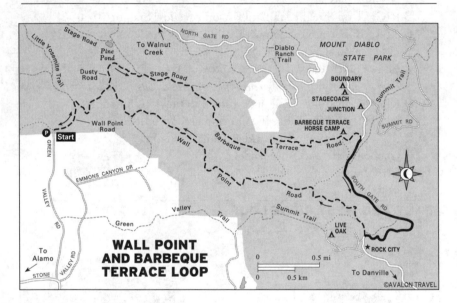

Ride the Devil. That's the attitude of most mountain bikers who come to pedal on "devilish" Mount Diablo. The great 3,849-foot peak is a butt-kicker for casual riders, due to steep and rugged fire roads, occasional stretches of single-track that require advanced technical skills, and the brutally hot temperatures that occur on these slopes during 4–5 months of the year. That said, the Wall Point and Barbeque Terrace Loop is one of the more manageable rides on the mountain, although it certainly has its share of ups and downs.

The trip starts at the Macedo Ranch trailhead and begins with a moderate climb up Wall Point Road. This is followed by a rocky descent into Pine Canyon, which may present some technical challenges to the less experienced. This downhill is known as "the staircase" because of its layers of exposed rock. Pine Canyon is especially lovely in winter when its stream flows, but the wet season also

A tough climb on Barbeque Terrace Road leads to a rewarding view looking out over Pine Canyon.

necessitates a few creek crossings. After a series of heavy storms, Pine Canyon can even become impassable. Call the park to check on trail conditions if you are visiting in the winter or early spring.

A tough climb ensues on Barbeque Terrace Road out of Pine Canyon, in which you must gain 900 feet in little more than a mile, often on a loose, pebbly surface. After that difficult ascent, which leaves many riders walking their bikes and weeping in the Diablo dust, the trail ends at Barbeque Terrace Group Campground. Admire the view from the trail gate and congratulate yourself for having made it up this hellacious hill. Then ride up the paved camp access road to South Gate Road for a fast downhill on pavement to Rock City. (A short single-track option is also possible here.)

Lock up your bike and take a brief walk at Rock City. Set among clusters of tall manzanita, foothill pines, madrones, and live oaks, Rock City is a jumble of eroded sandstone outcroppings that was formed 40 or 50 million years ago during the Eocene period, when Mount Diablo was buried under a great sea. Eventually the waters receded and the remaining sand hardened into a ridge of rocks. This rocky ridge has been weathered and eroded by centuries of wind and rain, creating odd-shaped boulders with small caves and Swiss cheese–style holes. They're fun to look at and climb around on.

After exploring the rocks, loop back to Macedo Ranch on Wall Point Road, a wide fire road that runs along a rocky ridgeline. As you pedal west, you'll have lovely views of Rock City and two concrete cities—Danville and Walnut Creek—to the west. You'll face a moderate climb for the first 1.6 miles, then it's downhill all the way back to the parking lot.

For more information, contact Mount Diablo State Park, 925/837-2525 or 925/837-0904, www.mdia.org or www.parks.ca.gov.

Driving Directions

From I-680 at Danville, take the Diablo Road exit and head east. Follow Diablo Road for 1.4 miles (turn right at 0.7 mile to stay on Diablo Road), then turn left at Green Valley Road. Drive 2 miles to the end of Green Valley Road and the Macedo Ranch trailhead.

Route Directions

0.0 Park at Macedo Ranch and start riding on the fire road by the signboard and water trough. This is Wall Point Road, but it is signed as Macedo Ranch to Summit Trail. *Supplies are available in Danville.*

0.3 RIGHT to stay on Wall Point Road.

0.9 LEFT on Dusty Road/Pine Canyon Trail (Wall Point Road goes right).

1.4 RIGHT on Stage Road.

1.8 RIGHT on Barbeque Terrace Road.

2.6 Tough climb begins.

3.7 Barbecue Terrace Group Campground; follow paved camp road uphill to paved South Gate Road. *Water is available at the group camp.*

4.0 RIGHT on South Gate Road. *If you prefer to ride on dirt, you can pick up single-track Summit Trail 0.2 mile down South Gate Road on the right, signed as Multi-Purpose Trail.*

5.7 RIGHT at Rock City/Live Oak parking lot. *Lock up your bike and explore the fascinating rocks.* TURN AROUND. Ride 50 yards uphill (backtracking) on South Gate Road to the start of Wall Point Road (across from the private residence and service area).

5.8 LEFT on Wall Point Road. *Water is available at the service area across from the start of Wall Point Road.*

8.3 RIGHT to stay on Wall Point Road.

8.5 LEFT to stay on Wall Point Road.

9.4 Arrive at starting point.

WALL POINT AND BARBEQUE TERRACE LOOP

32 MITCHELL AND DONNER CANYONS LOOP
Mount Diablo State Park near Clayton

DIRT ROADS AND SINGLE-TRACK

Difficulty: 4   **Total Distance:** 13.1 miles (or 8.6-mile option)

Riding Time: 2.5 hours   **Elevation Gain:** 2,900 feet

Summary: Tricky single-track, challenging climbs, and a variety of close-up and far-off scenery await riders on the back side of Mount Diablo.

This ride on the "back" (north) side of Mount Diablo isn't particularly long, but it is quite strenuous. Still, the rewards are great: The loop passes by some of the most diverse habitats that the old Devil's Mountain has to offer, including gangly Coulter and foothill pines with their heavyweight cones, a wide range of chaparral plants (sage, toyon, manzanita, yerba santa, and more) and lush streamside vegetation. Plus, with the completion of every gut-thumping ascent on this route, you are rewarded with wide views of the surrounding area.

Mitchell Canyon Fire Road starts out deceptively easy, with a gentle climb along Mitchell Creek. But just past the two-mile mark, things start to get ugly—I mean, challenging. Over the next stretch to Deer Flat, you'll gain 1,200 feet, much of it with average grades that reach into the mid-teens and almost no shade from the ruthless sun. If you are crying uncle by the time you reach Deer Flat, check out the *Options* section. Meanwhile, the intrepid rider will continue on a 1,000-foot

Make sure you choose a cool day for riding the shadeless stretches of the Mitchell and Donner Canyons Loop.

climb to Juniper Campground and the paved Summit Road, then climb some more, this time on blessedly smooth pavement, to a 3,400-foot-high point called the Devils Elbow.

Here, single-track lovers will be thrilled by North Peak Trail's one mile of technically tricky stuff, which throws plenty of rocks and tree roots in your path as it makes a speedy descent to a saddle at Prospectors Gap. This is a good place to repeat to yourself the Smart Mountain Biker's Mantra: "Caution is the better part of valor." It is also a good place to slow down and enjoy the views, which extend southwest to the windmills in Livermore and east to the Central Valley. You'll pass directly below the large rock outcrop called Devils Pulpit on Mount Diablo's summit.

At the saddle at Prospectors Gap, you'll follow yet another fire road very steeply downhill until you meet up with Meridian Ridge Road and then Meridian Point, an overlook with a wide view of Clayton and a glimpse at Suisun Bay to the northwest. Then it's onward to Donner Canyon Road, Murchio Road, and back to the trailhead at Mitchell Canyon.

For more information, contact Mount Diablo State Park, 925/837-2525 or 925/837-0904, www.mdia.org or www.parks.ca.gov.

Options

If you've had enough when you reach oak-shaded Deer Flat, you can always bail out and head back on Meridian Ridge Road, making an 8.6-mile loop with only a 0.5-mile additional ascent. By choosing this option, you can add a thrilling short hike to your day. Lock up your bike near Murchio Gap on Meridian Ridge Road and walk out and back on the Eagle Peak Trail to Eagle Peak, elevation 2,369 feet. The 0.8-mile-long trail leads along the narrow backbone of Bald Ridge, with steep drop-offs on both sides. From Eagle Peak's rocky summit, you'll gain wide vistas of Mount Diablo's North Peak, the Sacramento and San Joaquin Delta, Honker Bay, and Suisun Bay. Although you opted for the shorter bike ride, after visiting this impressive summit you can call yourself a real mountaineer.

Driving Directions

From I-680 heading north in Walnut Creek, take the Ygnacio Valley Road exit. Drive east on Ygnacio Valley Road for 7.5 miles to Clayton Road. Turn right (south) on Clayton Road and drive 1.5 miles to Mitchell Canyon Road. Turn right and drive to the end of the road and the trailhead.

Route Directions

0.0 Park at the Mitchell Canyon trailhead and begin riding on Mitchell Canyon Fire Road. *Supplies are available in Clayton.*

2.0 Begin serious climb.

3.8 RIGHT on Deer Flat Road at Deer Flat (three-way junction).

4.9 LEFT to stay on Deer Flat Road at junction with Burma Road.

5.4 Juniper Campground; follow the paved camp road out to Summit Road. *Water is available at Juniper Campground.*

5.6 LEFT on paved Summit Road.

7.1 RIGHT on North Peak Trail (single-track) at hairpin turn in road (Devils Elbow).

8.1 LEFT on Prospectors Gap Road.

9.4 RIGHT on Meridian Ridge Road.

10.8 LEFT on Donner Canyon Road at junction with Cardinet Oaks Road.

12.1 LEFT on Murchio Road; stay straight at next three junctions.

13.1 Arrive at starting point.

33 MOUNT DIABLO SUMMIT RIDE   BEST ☾
Blackhawk to Mount Diablo summit

PAVED ROADS WITH MODERATE CAR TRAFFIC

Difficulty: 4 | **Total Distance:** 29.6 miles

Riding Time: 4-5 hours | **Elevation Gain:** 3,200 feet

Summary: Pick a clear day – preferably the day after a winter storm – for a ride up Mount Diablo to its rewarding panoramic summit view.

Almost everybody thinks about making the trip to 3,849-foot Mount Diablo from time to time. After all, you see it from just about everywhere in the Bay Area. It's not the tallest mountain around San Francisco Bay (Mount Hamilton near San Jose is 360 feet taller; see ride 57, *Mount Hamilton*), but it has a way of making its presence known, looming in the background of the lives of millions of East Bay residents.

Although most people travel to the summit of Mount Diablo by car, a better way to get there is by bike. Sure, the ride is a long grind with a nearly nonstop elevation gain, but this is what you live for, right? You haven't really experienced Diablo's Summit Road until you've ridden it on a bike. With every curve in the winding pavement, the views are constantly changing.

Two roads—North Gate and South Gate—travel most of the way up the mountain; they join at Junction Ranger Station for the final 4.5 miles on Summit Road to the top. This ride follows South Gate Road from Blackhawk, elevation 738 feet; it's the easier of the two roads. Okay, full disclosure: It's only slightly easier. But when you take in the remarkable view from Diablo's summit, it's all worth it. On the clearest days, it's easy to spot the Farallon Islands, Lick Observatory on Mount Hamilton, Mount St. Helena in Calistoga, and even Mount Lassen to the north and the Sierra Nevada to the east. Bar none, it's the best view from any single spot in the East Bay.

Pick a cool day (forget summer on this shadeless "devil's mountain") and be encouraged by the fact that water and rest stops are plentiful all the way up the mountain (most roadside picnic areas and campgrounds have water).

The vistas change with every curve in the winding pavement that leads to the summit of Mount Diablo.

For more information, contact Mount Diablo State Park, 925/837-2525 or 925/837-0904, www.mdia.org or www.parks.ca.gov.

Options

If you want to shorten this ride, just drive your car farther up the mountain road and start from one of the parking areas within the state park, such as Curry Point or Rock City. And when you get to the summit of Mount Diablo, be sure to stop in at the Summit Museum (open 10 A.M.–4 P.M. daily, 925/837-6119, www.mdia.org/museum), a historic stone building that was built in the 1930s from sandstone blocks quarried in the park. The museum features permanent exhibits on the mountain's geology, natural history, and Native American history, as well as rotating art exhibits and an observation deck with telescopes.

Driving Directions

From the junction of I-680 and I-580 in Dublin, drive north on I-680 for five miles to the Crow Canyon Road exit. Drive east for four miles; Crow Canyon Road becomes Blackhawk Road at its junction with Tassajara Road. Park at or near the Blackhawk Plaza shopping center.

Route Directions

0.0 Park at or near Blackhawk Plaza shopping center and ride east on

Blackhawk Road, then pick up the bike/walking path alongside the road. *Supplies are available at the shopping center.*

3.4 RIGHT on Mount Diablo Scenic Boulevard.

4.5 Mount Diablo State Park gate.

7.1 Entrance kiosk; road changes names to South Gate Road.

7.6 Rock City region of the park.

8.2 Rock City parking area (good alternate starting point).

8.8 Curry Point parking area.

10.3 RIGHT on Summit Road at Junction Ranger Station.

12.8 Juniper Campground.

14.8 Mount Diablo summit and Summit Museum. TURN AROUND.

29.6 Arrive at starting point.

MOUNT DIABLO SUMMIT RIDE

34 ROUND VALLEY RAMBLE
Round Valley Regional Preserve near Clayton

DIRT ROAD

Difficulty: 1

Total Distance: 10.8 miles (or longer options)

Riding Time: 1.5 hours

Elevation Gain: 600 feet

Summary: A gentle ride through the Clayton countryside, this route is ideal for a spring day when the grasses are green and the wildflowers are blooming.

If you ever start to feel like the East Bay is too crowded, too congested, and has too much concrete, take a trip a little farther east to the northeast side of Mount Diablo. Here on the far eastern edge of the San Francisco Bay Area are wide-open spaces, spring wildflowers, and stately oak trees.

You'll find all this and more at Round Valley Regional Preserve, the 2,000-acre home of nesting golden eagles, burrowing owls, chubby ground squirrels, and the endangered San Joaquin kit fox. The bike riding here is mellow and easy, unless of course you show up at midday in August, when it can be more than 100 degrees.

From the preserve staging area, the trail starts out with a long bridge over Marsh Creek. At the far side of the bridge, a right turn puts you on Miwok Trail. Immediately you face the only real hill of the day; the remaining miles of this ride are mostly level.

The pastoral landscape of Round Valley makes for a pleasant ride and a chance for solitude.

In 0.5 mile, the wide dirt road meets up with Round Valley Creek. If you've timed your trip for the wet season, the stream will run cool and clear alongside you for much of your ride. You'll notice the remains of old farming equipment along the dirt trail; this land was farmed by the Murphy family from 1873 until 1988, when it was donated to the East Bay Regional Park District.

Stay on Miwok Trail through the entire length of the preserve, then turn right on Murphy's Meadow Trail. You'll loop back on the far side of Round Valley Creek. At a junction with Fox Tail Trail, follow Fox Tail uphill for a short out-and-back excursion. Head for the top of the hill, where you'll find a wide view of rolling hills and vast, unpopulated parkland. What a fine spot for a picnic lunch. When you've finished your meal, just turn around and retrace your tire treads back to your car.

Free maps available from the East Bay Regional Park District (510/562-7275 or 510/635-0135, www.ebparks.org) can get you where you want to go.

Options

Riders looking for more mileage can follow Miwok Trail out of the park, through a 1.6-mile stretch of Los Vaqueros Watershed, and into the east side of Morgan Territory Regional Preserve, where most trails are open to mountain bikes (see ride 35, *Volvon and Valley View Loop*).

Driving Directions

From I-580 in Livermore, take the Vasco Road exit and drive north 13 miles. Turn left (west) on Camino Diablo Road and drive 3.5 miles. Where Camino Diablo ends, continue straight on Marsh Creek Road for 1.5 miles to the Round Valley parking area on the left.

Route Directions

0.0 Park at Round Valley Staging Area and ride across the bridge. *Supplies are available in Clayton, eight miles west.*

0.1 RIGHT on Miwok Trail at far side of bridge.

0.5 STRAIGHT at junction with trail on right.

2.8 RIGHT on Murphy's Meadow Trail. *Miwok Trail leaves the park here and travels through the Los Vaqueros Watershed and into Morgan Territory Regional Preserve, for more riding options.*

3.7 RIGHT to stay on Murphy's Meadow Trail.

4.6 LEFT on Fox Tail Trail.

5.4 End of Fox Tail Trail. TURN AROUND.

10.8 Arrive at starting point.

35 VOLVON AND VALLEY VIEW LOOP
Morgan Territory Regional Preserve near Livermore

DIRT ROAD

Difficulty: 3   **Total Distance:** 8.4 miles

Riding Time: 2 hours   **Elevation Gain:** 1,200 feet

Summary: The Old West is still alive at this preserve on the far eastern edge of the East Bay, where cattle and horses roam among grasslands and oaks.

Morgan Territory—even this park's name sounds wild, like a holdover from the Old West. If you're wondering if anything wild might still exist in Contra Costa County, wonder no more. Come to Morgan Territory and rediscover the wild East Bay.

The drive to the trailhead is a trip in itself. You'll follow narrow, winding Morgan Territory Road north of Livermore to the preserve's main trailhead. Try not to get so wowed by the views that you drive right off the curvy, narrow road.

At the trailhead parking lot, you've climbed to 1,900 feet in elevation. (Okay, so your car has done the work.) Hopefully you've planned your visit for the cooler months of the year, because the open hills around Livermore bake in the summer. If you're riding in the warm season, make sure it is *very* early in the morning. Pick up a free trail map at the trailhead (the preserve has an overabundance of trail junctions) and follow Volvon Trail uphill and through a cattle gate.

© ANN MARIE BROWN

Morgan Territory's rolling hills are punctuated by magnificent oak trees and colorful spring wildflowers.

Successive trails—Volvon, Blue Oak, and Valley View—carry you up and down Morgan Territory's scenic, rolling hills, which are punctuated by magnificent oak trees and colorful lichen-coated rocks. In the spring, more than 90 wildflower species blossom along these grassy hillsides. Views to the west of Mount Diablo are fine, but what is most surprising is Valley View Trail's eastern perspective on the San Joaquin Valley. On the clearest days of winter, the snowcapped High Sierra can be seen, more than 100 miles away.

The route described makes a dogleg from Valley View to cruise a section of 1,700-foot Highland Ridge, where more views are yours for the taking. The final stretch of the route is a long, mostly level cruise back to the trailhead on Volvon Trail. Overall, the riding is generally easy here, with wide trails and few technical challenges except for the ruts and holes caused by the trampling feet of cattle. You'll probably see a few groups of cud-chewing bovines somewhere along the path. They usually flee from mountain bikers, or stop in mid-chew to stare at you.

For more information, contact East Bay Regional Park District, 510/635-0135 or 510/562-7275, www.ebparks.org.

Driving Directions

From I-580 in Livermore, take the North Livermore Avenue exit and turn north. Drive north for 4 miles, then turn right on Morgan Territory Road. Drive 5.6 miles to the entrance to Morgan Territory Preserve on the right. (The road is narrow and steep.)

Route Directions

0.0 Park at Morgan Territory Preserve trailhead. Start riding on the main, wide trail (Volvon Trail). *Supplies are available in Livermore; stock up before you drive out Morgan Territory Road.*

0.3 LEFT, then immediately RIGHT on Blue Oak Trail.

1.7 STRAIGHT on Volvon Trail.

1.8 RIGHT on Valley View Trail.

3.0 RIGHT on Volvon Loop Trail.

3.7 RIGHT on Eagle Trail.

4.1 LEFT on Highland Ridge Trail.

5.0 LEFT on Stone Corral Trail just before Highland Ridge Trail meets paved road.

6.1 RIGHT on Volvon Trail; stay on Volvon Trail at the next several junctions.

8.0 RIGHT, then immediately RIGHT again to stay on Volvon Trail.

8.4 Arrive at starting point.

VOLVON AND VALLEY VIEW LOOP

36 LAKE CHABOT LOOP

Lake Chabot and Anthony Chabot Regional Parks, east of San Leandro

DIRT ROAD AND PAVED BIKE PATH

Difficulty: 3   **Total Distance:** 13.3 miles (or 9-mile option)

Riding Time: 2 hours   **Elevation Gain:** 1,200 feet

Summary: This is a great training ride for East Bay mountain bikers looking to sharpen their skills, and an easy paved route around the lakeshore for families and those on skinny tires.

Lakeside trails are often level and somewhat predictable, but the trails around Lake Chabot never stop turning, twisting, climbing, and diving. You're either braking hard or pedaling hard the whole way. Still, with only 1,200 feet of elevation gain, the Lake Chabot Loop is suitable for all kinds of riders. The challenge of a few hills is compensated by the sheer fun of the ride. This is a good place to gain some experience on a mountain bike.

You will have to put up with some irritating signs of civilization, though. In addition to the lake's busy marina and campground, you'll ride near a golf course and a shooting range. And if this is your first time here, you must pay careful attention to trail junctions. There are a ton of them. Too many, you may surmise.

An advantage to the prolific junctions is that Lake Chabot's trails can be customized according to your desires and abilities. The route described here combines the

The popular bike trail around Lake Chabot is a mix of paved, fire, and single-track roads.

paved West and East Shore Trails with several dirt fire roads for a 13.3-mile round-trip. The two paved trails are surprisingly scenic; they skirt the lake's edge, sometimes rising up along its steep walls, sometimes tracing a line just a few feet from the water.

Following the loop below, East Shore Trail's pavement ends 1.8 miles beyond the marina. Mountain bikers continue onward, walking their bikes over a bridge to connect with Honker Bay Trail (some use Live Oak Trail to make their loop; I prefer Honker Bay because it stays along the lakeshore). Take a trail map with you (they're available for free at the trailhead) to negotiate the long stretch of Brandon Trail; it intersects annoyingly with what seems like a million other trails. Still, it offers some wide views of San Francisco Bay.

For more information, contact East Bay Regional Park District, 510/635-0135 or 510/562-7275, www.ebparks.org.

Options

Families with young children and skinny-tire riders will want to stick to the paved East and West Shore Trails for a nine-mile out-and-back. If you want to turn your bike ride into a day at the lake, Lake Chabot Marina (510/247-2526) has boats for rent, plus a small café that sells hot dogs and coffee. Lake Chabot is stocked with trout, bass, and catfish, and fishing prospects are quite good.

Driving Directions

From Oakland, drive east on I-580 and take the Dutton/Estudillo Avenue exit in San Leandro. Drive 0.5 mile, then turn left on Estudillo Avenue and drive 0.4 mile. Bear right at the Y with Lake Chabot Road and drive 2.5 miles to a T-junction. Turn left, then left again into Lake Chabot Marina.

Route Directions

0.0 Park at Lake Chabot Marina and head for the east side of the picnic area to the start of East Shore Trail. *Supplies are available at the marina store and café. A trail map is posted on a signboard next to the marina café.*

1.8 LEFT across narrow bridge at end of paved East Shore Trail; walk your bike.

1.9 LEFT on Honker Bay Trail.

3.5 Join paved campground road; ride through family campground on main road.

4.0 RIGHT on Towhee Trail.

4.8 LEFT on Brandon Trail (easy to miss—watch for it!).

4.9 Parking lot and restrooms; cross road and pick up Brandon Trail on other side.

5.5 LEFT on Logger's Loop Trail (or RIGHT to stay on Brandon Trail and save 0.9 mile).

6.6 Back on Brandon Trail.

8.4 LEFT and across stone bridge to LEFT on Jackson Grade to Goldenrod Trail.

8.8 Grass Valley Staging Area; stay on Goldenrod Trail.

10.2 RIGHT on Bass Cove Trail.

11.5 LEFT on paved West Shore Trail.

13.3 Arrive at starting point.

37 PALOMARES ROAD
east of Hayward and Fremont

PAVED ROAD WITH MINIMAL CAR TRAFFIC

Difficulty: 3   **Total Distance:** 20.2 miles

Riding Time: 1-2 hours   **Elevation Gain:** 1,900 feet

Summary: A fun training ride takes you on a winding road in the Sunol countryside, with the chance to stop for wine-tasting on weekends.

For a short stint in my life, I had the pleasure of living in the peaceful Sunol countryside, where on Sunday mornings I would awaken to the sounds of birds chirping and my roommate yelling, "Get up! Let's go ride Palomares Road."

And so we did, along with dozens of other East Bay cyclists, almost every Sunday, rain or shine. It was a happy habit that put some country into our urban lives.

The good news is that Palomares Road is still a peaceful country road, despite the fact that it's bordered by busy highways on both ends. The road is perfect for a quick 20-mile training ride after work or on the weekends. It's remote enough that it feels like a getaway even though it's remarkably close to home for riders in the southeast Bay Area.

Some cyclists make a loop out of Palomares Road by riding Dublin Canyon Road to the north and Niles Canyon Road (Highway 84) to the south, then using Foothill Road as the east connector. I don't recommend it. These three roads were viable for cyclists a decade or so ago, but are now heavily trafficked almost 24 hours a day. Besides, who wants to ride on a freeway frontage road after spinning though Palomares Road's lovely forested scenery?

Palomares Road ascends from both ends; the high point is almost exactly in the middle. That means you get an invigorating climb and a fun descent in both directions. In between, you have many rolling curves and a chance to ride as fast as 40 mph on the downhills, if you so choose.

© ANN MARIE BROWN

Palomares Road is a peaceful country lane bordered by busy highways on both ends.

Options

If you're more into savoring your rides than speeding through them, note that two wineries are open on Palomares Road: Chouinard Winery (510/582-9900, www.chouinard.com) and Westover Vineyards (510/537-3932, www.westoverwinery.com). Both offer drop-in wine-tasting on weekends noon–5 P.M.

Driving Directions

From Hayward, drive four miles east on I-580 and take the Eden Canyon Road/Palomares Road exit. Turn left, cross under the freeway, and park on the north side of the freeway in the dirt pullout (start of Eden Canyon Road).

Route Directions

0.0 Park in the dirt pullout at the start of Eden Canyon Road, by the I-580 freeway overpass. Ride under the overpass and cross Dublin Canyon Road to access Palo Verde Road. *Supplies are available in Hayward or Dublin.*

0.4 LEFT on Palomares Road.

5.4 Summit of Palomares Road.

6.3 Chouinard Winery.

6.6 Westover Vineyards.

10.1 End of Palomares Road at Highway 84. TURN AROUND.

20.2 Arrive at starting point.

PALOMARES ROAD

38 MORGAN TERRITORY ROAD
Livermore to Clayton

PAVED ROADS WITH MINIMAL CAR TRAFFIC

Difficulty: 4

Total Distance: 46.4 miles

Riding Time: 3-4 hours

Elevation Gain: 3,500 feet

Summary: If the hustle and bustle of the East Bay has started to wear you down, you need a ride on bucolic Morgan Territory Road.

One of the finest roads in the East Bay crosses through the Black Hills north of Livermore and passes by the eastern flank of mighty Mount Diablo and neighboring North Peak. Morgan Territory Road, as it is known, leaves the shopping centers and I-580 freeway traffic far behind as it carves a narrow path through hillside grasslands and scenic oak woodlands.

As an out-and-back ride, this route from Livermore to Clayton has a good hill climb in both directions, so a stop in Clayton for lunch is recommended, and also perhaps a rest stop near the road's summit at elevation 2,100 feet, near Morgan Territory Regional Preserve. (If traffic is heavy, you may want to ride this route in the opposite direction; see *Options*.) Your main concern is the weather—this kind of climbing in these sunny, exposed hills should be reserved for the cooler days of fall,

© ANN MARIE BROWN

Morgan Territory Road

winter, and spring. Another concern is the narrowness of Morgan Territory Road; one car and one bike makes a crowd. Fortunately cars are few and far between.

Although it seems sensible to make a loop out of this ride by returning from Clayton to Livermore on Marsh Creek Road and Vasco Road, a five-mile stretch of Vasco Road has been widened in recent years, making it as fast and hectic as a freeway. Intrepid riders may still want to make this loop, but be forewarned of the long hill climb on Vasco Road with cars peeling by you at 70 mph. Although the road's shoulder is wide, riding it is just plain stressful. An out-and-back on Morgan Territory Road is safer, more scenic, and far more relaxing.

For more information on Morgan Territory Regional Preserve, contact East Bay Regional Park District, 510/635-0135 or 510/562-7275, www.ebparks.org.

Options

Note that depending on what day of the week and what hour of the day you ride, you could face a daunting amount of car traffic on Marsh Creek Road. If that's the case, it's best to do this ride in reverse, so you are heading east and downhill on Marsh Creek Road and can keep pace with the cars. There is very little shoulder on this stretch, so you'll need to be in the car lane, and you'll need to ride fast.

Driving Directions

From Livermore on I-580, take the North Livermore Avenue exit and park at the shopping center just south of I-580 on North Livermore Avenue.

Route Directions

0.0 Park at the shopping center just south of I-580 on North Livermore Avenue and ride north, crossing under the freeway. Set your odometer on the north side of I-580. *Supplies are available in Livermore.*

3.5 LEFT on Manning Road.

4.0 RIGHT on Morgan Territory Road.

4.7 Road narrows to single lane.

9.5 Entrance to Morgan Territory Regional Preserve on right. *Water is available.*

15.0 Road widens to two lanes.

18.7 LEFT on Marsh Creek Road.

22.7 LEFT on Marsh Creek Road (also called Clayton Road in Clayton).

23.2 Arrive in Clayton historic district. TURN AROUND. *Supplies are available in Clayton.*

46.2 Arrive at starting point.

39 LIVERMORE WINERY RIDE
Livermore

PAVED ROADS WITH MODERATE CAR TRAFFIC

Difficulty: 2　　　　　**Total Distance:** 19.5 miles (or 24.5-mile option)

Riding Time: 2 hours　　　　　**Elevation Gain:** 800 feet

Summary: Nearly a dozen wineries await cyclists who choose to ramble through the Livermore countryside.

The town of Livermore, well known for being the home of Lawrence Livermore Laboratories and a huge collection of windmills, was founded in 1869 as a farming community. Cattle and sheep ranching and hay and grain production made the fertile area prosperous for more than a century. Even today the annual June rodeo is still the biggest show in town, although Livermore's agricultural legacy has largely shifted to vineyards and wine production. All the better for cyclists, who can ride this easy tour of rolling hills and stop to taste the products of nearly a dozen wineries.

While planning your ride, remember two things: First, if you want to do much wine-tasting, ride on Saturday or Sunday, because many smaller wineries are not open on weekdays. Second, consider the weather in Livermore. Pick a cool day and bring along a picnic for the ride's finale, when you return to shady Sycamore Grove Park (925/373-5770).

The route directions show only the mileage along the main roads from winery to winery. Each time you choose to stop at one of the wineries, your mileage will increase as you ride up and down its driveway. I'm assuming you won't stop to taste at every winery mentioned (if you did, your bike-handling skills would be severely compromised), so adjust your mileage according to your chosen stops. And if you want to shorten the ride, skip the out-and-back to Wente Vineyards on Arroyo Road (at 0.7 mile) and save 3.5 miles. Just go left on Arroyo Road instead.

If you can arrange it, try to get tickets in advance for one of the outdoor summer concerts at Wente Vineyards (5050 Arroyo Rd., 925/456-2300, www.wentevineyards.com). You can ride all afternoon, have dinner at a restaurant in town, and go to a show in the evening. Concerts are held June–September each year and feature well-known acts like Lyle Lovett and Chris Isaak.

Have fun. And don't forget to drink some water with that wine.

Options

If you feel like riding a bit more, Sycamore Grove Park has a 2.5-mile paved bike path through its grasslands and groves of sycamores. An out-and-back will add an easy, pleasant 5 miles to your day.

Driving Directions

From I-580 in Livermore, take the North Livermore Avenue exit and turn south. Drive 1 mile through downtown Livermore. Turn right on Stanley Boulevard (Highway 84), then left on Holmes Street. Follow Holmes Street for about 2 miles, then turn left on East Vallecitos Road (signed for the Veterans Hospital), which becomes Wetmore Road. Turn right into Sycamore Grove Park in 0.3 mile.

Route Directions

0.0 Park at Sycamore Grove Park, then ride out to Wetmore Road and turn RIGHT. *Supplies are available in Livermore and at several wineries along the route.*

0.3 Livermore Valley Cellars.

0.7 RIGHT on Arroyo Road.

2.5 Wente Vineyards, Golf Course, Restaurant, and Visitor Center. TURN AROUND.

4.2 STRAIGHT at junction of Wetmore and Arroyo Roads.

5.0 RIGHT on Marina Avenue. Watch for speed "humps" (not bumps!).

6.0 LEFT on Wente Street.

6.5 RIGHT on Concannon Boulevard.

6.9 RIGHT on South Livermore Avenue, which becomes Tesla Road.

7.6 Concannon Vineyard.

7.9 RIGHT on Mines Road.

8.2 Murrieta's Well Winery. TURN AROUND.

8.5 RIGHT on Tesla Road.

8.8 Steven Kent Winery.

8.9 Wente Estate Vineyards (different from Wente Vineyards).

9.6 Rios-Lovell Winery.

10.1 Cedar Mountain Winery.

10.5 Garre Vineyard and Café.

10.6 RIGHT on Greenville Road.

11.1 Poppy Ridge Golf Course.

11.6 Bent Creek Winery.

11.7 White Crane Vineyards. TURN AROUND.

13.0 LEFT on Tesla Road.

16.1 LEFT on Concannon Boulevard.

16.5 LEFT on Wente Street.

17.0 RIGHT on Marina Avenue.

18.0 LEFT on Arroyo Road.

18.8 RIGHT on Wetmore Road.

19.5 Arrive at starting point.

40 ALAMEDA CREEK TRAIL
Fremont to Coyote Hills Regional Park

PAVED BIKE PATH

Difficulty: 1   **Total Distance:** 24 miles (or longer options)

Riding Time: 2 hours   **Elevation Gain:** 200 feet

Summary: Enjoy miles of car-free riding on a paved trail that parallels Alameda Creek from Fremont to the shores of San Francisco Bay.

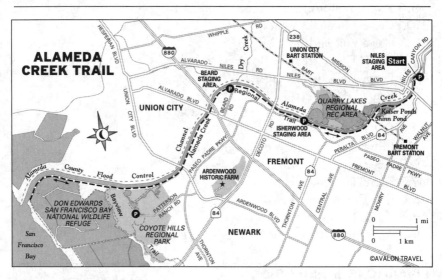

Alameda Creek, the largest stream in Alameda County, was once a valuable resource to the Ohlone Indians who settled along its banks. Today Alameda Creek Trail follows the creek from the mouth of Niles Canyon in Fremont 12 miles west to San Francisco Bay.

The trail is actually two parallel trails on the south and north banks of the creek. The south-side trail (paved) is for bikers, hikers, and runners, and the north side (unpaved) is for equestrians, too. The south-side trail, described here, accesses Coyote Hills Regional Park, where more riding is available.

Everything is in place here to make your ride easy. Unlike some trails in the East Bay's impressive system of paved recreation paths, the Alameda Creek Trail is unique in that it is uninterrupted by street intersections, so you have 12 miles of worry-free riding in both directions. Mileage markers are installed along the trail, and water and restrooms are available at several points. Even when the afternoon westerly wind comes up from the bay, it will be at your back for the slightly uphill ride home (provided you got an early start, of course).

© ANN MARIE BROWN

Don't forget your binoculars for birdwatching when you ride on the Alameda Creek Trail to Coyote Hills Regional Park.

Alameda Creek Trail passes under highway overpasses and alongside neighborhood backyards, so it isn't exactly a nature trail, although you will probably spot a variety of birds along the narrow-channeled creek. Snowy egrets are often seen in abundance.

For more information, contact East Bay Regional Park District, 510/635-0135 or 510/562-7275, www.ebparks.org.

Options

If you're clamoring for something more, well, natural, add on a ride in Coyote Hills Regional Park, a bayside park with lots of wildlife and fascinating Native American history. Skinny-tire riders are restricted to adding 3.5 paved miles on the park's Bayview Trail, but mountain bikers can pedal around on the numerous dirt trails that roll up and down Coyote's rounded hills. Those who enjoy steep ups and fast downs should not miss the Red Hill Trail in particular. Another great option is to connect from the Alameda Creek Trail to Quarry Lakes Park (at Isherwood Way, the Sequoia Bridge, or the Niles Gate). This lovely park has its own small network of biking trails as well as fishing and swimming opportunities at Horseshoe Lake and Rainbow Lake.

Driving Directions

From I-680 in Fremont, take the Mission Boulevard exit and drive northwest for four miles to Highway 84/Niles Canyon Road. Turn right, then right again on Old Canyon Road. The staging area is on the left.

Route Directions

0.0 Park at Niles Staging Area and follow the trail out of the parking lot. *Water and restrooms are available at the staging area and along the trail.*

1.4 Pass Kaiser and Shinn Ponds.

2.6 Bridge at end of Thornton Avenue.

3.5 Isherwood Staging Area.

4.3 Decoto Road.

5.4 End of Beard Road; Beard Staging Area.

6.1 I-880.

6.4 Alvarado Boulevard.

7.8 Newark Boulevard.

9.7 Sign at base of hill leading to Coyote Hills Regional Park.

12.0 Edge of San Francisco Bay. TURN AROUND. *Or take the 50-foot connector trail from Alameda Creek Trail to the paved Bayview Trail in Coyote Hills Regional Park, adding on a 3.5-mile paved loop. Mountain bikers can add on several miles of dirt riding in the park.*

24.0 Arrive at starting point.

41 SWEENEY RIDGE LOOP

Golden Gate National Recreation Area near Pacifica

DIRT ROAD AND PAVED ROADS WITH MODERATE CAR TRAFFIC

Difficulty: 3   **Total Distance:** 7.3 miles

Riding Time: 2 hours   **Elevation Gain:** 1,100 feet

Summary: This mostly dirt loop delivers sweeping ocean views – on rare clear days – and the chance to visit the San Francisco Bay Discovery Site.

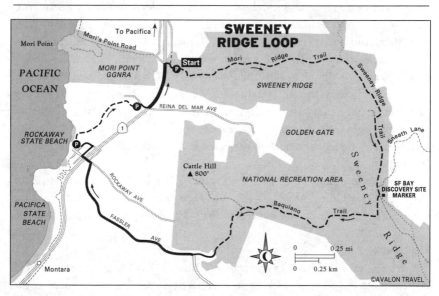

It's steep, it's fast, and it's well loved by Pacifica locals. The Sweeney Ridge Loop is the perfect length for a good bout of exercise, and it can be completed in a couple of hours. Better still, on clear days it offers one of the best views in the Bay Area, an incredible 360-degree panorama from the top of Sweeney Ridge. This vista takes in the Pacific coastline and San Francisco Bay as well as the landmass to the east, north, and south—including Montara Mountain, Mount Tamalpais, Mount Diablo, Mount Hamilton, Point Reyes, Point San Pedro, and the Farallon Islands. But remember, clear days are rare in Pacifica, especially in summer. If you want to see the view, ride here in one of the other seasons.

This loop route isn't for the aerobically challenged. It starts out with a serious climb on Mori Ridge Trail, an old dirt road, gaining 700 feet in 1.3 miles. Don't expect a warm-up; you just get into your lowest gear at the trailhead and crank uphill. The trail leads through open grasslands and coastal scrub, with occasional Monterey pines presenting a chance for shade. When Mori Ridge Trail meets up with Sweeney Ridge Trail, the heart-pumping work is over. Turn right for a much easier cruise to an old Nike missile site, then follow the paved trail south from the decaying military buildings to the San Francisco Bay Discovery Site. It was here, at the 1,220-foot summit on top of Sweeney Ridge, that Gaspar de Portolá first sighted San Francisco Bay on November 4, 1769. A stone monument commemorates the discovery.

You're back on dirt now and ready to start your descent on Baquiano Trail. The trail gets steeper and faster as it goes, so watch your speed. Remember: Hikers and dog walkers also use this trail, and they don't appreciate getting run over by bikes. You'll drop down to a gate at the end of Fassler Avenue in Pacifica, then continue steeply downhill to Highway 1, now on pavement and in the company of car traffic. Cross to the west side of the highway at Rockaway Beach Avenue, pick up the short but scenic bike path alongside Calera Creek, then cross Highway 1 again at Reina del Mar Avenue. The last stretch back to your car is, unfortunately, the least pleasant of the trip: a 0.3-mile stretch on the wide Highway 1 shoulder, then a steep 0.3-mile stint up the driveway to Shell Dance Nursery and back to the trailhead. But the rest of the loop makes it worth it.

For more information, contact the Golden Gate National Recreation Area Presidio Visitor Center, 415/561-4323, www.nps.gov/goga; or the Pacifica Visitor Center and Chamber of Commerce, 650/355-4122, www.pacificachamber.com.

Options

Bicyclists who would like to visit the San Francisco Bay Discovery Site and old Nike missile site without working so hard to do so can begin their ride at the Sneath Lane trailhead in San Bruno. From I-280, take the Sneath Lane/San Bruno Avenue exit and head west. Drive 1.9 miles on Sneath Lane to the trailhead parking area. The paved Sweeney Ridge Trail begins here and climbs a moderate 2.2 miles to the top of the ridge.

Driving Directions

From Highway 1 in Pacifica, turn east into the driveway for Shell Dance Nursery (north of Reina del Mar Avenue and south of Sharp Park Road). Drive 0.3 mile, past the nursery buildings, to the signed Sweeney Ridge trailhead parking area. (If you are driving south on Highway 1, you will have to make a U-turn and head north to enter the Shell Dance Nursery driveway.)

Route Directions

0.0 Park at the Sweeney Ridge trailhead by Shell Dance Nursery. Begin riding on the trail heading uphill from the trailhead sign. *Supplies are available in Pacifica.*

1.3 RIGHT at junction of Mori Ridge Trail and Sweeney Ridge Trail.

2.1 Nike missile site; dirt trail meets up with paved trail along the ridgetop; follow paved trail.

2.6 STRAIGHT on dirt trail where pavement turns sharply left.

2.7 RIGHT on Baquiano Trail at San Francisco Bay Discovery Site marker.

4.0 Go through gate.

4.1 LEFT at trail fork.

4.4 Pass water tank; trail becomes old paved road.

4.5 Go through gate at end of Fassler Avenue; watch for cars on downhill.

5.8 Cross Highway 1 to Rockaway Beach Avenue.

5.9 RIGHT on Dondee Way.

6.0 LEFT on San Marlo Way.

6.1 Parking lot by beach; pick up paved bike trail on right side of parking lot.

6.6 Bike trail meets the parking lot by Reina del Mar Avenue; ride out to Highway 1 and cross to its east side (don't stay on the bike trail, which travels on the west side of Highway 1).

6.7 LEFT on Highway 1; ride north using wide shoulder, passing police station.

7.0 RIGHT at Shell Dance Nursery driveway; steep uphill.

7.3 Arrive at starting point.

SWEENEY RIDGE LOOP

42 MONTARA MOUNTAIN

McNee Ranch State Park, north of Half Moon Bay

DIRT ROAD AND DETERIORATING PAVEMENT

Difficulty: 3   **Total Distance:** 9.6 miles

Riding Time: 2 hours   **Elevation Gain:** 2,000 feet

Summary: Each time you pause to catch your breath on this coastal summit ride, sublime ocean vistas await.

You like a long, sustained hill climb and a lightning-fast descent? You get them both on this ride from the Pacific Ocean to the top of Montara Mountain, elevation 1,898 feet. Make sure your body has plenty of fuel and water for the 4.8-mile climb up, and wear your sturdiest helmet for the ride down.

Aside from the heart- and leg-pumping work, there isn't much to think about on this ride, which has almost no intersections. Instead, you can focus on the views, which are downright spectacular on clear days. You ride with the ocean mostly at your back for the first 1.5 miles, heading deep into Montara Mountain's coastal canyon. Gradually the trail rises above the valleys and starts to show off glimpses of the blue Pacific. At the 2.2-mile mark, where two posts mark a side trail off-limits to bikes, the panorama opens wide, exposing the crashing surf and tall cliffs of Montara State Beach and Gray Whale Cove.

Here you can pause to consider how often the section of Highway 1 below you—aptly named Devil's Slide—has been closed due to landslides, effectively sealing off the people of Montara and nearby communities from most of the rest of the world and creating traffic nightmares on Highway 92, the only other nearby

© ANN MARIE BROWN

This view of the treacherous stretch of coast known as Devil's Slide is a good reason for a rest stop on the ascent up Montara Mountain.

access to the coast from the Peninsula. The most recent long-term closure was in 2006, when the road was closed April–August. Residents of the coast will continue to hold their breath until late 2012 or early 2013, when two tunnels through the base of Montara Mountain should be completed, which will completely eliminate this accident-prone stretch of Highway 1. At that time, the old highway and the land around it is scheduled to be made available for public recreation, which should give bikers even more to cheer about.

The views keep expanding as you pedal onward and upward. When at last you attain Montara Mountain's transmitter tower–littered summit, your view expands to include the north and east: Mount Tamalpais, the skyline of San Francisco, the famous sign on U.S. 101 proclaiming South San Francisco the Industrial City, San Mateo Bridge, San Francisco Bay, plus Mount Diablo in the background. This is one of the most all-encompassing views possible in the Bay Area.

The trail's grade is fairly moderate all the way up except for one 0.5-mile stretch at 2.6 miles, which is *really* steep (it gains 500 feet in 0.5 mile). Making matters worse, this stretch is also often extremely rutted. The path's first 2.4 miles are a mix of deteriorating pavement, gravel, and dirt (often squeezed into single-track by encroaching pampas grass). You're riding on old San Pedro Mountain Road, which used to be the route from Montara to Pacifica before precarious Highway 1 was built. The last 2.4 miles follow Montara Mountain Fire Road, a wide dirt road. Because of its rough surface, descending can be like riding on ball bearings;

it's difficult to control your speed. Move your butt way back off your seat or you'll go down for sure. Guess how I know?

For more information, contact Montara State Beach or McNee Ranch State Park, 650/726-8819 or 650/726-8820.

Driving Directions

From Half Moon Bay, drive north on Highway 1 for 10 miles to just north of Montara State Beach and La Costanera Restaurant and just south of Devil's Slide. The trailhead is marked by a yellow metal gate on the east side of the highway, with parking for about six cars. If this lot is full, park 0.2 mile farther south at Montara State Beach.

Route Directions

0.0 Park at McNee Ranch trailhead by the yellow metal gate. Begin riding on the wide road behind the gate (not the single-track trail). *Supplies are available in Montara, one mile south.*

0.2 LEFT at fork by ranger's house.

1.7 Dirt road merges in from the right.

2.2 Coastal viewpoint where hiker's trail leads west (signed as No Bikes).

2.4 RIGHT on dirt Montara Mountain Fire Road (deteriorating pavement veers to the left); prepare for brutal 0.5-mile climb.

3.5 Pass Montara Mountain Trail on left (hikers-only trail from San Pedro Valley County Park).

4.4 South Peak of Montara Mountain on left; continue straight.

4.8 Arrive at North Peak of Montara Mountain. TURN AROUND. *Climb up the rocky, short trail (about 20 feet) next to the communication towers for the best view of the day.*

9.6 Arrive at starting point.

43 SAWYER CAMP RECREATION TRAIL
Crystal Springs Reservoir near Hillsborough and Millbrae

BEST ☾

PAVED BIKE PATH

Difficulty: 1

Total Distance: 12 miles

Riding Time: 1 hour

Elevation Gain: 250 feet

Summary: A paved trail skirts the edge of Lower Crystal Springs Reservoir, offering easy pedaling and a good chance for wildlife sightings.

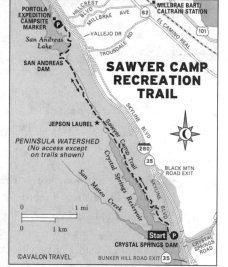

Few bike trails are as well loved and well used as the Sawyer Camp Trail. This paved, car-free recreation trail is long enough so you can feel like you got some exercise riding it, easy enough so that even the most casual rider can try it, and surprisingly scenic as well. Its only drawback is its popularity: With so many people living nearby on the northern Peninsula, the trail is almost always packed with walkers, runners, in-line skaters, and baby strollers, in addition to bikers. No matter; just get here early to avoid the crowds, especially on weekends.

The trail travels the length of Lower Crystal Springs Reservoir, then leads through marshlands to southern San Andreas Lake, ending just beyond the lake's dam at Hillcrest Boulevard in Millbrae. Unlike many paved recreation trails, it isn't as straight as a stick; it twists and curves gracefully around the reservoir's shoreline. You have a good chance of seeing deer, raptors, herons, and egrets somewhere along the route.

The ride is an easy cruise; you probably won't even shift gears for the first 4.5 miles. The only noticeable hill is in the last stretch near San Andreas Lake's dam. Be sure to make a stop to see the Jepson laurel tree, 3.5 miles in and 25 feet off the trail (near a picnic area). More than 600 years old and 55 feet tall, the tree is the oldest and largest living California laurel, named for botanist Willis Jepson.

Another of the trail's highlights is a plaque on a boulder at trail's end at Hillcrest

Cyclists share the six-mile Sawyer Camp Recreation Trail with joggers and other users.

Boulevard, which marks the spot where Captain Gaspar de Portolá made camp after his discovery of San Francisco Bay in 1769.

Options
Mountain bikers don't have to stop at the Sawyer Camp Trail's end at Hillcrest Boulevard; a dirt trail continues from there to Larkspur Drive, where the paved San Andreas Trail begins and runs alongside the western half of San Andreas Lake. Road and mountain bikers looking for more mileage can connect the Sawyer Camp Trail with a ride on Cañada Road, two miles south of the Sawyer Camp Trailhead, which is good for riding any time but especially good every Sunday, when four miles of its length are closed to cars. For more information on Cañada Road Bicycle Sunday, contact San Mateo County Parks and Recreation, 650/363-4020, www.eparks.net.

Driving Directions
From I-280 in San Mateo, take the Highway 92 exit west, then turn right (north) immediately on Highway 35. Drive 0.5 mile to Crystal Springs Road and the trail entrance.

Route Directions
0.0 Park in the small parking lot by the trailhead, or alongside the road. Ride through the signed gate to enter the trail. *Water is available along the trail.*

3.5 Restrooms, drinking water, and picnic area by short path to Jepson laurel tree.

4.8 Beginning of hill climb.

5.1 Cross dam over San Andreas Lake.

6.0 Arrive at gate at Hillcrest Boulevard. TURN AROUND. *Note historic marker for Gaspar de Portolá's camp just past the gate.*

12.0 Arrive at starting point.

SAWYER CAMP RECREATION TRAIL

44 HALF MOON BAY BACK ROADS
south of Half Moon Bay

PAVED ROADS WITH MINIMAL CAR TRAFFIC

Difficulty: 3

Total Distance: 24.1 miles

Riding Time: 2 hours

Elevation Gain: 1,500 feet

Summary: Forget the crowds at the annual Pumpkin Festival – this road ride will show you the real Half Moon Bay.

Many Bay Area residents complain that the coastal resort town of Half Moon Bay has left its country roots behind and become too much of a city. This loop ride on Half Moon Bay's back roads (with a mere 6.8-mile stretch on busy Highway 1) proves that there's still plenty of country left in this coastal town; you just have to know where to find it.

The ride begins at the Half Moon Bay firehouse at the junction of Main Street and Higgins Canyon Road. The toughest part is the first 100 yards, in which you must use impeccable judgment when crossing the stream of cars on Highway 1. With this accomplished, you face a quick, level jaunt south on the highway, followed by another careful crossing and a left turn on Tunitas Creek Road. Now you're in the country, and you'll face nothing but quiet roads and pastoral scenery for the rest of your ride.

The only serious hill appears at mile 19.8, when Purisima Creek Road becomes Higgins Canyon Road at a hairpin turn in the road. Here you'll gain 400 feet in about two miles, then lose it again on your way back into town. Otherwise, there's a bit of climbing on Lobitos Creek Road, but it's nothing to complain about. The views of the remote coastal canyons will more than compensate.

Driving Directions

From Half Moon Bay at the junction of Highway 92 and Highway 1, head south on Highway 1 for 1.2 miles to Higgins Purisima Road (by the firehouse). Turn left and park along Main Street near the firehouse.

Route Directions

0.0 Park on the south end of Main Street in Half Moon Bay, near its junction with Higgins Canyon Road and Highway 1. Ride out the last few yards of Higgins Canyon Road and cross Highway 1 to head south. *Supplies are available on Main Street or Highway 1 in Half Moon Bay.*

1.9 Pass Cowell Ranch Beach turnoff.

6.8 LEFT on Tunitas Creek Road.

8.8 RIGHT at junction with Lobitos Creek Cutoff.

9.8 Enter redwoods.

10.4 LEFT on Lobitos Creek Road (a very sharp left turn).

14.6 RIGHT on Verde Road (parallels Highway 1 with nice views of the ocean).

16.2 RIGHT on Purisima Creek Road.

19.8 Pass entrance to Purisima Creek Redwoods Open Space Preserve at hairpin turn; road changes names to Higgins Purisima Road.

24.1 Arrive at starting point.

HALF MOON BAY BACK ROADS

45 PURISIMA REDWOODS LOOP

off Skyline Boulevard near Woodside

DIRT ROAD AND SINGLE-TRACK; PAVED ROAD WITH MODERATE CAR TRAFFIC

Difficulty: 3

Total Distance: 10 miles

Riding Time: 2-3 hours

Elevation Gain: 1,600 feet

Summary: Enjoy a redwood fantasy ride just a few miles south of San Francisco.

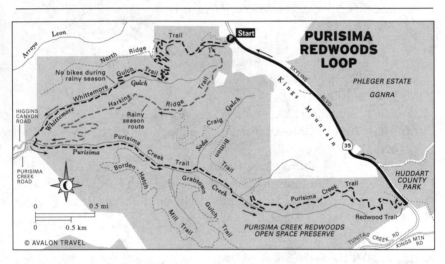

It might seem more sensible to start this loop ride from its lowest point, at the Purisima trailhead south of Half Moon Bay, so that you could climb uphill when you're fresh and save the downhill for the way home. But there's room for only a few cars at the Half Moon Bay trailhead, and these spaces are almost always filled. Unless you live in or near Half Moon Bay, it's not worth the drive to the trailhead only to discover there is no place to park.

Instead, start this ride at the top of the loop, at the large Purisima parking lot on Skyline Boulevard near Woodside. Folks who live in San Francisco and the northern Peninsula will find that this trailhead is close enough that they can show up after work on the long days of summer and still have enough daylight to complete the ride.

Summer is a key word here, because the Whittemore Gulch section of this trail is closed to bikes during the rainy season. It's a beautiful single-track trail tunneling through a flower-filled Douglas fir forest, with lots of fun twists and tight turns. (You access it 0.8 mile from the trailhead, after a rather bumpy ride on North Ridge Trail, a dirt road.)

The upper section of Whittemore Gulch Trail provides long-distance views of the Half Moon Bay coast, or Half Moon Bay fog, depending on the weather. The trail keeps descending until, at about two miles from the start, you enter a deep, dark redwood canyon. The area was logged in the late 1800s, so these are second- and third-growth trees, but impressive nonetheless. The return leg of the loop is uphill on Purisima Creek Trail, a gradual but steady climb alongside a pretty stream and some very large redwoods, followed by a quick, two-mile stint on paved Skyline Boulevard.

© ANN MARIE BROWN

The single-track Whittemore Gulch Trail is a favorite route of mountain bikers in Purisima Creek Redwoods Open Space Preserve.

Options

If you must ride in the wet season, you can follow an alternate route in Purisima from the same trailhead: downhill on Harkins Ridge Trail and uphill on Purisima Creek Trail. The Midpeninsula Regional Open Space District (650/691-1200, www.openspace.org) keeps these wide trails open no matter what the weather. There's no comparison, though; Whittemore Gulch is the trail to ride in this park.

Driving Directions

From San Francisco, drive south on I-280 for 19 miles to the Highway 92 west exit. Go west on Highway 92 for 2.7 miles, then turn left (south) on Highway 35 (Skyline Boulevard). Drive 4.3 miles to the Purisima Creek Redwoods Open Space Preserve parking area on the right.

Route Directions

0.0 Park at Purisima Preserve parking lot on Skyline Boulevard. Follow North Ridge Trail (dirt road) from the parking lot (not the hikers-only trail). *Supplies are available eight miles south on Skyline Boulevard at Skylonda.*

0.3 Straight at junction with Harkins Ridge Trail.

0.8 LEFT on Whittemore Gulch Trail.

1.4 LEFT to stay on Whittemore Gulch Trail.

2.8 Cross footbridge; trail widens and levels out.

3.7 STRAIGHT at junction with Harkins Ridge Trail. Cross wide bridge ahead.

3.8 LEFT on Purisima Creek Trail on far side of bridge.

4.8 STRAIGHT at junction with Borden Hatch Mill Trail.

5.1 STRAIGHT at junction with Grabtown Gulch Trail.

6.1 RIGHT at junction with Soda Gulch/Craig Britton Trail.

7.8 RIGHT on Redwood Trail.

8.0 LEFT on Skyline Boulevard.

10.0 Arrive at starting point.

46 EL CORTE DE MADERA CREEK LOOP
off Skyline Boulevard near Woodside

DIRT ROAD AND SINGLE-TRACK

Difficulty: 3

Riding Time: 2 hours

Total Distance: 10.5 miles

Elevation Gain: 1,400 feet

Summary: Miles of single-track trails await among the second- and third-growth redwoods in El Corte de Madera Creek canyon.

Of all the beautiful open-space lands on Skyline Boulevard, El Corte de Madera Creek Open Space Preserve is the one most favored by mountain bikers. Partly it's because almost every trail is open to bikes, and partly it's because so many of those trails are single-track. To sweeten the pot, the trail is densely shaded with second- and third-growth redwoods, making it a good choice for warm summer days when you want to ride where you won't bake in the sun.

The loop described below is designed to string together an abundance of single-track, but that means you have to put up with a lot of trail directions. One thing this preserve has plenty of, besides redwood trees, is junctions. It's common to see riders stopped at intersections here—they're usually consulting a map, or each other.

This route is also designed to keep you away from the many hikers who walk

honeycomb patterns in tafoni sandstone

the short trail to the preserve's main attraction, a tafoni sandstone formation. Except for a brief stretch where your paths may intersect, you should be far from the vast majority of pedestrians on this loop. Don't forget to bring a bike lock so you can chain up your wheels and walk the short path to see this cluster of 50-foot-high sandstone outcrops. Tafoni is a type of sandstone that is formed by years of weathering. The "glue" that holds the sandstone's individual sand grains together slowly erodes away, leaving honeycomb patterned, lace-like crevices and holes in the smooth rock. From an observation deck at the end of this 0.2-mile trail, you have a good vantage point for gazing in awe at the tafoni. Just don't think about riding your bike on this trail; it's for hiking only.

Another attraction this loop visits is the Old Growth Redwood, the only one left standing in this preserve. The tree is noticeably larger than its hundreds of second- and third-growth compatriots at El Corte de Madera Creek.

But mostly it's the riding you'll enjoy here. Highlights include the too-short romps on Giant Salamander and North Leaf Trails and a challenging climb on Resolution Trail (all single-track). Note that many of the trails are quite steep (even the single-tracks), so if you don't enjoy a lot of ups and downs, you won't be happy here. Overall, this is not a place for beginners to ride because of technical challenges, but intermediates will have a great time on the frequent sharp corners, steep ascents and descents, tree roots, and rocky and loose trail surfaces.

One more caveat: This preserve is subject to seasonal trail closures. During the rainy season, Leaf Trail, Methuselah Trail, Giant Salamander Trail, and a few others are often closed, and if so you'll have to limit your fun to the dry season from May to October.

For more information, contact the Midpeninsula Regional Open Space District, 650/691-1200, www.openspace.org.

Driving Directions

From San Francisco, drive south on I-280 for 19 miles to the Highway 92 west exit. Go west on Highway 92 for 2.7 miles, then turn left (south) on Highway 35 (Skyline Boulevard). Drive 8.9 miles to the trailhead parking on the west side of the road, 0.4 mile south of Skeggs Vista Point. (If this small lot is full, park at the vista point lot and ride south to this trailhead.)

Route Directions

0.0 Park at the CM02 gate and ride to your right (north) on Sierra Morena Trail. *Supplies are available in Skylonda, 3.4 miles south on Skyline Boulevard.*

0.6 RIGHT on Fir Trail.

0.8 Gate at Skyline Boulevard; turn sharply LEFT on Tafoni Trail.

0.9 RIGHT on El Corte de Madera Creek Trail.

1.6 LEFT to stay on El Corte de Madera Creek Trail (turns to single-track).

2.4 LEFT on Tafoni Trail.

3.2 Hiker's trail to tafoni sandstone formation on left. *Lock up your bike and walk the 0.2-mile trail to the see the tafoni.*

3.3 RIGHT (sharp) on Fir Trail at four-way junction.

3.5 LEFT at Vista Point Trail to stay on Fir Trail.

3.6 RIGHT on Resolution Trail (single-track).

4.7 LEFT on El Corte de Madera Creek Trail.

5.2 Cross El Corte de Madera Creek.

5.6 LEFT on North Leaf Trail (single-track).

6.7 LEFT on Methuselah Trail (single-track).

6.8 Cross El Corte de Madera Creek.

7.1 RIGHT on Giant Salamander Trail (single-track).

8.0 LEFT on Timberview Trail.

8.1 Old Growth Redwood. *Pay homage to the big tree.*

8.6 LEFT on Manzanita Trail (single-track).

9.7 RIGHT on Methuselah Trail at four-way junction.

10.1 LEFT to stay on Methuselah Trail.

10.5 Arrive at starting point.

47 WOODSIDE TO SKYLINE SHORT LOOP
Woodside to Skylonda

PAVED ROADS WITH MODERATE CAR TRAFFIC

Difficulty: 4

Riding Time: 1.5-2 hours

Total Distance: 20 miles

Elevation Gain: 2,200 feet

Summary: The bike-obsessed town of Woodside is the start of this popular 20-mile training loop.

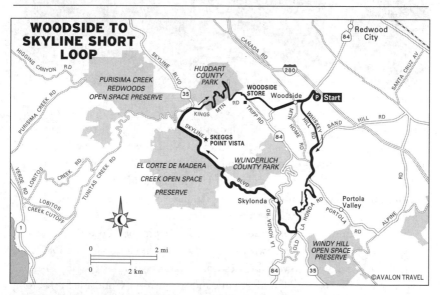

The Woodside to Skyline Short Loop is as close to a perfect 20-mile training ride as you can get. It supplies a killer 3.4-mile hill (Old La Honda Road from Woodside to Skyline Boulevard) and just enough mileage to keep your heart rate up for an hour or two. Yet it's remarkably scenic, provides convenient places to stop for fuel or rest, and offers a mix of wide bike lanes and less-traveled country roads. You'll have to put up with some traffic on Skyline Boulevard, but the payoff is worth it.

First, know that the tony community of Woodside is Bike Central. There isn't a more bike-friendly town anywhere in the Bay Area, a region filled with bike-friendly towns. And there isn't a more likely place to spot the most expensive bikes, the hottest gear, and the tautest leg muscles. It seems that people who can afford to live in Woodside have plenty of time for recreation and fitness. Try not to hold it against them.

Whiskey Hill and Sand Hill Roads both have wide bike lanes that will get you through the busy Woodside corridor. Then you begin your epic climb on

The historic Woodside Store (now a museum) is filled with local history.

extremely narrow Old La Honda Road, a former logging toll road that today twists and turns through second- and third-growth redwoods. On any weekend day you'll find members of local cycling clubs racing each other up this one-lane hill. Fortunately few car drivers use Old La Honda Road except for those who live on it. It's so steep and narrow that at its high terminus on Skyline Boulevard, it is signed "Downhill Bicycling Not Recommended."

The climb continues, more gradually now and with one 400-foot dip, as you cruise north on Skyline Boulevard. You can stop in Skylonda for a cool drink, or just continue onward to your big descent on Kings Mountain Road. Then it's back to Woodside, passing Huddart Park and the historic Woodside Store along the way. Stop in if it's open; the old store is now a museum with fascinating artifacts from the area's pioneer past.

Options

For more mileage and hills in the Woodside area, see ride 48, *Woodside to Coast Long Loop.*

Driving Directions

From I-280, take the Highway 84/Woodside exit and drive west for less than 0.25 mile to the Park and Ride lot.

Route Directions

0.0 Park at the Woodside Park and Ride lot. Ride west on Woodside Road (Highway 84). *Supplies are available in Woodside.*

0.5 LEFT on Whiskey Hill Road.

1.8 RIGHT on Sand Hill Road at Y-junction.

3.2 RIGHT on Old La Honda Road.

6.6 RIGHT on Skyline Boulevard.

8.1 Skylonda market and Alice's Restaurant at junction of Skyline and Highway 84. *Supplies are available.*

11.9 Skeggs Vista Point on right.

13.6 RIGHT on Kings Mountain Road.

16.5 Entrance to Huddart Park on left. *Water is available.*

17.7 LEFT at stop sign at Entrance Way.

17.9 Historic Woodside Store at Tripp Road junction. *Stop in to the museum to see the local history exhibits.*

18.6 LEFT on Woodside Road (Highway 84).

19.4 Downtown Woodside. *Supplies are available.*

19.5 STRAIGHT at junction with Whiskey Hill Road (start of loop).

20.0 Arrive at starting point.

WOODSIDE TO SKYLINE SHORT LOOP

48 WOODSIDE TO COAST LONG LOOP BEST ◖

Woodside to Pescadero

PAVED ROADS WITH MODERATE CAR TRAFFIC

Difficulty: 5   **Total Distance:** 57.1 miles

Riding Time: 5-7 hours   **Elevation Gain:** 5,800 feet

Summary: For an epic cycling adventure in the San Francisco Bay Area, this demanding loop can't be beat.

A lot of hill climbing and a lot of scenery make up this all-day ride from Woodside to the coast. With 5,800 feet of elevation gain, it's not for the faint of heart. But there are enough serious cyclists living on the Peninsula that every weekend, hundreds of them take this epic ride, many pedaling in groups of 20 or more.

The ride's first 6.6 miles mimic those of the *Woodside to Skyline Short Loop,* ride 47 in this chapter. But where riders on the short loop head north on Skyline Boulevard, you'll head south, passing by Windy Hill and Russian Ridge Open Space Preserves while gaining another 500 feet, then turn west on Alpine Road. I hope your brakes are in good working order, because you're going to descend 2,000 feet in the next seven miles. Most of it is in open grasslands, but you also pass through a stretch of old-growth redwoods called the Heritage Grove in Alpine Road's last two miles. Lock up your bike and take a short walk through these magnificent trees.

A cycling club gathers on Skyline Boulevard after the climb from Woodside.

© ANN MARIE BROWN

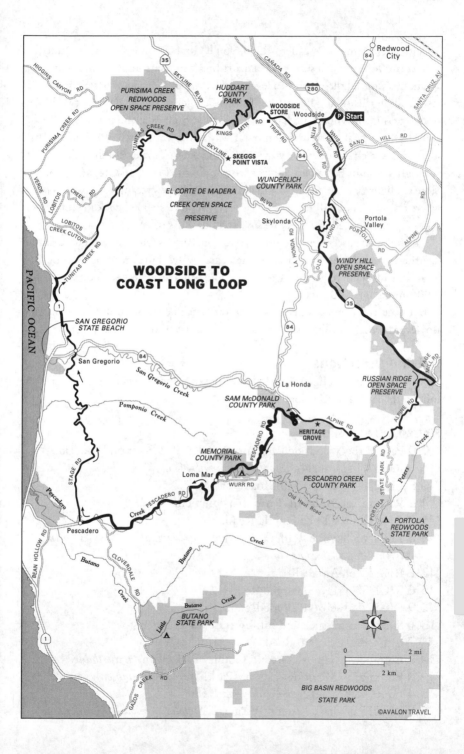

With a left turn on Pescadero Road, you'll climb again over a steep grade for almost two miles, which seems like a heart-breaking injustice. But then you drop again, this time all the way to sea level in the town of Pescadero. After a food and rest break in this small village (there's so much good stuff to eat in a two-block stretch of this tiny village, it's hard to get back on your bike and ride), Stage Road and Highway 1 take you over comparatively easy terrain (two 300-foot climbs) to Tunitas Creek Road, where you will begin your last major climb of the day. If you didn't stop in Pescadero, make sure you do so at the San Gregorio General Store at Highway 84 and Stage Road (650/726-0565, www.sangregoriostore.com), where the ambience will make you feel like you have stepped back in time. Bike shoes are not allowed inside, so be sure to take yours off.

The following ascent, a nine-mile stretch on Tunitas Creek Road, is one of the favorite training rides of cyclists on the coast. Why? Three reasons: The majority of it is in shady redwoods, the climb holds an average 6 percent grade (total 2,000-foot gain), and cars are a rarity.

But wait, this ride's best news is saved for last: The last six miles from Skyline Boulevard are all downhill back to your car. And a well-deserved downhill at that.

Driving Directions

From I-280, take the Highway 84/Woodside exit and drive west for less than 0.25 mile to the Park and Ride lot.

Route Directions

0.0 Park at the Woodside Park and Ride lot. Ride west on Woodside Road (Highway 84). *Supplies are available in Woodside.*

0.5 LEFT on Whiskey Hill Road.

1.8 RIGHT on Sand Hill Road at Y-junction.

3.2 RIGHT on Old La Honda Road.

6.6 LEFT on Skyline Boulevard. *Supplies are available 1.5 miles north (right) in La Honda.*

12.2 RIGHT on Alpine Road.

15.6 RIGHT to stay on Alpine Road.

15.9 RIGHT to stay on Alpine Road.

18.4 Small parking area and hiking trail at Heritage Grove.

19.7 LEFT on Pescadero Road.

20.2 Entrance to Sam McDonald County Park. *Water is available.*

24.1 Entrance to Memorial County Park. *Water is available.*

25.4 Loma Mar Store. *Supplies are available.*

31.5 RIGHT on Stage Road in Pescadero. *Supplies are available in Pescadero.*

38.7 Cross Highway 84 and stay on Stage Road. *Supplies are available at San Gregorio Store.*

39.8 RIGHT on Highway 1.

41.4 RIGHT on Tunitas Creek Road.

43.4 RIGHT at junction with Lobitos Creek Cutoff.

45.0 RIGHT at junction with Lobitos Creek Road.

50.5 Cross Skyline Boulevard and continue on Kings Mountain Road.

53.6 Entrance to Huddart Park on left. *Water is available.*

54.8 LEFT at stop sign at Entrance Way.

55.7 LEFT on Woodside Road (Highway 84).

56.5 Downtown Woodside. *Supplies are available.*

56.6 STRAIGHT at junction with Whiskey Hill Road.

57.1 Arrive at starting point.

49 RUSSIAN RIDGE AND COAL CREEK LOOP
off Skyline Boulevard near Palo Alto

DIRT ROAD AND SINGLE-TRACK

Difficulty: 2

Riding Time: 1.5 hours

Total Distance: 7.3 miles

Elevation Gain: 800 feet

Summary: The flower-filled days of spring on Skyline Boulevard are ideal for this easy mountain bike ride.

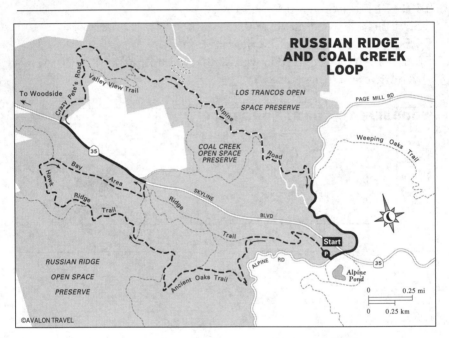

Russian Ridge is one of the few open-space preserves on Skyline Boulevard where beginning mountain bikers have a chance to ride without becoming discouraged by the technical nature of the trails. Conveniently, it's also more than 1,500 acres of windswept ridgetop paradise that will charm you in every season of the year. In summer and fall, the hillsides turn gold and the grasses sway in unison to the ridgetop winds. In winter, the trunks of the moss-covered oaks and laurels turn a bright, verdant green. And in spring, the grasslands explode in a fireworks display of colorful mule's ears, poppies, lupine, goldfields, Johnny-jump-ups, and blue-eyed grass.

This loop route combines a ride through Russian Ridge Open Space Preserve with a ride through neighboring Coal Creek Open Space Preserve, directly across

© ANN MARIE BROWN

Russian Ridge Open Space Preserve offers easy-to-moderate trail riding through grasslands and spring wildflowers.

Skyline Boulevard. You'll get to try out your skills on mostly wide fire roads, with a few stints on manageable single-track. This loop is a great place to become more confident on two wheels and at the same time enjoy some beautiful scenery. If you feel like you're getting in over your head at any point, don't be afraid to dismount your bike and walk.

Although each stretch of this loop has its own rewards, a few trails deserve special mention. Ancient Oaks Trail in Russian Ridge is a single-track that leads through a remarkable forest of gnarled, moss-covered oak trees interspersed with equally gnarled Douglas firs, plus some madrones and ferns. You may want to linger for a while in this strange, enchanted woodland. The route also follows a historic road in Coal Creek Open Space Preserve—the old Alpine Road on the east side of Skyline Boulevard, which was closed to cars in the late 1960s. The road was originally built by San Mateo County as a way of encouraging commerce from Santa Cruz County, while bypassing Santa Clara County. (Alpine Road on the west side of Skyline is still open to cars.) The stretch that is covered in this loop—from Crazy Pete's Road to Page Mill Road—looks much more like a trail than a road. It's fun to imagine cars negotiating its narrow turns.

For more information, contact the Midpeninsula Regional Open Space District, 650/691-1200, www.openspace.org.

Driving Directions
From I-280 in Palo Alto, take the Page Mill Road exit west. Drive 8.9 winding

miles to Skyline Boulevard (Highway 35). Cross Skyline Boulevard to Alpine Road. Drive 200 feet on Alpine Road and turn right into the Russian Ridge entrance.

Or, from the junction of Highways 35 and 9 at Saratoga Gap, drive seven miles north on Highway 35 (Skyline Boulevard). Turn left on Alpine Road and then right into the preserve entrance.

Route Directions

0.0 Park at the Russian Ridge main trailhead at Alpine Road and Skyline Boulevard. Ride north on Bay Area Ridge Trail (near restroom). *Supplies are available in Skylonda, 7.5 miles north on Skyline Boulevard.*

0.5 LEFT on connector trail to Ancient Oaks Trail.

0.8 RIGHT on Ancient Oaks Trail.

1.6 RIGHT on Mindego Ridge Trail (wide road).

1.9 STRAIGHT at junction.

2.1 RIGHT on Hawk Trail.

2.7 RIGHT on Bay Area Ridge Trail.

3.2 LEFT to ride out to Skyline Boulevard.

3.3 LEFT (north) on Skyline Boulevard.

4.0 RIGHT on Crazy Pete's Road.

4.4 RIGHT at junction (go through gate).

5.1 RIGHT at junction to stay on Crazy Pete's Road.

5.4 RIGHT on old Alpine Road.

6.5 RIGHT on Page Mill Road (paved road).

7.1 Cross Skyline Boulevard to Alpine Road.

7.2 RIGHT into trailhead parking area.

7.3 Arrive at starting point.

RUSSIAN RIDGE AND COAL CREEK LOOP

50 STANFORD AND PORTOLA VALLEY LOOP
Palo Alto to Portola Valley

PAVED ROADS WITH MODERATE CAR TRAFFIC

Difficulty: 2

Riding Time: 1.5 hours

Total Distance: 18 miles

Elevation Gain: 750 feet

Summary: For Stanford Cardinal fans, or any cyclist who finds him or herself in the Palo Alto area, this popular exercise ride circles the famous university.

This road ride is more urban than many others in this book, yet it covers some of the most bicycled territory in the Peninsula, the site of millions of after-work or in-between-classes rides. On "The Loop," as it's known, you'll find cyclists at every hour of any day working off a little stress from their high-tech jobs or harried Stanford studies. If you choose to ride your mountain bike here, you can take off from the paved roads onto dirt trails in Arastradero Preserve and/or Windy Hill Open Space Preserve.

Cyclists start this ride from all over the Stanford and Palo Alto area; for convenience, this route begins at the Stanford Shopping Center. If you feel daunted by the first stint on busy Sand Hill Road's bike lane, fear not; you'll soon reach a much quieter stretch on Portola Road and Alpine Road.

In addition, I've added to the traditional loop a peaceful, two-mile, country-lane stretch on Arastradero Road, passing the grassy hills of Arastradero Preserve. This out-and-back begins at the historic Alpine Inn (650/854-4004), formerly Rossotti's (also known as Zot's), reputed to be the oldest roadhouse in continuous operation in California. In the late 1800s, officials at Stanford tried to have the drinking and gambling establishment shut down, fearing its bad influence on

The popular Alpine Inn is a cyclist's landmark on the Stanford and Portola Valley Loop.

students. They didn't succeed, and, of course, the Alpine Inn has been a popular Stanford beer-and-burger hangout ever since.

On the return leg on Alpine Road, you can opt to pick up the recreation trail that runs alongside the road, starting just past Los Trancos Road. The paved surface is a bit rough, however, so many cyclists stick to the wide shoulder of Alpine Road.

Options

When you ride through the pleasant, small town of Portola Valley, you might want to stop to see the little red Portola schoolhouse next to the town hall and library. Built in 1909, it now serves as an art gallery. The dirt trails of Windy Hill Open Space Preserve are also accessible from the roadside parking lot in Portola Valley (mile 7.6).

Driving Directions

From I-280 in Woodside, take the Sand Hill Road exit and drive east 2.8 miles to Arboretum Road and the Stanford Shopping Center.

Route Directions

0.0 Park at the Stanford Shopping Center near the junction of Arboretum Road and Sand Hill Road (near Nordstrom's). Ride west on the Sand Hill Road bike lane. *Supplies are available in Stanford Shopping Center.*

2.8 Cross under I-280.

5.1 Sand Hill Road becomes Portola Road (stay straight).

7.6 Parking area on right for Windy Hill Open Space Preserve in Portola Valley. *Mountain bikers can ride trails here.*

8.4 LEFT on Alpine Road. *Café and stores available at this junction.*

9.5 RIGHT on Arastradero Road; the Alpine Inn is immediately on the right. *Food and drinks are available at the Alpine Inn.*

10.9 Arastradero Preserve on left (main entrance). *Mountain bikers can ride trails here.*

11.5 Arastradero Road ends at Page Mill Road. TURN AROUND.

13.5 RIGHT on Alpine Road (back at Alpine Inn).

15.3 Cross under I-280.

16.5 STRAIGHT at stoplight onto Santa Cruz Avenue.

16.6 RIGHT on Sand Hill Road.

18.0 Arrive at starting point.

51 PESCADERO AND SAN GREGORIO LOOP

BEST ☾

San Mateo County coast, south of Half Moon Bay

PAVED ROADS WITH MODERATE CAR TRAFFIC

Difficulty: 3

Total Distance: 28.7 miles

Riding Time: 2 hours

Elevation Gain: 1,200 feet

Summary: Two of San Mateo County's most charming towns and the historic Pigeon Point Lighthouse are visited on this coastal back road loop.

There's one rule about riding coastal Highway 1 south of Half Moon Bay: Ride south, not north, to avoid an often ferocious headwind. This loop around the town of Pescadero allows you to experience the best of Highway 1—heading in the direction of the prevailing winds, while riding on the ocean side of the highway in the safety of a mercifully wide shoulder. The return leg of the loop traces an inland route on mellow country lanes.

Early morning or weekday rides are recommended to avoid potentially heavy beach traffic. This loop makes a great Sunday morning ride with an early start, with time allotted for coffee or breakfast stops in the charming towns of Pescadero and San Gregorio.

Although the mileage isn't high, three long, slow hills in the first six miles of Highway 1 will give you a workout. (Two more hills await on Stage Road, plus one on Cloverdale Road.) The coastal scenery on the first half of the loop is as good as it gets, with nearly nonstop views of the surging sea pounding against a rocky shoreline. A highlight is a visit to Pigeon Point Lighthouse, built in 1871 and now operated as an overnight hostel. Lighthouse tours are often available on weekends for a small fee, but you can always enjoy the views from the lighthouse grounds, and the windswept coast at neighboring Whaler's Cove.

© ANN MARIE BROWN

Pigeon Point Lighthouse, built in 1871, is one of the highlights of the Pescadero and San Gregorio Loop.

Heading south from the lighthouse, you'll turn inland at Gazos Creek Road and enjoy a rolling ride through rural coastal hills. Pedaling north toward Pescadero, you'll pass by the entrance road to Butano State Park, a pretty redwood park with a campground and hiking trails. If you have energy to burn, it's worth a ride in for a look.

In the small town of Pescadero, historic Duarte's Tavern (202 Stage Rd., 650/879-0464, www.duartestavern. com) is a favorite breakfast and lunch stop for cyclists, and two nearby markets sell fresh-baked breads and other goodies. The ride concludes with a 7.2-mile stint on Stage Road, which, before Highway 1 was built, was the only route from Pescadero to San Gregorio.

For more information, contact Pigeon Point Lighthouse, 650/879-2120, www.parks.ca.gov; or Butano State Park, 650/879-2040, www.parks. ca.gov.

Driving Directions

From Highway 1 in Half Moon Bay, drive south for 13 miles to San Gregorio State Beach, just south of the junction with Highway 84. Park in the state beach parking lot.

Route Directions

0.0 Park at San Gregorio State Beach and turn right out of the lot, heading south on Highway 1. *Supplies are available in Half Moon Bay,*

13 miles north on Highway 1, or in San Gregorio, 0.75 mile east on Highway 84.

1.6 Pomponio State Beach.

3.5 Pescadero State Beach and Pescadero Marsh.

4.5 STRAIGHT at junction with Pescadero Road.

6.1 Pebble Beach.

7.0 Bean Hollow State Beach.

9.4 RIGHT on Pigeon Point Road; seaside riding on a quiet access road.

10.1 Pigeon Point Lighthouse. *Lighthouse tours are sometimes available on weekends.*

10.3 RIGHT on Highway 1.

12.5 LEFT on Gazos Creek Road. *Supplies are available at store 50 yards south on Highway 1.*

14.6 LEFT on Cloverdale Road.

15.8 Butano State Park turnoff on the right.

20.1 LEFT on Pescadero Road.

20.6 RIGHT on Stage Road. *Supplies are available in Pescadero (two blocks of shops).*

27.8 LEFT on La Honda Road. *Supplies are available at San Gregorio Store, straight ahead at intersection.*

28.5 LEFT on Highway 1.

28.7 Arrive at starting point.

PESCADERO AND SAN GREGORIO LOOP

52 OLD HAUL ROAD LOOP

Pescadero Creek County Park, Loma Mar

DIRT ROAD AND PAVED ROADS WITH MINIMAL CAR TRAFFIC

Difficulty: 3   **Total Distance:** 17.6 miles (or 10-mile option)

Riding Time: 3 hours   **Elevation Gain:** 2,100 feet

Summary: A redwood-lined old railroad bed serves as the basis for this scenic loop on San Mateo County's back roads.

The Old Haul Road is an old logging route that runs for five miles between Pescadero Creek County Park and Portola Redwoods State Park. The historic railroad bed tunnels through a thick forest of second-growth redwoods, providing a smooth, easy ride that gains only 500 feet in elevation. Although plenty of beginning mountain bikers simply pedal it out-and-back, those who want a more strenuous ride with greater variety can use the Old Haul Road to connect to paved Portola State Park Road and Alpine Road, home of the awe-inspiring Heritage Grove of old-growth redwoods.

On the Pescadero Creek County Park side, the Old Haul Road starts by a small picnic area near the rushing creek gorge, then heads east. You'll see plenty of big stumps along the route—reminders of this forest's earlier state—and many tiny streams that run down the hillsides to empty into Pescadero Creek. The hard-packed dirt-and-gravel road is well signed and easy to follow the whole way. Your only concern is to watch out for equestrians and hikers, who also use this trail.

Once you reach the Old Haul Road's terminus at Portola Redwoods State Park, you face a long, slow climb of 900 feet over four miles on the park's paved

Mountain bikers can ride an easy out-and-back trail on Old Haul Road or do a more strenuous loop.

entrance road. It is followed by a long, fast descent on Alpine Road to the Heritage Grove. After enjoying the grandeur of the mighty trees, you face a second climb, this time with a steeper grade, as Pescadero Road ascends mercilessly for just under two miles. (Prepare to use your granny gear.) The last two miles are an easy downhill cruise back to your car. Although the roads on this loop are quite narrow, they get little traffic, so you won't have to worry much about cars.

For more information, contact San Mateo County Parks and Recreation, 650/363-4020, www.eparks.net; or Portola Redwoods State Park, 650/948-9098, www.santacruzstateparks.org.

Options

If you want to get a novice hooked on mountain biking, take them for a 10-mile out-and-back ride on the Old Haul Road.

Driving Directions

From Highway 1, 15 miles south of Half Moon Bay, drive east on Pescadero Road for 9.8 miles. Turn right at the second entrance to Wurr Road, 0.25 mile past the entrance to Memorial Park. Drive 0.25 mile to the Hoffman Creek Trailhead, where Old Haul Road begins. (Or, from I-280 at Woodside, take Highway 84 west for 13 miles to La Honda. Turn left on Pescadero Road and drive 1 mile, then bear right to stay on Pescadero Road. Continue 4.2 miles to Wurr Road on the left. Turn left and drive 0.25 mile to the trailhead.)

Route Directions

0.0 Park at the Wurr Road entrance to Pescadero Creek County Park. Begin riding at the entrance gate. *Supplies are available at the Loma Mar Store, 1.5 miles west on Pescadero Road.*

0.5 STRAIGHT at junction with Pomponio Trail.

1.1 STRAIGHT at junction with Towne Trail.

3.2 Reach high point in the trail and start to descend.

3.9 STRAIGHT at junction with Bridge Trail on left and Butano Ridge Trail on right.

5.0 LEFT at service road to Portola Redwoods State Park; descend and continue past the gate onto paved road.

6.0 Portola State Park visitor center and restrooms on the left. *Water is available.*

6.4 Exit out of Portola State Park and follow Portola State Park Road.

9.3 LEFT on Alpine Road.

9.6 RIGHT to stay on Alpine Road.

12.1 Heritage Grove. *Take a short walk through these magnificent trees.*

13.3 LEFT on Pescadero Road.

13.8 Entrance to Sam McDonald County Park. *Water is available.*

17.4 LEFT on Wurr Road.

17.6 Arrive at starting point.

53 BIG BASIN AND BOULDER CREEK LOOP

Santa Cruz Mountains and Big Basin Redwoods State Park

PAVED ROADS WITH MODERATE CAR TRAFFIC

Difficulty: 4   **Total Distance:** 43 miles

Riding Time: 3-4 hours   **Elevation Gain:** 3,300 feet

Summary: This road ride winds through one of the least developed regions of the South Bay, from the redwoods of Big Basin to the vineyards of Bear Creek Road.

A shoulderless stretch of Highway 9 leads to Big Basin Redwoods State Park.

This road ride explores the ridges and forests of the Santa Cruz Mountains and includes a visit to California's first state park, Big Basin Redwoods. You'll see plenty of redwoods along the route, plus ridgeline forests of madrone and oak. Long climbs and descents are part of the package, and you'll have to put up with auto traffic on narrow, shoulder-less roads. But it's worth it to complete this 43-mile epic trip through some of the South Bay's most remote countryside.

The loop ride begins at Saratoga Gap at the junction of Highway 9 and Skyline Boulevard (Highway 35) and heads southwest to Big Basin Redwoods State Park. A 6-mile descent from Saratoga Gap at 2,634 feet to Waterman Gap at 1,267 feet is your warm-up for the day. Continuing straight on narrow, twisting Highway 236, you'll face a moderate up-and-down ride to state park headquarters. Lock up your bike at the parking lot and take the 0.5-mile walk on Redwood Trail, which shows off some of the park's largest and oldest redwoods, including the Mother of the Forest (329 feet tall) and the Santa Clara Tree (17 feet in diameter). Nothing compares to the humbling feeling of walking in the shadows of 2,000-year-old giants.

Back on your bike, you'll exit the park and continue south on Highway 236, climbing briefly and then dropping down to the town of Boulder Creek. After a food and rest stop, and maybe a triple espresso, you face a strenuous climb from Boulder Creek (500 feet in elevation) to North Summit Road near Los Gatos (2,200 feet in elevation). You'll pass two wineries along the way. Byington Vineyard (408/354-1111, www.byington.com) offers wine tastings Tuesday–Sunday 11 A.M.–5 P.M., picnic facilities, and a bocce ball court. David Bruce Winery (408/354-4214, www.davidbrucewinery.com) holds wine tastings Thursday–Monday noon–5 P.M.

If you can somehow pull yourself through this unforgiving stretch (and no, a little wine won't help), the remaining miles on narrow North Summit Road and Skyline Boulevard will seem relatively easy. Thankfully, the last two miles on Skyline Boulevard to your car at Saratoga Gap are actually downhill.

For more information, contact Big Basin Redwoods State Park, 831/338-8860, www.santacruzstateparks.org.

Driving Directions
From I-280 in Palo Alto, take Page Mill Road west for 8.9 miles to Skyline Boulevard (Highway 35). Turn left (south) on Skyline and drive 10.5 miles to the junction with Highway 9. The parking lot is on the left. Or, from Saratoga, take Highway 9 west for 7.5 miles to its junction with Skyline Boulevard.

Route Directions
0.0 Park at the large parking lot at the junction of Highway 9 and Highway 35. Ride west on Highway 9. *A vendor sells hot dogs and drinks in the parking lot on most weekends. Other supplies are available in Saratoga.*

1.8 Overlook point and restrooms on left.

6.1 RIGHT on Highway 236 at Waterman Gap.

10.8 STRAIGHT at junction with China Grade.

14.2 Big Basin Redwoods State Park headquarters. *Lock up your bike and take a hike on the 0.5-mile Redwood Trail from the main parking lot. Water, restrooms, and a small store are available (open most of the year).*

20.6 Pass golf course.

23.5 LEFT onto Highway 9 at stop sign. *Supplies are available in town of Boulder Creek.*

23.6 RIGHT on Bear Creek Road.

28.3 Begin major climb.

31.0 Byington Vineyard & Winery on right.

31.6 David Bruce Winery on left.

32.6 LEFT on North Summit Road (unsigned except for the spray-painted word Skyline and an arrow); end of major climb.

36.5 STRAIGHT at junction with Black Road; North Summit Road widens and becomes Skyline Boulevard.

40.4 Castle Rock State Park entrance.

43.0 Arrive at starting point.

54 SARATOGA GAP LOOP

off Skyline Boulevard near Saratoga

DIRT ROAD AND SINGLE-TRACK

Difficulty: 3

Riding Time: 2-3 hours

Total Distance: 12.9 miles

Elevation Gain: 1,600 feet

Summary: Hone your mountain bike skills on a deservedly popular loop of mostly single-track riding through three separate Skyline-area parks.

The ride through Long Ridge Open Space Preserve is one of the easier stretches of the Saratoga Gap Loop.

When I was first getting acquainted with mountain biking, I met a pro rider on the trail who gave me one piece of advice: "If you want to learn how to handle single-track, ride Saratoga Gap Trail—often."

It was sage advice. I'm still not the world's greatest single-track rider (not even close), but I know where to go to sharpen my skills.

So does everyone else. This loop is one of the most popular in the South Bay, and for good reason. It starts at the busy junction of Highways 9 and 35, with easy access from most of Silicon Valley and the Peninsula, and carves its way through three separate parks and preserves: Saratoga Gap, Long Ridge, and Upper Stevens Creek.

The loop can be ridden in only one direction because one leg is open to uphill traffic only. If you can take your eyes off the six-foot space in front of your front tire, you'll find that the surrounding foothill scenery is lovely: open grassland ridges, fern-filled forests of handsome Douglas firs, wide views of wooded hillsides, and even a visit to a trickling creek in Stevens Canyon, which makes a perfect mid-loop rest stop.

Aside from the technical challenges of single-track on Saratoga Gap, Peters Creek, and Table Mountain Trails, the only major difficulty on this ride is the long climb out on Charcoal Road, a 1.3-mile workout. But since it is preceded by a steep descent on Grizzly Flat Road to Stevens Canyon, you are clearly forewarned that the uphill is coming. More than a few riders have been spotted walking their bikes here.

Note that this is a dry-season-only loop; many of the trails are closed during wet weather. Please don't ride them illegally.

For more information, contact Midpeninsula Regional Open Space District, 650/691-1200, www.openspace.org.

Driving Directions

From I-280 in Palo Alto, take Page Mill Road west for 8.9 miles to Skyline Boulevard (Highway 35). Turn left (south) on Skyline and drive 10.5 miles to the junction with Highway 9. The parking lot is on the left. Or, from Saratoga, take Highway 9 west for 7.5 miles to its junction with Skyline Boulevard.

Route Directions

0.0 Park at the large parking lot at the junction of Highway 9 and Highway 35. Ride across Highway 9 carefully to access Saratoga Gap Trail. *A vendor sells hot dogs and drinks in the parking lot on most weekends. Other supplies are available in Saratoga.*

2.0 Single-track Saratoga Gap Trail ends at Highway 35; cross the highway and go RIGHT on Bay Area Ridge Trail.

3.2 RIGHT on single-track (signed for Grizzly Flat parking).

3.3 STRAIGHT at junction with Ward Road on left.

3.4 RIGHT on single-track Peters Creek Trail at major junction of Ward Road, Long Ridge Road, and Peters Creek Trail.

4.3 RIGHT to stay on Peters Creek Trail. Keep to right at next two forks to come out to Highway 35.

5.3 Cross Highway 35 and pick up Grizzly Flat Road on other side; steep and long descent.

7.8 Cross Stevens Creek.

8.0 RIGHT on Canyon Trail.

8.3 RIGHT on Table Mountain Trail (single-track signed To Saratoga Gap).

9.5 RIGHT on Table Mountain Trail/Charcoal Road (wide road).

9.9 RIGHT on Charcoal Road; begin major hill climb.

10.4 RIGHT to stay on Charcoal Road.

11.2 LEFT at junction with Saratoga Gap Trail. *Check out the Miwok grinding stones near this junction.*

12.9 Arrive at starting point.

55 MONTE BELLO LOOP   BEST ☾

Saratoga to Monte Bello Ridge

DIRT ROAD AND SINGLE-TRACK; PAVED ROADS WITH MODERATE CAR TRAFFIC

Difficulty: 4   **Total Distance:** 27 miles (or 21.2-mile option)

Riding Time: 3 hours   **Elevation Gain:** 2,300 feet

Summary: Views from Monte Bello's high ridge and a picnic at Ridge Winery are your rewards for a serious climb from downtown Saratoga.

The roads around Stevens Creek Reservoir and throughout Stevens Creek Canyon are well traveled by cyclists from the Silicon Valley every day of the week. The proximity of this lovely, tree-lined canyon to the hustle and bustle of Cupertino makes it perfect for after-work, lunchtime, and weekend rides.

The ride described here is designed to allow for the most scenery with the least traffic. The route travels up Pierce Road from Saratoga through a mix of vineyards, red-tile-roofed mansions, and older farmhouses, then cruises through the foothills of Mount Eden Road and creekside Stevens Canyon Road to Monte Bello Road. Following this path, you'll encounter two brief climbs, then nothing but climbing on Monte Bello's increasingly narrow road. The road gains 1,500 feet over 4.3 miles, with grades occasionally as steep as 13 percent.

Achieving Monte Bello's high ridge is your reward, with its spreading views overlooking the Santa Clara Valley and a chance for wine-tasting and a picnic at Ridge Winery (weekends only). Skinny-tire riders can continue for another mile beyond the vineyards to where the pavement ends, but then they'll have to turn

Bikes of all shapes and sizes can be ridden to the summit of Monte Bello Road.

around (see *Options*). Mountain bikers stay on Monte Bello Road to the Water-wheel Creek Trail in Monte Bello Open Space Preserve, then follow that trail to the dirt section of Monte Bello Road. Shortly, you're at the microwave-covered summit of 2,800-foot Black Mountain, the highest point on Monte Bello Ridge. Views are good in all directions, but the best vista is to the west, as seen from near the 15-mph speed limit sign at an obvious outcrop of scattered rocks: Stevens Creek Canyon lies below you. Untrammeled grassland hills spread to the north and south along Skyline Ridge. The Pacific Ocean glimmers from afar. In springtime, the grassland wildflowers explode in a riot of colors.

The all-dirt downhill is exciting and fast; be careful not to mow over cyclists riding in the opposite direction. Indian Creek Trail drops 850 feet over 1.2 miles, then Canyon Trail descends almost as fast, adding a little single-track to the mix. Where the dirt ends, you follow paved Stevens Canyon Road to Mount Eden Road, then retrace your tracks to Saratoga.

If you're out on Sunday, you may be able to stop after your ride at the Picchetti Winery for a well-deserved rest and some live music. The winery (408/741-1310, www.picchetti.com) is located at 13100 Monte Bello Road. Ridge Winery (408/867-3233, www.ridgewine.com) is located at 17100 Monte Bello Road.

For more information on Monte Bello Open Space Preserve, contact Midpeninsula Regional Open Space District, 650/691-1200, www.openspace.org.

Options

Road cyclists can enjoy a 21.2-mile out-and-back on pavement by following this same route up to Ridge Winery, then retracing their tire treads. The route has a 2,000-foot elevation gain.

Driving Directions

From San Jose, take Highway 17 south for 6 miles to the Highway 9 exit in Los Gatos. Take Highway 9 northwest 2.5 miles into Saratoga and park in downtown.

Route Directions

0.0 Park in downtown Saratoga in any of the public parking lots one block off Highway 9. Ride west on Highway 9. *Supplies are available in Saratoga.*

1.6 RIGHT on Pierce Road (signed for Mountain Winery).

2.6 LEFT on Mount Eden Road.

3.1 Mount Eden Vineyards.

3.5 Garrod Farm Stables.

4.1 Mount Eden Trailhead on the left (no bikes).

4.9 STRAIGHT on Stevens Canyon Road at stop sign.

6.3 LEFT on Monte Bello Road.

6.8 Picchetti Ranch and Winery at Monte Bello Open Space Preserve (live music on Sunday).

8.3 Road narrows considerably.

10.6 Ridge Winery on the left. *Wine-tasting on weekends; restrooms and water are available.*

11.5 LEFT on Waterwheel Creek Trail (gated dirt trail).

12.9 LEFT on Monte Bello Road (dirt).

13.8 Summit of Black Mountain.

14.1 LEFT on Indian Creek Trail.

15.0 LEFT on Canyon Trail, stay left at next two junctions to stay on Canyon Trail.

18.5 Gate and start of Stevens Canyon Road.

20.4 LEFT to stay on Stevens Canyon Road.

22.1 RIGHT on Mount Eden Road.

27.0 Arrive at starting point.

56 COYOTE CREEK TRAIL

San Jose to Morgan Hill

PAVED BIKE PATH

Difficulty: 2 **Total Distance:** 29.4 miles

Riding Time: 2-3 hours **Elevation Gain:** 400 feet

Summary: This paved recreation trail starts at San Jose's velodrome and is long enough to rack up some serious training miles.

Think San Jose and you probably think industrial parks. It's true, San Jose has more than its share of these mammoth concrete complexes, but it also has peaceful farmlands, orchards, and gurgling creeks. The Coyote Creek Trail passes by all of these on its 14.7-mile length from Coyote Hellyer County Park south to Anderson Lake County Park. This makes a level, 29.4-mile round-trip on a paved recreation trail. If you simply want to crank out some level miles on your bike without worrying about cars or trail junctions, this is a good place to do it, and it's close to home for millions of Bay Area residents.

The trail begins at Coyote Hellyer County

Park, home of the only velodrome in Northern California. Bike races are usually held on Wednesday, Thursday, and Friday nights in summer. The open-air velodrome was built in 1962 as a training site for the Pan American Games. A single lap around the track is 335 meters, or about 0.2 mile, and the corners are sharply banked. If you've never watched bike racing in a velodrome, you have to check it out.

In the trail's first 0.5 mile, you'll ride past small Cottonwood Lake on the left, a popular spot with shore anglers. The lake, which was developed out of an old rock quarry, is stocked with rainbow trout. Shortly beyond it, the trail crosses under U.S. 101 to the highway's east side. You'll cross the highway twice more along the route.

As you ride, ignore the numerous side bridges over Coyote Creek that access San Jose neighborhoods. Stay on the main path, which for a paved trail is a bit rough in places. You'll have to put up with the steady hum of road noise from U.S. 101 and Monterey Highway, which are never far away. But you'll also have the fine companionship of shady sycamores, cottonwoods, and live oaks along Coyote Creek, plus occasional scrub jays and ground squirrels. South of Metcalf Road, an equestrian trail parallels the paved trail, so you may see some horses, too.

The trail ends by the ranger station at Anderson Lake County Park, site of Santa Clara County's largest reservoir. You might want to lock up your bike here and take a walk on the one-mile, self-guided nature trail that runs to Malaguerra Avenue. It, too, follows Coyote Creek; a printed trail guide interprets the creek's riparian habitat.

For more information, contact Santa Clara County Parks and Recreation Department, 408/355-2200 or 408/225-0225, www.parkhere.org.

Options

If you've ever dreamed of riding on a velodrome track, your dreams can come true at Hellyer Park. Beginner sessions are held every Saturday morning. You can rent a fixed-gear track bike and will receive basic track instruction, all for about $10. For more information, visit www.ridethetrack.com.

Driving Directions

From San Jose, drive 4 miles south on U.S. 101 and take the Hellyer Avenue exit. Drive 0.25 mile to the Coyote Hellyer County Park entrance. Just beyond the entrance kiosk, bear left at the fork and park at the velodrome parking lot.

Route Directions

0.0 Park at the velodrome parking lot. The bike path begins by the restrooms. *Water is available at the park.*

0.4 Cottonwood Lake on the left.

0.8 Cross under U.S. 101.

3.0 LEFT at tricky intersection on far side of bridge.

5.5 Cross under U.S. 101.

6.8 Cross Metcalf Road to Coyote Ranch Road; go right to continue on path.

7.7 LEFT on Coyote Ranch Road, then RIGHT back onto path.

10.6 Cross Riverside Golf Course road.

14.0 Cross under U.S. 101.

14.7 Arrive at the ranger station for Anderson Lake County Park. TURN AROUND. *Water is available at the park.*

29.4 Arrive at starting point.

57 MOUNT HAMILTON   BEST

Joseph D. Grant County Park, southeast of San Jose

PAVED ROAD WITH MINIMAL CAR TRAFFIC

Difficulty: 4   **Total Distance:** 23 miles (or longer options)

Riding Time: 2 hours   **Elevation Gain:** 2,700 feet

Summary: Put your granny gear to work on this strenuous climb to the top of the Bay Area's loftiest peak.

The summit of Mount Hamilton, at 4,209 feet, is high enough so that on those rare winter days when snow falls in the Bay Area, it is gloriously crowned in white. It's the Bay Area's loftiest peak, and the highest you can drive to—or ride your bike to. It's also the home of Lick Observatory, where astronomers from the University of California keep a watch on the stars. Constructed in 1887 by James Lick, the observatory was once famous for its 36-inch telescope, the world's largest at that time.

The ascent to Mount Hamilton's summit is challenging, but not impossibly so, thanks to the curving, twisting, switchbacking, steady 5–7 percent grade of Mount Hamilton Road. Beginning from Joseph D. Grant County Park, you have 11.5 miles to gain 2,700 feet in elevation to the summit (this includes a 300-foot descent to Smith Creek, which you must regain).

Junctions are few and far between on this road, so you don't have route directions to worry about. Just follow the pavement uphill, through a landscape of grasslands, buckeyes, and mistletoe-draped oaks. In spring, the mountain is well known for its wildflower displays, and in autumn, the fall colors on the upper slopes can be delightful. As you ascend the mountain, you'll notice the foliage change: Coulter pines with their big, heavy cones appear among the manzanita, plus leafy black oaks. It gets cooler the higher you go, and the views of Santa Clara Valley get better and better.

For more information, contact Joseph D. Grant County Park, 408/274-6121, www.parkhere.org. The Lick Observatory (408/274-5061, www.ucolick.org) is open daily in summer noon–5 P.M. and Thursday–Sunday in winter noon–5 P.M.

Options

If you want to keep riding beyond the summit, help yourself. San Antonio Valley Road rolls, winds, and gradually descends until it changes names to Mines Road and eventually winds up in Livermore, 45 miles later. Almost no cars travel this stretch of road, so it's all yours. If you happen to know someone in Livermore who will give you a ride back to Joseph Grant Park, you're in for a fine day. Another way to add mileage is to start your ride at the junction of Alum Rock Avenue and Mount Hamilton Road, where there are pullouts on the side of Alum Rock Avenue with space for about 20 cars. This will add another 15.6 miles to your round-trip summit ride.

wild pig warning on Mount Hamilton Road near Lick Observatory

© ANN MARIE BROWN

Driving Directions

From I-680 in San Jose, take the Alum Rock Avenue exit and drive east 2.2 miles. Turn right on Mount Hamilton Road and drive 7.8 miles to the main entrance to Joseph D. Grant County Park on the right. Park in the county park lot (fee charged) or alongside the road in pullouts (no fee).

Route Directions

0.0 Park near the entrance to Joseph D. Grant County Park and ride southeast on Mount Hamilton Road. *Water is available in the park campground; supplies are available in San Jose.*

3.5 Twin Gates Trailhead and start of descent to Smith Creek. *Now or on the return trip, take a walk on Cañada de Pala Trail to see an abundance of blue-eyed grass, Johnny-jump-ups, brodiaea, shooting stars, and goldfields (springtime only).*

4.4 Smith Creek bridge.

5.6 STRAIGHT at junction with Kincaid Road on left.

10.9 RIGHT at Lick Observatory junction.

11.5 Arrive at main building and visitor area of observatory. TURN AROUND. *Water and snack machines are available when the visitor*

center is open, weekday afternoons and weekends 10 A.M.–5 P.M. Public tours are available.

23.0 Arrive at starting point.

MOUNT HAMILTON

58 GRANT RANCH LOOP

Joseph D. Grant County Park, southeast of San Jose

DIRT ROAD

Difficulty: 3

Total Distance: 10.9 or 12 miles

Riding Time: 2 hours

Elevation Gain: 1,600 feet

Summary: A series of ranch roads carve their way through the grasslands and past magnificent oaks in this pastoral county park.

Joseph D. Grant County Park, called Grant Ranch by the locals, lies due north of better known Henry Coe State Park, and it shares the same summer weather—hot as Hades. Plan your trip for the cooler months, preferably April or May when the grasslands are green and the slopes are gilded with wildflowers.

The park's trails are predominantly multiuse dirt roads that are used by mountain

At Joseph D. Grant County Park, most of the riding is on old ranch roads with steep hills on parts of the trails.

bikers more than anybody else. Almost every trail is an old ranch road, so if you are a single-track snob, you won't be happy here.

This challenging figure-eight loop trip takes you to the highest point in the park, Antler Point at 2,995 feet. The first two miles include some memorably steep uphill pitches, but the rest of the trip is more moderate. The ride starts at the Grant Lake Trailhead and follows Halls Valley Trail (open to bikes in the uphill direction only). The next 2.1 miles are the toughest of the ride, but as you gain elevation, you also gain surprising views of the South Bay's distant shimmering waters.

Where the trail tops out at Cañada de Pala Trail, turn left and enjoy an easier, more rolling grade. More views of the South Bay are seen to the northwest, and Mount Hamilton shows up to the east. Look for abundant displays of spring wildflowers on this high, bald ridge.

Your destination, Antler Point, is visible straight ahead, the highest hill around. Follow Pala Seca Trail through grasslands and occasional grazing bovines to Antler Point's spur trail. This grassy overlook supplies the day's best view of the South Bay, San Jose, Grant Park's rolling grasslands, and Lick Observatory on top of 4,209-foot Mount Hamilton.

For your return trip, loop back on Cañada de Pala Trail, enjoying more high views. You have some choices for the final leg: Los Huecos Trail (a very fast and steep downhill for a 10.9-mile loop) or Yerba Buena Trail (a more gentle downhill for a 12-mile loop). The latter will get you away from the biking crowds, but if you love screaming downhills, Los Huecos Trail is the only way to go.

For more information, contact Joseph D. Grant County Park, 408/274-6121, www.parkhere.org.

Driving Directions

From I-680 in San Jose, take the Alum Rock Avenue exit and drive east 2.2 miles. Turn right on Mount Hamilton Road and drive 7.8 miles to the sign for Joseph D. Grant County Park on the right. Don't turn here; continue another 100 yards to the Grant Lake parking lot on the left.

Route Directions

0.0 Park at the Grant Lake parking area. Follow the trail to the left to Grant Lake. *Water is available at the park campground.*

0.3 RIGHT on connector trail to Halls Valley Trail.

0.6 Straight on Halls Valley Trail and begin steep climb.

2.7 LEFT on Cañada de Pala Trail.

3.1 RIGHT on Pala Seca Trail.

4.8 RIGHT on Antler Point Trail (walk your bike 0.2 mile uphill to this 2,995-foot viewpoint).

4.9 Arrive at Antler Point. TURN AROUND.

5.1 RIGHT at junction with Pala Seca Trail.

8.1 LEFT to stay on Cañada de Pala Trail.

8.5 RIGHT on Los Huecos Trail; begin fast, steep descent. *If you prefer a gentler descent, continue on Cañada de Pala Trail for 1.3 miles farther and turn right on Yerba Buena Trail; this gets you back to your car in a 12-mile round-trip.*

10.3 STRAIGHT to return to Grant Lake.

10.6 LEFT to return to parking lot.

10.9 Arrive at starting point.

GRANT RANCH LOOP

59 MIDDLE RIDGE LOOP   BEST ☾
Henry W. Coe State Park, east of Morgan Hill

DIRT ROAD AND SINGLE-TRACK

Difficulty: 4   **Total Distance:** 10.8 miles

Riding Time: 2 hours   **Elevation Gain:** 2,100 feet

Summary: This huge state park is a great place to get away from it all and enjoy some great single-track riding and steep climbs and descents.

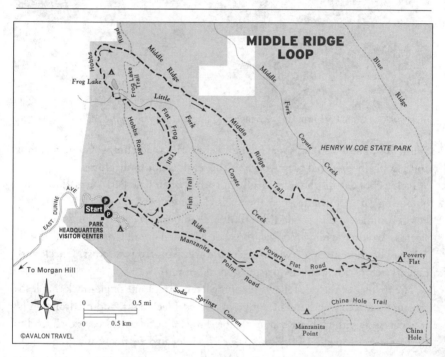

The closest thing to a wilderness park in the South Bay area is Henry W. Coe State Park. This well-known but little-traveled state park is the second largest in California (the largest is Anza-Borrego Desert State Park near San Diego). Composed of tall ridges bisected by deep, steep ravines, the park is notoriously hilly. Its varied terrain includes grasslands, oaks, chaparral, pines, and mixed hardwoods.

Henry Coe is so large—80,000 acres—and its terrain is so rugged that to see much of it, you need to pack your bike's panniers and plan to stay for a few days. But day visitors can tour the western part of the park on this 10.8-mile loop around Middle Ridge. The ride has some of the finest single-track to be found in the

Henry W. Coe State Park provides a challenging single-track ride on the Middle Ridge Loop.

South Bay, but it also has some of the steepest fire road climbs. Come mentally and physically prepared for a workout; this park is not for beginners.

Pick a cool day for the ride, ideally in spring when Coe Park's wildflowers are blooming, or in autumn when the air is clear and cool. The park is extremely hot in summer, and its single-track trails are temporarily closed after winter rainstorms. Also in the rainy months, the wide Middle Fork of Coyote Creek at mile 7.2 may be more than a few feet deep and too dangerous to cross. Check with rangers before riding this loop after a period of rain.

The first leg of the ride follows Flat Frog Trail, a pleasant single-track that leads through a mixed woodland of ponderosa pines, black oaks, and madrones. The trail connects with Hobbs Road just before Frog Lake; take the steep ranch road to the former cattle pond. (A backpacking camp is located nearby.) Tiny Frog Lake is spring fed; it supports a few bass and bluegill. Frequently, the surface of the water is completely covered with green algae. Cross Frog Lake's inlet and continue steeply uphill to Middle Ridge. The oak-dotted grasslands above Frog Lake support colorful wildflowers, which give you something to look at while you stop to catch your breath.

Once you reach Middle Ridge, look forward to a roller-coaster descent with many fine views of Coyote Creek canyon. Although Middle Ridge Trail initially leads through alternating grassy clearings and groves of pines and black oaks, it later enters a grove of giant, tree-sized manzanitas growing 15 feet tall. The trail loses 1,700 feet over 3.4 miles (with one short but steep uphill), and becomes more technical as it drops. In its final mile, it is downright treacherous—steep, loose, narrow, rocky, and rutted.

After crossing the Middle Fork of Coyote Creek, get ready to pay the price for all the fun you've had: You face a 1.8-mile climb on rocky Poverty Flat Road with a 1,400-foot elevation gain (12 percent average grade). Sometimes mountain biking is hell, and this is one of those times. When at last you reach Manzanita Point Road, the punishment is over, and you have an easy ride back to your car.

For more information, contact Henry W. Coe State Park, 408/779-2728, www. coepark.org.

Driving Directions

From U.S. 101 in Morgan Hill, take the East Dunne Avenue exit and drive east for 13 miles to Henry W. Coe State Park headquarters.

Route Directions

0.0 Park at the lot near park headquarters. Follow paved Manzanita Point Road from near the headquarters building (pavement ends shortly). *Water is available at the trailhead; supplies are available in Morgan Hill.*

0.5 RIGHT to stay on Manzanita Point Road at junction with Hobbs Road.

0.7 LEFT on Flat Frog Trail.

2.9 RIGHT on Hobbs Road.

3.2 Frog Lake. Cross the dam and join trail to Middle Ridge (steep climb uphill).

3.8 RIGHT on Middle Ridge Trail; begin long, steep descent.

5.1 STRAIGHT on Middle Ridge Trail at junction with Fish Trail.

7.2 Cross Middle Fork of Coyote Creek at Poverty Flat.

7.3 RIGHT on Poverty Flat Road; begin long, steep climb out.

9.1 RIGHT on Manzanita Point Road.

10.3 LEFT to stay on Manzanita Point Road.

10.8 Arrive at starting point.

MIDDLE RIDGE LOOP

60 BERRY CREEK FALLS BIKE AND HIKE (SKYLINE-TO-THE-SEA TRAIL) BEST ☾
Big Basin Redwoods State Park, south of Pescadero

DIRT ROAD AND SINGLE-TRACK

Difficulty: 2

Total Distance: 11.6 miles (plus 1.2-mile hike)

Riding Time: 2.5 hours

Elevation Gain: 550 feet

Summary: Take a jaunt to one of the Bay Area's prettiest waterfalls by bike and on foot, easy enough for the whole family to enjoy.

You can see Berry Creek Falls the hard way, by hiking 5.5 hilly miles from park headquarters at Big Basin Redwoods State Park, or you can see Berry Creek Falls the easy way, by riding your bike 5.8 nearly level miles from the coast near Davenport, then walking the last 0.6 mile.

The 70-foot falls are worth seeing no matter how you get there, but if you have children in tow, or if you aren't anywhere near the Boulder Creek entrance to the park, or if you'd just rather ride than walk, the bike route is a smart choice. Riders of almost any ability can handle the wide dirt road, and the trip begins and ends at an easy-access trailhead right on Highway 1.

The trail, which is the western section of the 38-mile-long Skyline-to-the-Sea Trail, used to be even easier to ride, but a series of heavy rains in the 1990s washed parts of it into Waddell Creek, forcing one stretch to be rerouted as narrow single-track with a few ludicrously tight turns. The vast majority of riders simply walk their bikes through this 100-yard stretch.

The old ranch road begins by the highway, passes by Big Basin's Rancho del Oso visitor center and a few private farms, then enters the redwoods. The entire route parallels Waddell Creek until the final walk to the falls, where the trail follows Berry Creek. Several

© ANN MARIE BROWN

An easy ride through the redwoods leads to the beautiful Berry Creek Falls.

backpacking camps are located a few yards off the route, used mostly by hikers following the entire length of Skyline-to-the-Sea Trail.

Make sure you bring a bike lock so you can secure your wheels at the bike rack and take the 15-minute hike to the waterfall (bikes are not allowed). A bench on the viewing platform at Berry Creek Falls makes a perfect spot for lunch, if it isn't already in use by somebody else. Not surprisingly, this is a popular spot year-round. Plan a weekday trip if at all possible.

For more information, contact Big Basin Redwoods State Park, 831/338-8860, www.santacruzstateparks.org.

Driving Directions

From Half Moon Bay at the junction of Highway 92 and Highway 1, drive south on Highway 1 for 30 miles to the Rancho del Oso area of Big Basin Redwoods State Park (across from Waddell Beach, 7.5 miles north of Davenport). Park on the east side of the highway by the Rancho del Oso gate.

Route Directions

0.0 Park at Rancho del Oso trailhead and ride into the parking lot and past the visitor center. *Supplies are available in Davenport.*

0.4 Pass the Rancho del Oso nature center (open most weekends).

3.0 Trail washout creates tricky section with tight switchbacks. May have to walk your bike.

3.3 Cross Waddell Creek; follow the single-track trail on the right to a bridge if the stream is too high to cross.

5.8 Bike rack; TURN AROUND. *Lock up your bike and follow the hiking trail across the creek for 0.6 mile to Berry Creek Falls.*

11.6 Arrive at starting point.

BERRY CREEK FALLS BIKE AND HIKE (SKYLINE-TO-THE-SEA TRAIL)

MONTEREY AND BIG SUR

© ANN MARIE BROWN

BEST BIKE RIDES

❰ Butt-Kickers
Nacimiento-Fergusson Road to the Mission,
    page 512.

❰ Historic Rides
Aptos Creek Fire Road to Sand Point, **page 482.**

❰ Oceanfront Rides
Wilder Ranch Bluffs Ride, **page 476.**
17-Mile Drive, **page 497.**

❰ Paved Bike Paths
Monterey Recreation Trail, **page 494.**

❰ Single-Track Rides
Soquel Demonstration State Forest, **page 485.**

❰ Wildlife-Viewing
Davenport to Santa Cruz Loop, **page 470.**
Big Sur to Lucia, **page 509.**

❰ Wine-Tasting
Davenport to Santa Cruz Loop, **page 470.**

It wouldn't be easy to choose the most spectacular stretch of California coastline, but if pressed, most beach connoisseurs would agree there is nothing quite as visually stunning as the 130 miles of cliffs, rocks, and waves that run from Davenport to San Simeon. Cyclists have been traveling this stretch of Highway 1 ever since the road was built in the 1930s. Along the way, they pause on top of 200-foot-high cliffs to admire the crashing surf, cross over concrete bridges spanning precipitous river gorges, and experience mile after mile of postcard-quality coastal scenery.

There is nothing to dislike here, from the mild climate to the wild landscape. Much of this area is isolated, undeveloped, and difficult to access, with high cliffs and few roads. Visiting this land means wandering along gravel beaches, watching sunsets over glimmering seas, and walking in the shadows of giant redwoods. South of Carmel, services are clustered in a few small towns: Big Sur, Lucia, Gorda, and San Simeon. In between are silence, solitude, and the sea.

In the midst of all this splendor, every winter and spring, like clockwork, a great natural spectacle occurs: Gray whales pass by on their long migrations. Traveling from their summer home in Alaska's Bering Sea to their winter breeding grounds in Baja, then back again a few months later, they leave hundreds of frothy spouts and occasional glimpses of fins or tails as their calling cards. Any spot along the Monterey and Big Sur coastline is a good place to observe the more than 18,000 gray whales as they cruise by – but the bluffs of Andrew Molera State Park, open to mountain bikers, and the stretch of Highway 1 between Big Sur and Lucia, popular with road cyclists, are two of the better sighting areas. Whale-watching is at its best December–May, on days when the sea is flat and deep blue, with no wind or whitecaps.

Besides watching whales, there's much more to keep a bicyclist occupied in the Monterey and Big Sur region. To the north, mountain bikers cruise the trails of Wilder Ranch and Forest of Nisene Marks State Parks near Santa Cruz, or head for the more remote single-track of Soquel Demonstration State Forest and Fort Ord. To the south, they ride the dirt roads of Los Padres National Forest, including the spectacular trek up to Cone Peak Fire Lookout. Road cyclists have myriad coastal and inland routes to choose from in and around Monterey Bay, including the world-famous 17-Mile Drive with its ocean lookouts, golf courses, and mansions. And riders of all styles and abilities can pedal on the 18-mile Monterey Recreation Trail that runs from Castroville to Pacific Grove, passing by highlights such as the Monterey Bay Aquarium and Cannery Row.

Whatever kind of riding you enjoy, you'll find the right trail in the Monterey and Big Sur region. Here at "the greatest meeting of land and sea" lies a world of bicycling opportunities.

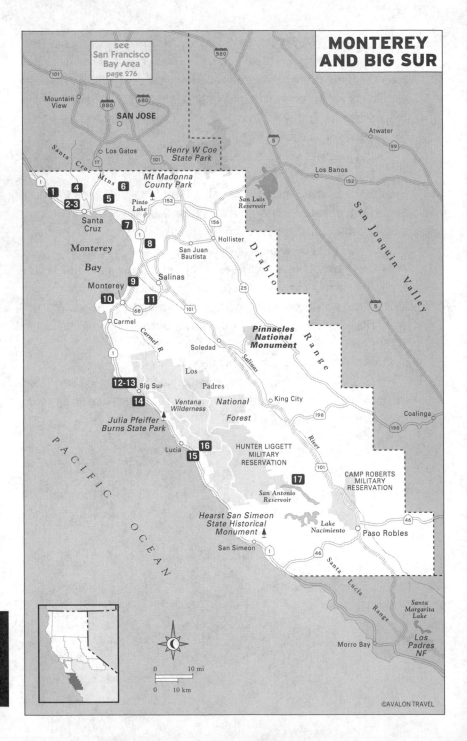

MONTEREY AND BIG SUR

©AVALON TRAVEL

TRAIL NAME	LEVEL	DISTANCE	TIME	ELEVATION	PAGE
1 Davenport to Santa Cruz Loop	3	31.4 mi	3 hr	1,900 ft	470
2 Wilder Ranch Inland Loop	2	9.1 mi	2 hr	800 ft	473
3 Wilder Ranch Bluffs Ride	1	7.6 mi	1.5 hr	200 ft	476
4 Henry Cowell Redwoods Ramble	2	7.4 mi	1.5 hr	850 ft	479
5 Aptos Creek Fire Road to Sand Point	3	13.8 mi	3 hr	1,400 ft	482
6 Soquel Demonstration State Forest	4	14.1 mi	3 hr	2,100 ft	485
7 Sunset Beach to Rio del Mar	2	20.2 mi	2 hr	800 ft	488
8 Elkhorn Slough Loop	2	21.8 mi	2 hr	900 ft	491
9 Monterey Recreation Trail	2	29 mi	2-3 hr	800 ft	494
10 17-Mile Drive	2	17.4 mi	1.5-2 hr	900 ft	497
11 Fort Ord Loop	3	10.7 mi	1.5 hr	1,300 ft	501
12 Andrew Molera Ramble	2	7 mi	1.5 hr	1,000 ft	504
13 Old Coast Road Loop	4	18.8 mi	3-4 hr	2,600 ft	506
14 Big Sur to Lucia	4	51 mi	5 hr	3,300 ft	509
15 Nacimiento-Fergusson Road to the Mission	5	58.8 mi	5-6 hr	4,200 ft	512
16 Cone Peak Lookout Bike and Hike	3	10.8 mi	2 hr	1,100 ft	515
17 Lake San Antonio Loop	4	53.2 mi	5 hr	2,200 ft	518

1 DAVENPORT TO SANTA CRUZ LOOP BEST ☾
north of Santa Cruz

PAVED ROADS WITH MODERATE CAR TRAFFIC

Difficulty: 3

Riding Time: 3 hours

Total Distance: 31.4 miles

Elevation Gain: 1,900 feet

Summary: Shoreline cruising and serious hill climbing take you past a surfing museum, a monarch butterfly preserve, and a winery perched high on a ridge above Santa Cruz.

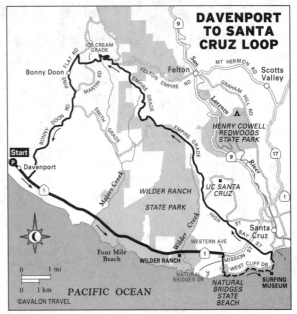

This loop road ride has a little bit of everything: coastal riding along Highway 1, a car-free recreation path along the beaches of Santa Cruz, and a hill climb workout on the forested back roads northeast of Santa Cruz.

You might want to start your ride with a hearty breakfast at the Davenport Roadhouse (831/426-8801, www. davenportroadhouse. com, closed Mondays). Then take off south on Highway 1, passing the entrance to Wilder Ranch State Park on your way to Santa Cruz. You'll be able to get off the highway and onto a paved recreation trail at Wilder Ranch; it will take you all the way into the north end of Santa Cruz. Soon thereafter, you can pick up the recreational trail that runs through Natural Bridges State Beach and alongside West Cliff Drive. There you'll enjoy glorious coastside cruising with blue-water views. This is a popular path, though, so watch out for the usual gamut of baby strollers, in-line skaters, walkers, and the like. For some local color, stop at the Santa Cruz surfing museum in the old lighthouse building at mile 11.6. In the autumn and winter months, even brighter local color is found at Natural Bridges, where monarch butterflies nest in the eucalyptus trees.

A busy stretch of the Davenport to Santa Cruz Loop runs along West Cliff Drive.

Gear down for a climb up Bay Street and Empire Grade, passing by the entrance to the University of California, Santa Cruz. If you tire of the steady ascent, you can take a shortcut on Smith Grade at mile 19.3; otherwise, continue onward to Ice Cream Grade. This is a fun descent on a narrow, winding road. A left turn on Pine Flat Road brings you to Beauregard Vineyards (831/425-7777, www.beauregardvineyards.com), where you can sample varietals and enjoy the view from the picnic area. Then check your brakes, because you're heading for a 10 percent downhill grade on Bonny Doon Road, dropping down to Highway 1. One final northward mile brings you back to Davenport, but you might choose to simply cross Highway 1 instead and head for the beach.

Options

Although this ride is described as starting in the quaint coastal town of Davenport, you could just as easily join the loop from the University of California, Santa Cruz or downtown Santa Cruz.

Driving Directions

From Santa Cruz, drive north on Highway 1 for 11 miles to Davenport.

Route Directions

0.0 Park in downtown Davenport. Ride south on Highway 1. *Supplies are available in Davenport.*

7.0 Wilder Ranch State Park on the right. After passing the entrance, you can get off the highway and onto the parallel paved recreation trail that heads south into Santa Cruz. *Water is available at Wilder Ranch.*

8.7 RIGHT on Western Drive.

8.8 RIGHT on Mission Street.

8.9 LEFT on Natural Bridges Drive.

9.2 STRAIGHT through gate into Natural Bridges State Beach (follow pavement). *Lock up your bike and walk the short trail to see the monarch butterflies September–December.*

9.7 STRAIGHT on West Cliff Drive (exit Natural Bridges State Beach). Follow paved recreation trail alongside the road.

11.6 Surfing museum and Seal Rock on the right.

12.3 LEFT on Bay Street. Begin climb.

13.3 Cross Highway 1.

14.4 LEFT on High Street at entrance to the University of California, Santa Cruz; High Street becomes Empire Grade.

19.3 STRAIGHT at junction with Smith Grade on left. *Shortcut is possible by turning left here; it cuts off three miles.*

22.6 LEFT on Ice Cream Grade.

25.2 LEFT on Pine Flat Road at T-junction.

26.9 STRAIGHT on Bonny Doon Road; Beauregard Vineyards is on the left. *Wine-tasting is available 11 A.M.–5 P.M. daily.*

30.4 RIGHT on Highway 1. *Or cross the highway and head for the beach on the other side of the railroad tracks.*

31.4 Arrive at starting point.

DAVENPORT TO SANTA CRUZ LOOP

② WILDER RANCH INLAND LOOP
Wilder Ranch State Park, north of Santa Cruz

DIRT ROAD AND SINGLE-TRACK

Difficulty: 2   **Total Distance:** 9.1 miles (or 10.7-mile option)

Riding Time: 2 hours   **Elevation Gain:** 800 feet

Summary: The wide variety of trails at Wilder Ranch State Park make it a hot spot for coastal mountain biking.

Wilder Ranch State Park's 5,100-acre north side is almost completely the domain of mountain bikers. The experience here is a lot like visiting a mountain bike park at the ski areas around Tahoe or Mammoth. Looking upward from the bottom of Wilder's coastal hills, you'll see dozens of bikers racing toward you, each

The inland trails at Wilder Ranch State Park provide wide views of coast and hills.

carving perfect S-turns on their descent down the slope. The park's 30 miles of trails seem to have been built with mountain biking in mind: They rollercoaster up and down with plenty of twists, turns, and a number of technical challenges, including stream crossings and rock beds.

Not surprisingly, it's a popular place, but there's no reason to be intimidated by the crowds, even on sunny, busy weekends. The park is large enough to accommodate everybody. A major plus is the great view of Monterey Bay and the Pacific Ocean, visible from several high points in these coastal hills. You just have to be willing to climb a bit.

A wide range of possible loops exist at Wilder, but most start with an ascent on wide Wilder Ridge Trail. The loop outlined here is a solid intermediate ride with a good dose of single-track and some challenges to test your skills. The single-track begins at mile 1.2 where Wilder Ridge Loop Trail meanders around the open coastal hills through dozens of curves and turns. Next comes a stint on Zane Gray, with some steep uphill challenges, followed by more uphill on wide Wilder Ridge Fire Road. Then you'll experience some fun single-track on Eucalyptus Loop and Old Cabin Trail, both of which head steeply down, then up, a wooded gulch.

For more information, contact Wilder Ranch State Park, 831/423-9703, www.santacruzstateparks.org or www.parks.ca.gov.

Options

If you want to add a couple more miles, tack on to this loop the 1.6-mile Enchanted Loop, which starts and ends at the rather confusing junction at mile 4.5. Its steep single-track and fire road pitches up and down through a dense redwood forest lined with sorrel and ferns along Baldwin Creek. This is what mountain biking was meant to be.

Driving Directions

From Santa Cruz, drive north on Highway 1 for four miles. Turn left into the entrance for Wilder Ranch State Park, then follow the park road to its end at the main parking area.

Route Directions

0.0 Park at the main lot at Wilder Ranch. Walk your bike on the paved trail from the parking lot to the cultural preserve/ranch buildings. Walk past the buildings and picnic area, then ride your bike through the tunnel to the east side of Highway 1. *Supplies are available in Davenport to the north or Santa Cruz to the south.*

0.4 Hairpin LEFT on Wilder Ridge Fire Road.

1.2 LEFT on Wilder Ridge single-track.

3.0 RIGHT on Zane Gray single-track.

3.9 LEFT on Wilder Ridge Fire Road.

4.5 STRAIGHT on paved road toward Eucalyptus Loop at confusing junction. Or, to add on 1.6 miles, turn left on Enchanted Loop, which will bring you back to this junction.

4.7 RIGHT on Eucalyptus Loop single-track.

5.9 RIGHT on connector to Old Cabin Trail.

7.0 RIGHT on fire road.

7.2 LEFT on Wild Boar Trail.

7.5 RIGHT on Engelsman Loop Trail.

8.7 STRAIGHT at junction with Wilder Ridge Fire Road. Ride past corrals, through tunnel, then walk bike through cultural center.

9.1 Arrive at starting point.

WILDER RANCH INLAND LOOP

3 WILDER RANCH BLUFFS RIDE   BEST
Wilder Ranch State Park, north of Santa Cruz

DIRT ROAD AND SINGLE-TRACK

Difficulty: 1   **Total Distance:** 7.6 miles

Riding Time: 1.5 hours   **Elevation Gain:** 200 feet

Summary: For beginners and those riding beach cruisers, this is an easy and view-filled jaunt on the coastal bluffs at Wilder Ranch.

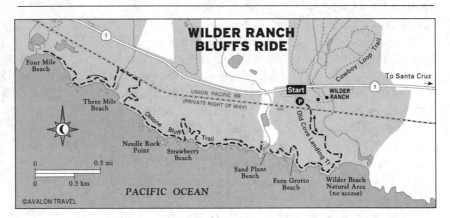

Old Cove Landing and Ohlone Bluff Trails are exactly the opposite of all other trails at Wilder Ranch State Park. These trails are coastal; the park's other trails are inland. These trails are almost completely level; the park's other trails are roller-coaster climbs and descents.

For easy riding, a cruise on Old Cove Landing and Ohlone Bluff Trails is a great way to spend an afternoon at Wilder Ranch State Park. The trails reveal many surprises, including dramatic cliffs and sea arches, a seal rookery, windswept beaches, and a hidden fern cave.

Old Cove Landing Trail begins from the main parking lot to the right of the restrooms. Begin riding on a level ranch road through the park's agricultural preserve—nearly 900 acres of Brussels sprout fields. The trail travels toward the coast, then turns right to parallel it. You're pedaling on top of sandstone and mudstone bluffs, the remains of an ancient marine terrace. In short order you'll pass a wooden platform overlooking Wilder Beach, a critical habitat area for the endangered snowy plover, followed by the trail's namesake, the old landing cove—a remarkably narrow inlet where small schooners pulled in and anchored to load lumber in the late 1800s.

Continuing onward, you'll cruise by a huge flat rock where harbor seals

© ANN MARIE BROWN

Old Cove Landing and Ohlone Bluff Trails trace the edge of oceanside cliffs at Wilder Ranch State Park.

hang out, lying around in the sun to warm their flippers. At a wooden post marked as number 8, look down on Fern Grotto Beach, a small sandy cove. Tucked into its back wall is a shallow cave filled with sword and bracken ferns. A spur trail takes you there; you can carry your bike down and explore the cave if you please.

Beyond Fern Grotto Beach lie several more beaches. Accessing them, however, requires a little upper body strength. At Sand Plant Beach, a sign directs you down to the beach and across the sand. You'll have to carry your bike. Then follow another trail back up to the bluffs on the beach's south side. (The bluffs above Sand Plant Beach are private farming property; most of the year, bikers are not permitted to ride through.)

Once you're back on the bluffs south of Sand Plant, the trail name changes to Ohlone Bluff Trail and travels 2.5 miles farther, past Strawberry Beach, Needle Rock, Three Mile Beach, and finally Four Mile Beach, a strip of sand well known for its clothing-optional tendencies. At Four Mile, the trail turns inland, crosses the railroad tracks, then passes through a tunnel under Highway 1 to connect to Baldwin Loop Trail on the east side of the park. Some riders connect to the inland trails this way, but the majority turn around and head back the way they came, enjoying the coastal scenery from the opposite perspective.

For more information, contact Wilder Ranch State Park, 831/423-9703, www.santacruzstateparks.org or www.parks.ca.gov.

Driving Directions

From Santa Cruz, drive north on Highway 1 for four miles. Turn left into the entrance for Wilder Ranch State Park, then follow the park road to its end at the main parking area. For trail map and elevation profile, see ride 2, *Wilder Ranch Inland Loop.*

Route Directions

0.0 Park at the main lot at Wilder Ranch. Take the signed Old Cove Landing Trail from the right side of the restrooms. *Supplies are available in Davenport to the north or Santa Cruz to the south.*

1.0 Fern Grotto Beach at marker 8.

1.3 Sand Plant Beach. Follow trail down to beach, across sand, and back up bluffs on other side (carry your bike).

1.9 Strawberry Beach.

2.6 Three Mile Beach

3.8 Four Mile Beach. TURN AROUND.

7.6 Arrive at starting point.

4 HENRY COWELL REDWOODS RAMBLE
Henry Cowell Redwoods State Park in Felton

DIRT ROAD AND PAVED BIKE PATH

Difficulty: 2

Total Distance: 7.4 miles (or 9.7-mile option)

Riding Time: 1.5 hours

Elevation Gain: 850 feet

Summary: A paved trail leads deep into the redwood forest, then joins with a network of dirt paths that lead to swimming holes in the San Lorenzo River.

Henry Cowell Redwoods State Park is celebrated for its ancient groves of coast redwoods. It's famous for its Roaring Camp Railroad steam trains, which roar over tracks carving through the center of the park. And it's well known for the San Lorenzo River, which provides good swimming for park visitors in summer, and rushing waters for salmon and steelhead in winter.

But while bicyclists may enjoy all these aspects of Henry Cowell Redwoods State Park, what they'll really like is Pipeline Road, a paved service road that travels the park's length. A few dirt roads branch off the paved route, giving mountain bikers a chance to see more of the park.

The initial, paved part of the ride travels through a forest of second- and third-growth redwoods, Douglas firs, and bay laurel, and passes by a railroad trestle crossing over the San Lorenzo River. (Don't be surprised if a steam train comes barreling through.) Although the river is only a few inches deep in summer, it can be 20 or 30 feet deep during winter rains.

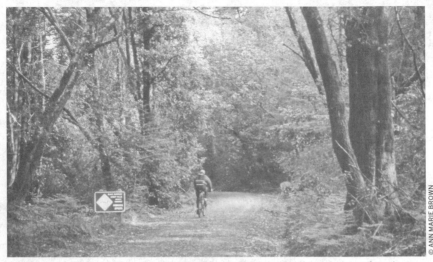

Pipeline Road in Henry Cowell Redwoods State Park meanders through dense forest.

The second mile of pavement climbs steeply to a ridgeline, from which you can see all the way down the San Lorenzo River canyon to Monterey Bay and the Pacific Ocean. At a major junction of trails at mile 2.3, take Powder Mill Fire Road uphill (expect to encounter some annoying sandy patches where you'll lose traction) to a concrete observation deck. There you'll find a picnic table and water fountain, plus two surprising types of trees—knobcone pines and ponderosa pines. The latter, with its distinctive jigsaw-puzzle bark, usually is found at much higher elevations in places like the Sierra Nevada. Walk up the observation deck's stairs and you'll have a somewhat obstructed view of Monterey Bay. (The trees have grown up since the deck was built.)

The park map makes it seem obvious to loop back from the observation deck by continuing on Ridge Fire Road, but this stretch can't be ridden (except by an elite few) due to deep sand and foot-high stairsteps (drain bars). Instead, retrace your tire tracks down Powder Mill Fire Road and Pipeline Road, then take Rincon Fire Road to Cathedral Redwoods, a peaceful grove of big trees. This is the suggested turnaround for this ride, but if you don't mind losing (and then having to regain) another 400 feet in elevation in the next 0.5 mile, you could continue down to the San Lorenzo River, where swimming holes abound in summer.

For more information, contact Henry Cowell Redwoods State Park, 831/335-4598 or 831/335-2974, www.santacruzstateparks.org or www.parks.ca.gov.

Options

From the swimming holes at the San Lorenzo River, some riders choose to loop back on Highway 9 rather than climbing back up the steep hill they just descended. If you are a sensible sort, the heavy highway traffic should deter you. But if you insist on taking the shortcut, you must carry your bike across the river, follow the service road for 0.5 mile, then turn right on Highway 9 and ride 3 miles back to the park, for a 9.7-mile round-trip.

Driving Directions

From Santa Cruz at the junction of Highways 1 and 9, take Highway 9 north six miles to the right turnoff for Henry Cowell Redwoods State Park. Continue past the entrance kiosk to the visitor center and main parking lot.

Route Directions

0.0 Park at the main day-use lot, then follow the signs to the Redwood Grove and Nature Center. Take the paved road that leads to the right of the nature center to connect to Pipeline Road (behind the nature center). *Supplies are available in Felton. Water is available in the park.*

0.6 Pass railroad bridge over San Lorenzo River.

2.3 LEFT on Powder Mill Fire Road.

2.9 LEFT on Ridge Fire Road.

3.1 Observation deck. TURN AROUND. *Water is available.*

3.3 RIGHT on Powder Mill Fire Road.

3.9 RIGHT on Pipeline Road.

4.7 LEFT on Ridge Fire Road.

4.9 LEFT on Rincon Fire Road.

5.3 Cathedral Redwoods. TURN AROUND. *Or continue steeply downhill for 0.5 mile to swimming holes in the San Lorenzo River. See possible loop option in Options above.*

5.7 RIGHT on Ridge Fire Road.

5.9 LEFT on Pipeline Road.

7.4 Arrive at starting point.

HENRY COWELL REDWOODS RAMBLE

5 APTOS CREEK FIRE ROAD TO SAND POINT

BEST ☾

The Forest of Nisene Marks State Park, east of Santa Cruz

DIRT ROAD

Difficulty: 3 (4 for longer option)

Total Distance: 13.8 miles (or 20.8-mile option)

Riding Time: 3 hours   **Elevation Gain:** 1,400 feet (or 2,400-foot option)

Summary: Follow a winding railroad grade past the epicenter of the Loma Prieta earthquake to a high overlook above Monterey Bay.

Two major forces have shaped the land at The Forest of Nisene Marks State Park: the railroad and unstable geology. Old-growth redwoods remained untouched in this steep and winding canyon for hundreds of years until the Loma Prieta Lumber Company came into ownership in 1881. Teaming up with the Southern Pacific, they built a railroad along Aptos Creek and worked the land with trains, oxen, skid roads, inclines, horses, and as many men as they could hire, removing 140 million board feet of lumber over the course of 40 years. In 1922, when the loggers finally put their saws down, there were no trees left.

Luckily, Mother Nature has been busy in the last century. Today the canyon is filled with second-growth redwoods and Douglas firs, and the higher ridges are lined with oaks, eucalyptus, and madrones.

Mother Nature was especially busy on October 17, 1989, when the park was the epicenter of the famous Loma

Prieta earthquake, which forcefully shook the entire San Francisco Bay Area. Although there's nothing much to see, you'll ride past the earthquake epicenter

Tall redwoods and leafy ferns line Aptos Creek.

on this out-and-back tour, which follows Aptos Creek Fire Road to Sand Point Overlook.

The ride is simple to follow, shaded all the way, and without a lot of technical challenges. The first 2.6 miles are inevitably the most crowded; the grade is so mellow here that even children can ride it. From George's Picnic Area, the hard-packed dirt road parallels Aptos Creek, climbing almost imperceptibly. After crossing a steel bridge and passing the earthquake epicenter area, the road's grade abruptly intensifies. You're entering a stretch known as the Molino Incline, which makes several hairpin turns as it ascends 660 feet in slightly over a mile. An incline railway just west of the road once lowered logs straight down the ridge to the mill on Aptos Creek.

If you can make it to the "Top of the Incline" at 3.9 miles, the rest of the route seems easier. From the "Top of the Incline" to Santa Rosalia Mountain, Aptos Creek Fire Road follows the route of the loggers' narrow-gauge railroad. It ascends more gently for the final 3 miles to Sand Point Overlook at 1,617 feet in elevation. The view from the benches at Sand Point is an open vista of Monterey Bay and the tree-filled canyons and ridges of the Santa Cruz Mountains. You'll probably share the overlook with a posse of other happy riders, especially on weekend afternoons.

For more information, contact Sunset State Beach (managers for The Forest of Nisene Marks State Park), 831/763-7062 or 831/763-7063, www.santacruzstateparks.org or www.parks.ca.gov.

Options

If you haven't had your fill of climbing, you can continue uphill from Sand Point; Aptos Creek Fire Road continues another 3.5 miles to Santa Rosalia Overlook, elevation 2,529 feet. The trail section above Sand Point is known as "The Ladder" because it steepens, then levels out, then steepens, and so on. You'll even have a few downhills just before you reach Santa Rosalia Overlook, which is located at a wide clearing with blue-water views of Monterey Bay. This time you'll share the vista with less company.

Driving Directions

From Santa Cruz, drive south on Highway 1 for 6 miles to the Aptos/State Park Drive exit. Turn left at the exit, cross over the highway, then turn right on Soquel Drive and drive 0.5 mile. Turn left on Aptos Creek Road and drive 1.8 miles to George's Picnic Area.

Route Directions

0.0 Park at George's Picnic Area. *Supplies are available in Aptos.*

2.6 Sign may be in place that reads "Epicenter Area, 7.1 Earthquake, 5:04 P.M., October 17, 1989." *A bike rack is located here. A hiking trail leads 0.5 mile from this sign to the exact epicenter.*

3.9 "Top of the Incline."

6.9 Arrive at Sand Point Overlook. TURN AROUND. *Or continue uphill 3.5 miles farther to Santa Rosalia Overlook; see Options.*

13.8 Arrive at starting point.

APTOS CREEK FIRE ROAD TO SAND POINT

6 SOQUEL DEMONSTRATION STATE FOREST

BEST ☾

north of Santa Cruz

DIRT ROAD AND SINGLE-TRACK; PAVED ROAD WITH MINIMAL CAR TRAFFIC

Difficulty: 4

Total Distance: 14.1 miles

Riding Time: 3 hours

Elevation Gain: 2,100 feet

Summary: Amid a dense forest setting, miles of single-track await experienced mountain bikers looking for technical challenges.

This ride in Soquel Demonstration State Forest is challenging, both in terms of elevation gain and the skills needed to ride its steep, technical single-track. But it's worth it. The state forest is in a remote area of the Santa Cruz Mountains on the northeast boundary of The Forest of Nisene Marks State Park. The terrain is much like Nisene Marks—dense forests of redwoods, tan oaks, and madrones—but the trails are as different as can be, with miles of gnarly single-tracks that twist, turn, and pitch steeply up and down. This is the kind of trail that the true mountain biker lives for.

The ride begins with a climb on paved Highland Way, following pretty Soquel Creek. Two right turns and more climbing on dirt roads bring you to the Santa Rosalia Overlook in The Forest of Nisene Marks State Park. Enjoy the wide view of Monterey Bay from the clearing, then get ready for a long roller-coaster ride on single-track, heading back into the state forest. Ridge Trail pitches up and down steeply for 3.5 miles, supplying more ocean views at openings between the trees. Around the 8.3-mile mark, the trail suddenly becomes too steep for anyone to ride. After pushing your bike for a 100-yard stretch, you'll follow Ridge Trail to the right as it becomes Sawpit Trail, one of the most amazing stretches of single-track in Northern California. It is a gross understatement to say that the next 1.2 miles are an extremely steep descent. (Lowering your seat is more than a good idea.) In addition, the trail is littered with every imaginable kind of obstacle, including redwood trees, ruts, hairpin turns, and poison oak. If this trail doesn't scare the daylights out of you, you're going to have a ball.

The final stretch of the loop is a rather pedestrian climb on dirt Hihn's Mill Road back to your car. But after all the excitement you've just had, you'll probably be relieved to ride on a plain old dirt road.

For more information, contact Soquel Demonstration State Forest, 831/475-8643.

Driving Directions

From Santa Cruz, take Highway 17 north for 13 miles to the Summit Road exit. Drive southeast on Summit Road for 5 miles, where it becomes Highland Way. Continue on Highland Way for 4.7 more miles. A small sign by a bridge and a dirt road junction marks the parking area for Soquel Demonstration State Forest.

Route Directions

0.0 Park at the Soquel Forest parking lot on Highland Way, then ride to your right (south) on paved Highland Way. *Supplies are available at the Summit Store on Summit Road.*

1.9 RIGHT on Buzzard Lagoon Road (dirt road).

2.9 RIGHT on Aptos Creek Fire Road.

4.1 Gate for The Forest of Nisene Marks State Park.

5.1 RIGHT on single-track Ridge Trail at Santa Rosalia Overlook (wide, flat clearing with view of Monterey Bay). Stay LEFT on Ridge Trail at next three junctions.

7.4 Overlook point.

8.3 Impossible stretch; plan on walking.

8.5 RIGHT on Sawpit Trail (Ridge Trail simply turns right and becomes Sawpit Trail—not really a junction).

9.7 RIGHT on Hihn's Mill Road (dirt road).

14.1 Arrive at starting point.

7 SUNSET BEACH TO RIO DEL MAR
south of Santa Cruz

PAVED ROADS WITH MODERATE CAR TRAFFIC

Difficulty: 2

Total Distance: 20.2 miles

Riding Time: 2 hours

Elevation Gain: 800 feet

Summary: This road ride connects some of Santa Cruz's most scenic beaches: Sunset, Seacliff, Rio del Mar, and Manresa.

Despite their location between the bustling tourist towns of Santa Cruz and Monterey, the state beaches of Seacliff, Rio del Mar, Manresa, and Sunset have a remote feeling about them. The parks are set on high bluffs overlooking Monterey Bay and contain secluded groves of cypress and pine trees, grass-covered dunes, and long strands of white sand beaches. On the inland side, the beach parks are surrounded by green agricultural fields and small seaside villages.

This ride tours the four state beaches, starting at the southern end at Sunset State Beach (831/763-7062), a popular camping spot in the summer months. (If you're camping at Sunset, you can ride from your tent site and skip the first hill from the beach day-use area.) You could also begin this ride from any of the other beach parks or campgrounds, or in the nearby towns of Aptos, Rio del Mar, Seascape, or La Selva. It's a take-your-pick deal. This is a ride for dawdling, with many places to stop for supplies, and even more places to pause and enjoy the coastal scenery or plop down on a beach. Hills are few and far between, traffic is generally light, and bike lanes are wide. Don't forget your bike lock.

Among other highlights, you'll want to visit Seacliff State Beach's (831/685-6444) unusual pier, which is attached to a cement ship, the *Palo Alto*. The ship

A unicyclist pedals the paved path alongside Rio del Mar Beach.

was constructed as a supply tanker for World War I but never saw active duty. After being towed to Santa Cruz, it briefly served as a nightclub and amusement park. Years of storms have taken their toll, and today the ship is reserved for the pelicans and seagulls.

A biking/pedestrian path links Seacliff State Beach to Rio del Mar Beach, where Cafe Rio (831/688-8917, www.caferioaptos.com), a hip-looking seafood restaurant, is only a few feet from the sand. An espresso bar and sandwich deli is next door, and a small grocery store is on the same block. You'll also find restaurants and stores in Seascape.

Driving Directions

From Highway 1 south of Aptos, take the Buena Vista Drive exit and drive west 2.4 miles. Turn left on San Andreas Road, drive 1.3 miles and turn right on Sunset Beach Road. Follow the road 2.2 miles, past the park entrance kiosk to its end at the beach parking lot.

Route Directions

0.0 Park at the beach day-use parking area at Sunset State Beach.
Mileage begins at the parking lot restrooms. Ride uphill on the park road. *Supplies are available in Seascape, Rio del Mar, and Aptos. Water is available at the trailhead.*

1.4 RIGHT at entrance kiosk.

2.2 LEFT on San Andreas Road (follow bike lane).

4.6 Manresa Uplands campground on left. *Water is available.*

5.3 Manresa State Beach on left. *Water is available.*

6.0 STRAIGHT at stop sign at Mar Monte Avenue.

6.8 LEFT on Seascape Boulevard.

7.5 Seascape Village shopping center. *Supplies are available.*

7.6 RIGHT on Sumner Avenue.

8.1 STRAIGHT at junction with Clubhouse.

9.3 LEFT on Rio del Mar Boulevard.

10.1 Rio del Mar Beach. TURN AROUND. *Supplies and a restaurant are available. Walk or ride your bike to the pier and concrete ship at neighboring Seacliff State Beach.*

20.2 Arrive at starting point.

8 ELKHORN SLOUGH LOOP

east of Moss Landing

PAVED ROADS WITH MODERATE CAR TRAFFIC

Difficulty: 2   **Total Distance:** 21.8 miles

Riding Time: 2 hours   **Elevation Gain:** 900 feet

Summary: Bring your field glasses for this bird-intensive loop around Elkhorn Slough.

The roads east of Moss Landing and surrounding the waters of Elkhorn Slough are immensely popular with road cyclists. The mostly level country thoroughfares see only moderate traffic and allow the creation of several varied loops, with possible starting points in Pajaro, Prunedale, Moss Landing, or Castroville. This 21.8-mile loop starts at the visitor center at Elkhorn Slough National Estuarine Reserve (831/728-2822, www.elkhornslough.org), a terrific place to take a short bird-watching walk, have a picnic, or get educated about the natural history of Elkhorn Slough.

The slough is the equivalent of a bed-and-breakfast for migrating birds on the Pacific Flyway. Here they find nourishment from the rich tidal waters and rest from their long journeys. The main channel of the slough winds inland nearly seven miles and encompasses 2,500 acres of marsh and tidal flats. This loop's final stretch on Elkhorn Road gives you the best look at the long, narrow channel. You won't even need binoculars to spot grebes, coots, ducks, geese, egrets, and herons as you ride.

The ride features only a few small hills, including one short but steep challenge leading up to Royal Oaks Park on Mahler Road. With its brief, mostly level

© ANN MARIE BROWN

The Elkhorn Slough Loop passes by miles of marshes and tidal flats.

mileage, this road ride can be enjoyed by cyclists of almost every ability. The only downside is the car traffic. Although it isn't particularly heavy, most roads are narrow and without bike lanes, and cars tend to travel fast.

If you're in the mood, make a rest stop at Royal Oaks Park, a pretty spot lined with coast live oaks. You'll find water fountains, restrooms, and plenty of picnic spots in addition to softball fields and tennis courts.

Driving Directions

From Highway 1 at Moss Landing, turn east on Dolan Road (by the power plant) and drive 3 miles. Turn left (north) on Elkhorn Road and drive 2.1 miles to Elkhorn Slough Reserve on the left.

Route Directions

0.0 Park at the visitor center parking lot at Elkhorn Slough, then ride out the entrance road to Elkhorn Road. If you arrive on Monday or Tuesday, when the visitor center is closed, park in one of the pullouts to the north along Elkhorn Road. *Supplies are available in Moss Landing or at Elkhorn Superette, 1.3 miles south on Elkhorn Road.*

0.1 RIGHT on Elkhorn Road.

1.3 Store on right. *Supplies are available.*

2.2 LEFT on Castroville Boulevard.

3.5 LEFT on Paradise Road.

6.4 RIGHT on San Miguel Canyon Road (Road G-12).

6.7 LEFT on Echo Valley Road.

7.1 LEFT on Mahler Road.

8.3 Royal Oaks County Park on right. *Water is available.*

10.1 LEFT on Tarpey Road, then immediate RIGHT on San Miguel Canyon Road.

12.6 LEFT on Vega Road.

14.9 RIGHT on Lewis Road.

15.1 LEFT on Garin Road.

16.5 LEFT on Elkhorn Road.

16.8 RIGHT to stay on Elkhorn Road.

19.2 Kirby Park access to Elkhorn Slough.

21.7 RIGHT into main entrance to Elkhorn Slough.

21.8 Arrive at starting point.

ELKHORN SLOUGH LOOP

9 MONTEREY RECREATION TRAIL BEST (

Marina to Pacific Grove

PAVED BIKE PATH

Difficulty: 2   **Total Distance:** 29 miles (or 36-mile option)

Riding Time: 2-3 hours   **Elevation Gain:** 800 feet

Summary: One of California's most popular paved recreational trails skirts the coast from Marina to Pacific Grove.

Good news came to cyclists at the close of the 20th century: After 25 years of red-tape wrangling, a final link in the Monterey Peninsula Recreation Trail was built through Sand City, making the trail a nearly complete 14.5 miles of car-free riding (29 miles round-trip). Nearly complete? Well, close enough: There is a short stretch in which you follow bike lanes through Seaside's shopping center, but otherwise, you're largely free of the dreaded gas-guzzler, except for street and parking lot crossings.

Most people don't ride the entire trail, but it's nice to know it's an option. Obvious starting points are at the trail's north terminus in Marina and the trail's southwest terminus at Lover's Point Park in Pacific Grove. (Parking is difficult in Pacific Grove; the route directions below begin from the north end of the trail.) Many local riders begin mid-trail at Laguna Grande Park in Seaside or a few blocks away at the aforementioned shopping center, where parking is free and easy.

The most congested trail section is the southwest end, where Cannery Row, Fisherman's Wharf, and the Monterey Bay Aquarium are located. The biggest

© ANN MARIE BROWN

A stretch of the Monterey Recreation Trail skirts the sandy shore north of Sand City.

obstacle there, besides the sheer number of walkers, bikers, joggers, and in-line skaters, are the four-wheeled, canopy-covered rental bikes that take up more than half the trail. Still, in between the bustling tourist areas are quiet stretches that belong only to you and the sea.

South of Cannery Row, the trail leads into the wealthy neighborhood of Pacific Grove, with its bed-and-breakfast hotels; restaurants; rugged, rocky coastline; and white sand beaches. This part of the trail is quintessential Monterey: Sea lions poke their heads out of the water, kayakers paddle by and wave, and sea otters float by on their backs munching on abalone. The trail ends near Lover's Point, an enchanting seaside park.

Not all of the trail is so lovely. The route through downtown Marina is commonplace at best, a stretch north of Sand City runs too close to noisy Highway 1, and the overall trail suffers from too many street intersections. But with this much car-free riding in beautiful Monterey, who's complaining?

For more information, contact the City of Monterey Recreation Services Department, 831/646-3866, www.monterey.org; or the Pacific Grove Recreation Department, 831/648-5730.

Options

This 14.5-mile stretch of the Monterey Recreation Trail can also be combined with another 3.5-mile stretch that runs to the north from Marina to Castroville, for a 36-mile round-trip.

Driving Directions

To access the north end of the trail, from Highway 1 south of Moss Landing take the Marina/Del Monte Boulevard exit. Cross over to the east side of the highway; the trail begins at the junction of Del Monte Boulevard and Lapis Road, about 100 yards from Highway 1 (a dirt parking area is located there).

Route Directions

0.0 Park at the northern terminus of the trail at the junction of Del Monte Boulevard and Lapis Road in Marina. *Supplies are available all along the trail.*

2.7 Trail crosses Reservation Road in Marina and passes through downtown (trail parallels Del Monte Boulevard).

3.3 Trail crosses under Highway 1.

7.9 RIGHT then immediate LEFT where trail ends at California Avenue/Monterey Road junction; follow bike lane along California Avenue.

8.2 RIGHT on Playa Avenue (follow bike lane).

8.4 Bike trail resumes at end of Playa Avenue.

12.3 Fisherman's Wharf.

13.5 Monterey Bay Aquarium.

14.5 Lover's Point Park; TURN AROUND.

29.0 Arrive at starting point.

10 17-MILE DRIVE

BEST ☾

north of Carmel and south of Pacific Grove

PAVED ROADS WITH MODERATE CAR TRAFFIC

Difficulty: 2   **Total Distance:** 17.4 miles (or 15-mile option)

Riding Time: 1.5-2 hours   **Elevation Gain:** 900 feet

Summary: Ride the world-famous 17-Mile Drive in the off-season and enjoy the coastal scenery without the crowds.

One of the top reasons to ride your bike on the world-famous 17-Mile Drive is because it costs 10 bucks to drive your car on it, but biking is free. Another reason is because it's gorgeous. Before cars became the normal mode of transportation, the 17-Mile Drive was navigated by horse-drawn carriages from Monterey's Hotel Del Monte. Tourists staying at the hotel in the late 1800s would

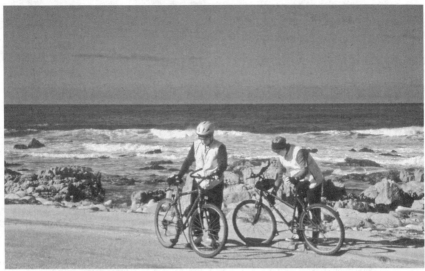

The coastside leg of the 17-Mile Drive offers close-up views of the crashing surf.

be driven through Del Monte Forest and down to the same exquisite coastline that we see today, minus the sprawling golf courses (Pebble Beach Golf Links was opened in 1919).

As you ride the 17-Mile Drive, you may wish for those days of carriages instead of cars, because in the summer tourist season this road is extremely congested. Although nobody drives the scenic route fast (after all, drivers want to get their money's worth), I don't recommend riding it in summer, except perhaps in the early morning on weekdays. I would especially avoid weekends and holidays. Some of the route follows roads without any shoulder, and the vast majority of drivers are gawking at the scenery, not watching for cyclists.

The route described below begins at the Pacific Grove gate to the 17-Mile Drive. Two other gates also access the drive: the Highway 1 gate at the junction of Highway 1 and Highway 68, and the Carmel gate off Ocean Avenue in Carmel.

The 17-Mile Drive is signed like crazy, so there is no chance of getting lost, despite numerous turns. To orient yourself, you can pick up a full-color map at the entrance gate when you sign your liability waiver to bicycle the 17-Mile Drive. Many riders choose to ride the seven-mile coastal section of the drive as an out-and-back (see *Options*), rather than looping inland over several miles that are hilly and far less scenic—comprised mostly of suburban-looking homes and cypress forests. Be forewarned that if you keep on the loop, the stretch between miles 8.9 and 10.5 is a 1.6-mile uphill grind. Honestly, the coastal section is what everyone comes here for: ocean lookouts, impossibly green and fine-trimmed golf courses, showy mansions belonging to movie stars and the very wealthy, and the white sands and turquoise waters of Monterey Bay.

For more information, contact the Pacific Grove Chamber of Commerce, 831/373-3304.

Options

If you opt for an out-and-back instead of the loop, turn around near mile 7.5 at Pebble Beach, before the route climbs uphill and heads inland. This will result in a 15-mile round-trip.

Driving Directions

From the junction of Highway 1 and Highway 68 north of Carmel, take Highway 68 northwest to Pacific Grove. Highway 68 ends at the Pacific Grove gate to the 17-Mile Drive and the start of Sunset Drive. Parking is available on side streets off Sunset Drive or at Asilomar State Beach on Sunset Drive.

Route Directions

0.0 Park off Sunset Drive or near Asilomar State Beach in Pacific Grove. Mileage begins at the junction of Sunset Drive and 17-Mile Drive. *Supplies are available at the small store on Sunset Drive near the 17-Mile Drive junction.*

0.2 Sign in at the 17-Mile Drive entrance gate.

1.1 RIGHT on Spanish Bay Road (17-Mile Drive).

3.5 Bird Rock and Seal Rock Picnic Area.

4.9 Cypress Point Lookout.

6.5 Ghost Tree and Pescadero Point.

6.8 RIGHT for Pebble Beach lodge, golf course, etc. *Supplies are available at Pebble Beach Market.*

7.5 RIGHT to exit Pebble Beach area (warning sign for cyclists: narrow road; no bike lane ahead). *Cyclists who would prefer to stick to the coastal side of the 17-Mile Drive should turn around here and head back.*

8.9 Start of climb.

10.5 Highway 1 entrance gate; cross Highway 68.

11.4 Shepherd's Knoll overlook.

12.7 Huckleberry Hill ocean view.

14.0 RIGHT then LEFT (follow signs).

14.8 RIGHT (follow signs).

15.0 Poppy Hills golf course, restaurant, bar.

16.1 RIGHT (follow signs).
16.7 RIGHT to return to Pacific Grove entrance gate.
17.4 Arrive at starting point.

11 FORT ORD LOOP

east of Monterey and west of Salinas

DIRT ROAD AND SINGLE-TRACK

Difficulty: 3

Riding Time: 1.5 hours

Total Distance: 10.7 miles

Elevation Gain: 1,300 feet

Summary: The trails traversing the inland hills of Monterey at Fort Ord are as good as those at any mountain biking park.

Fort Ord, a U.S. Army base dating back to 1917, has become a world-class recreation area for mountain bikers, hikers, horseback riders, and others of that ilk. The base, located just east of Monterey, was abandoned in 1994 and its management turned over to the Bureau of Land Management. The BLM maintains 7,200 acres of the old base for recreational use, including 50 miles of tight single-track and wide multiuse roads that wind through grassland hills, dense oaks, and coastal chaparral.

© ANN MARIE BROWN

An interesting mix of single-track and fire roads run through the grass-covered hills on the Fort Ord Loop.

That said, it's hard to figure out where to ride at Ford Ord. Signed and un-signed trails meander all over the place, and on weekends, people seem to ride all over the place. The best advice I got from a BLM recreation officer was to "follow Toro Creek Road and then take any trail that doesn't look too steep." The best advice I got from local riders was "try anything; it's all good."

So here is the loop I assembled, containing a fair mix of single-track and wide road, some steep ups and downs, and a few places where I wound up walking. Trails at Fort Ord are often sandy and dusty, especially late in the summer sea-son, which can derail your chance of gaining any traction. This was a bit irritat-ing at times, but aside from that one drawback, I couldn't wipe the smile off my face. Two highlights: Skyline Road, a smooth ridgeline road; and Goat Trail, also known as Trail 41, a 2.8-mile dream of a single-track. It's smooth and rollercoast-ering, like a well-constructed trail at a mountain bike park.

Note that no matter how foggy the Monterey coast may be, it will probably be sunny here at Fort Ord. Summer riding can be quite hot. Think Southern Cali-fornia and you get a good idea of the landscape—few trees, lots of chaparral, and dry sandstone earth. Spring is the optimal time to visit, when the wildflowers bloom and the grasses are green.

For more information, contact the Bureau of Land Management's Fort Ord Office, 831/394-8314, www.blm.gov/ca/hollister/fort_ord.

Driving Directions

From Highway 1 heading south in Marina, take the Marina/Reservation Road exit and drive east 0.25 mile. Turn right on Reservation Road and drive 8.8 miles. Turn right (west) on Highway 68 and drive 3 miles to the dirt parking area on the right.

Or, from Monterey at the junction of Highways 1 and 68, drive northeast on Highway 68 for 9.9 miles, past the entrance to Laguna Seca Recreation Area. Watch for the junction with San Benancio Road; the dirt parking area is 150 yards farther on the left.

Route Directions

0.0 Park at the Fort Ord parking lot on Highway 68 and take the main trail from the lot. *Supplies are available in Monterey.*

0.1 RIGHT on Toro Creek Road.

0.9 LEFT on Trail 45 (steep climb uphill).

1.3 LEFT on Oil Well Road.

2.5 RIGHT on Skyline Road.

4.0 RIGHT on Trail 43 (climb on single-track).

4.6 LEFT on Trail 41/Goat Trail at major junction of trails.

7.4 RIGHT on Oil Well Road.

9.2 LEFT on Toro Creek Road.

10.6 LEFT at spur trail to parking lot.

10.7 Arrive at starting point.

FORT ORD LOOP

12 ANDREW MOLERA RAMBLE
Andrew Molera State Park, north of Big Sur

DIRT ROAD AND SINGLE-TRACK

Difficulty: 2	**Total Distance:** 7 miles
Riding Time: 1.5 hours	**Elevation Gain:** 1,000 feet

Summary: Mellow two-wheeled meandering on Andrew Molera's coastal bluffs makes Big Sur a place to relax and enjoy the ride.

Mountain bikers can't make a loop out of the trails at Andrew Molera State Park, and as a result, the park is largely underused by them, although it's quite popular with hikers. But this is one park where making a loop is unnecessary; the scenery is so grand that an out-and-back is just fine. You'll want to see the park's ocean views, wildflowers, and roller-coaster ridgelines more than once.

The main pedaling is on Ridge Trail, an alternating wide and narrow ranch road that climbs quite steeply to a panoramic overlook. You access Ridge Trail by crossing a footbridge from the main parking lot, then following Beach Trail through Creamery Meadow. The level Beach Trail sees plenty of traffic from beachgoers, while steep Ridge Trail offers more solitude and a solid workout. Most of Ridge Trail is surrounded by low-growing chaparral, allowing open views of the ocean to the west and the chalky peak of Pico Blanco to the east. One surprising stretch enters an oak forest in a tangle of curving branches, followed by a short stint in redwoods. Ridge Trail ends at a bench with a fine view of the Pacific. (Hikers can loop back to the beach from here on Panorama Trail, but bikes are not permitted.)

Riding on Ridge Trail is a strenuous climb (10 percent grade), but has little in the way of technical challenges. That's convenient, because you'll want to keep your eyes on the coastal views and chaparral-covered headlands, not the trail.

Note that you won't be able to access any of Andrew Molera's coastside trails during the rainy season (usually Nov.–Apr.) without facing an icy-cold portage of the Big Sur River; the footbridge by the main parking lot is removed during the wet months. But for bikers, this is the best time to visit Andrew Molera. If you can stand taking off your shoes and socks and carrying your bike across a knee-high, 25-foot-wide frigid river running over rounded rocks, you'll practically have the trails to yourself.

For more information, contact Big Sur Station, 831/667-2315, www.parks.ca.gov.

Options

If you want to add more miles or more of a challenge to your day, you can combine this ride with ride 13, the Old Coast Road Loop, which begins across Highway 1 from this trailhead. Or consider an out-and-back on East Molera Trail, which runs from the east side of Highway 1 up into the coastal hills. A steep 1.5-mile climb will bring you to a small, secluded redwood grove. Pick up a park map at the entrance kiosk before you go.

Driving Directions

From Carmel, drive 20 miles south on Highway 1 to the entrance to Andrew Molera State Park on the right (4our miles north of Big Sur).

Route Directions

0.0 Park at the main lot at Andrew Molera and walk your bike across the footbridge to access the trails. In winter, you may have to ford; see route description above. *Supplies are available in Big Sur. Water is available at the trailhead.*

0.2 STRAIGHT on Beach Trail at junction with River Trail (confusing junction; head west toward the beach).

0.8 LEFT on Ridge Trail. Steep climb uphill.

0.9 LEFT to stay on Ridge Trail at junction with Bluffs Trail.

3.5 Bench at overlook point and junction of trails. TURN AROUND.

7.0 Arrive at starting point.

ANDREW MOLERA RAMBLE

13 OLD COAST ROAD LOOP
north of Big Sur and south of Carmel

DIRT ROAD AND PAVED ROAD WITH MODERATE CAR TRAFFIC

Difficulty: 4

Total Distance: 18.8 miles

Riding Time: 3-4 hours

Elevation Gain: 2,600 feet

Summary: Follow the historic Old Coast Road for a close-up look at the inland hills of Big Sur.

One of the most photographed icons of the Big Sur coast is the long, graceful span of the Bixby Bridge on Highway 1. But before that single-arch bridge was built in 1932, the thoroughfare that ran from Carmel to Big Sur was the Old Coast Road, which made a long arc inland before it could cross the deep gorge of Bixby Creek. That "pre-bridge" road still exists today, largely ignored by Highway 1 travelers but ideal for mountain bikers wanting to log some scenic miles.

To make a loop out of the Old Coast Road, it's best to start on its southern end by Andrew Molera State Park, where parking is ample. You follow the dirt-and-gravel Old Coast Road north, with no turns or junctions to concern you until you come out at Highway 1 at the Bixby Bridge, 10.5 miles later. There you ride south on Highway 1 to finish out the loop, with the prevailing westerly winds at your back and the sparkling Pacific on your side of the road.

You will face a heck of a climb at the start of this ride, but the surface is hard-packed gravel and dirt, which at least bestows some traction. The road climbs for the first 2.5 miles, providing ocean views. Then it drops for 2 miles and climbs again, more steeply and on a much looser surface, for 2 miles. By about mile 6.5,

Enjoy views of the Big Sur coast on the Old Coast Road Loop.

you may wish you were driving this road instead of riding it, or you may wish you weren't here at all but just sitting on the beach in Big Sur. But suddenly, the road leaves the hot, dusty sunshine and makes a cool, 3-mile descent through a redwood and fern forest. Suddenly you've achieved mountain biking nirvana.

After one more short climb at mile 9.5, you begin your descent to Highway 1, which is filled with the kind of scenery that makes Big Sur famous. A left turn on-to the busy highway and 8.3 miles alongside it lead you back to your car at Andrew Molera State Park. If it's a weekend, you might want to stop at Point Sur Lighthouse (www.pointsur.org) along the way for a tour. Or just head for the state park and its lovely beach, accessed by a 0.5-mile, level walk.

Driving Directions

From Carmel, drive 12 miles south on Highway 1 to the Bixby Bridge and the north end of Old Coast Road on the left. Take note of this junction, then continue another 8.5 miles south to the entrance to Andrew Molera State Park on the right, and the south end of Old Coast Road on the left.

Route Directions

0.0 Park at Andrew Molera State Park, then ride across Highway 1 to the start of Old Coast Road. *Supplies are available in Big Sur, four miles south.*

0.1 Start of Old Coast Road.

6.5 Summit and start of long descent in redwoods.

10.5 LEFT on Highway 1.

16.0 Right turnoff for Point Sur Lighthouse; weekend tours are available.

18.8 Arrive at starting point.

14 BIG SUR TO LUCIA

Big Sur coast

BEST C

PAVED ROAD WITH MODERATE CAR TRAFFIC

Difficulty: 4

Riding Time: 5 hours

Total Distance: 51 miles

Elevation Gain: 3,300 feet

Summary: This ride follows one of the few stretches of coastal Highway 1 that is well suited for two-wheeled travel, with plenty of places to stop and enjoy the Big Sur experience.

While it's true that thousands of cyclists ride coastal Highway 1 in its entirety every year, it's also true that many who do so admit that it's overrated. Common complaints include: too many cars, too narrow road shoulders, too much wind, and too few chances to enjoy the spectacular coastside scenery because you're too worried about staying alive.

Still, one stretch of the coastal highway that gets a big thumbs

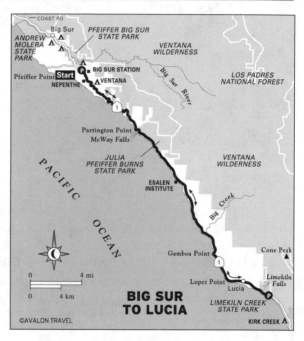

up from just about everybody is the 25 miles from Big Sur to Lucia. This area sees somewhat less traffic than other stretches of Highway 1 because the majority of drivers coming from the San Francisco Bay Area stop in Big Sur, and the majority of drivers coming from the Los Angeles area stop in Cambria or San Simeon. This leaves a glorious length of coastline in between. By simple good fortune, this highway stretch has an adequate shoulder through its entire length (a rarity on Highway 1), and is not especially hilly. The coastal scenery is as good as it gets anywhere in California, with nonstop views of crashing waves and a dramatic, rocky shoreline. It is not uncommon to spot gray whales or dolphins swimming past, or sea otters frolicking in the kelp beds.

Cyclists head south on Highway 1 in Big Sur with fully loaded panniers.

Chances are you'll start this ride from wherever you are staying in Big Sur, which is likely within a 3-mile radius of Big Sur Station (0.5 mile south of Pfeiffer Big Sur State Park and Big Sur Lodge). I describe this ride starting at Big Sur Station, an ideal location for getting updated information about road and park conditions. The route directions below note some of the highlights of the ride, which are numerous. Only one section is without services for any length, and that's the 13 miles from Julia Pfeiffer Burns State Park to Lucia Lodge. Otherwise, there are plenty of places to stop, relax, and enjoy the scenery. Bring a bike lock, plan to take a lot of breaks, and expect to eat well at the many restaurants and cafés along the route. There's no reason to hurry here; take your time and make a day of it.

For more information, contact Big Sur Station, 831/667-2315.

Driving Directions

From Carmel, drive 25 miles south on Highway 1 to Big Sur. Continue south through town to Big Sur Station on the right, 0.5 mile south of Pfeiffer Big Sur State Park.

Route Directions

0.0 Park at Big Sur Station, 0.5 mile south of Pfeiffer Big Sur State Park and Big Sur Lodge. Ride south on Highway 1. *Supplies are available at stores to the north or south in Big Sur.*

1.1 Big Sur Bakery and Restaurant. *Supplies are available.*

1.8 Post Ranch Inn and Ventana Campground. *Supplies are available.*

2.4 Nepenthe Restaurant and Cafe Kevah. *Snacks and drinks are available. If you're ready for a meal, get the scallop and shrimp salad and sit outside on the deck at Nepenthe.*

2.7 Henry Miller Library. *Lock up your bike and take a look at the exhibits on this famous American writer, who spent many years living in Big Sur.*

3.3 Deetjen's Big Sur Inn.

5.6 Coast Gallery and Cafe. *Snacks and drinks are available.*

10.5 Julia Pfeiffer Burns State Park. *Lock up your bike and take the 0.5-mile walk to McWay Falls.*

23.6 Lucia Lodge, store, restaurant. *Supplies and meals are available; the restaurant's deck has a marvelous view.*

25.5 Limekiln State Park. TURN AROUND. *Lock up your bike and head for the beach, or hike the one-mile trail to the park's historic lime kilns or beautiful Limekiln Falls.*

51.0 Arrive at starting point.

BIG SUR TO LUCIA

15 NACIMIENTO–FERGUSSON ROAD TO THE MISSION

BEST ☾

Big Sur coast to Jolon, west of King City

PAVED ROADS WITH MINIMAL CAR TRAFFIC

Difficulty: 5

Total Distance: 58.8 miles

Riding Time: 5-6 hours

Elevation Gain: 4,200 feet

Summary: This back-road ride travels from the Pacific coast to the inland valleys, making a stop at the historic Mission San Antonio de Padua.

There's a marvelous country road that runs from Highway 1 south of Big Sur to Highway 101 near King City, and those who know of it wouldn't dream of heading inland any other way. It's Nacimiento–Fergusson Road, a narrow, winding, and twisting thoroughfare that climbs up from the Pacific Ocean to Nacimiento Summit, then drops down the east side to the grasslands and oaks of the Central Coast. Riding it out and back is challenging in both directions, certainly, but it's also filled with rewards.

© ANN MARIE BROWN

a dizzying descent to Highway 1 and the coast on Nacimiento-Fergusson Road

The destination of this ride is Mission San Antonio de Padua (831/385-4478, www.missionsanantonio.net), founded in 1771 and the third of 21 missions began in California by Franciscan padres. San Antonio Mission is open to the public every day of the year, and Sunday mass is held weekly.

The mission has an unusual location: It sits in the middle of 170,000-acre Fort Hunter Liggett Military Reservation (831/386-3000), a land of rolling, oak-covered hills and extensive military operations. Because this is an active base, expect the unexpected on the roads: gates, delays due to closures, the sudden appearance of jeeps and tanks, you name it. Military personnel are accustomed to bicyclists and are generally quite friendly and helpful, but you have to follow their rules.

The best season to take this ride is in spring when the wildflowers are blooming, or at least in the cooler months of year. The western miles of the ride travel through the wild lands of Los Padres National Forest and are completely without services, so you must be self-reliant for this trip. (You might be able to get water at one of two Forest Service campgrounds along the road.) As for the elevation gain, well, this isn't a ride for cyclists who don't like to climb. You'll gain 2,600 feet over seven miles from the ocean to Nacimiento Summit (mostly in the open sunshine), then lose 1,600 feet on the descent to the mission (mostly in a shady forest). Reversing it on the way back makes your return trip easier. Plus, the final downhill to the coast is one of the most breathtaking road rides in California. Check your brakes before you go.

Driving Directions

From Big Sur, drive 27 miles south on Highway 1 to Kirk Creek Campground and the left turnoff for Nacimiento–Fergusson Road. Park off the road (and out of the campground unless you're camping there).

Route Directions

0.0 Park near the junction of Highway 1 and Nacimiento–Fergusson Road. *Supplies are available in Lucia, four miles north.*

7.0 Four-way junction with South Coast Ridge and Central Coast Ridge Roads.

10.8 Nacimiento Campground.

13.3 Ponderosa Campground. *Water is available when the campground is open.*

16.3 Enter Fort Hunter Liggett Military Reservation.

27.0 LEFT on Mission Road. *Supplies are available in Jolon, three miles to the right at this junction.*

29.4 Mission San Antonio de Padua. TURN AROUND. *A small shop is located in the mission, and water is available.*

58.8 Arrive at starting point.

NACIMIENTO-FERGUSSON ROAD TO THE MISSION

16 CONE PEAK LOOKOUT BIKE AND HIKE
Los Padres National Forest south of Big Sur

DIRT ROAD

Difficulty: 3   **Total Distance:** 10.8 miles (plus 5-mile hike)

Riding Time: 2 hours (plus 2-hour hike)   **Elevation Gain:** 1,100 feet

Summary: For a panoramic coastal view, visit the historic fire lookout perched at 5,155 feet on top of Big Sur's Cone Peak.

The trip to Cone Peak Lookout is a must for campers staying at Kirk Creek or Plaskett Creek Campgrounds, or for anyone who wants to see some of the backcountry of the Big Sur coast. You can drive all the way to the 2.5-mile, hikers-only trail to the summit and lookout tower, but the route is far more enjoyable on a bike. With few cars and a steady but moderate grade, the 5.4-mile uphill from Nacimiento Summit is manageable for anyone in good cardiovascular shape. The dirt road presents no technical challenges, but provides many fine views of the inland ridges and valleys of the Ventana Wilderness, plus a few surprising looks at the Pacific Ocean—far, far, away. Some sections of the road are densely forested with madrones, oaks, and bay laurel.

As you ride, keep your eyes open for the Cone Peak Lookout Trail on your left at mile 5.4, so you don't bypass it and continue uphill unnecessarily. It seems as if the road you're following would eventually reach the summit, but instead it ends at a Ventana Wilderness trailhead about a mile beyond Cone Peak Lookout's trailhead. Of course, if you're enjoying the ride and the wilderness vistas, you can pedal this last mile just for grins.

Make sure you bring a bike lock or are prepared to stash your bike so you can hike the final 2.5 miles to the summit, which gains another 1,300 feet. This stretch on your feet feels much steeper than what you've just accomplished on your bike, but it's completely worth it. From the historic lookout tower, built on view from an open clearing on the dirt road to Cone Peak

tinker-toy-style stilts in 1923, you can see as far as 100 miles on clear days. Perched at the lofty elevation of 5,155 feet, the tower looks down the west side of Cone Peak almost a vertical mile to the ocean.

The lookout is usually staffed in the summer and fall months. In case you are wondering, the staff person reaches the tower the same way you did—on foot via the 2.5-mile hiking trail. Supplies are brought in by helicopter.

For more information, contact the Monterey Ranger District of Los Padres National Forest, 831/385-5434, www.fs.fed.us/r5/lospadres.

Driving Directions

From Big Sur, drive 27 miles south on Highway 1 to Kirk Creek Campground and the left turnoff for Nacimiento–Fergusson Road. Turn left and drive seven miles (paved) to a four-way junction. Park off the road in the pullout.

For a trail map, see ride 15, *Nacimiento–Fergusson Road to the Mission.*

Route Directions

0.0 Park at Nacimiento Summit, at the junction of Nacimiento–Fergusson Road, South Coast Ridge Road, and Central Coast Ridge/Cone Peak Road. Ride north (left) on Cone Peak Road (dirt road 20S05). *Supplies are available at Lucia Lodge on Highway 1.*

3.7 Pass trail sign on left for trail to Vicente Flat.

3.9 Pass trail sign on right for San Antonio Trail.

4.0 Pass white marble outcroppings along road.

5.0 Ocean view at clearing.

5.4 Trail to Cone Peak Lookout on left (dirt road continues straight ahead but doesn't go to lookout tower). *Lock up your bike and hike 2.5 miles one-way to the lookout tower on the 5,155-foot summit.* TURN AROUND.

10.8 Arrive at starting point.

17 LAKE SAN ANTONIO LOOP
south of King City and north of Paso Robles

PAVED ROADS WITH MODERATE CAR TRAFFIC

Difficulty: 4

Total Distance: 53.2 miles

Riding Time: 5 hours

Elevation Gain: 2,200 feet

Summary: This challenging road ride, best done in the cooler months, visits two large reservoirs on the central coast: Lakes San Antonio and Nacimiento.

This hilly loop around Lake San Antonio presents a good workout combined with fetching views of the long, narrow lake and also nearby Lake Nacimiento. Both water bodies are county-owned reservoirs that are popular for waterskiing and fishing in summer, but largely deserted in the cooler seasons. Bicycling is best here October–April, when there is little traffic on the roads and the air temperature is cool. Springtime displays of wildflowers and verdant grasslands in these sprawling hills are worth planning your trip around.

The ride starts at the marina on the north shore of Lake San Antonio. In addition to being the site of the annual Wildflower Triathlon in May and popular all summer for water sports, San Antonio is well known as a major habitat area for eagles, both bald and golden. The county parks department runs Eagle Watch boat tours in the winter months.

In any season, don't be surprised to see two unusual creatures along the roadways: wild turkeys and wild pigs. Both frequent the area.

Say good-bye to the water as you start your ride: You'll be heading out into the dry, grassy hills. Ride back out the marina road, then turn right and follow Jolon Road east as it rolls up and down small hills. Almost at U.S. 101, a right turn on

Nacimiento Road takes you across the San Antonio River. You'll soon commence to climb, and continue to do so as you near the northeast edge of Lake Nacimiento. After a total four-mile ascent, enjoy a swooping descent to the hamlet of Bee Rock.

The next leg of the ride travels roughly parallel to Lake San Antonio's south shore. With 16 quiet miles of mostly level riding, you'll reach the town of Lockwood (store and café available), then make your final cruise back to the north shore. After all these miles, you might find yourself thinking that it's time for a swim.

Driving Directions

From U.S. 101 north of Bradley, take the Jolon Road/G-18 exit west. Drive 8.7 miles west on Jolon Road (G-18) to New Pleyto Road. Turn left and drive 5 miles to Lake San Antonio's north shore and marina.

Route Directions

0.0 Park at the marina on the north shore of Lake San Antonio. Ride back out the way you drove in. *Supplies are available at the marina store.*

5.0 RIGHT on Jolon Road (G-18).

13.7 RIGHT on Lake Nacimiento Road (G-19) near U.S. 101.

18.7 Cross San Antonio River on steel bridge.

20.5 LEFT to stay on Lake Nacimiento Road just before the dam.

22.2 RIGHT on Interlake Road (G-14).

26.8 Hamlet of Bee Rock. *Supplies are available.*

42.2 RIGHT on Jolon Road (G-18) in town of Lockwood. *Supplies are available.*

48.2 RIGHT on New Pleyto Road to marina, store, and lake. *Supplies are available.*

53.2 Arrive at starting point.

LAKE SAN ANTONIO LOOP

YOSEMITE AND MAMMOTH LAKES

© ANN MARIE BROWN

BEST BIKE RIDES

Plunging waterfalls, stark granite, alpine lakes,
pristine meadows, giant Sequoias, and raging rivers – you'll find them all
in the Yosemite and Mammoth Lakes region, which encompasses not only
world-famous Yosemite National Park but also the popular recreation areas
of Mammoth Lakes and the eastern Sierra.

The centerpiece of this region, of course, is Yosemite National Park,
a must-see on every traveler's itinerary. And what better way to see it
than on two wheels, pedaling along the Yosemite Valley Bike Path? On a
bicycle, you can enjoy unencumbered views of Yosemite Valley's famous
waterfalls, three of which are among the tallest in the world, plus the
towering granite of El Capitan, Half Dome, and Sentinel Rock. Those who
seek more of a challenge can ride Glacier Point Road to its end at a vista
that can only be described in superlatives. But then, almost everything
about Yosemite inspires verbal extravagance.

As scenic as the national park itself are the resort areas just to the east,
particularly Mammoth Lakes and June Lake on the U.S. 395 corridor. Best
known for skiing and snowboarding in winter, the eastern Sierra is also
ideal for cycling in the warmer seasons. One of the greatest challenges for
both road and mountain bikers is dealing with the thin air at this altitude,
which ranges 7,000–9,200 feet. Road and trail rides include easy loops
near towns and more strenuous rides through alpine meadows, fir and
pine forests, and sagebrush-covered plains.

Surrounding Mammoth and June Lakes, the lands of Inyo National Forest
are suited for two-wheeled use. The area east of June Lake is dominated

by the Mono Basin and Mono Lake, an ancient and majestic body of water covering 60 square miles. At more than 700,000 years old, Mono Lake is one of the oldest lakes in North America.

Just west of Mammoth Lakes is Devils Postpile National Monument, an 800-acre national park that preserves 60-foot-high basalt columns, remnants of an ancient lava flow, and breathtaking 101-foot Rainbow Falls. The road into the monument provides one of the most exciting bike rides on Northern California pavement, featuring a steep and fast descent on a narrow, twisty grade. Fortunately, a mandatory shuttle bus system minimizes auto traffic, making the road safer and more peaceful for cyclists.

Key to enjoying your experience in Yosemite and Mammoth is planning your visit for the least crowded months of the year. Summer is the busiest time and best avoided, especially in the national park. Springtime in Yosemite is ideal for viewing the valley's spectacular waterfalls. A visit before school lets out for the summer gives you a chance to see the valley without the masses.

Fall, too, is a fine time for cycling in and around Yosemite, and likewise, if there is a perfect time to visit the eastern Sierra, it's in the transition between summer and winter. Autumn transforms the scenic canyons and pristine lakeshores into a wave of blazing color. Aspens, willows, and cottonwoods turn showy hues of orange, yellow, and red. The trees generally begin their color change early in September; peak viewing is usually in late September and early October. With an autumn show like this, why go to New England?

YOSEMITE AND MAMMOTH LAKES

TRAIL NAME	LEVEL	DISTANCE	TIME	ELEVATION	PAGE
1 Twin Lakes Loop	2	8.3 mi	1.5 hr	400 ft	526
2 Glacier Point Road	4	31.6 mi	3-4 hr	2,700 ft	529
3 Yosemite Valley Bike Path	1	8.2 mi	1 hr	450 ft	532
4 Moraines and Meadows Loop	3	11.4 mi	2 hr	1,200 ft	535
5 Panorama Mountain Trail	3	10.7 mi	2 hr	1,100 ft	538
6 June Lake Loop Ramble	2	28.8 mi	2-3 hr	1,000 ft	540
7 Devils Postpile	3	19.6 mi	2-3 hr	1,500 ft	543
8 Mountain View Trail	3	11 mi	2 hr	800 ft	546
9 Mammoth Lakes Basin and Horseshoe Lake	1	12.2 mi	1.5 hr	700 ft	549
10 Mammoth Creek Park/Sherwin Creek Loop	2	6.3 mi	1 hr	500 ft	552
11 Lower Rock Creek	4	7.9 mi	1.5 hr	0 ft (2,000-foot loss)	555

1 TWIN LAKES LOOP
west of Bridgeport

**DIRT ROAD AND SINGLE-TRACK; PAVED ROAD
WITH MODERATE CAR TRAFFIC**

Difficulty: 2   **Total Distance:** 8.3 miles (or 30.3-mile option)

Riding Time: 1.5 hours   **Elevation Gain:** 400 feet

Summary: Gaze at the serrated peaks of the Sawtooth Range from the tranquil shores of Twin Lakes.

Bridgeport's Twin Lakes, elevation 7,100 feet, are a fine place for anglers to toss their lines in the water, gaze up at the jagged peaks of the Sawtooth Range, and forget their troubles for a while. The two scenic lakes are also just right for mountain bikers who want to string together a loop ride that circumnavigates the lakes, providing many unforgettable views of blue water and granite. The ride is mostly level and easy, leaving you free to focus on the glorious alpine scenery instead of the trail.

The ride takes off from Lower Twin Lakes Resort and immediately turns onto South Twin Road, skirting a few Forest Service campgrounds. Where the pavement ends, you follow a well-graded dirt road along the lakeshore, passing some summer homes and cabins. Soon the dirt road ends, too, and you follow a single-track trail for a short, technical stretch along the lake's edge, crossing Cattle Creek a few times. At the western end of Upper Twin Lake, the trail curves around Horse Creek. Follow the trail signs to cross a bridge over the creek and access the edge of a campground.

And what a campground it is. The peace and quiet of your lakeside ride is shattered upon entering Annett's Mono Village Resort, an absolute zoo of a vacation spot. The place is a miniature city, with a 300-site campground, cabins, motel rooms, a grocery store, marina, and the like. It will take you a few minutes to negotiate a path through this party scene and find your way back to paved Twin Lakes Road, where all is peaceful once more. Enjoy the final smooth miles on pavement back to your car at Lower Twin Lakes Resort.

The Twin Lakes Loop combines dirt, paved, and single-track roads.

For more information, contact the Bridgeport Ranger District of Humboldt–Toiyabe National Forest, 760/932-7070, www.fs.fed.us/r4/htnf.

Options

If you want a longer ride, park in downtown Bridgeport and ride out Twin Lakes Road to the start of this loop. You'll add on 11 paved miles each way on a very moderate grade (only 600 feet of elevation gain). The ride travels through pastures and grazing lands into Twin Lakes' canyon, and affords excellent views of Sawtooth Ridge and Matterhorn Peak.

Driving Directions

From Lee Vining, drive north on U.S. 395 for 25 miles to Bridgeport. Turn left (west) on Twin Lakes Road and drive 11 miles to Twin Lakes Resort on the right (on Lower Twin Lake).

Route Directions

0.0 Park at Twin Lakes Resort, then backtrack 0.25 mile on Twin Lakes Road (head east) and turn right on South Twin Road. *Supplies are available at the store at Twin Lakes Resort.*

0.5 Paved road turns to dirt past the campgrounds.

2.6 RIGHT at junction. Ride downhill between the two Twin Lakes.

2.8 LEFT at junction to stay on southeast side of lakes.

3.3 Pick up single-track at end of dirt road.

4.0 Cross bridge to Annett's Mono Village Resort and campground. Ride through the maze of buildings to the entrance station (stay to the right, close to the lakeshore).

4.7 Back on Twin Lakes Road.

8.3 Arrive at starting point.

2 GLACIER POINT ROAD   BEST **C**

Yosemite National Park

PAVED ROAD WITH MODERATE CAR TRAFFIC

Difficulty: 4   **Total Distance:** 31.6 miles

Riding Time: 3-4 hours   **Elevation Gain:** 2,700 feet

Summary: Glacier Point Road delivers you to one of the grandest views in the West — an overlook directly across from Half Dome and Vernal and Nevada Falls.

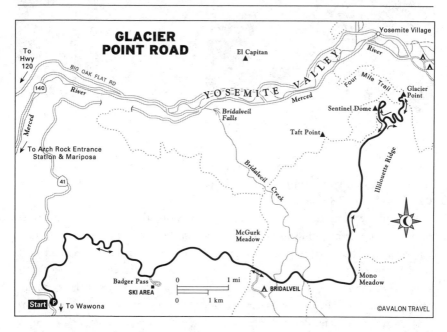

The view from Glacier Point—looking down 3,200 feet at Yosemite Valley and directly across at Half Dome and its granite neighbors, plus Vernal and Nevada Falls—is perhaps the most striking panorama of any in Yosemite National Park, a place that does not lack outstanding views. Getting there on a bike instead of in a car only adds to the grandeur.

The ride is less than ideal on summer weekends, however, when the park is overflowing with visitors, most of whom are driving around in cars. Weekdays are advisable, and early in the day is wise. The fewer cars you see on this often narrow, steep road, the more you'll be able to enjoy the world-class scenery.

From the start of Glacier Point Road, you begin to climb immediately, with the sweet scent of bear clover (a small shrub also called mountain misery)

© ANN MARIE BROWN

The view of Half Dome from Glacier Point is one of the most photographed sights in the western United States.

accompanying you. It lines the roadsides, forming a low-growing understory for the pines and firs. You won't see much but forest for the first several miles, so just focus on your climbing. If you need water, make a stop at Bridalveil Campground at 7.8 miles.

Beyond the camp turnoff, you start to get occasional peeks through the trees of the granite domes and summits ahead and to the south. Note the Taft Point and Sentinel Dome parking lot at mile 13.2; stop here for an easy hike on your return trip. The final 2 miles comprise a steep, circuitous descent to Glacier Point, passing Washburn Point Overlook along the way. The vista from here is enough to make you fly right off the pavement, but hold on to your handlebars for the final stretch to Glacier Point's parking lot. Then lock up your bike and go enjoy the famous view (and maybe a hot dog from the snack stand) with everybody else.

For your return trip, the first two miles present a tough workout, but with the exception of one more short climb near Summit Meadow, you'll hardly pedal at all back down to Chinquapin.

Keep in mind that the season to ride Glacier Point Road is short; the road is often snow covered as early as November and as late as May.

For more information, and to check on road conditions, contact Yosemite National Park, 209/372-0200, www.nps.gov/yose.

Driving Directions

From Yosemite Valley, take the Highway 41/Wawona/Fresno turnoff (near

Bridalveil Fall) and drive nine miles to the left turnoff for Glacier Point Road at Chinquapin Junction.

Route Directions

0.0 Park at the small parking area at the junction of Wawona Road and Glacier Point Road (Chinquapin Junction). *Supplies are available in Yosemite Valley or Wawona.*

7.8 Turnoff for Bridalveil Campground on right. *Water is available.*

13.2 Trailhead for Taft Point and Sentinel Dome on left. *On your return trip, lock up your bike and take one or both hikes to these two panoramic overlooks (each hike is 2.2 miles round-trip).*

14.7 Washburn Point Overlook.

15.8 Glacier Point parking lot. TURN AROUND. *Lock up your bike and visit the overlook area and snack bar. Food and supplies are available.*

31.6 Arrive at starting point.

GLACIER POINT ROAD

❸ YOSEMITE VALLEY BIKE PATH   BEST ☾
Yosemite National Park

PAVED BIKE PATH

Difficulty: 1	**Total Distance:** 8.2 miles
Riding Time: 1 hour	**Elevation Gain:** 450 feet

Summary: The best way to visit car-choked Yosemite Valley is to ride your bike past its spectacular granite walls and waterfalls.

It's congested, it's crowded, and it can be a zoo on summer weekends, but Yosemite Valley is still one of the greatest shows on earth. If you witness it from your bicycle seat rather than your car window, you'll see it in the best possible way.

To optimize the experience, ride this trail as early in the morning as you can. Better yet, ride this trail before or after the summer vacation season (in April or May when the valley waterfalls are at their peak, or any time in fall or winter when there is no snow or ice on the ground).

Start your bike trip at the Swinging Bridge picnic area on the south side of the valley. Head straight for the picturesque wooden bridge across the Merced River, then ride through the big meadow that faces Yosemite Falls. The drama begins immediately with the sight of this stunning waterfall and the immense granite walls that frame it.

At the Lower Yosemite Falls Trailhead, make use of the bike rack and take the one-mile loop hike to the falls. In early spring, the waterfall flows with such force that onlookers get showered with spray, even standing 50 yards away.

Steel yourself for the ride past the visitor center and through Yosemite Village, where the path gets very congested. Watch for stop signs at street intersections; cars are plentiful on the cross streets, and they don't necessarily stop for

There's no better way to see Yosemite Valley than on the seat of a bike.

bicyclists. Also, be cautious of other trail users, particularly pedestrians, who are often completely oblivious.

Shortly beyond the village is the right turnoff for Curry Village; ignore it and bear left to cross the Merced River two more times and pass through a peaceful area of pine forest, campgrounds, and no cars. Beyond the last of the campsites, the bike trail turns right to head for Happy Isles and the east side of Curry Village; you go straight on the paved road to Mirror Lake. The road is closed to cars but open to Yosemite Valley's free shuttle buses, which pass by occasionally.

Here you meet the only hill of your ride. If you've rented your bike in Yosemite Village, you must park your bike at the rack and walk up the hill (for insurance reasons). If you're on your own bike, pedal away. At the top, take a moment to enjoy Mirror Lake, a large, shallow pool in Tenaya Creek, which varies in size from season to season. Most of the year, it's more of a meadow than a lake. Nonetheless, the view of Half Dome's 4,700-foot perpendicular face, seen from its base, is awe-inspiring.

For your return trip, you'll loop back via Happy Isles and Curry Village, then rejoin your previous path just before Yosemite Village.

For more information, contact Yosemite National Park, 209/372-0200, www.nps.gov/yose.

Driving Directions

From the Arch Rock entrance station on Highway 140 in Yosemite Valley, drive east into the valley for 9.5 miles. Park in pullouts near the Four-Mile Trailhead (on the right), or at the Swinging Bridge picnic area just past this trailhead (on the left). The bike trail begins at the picnic area.

Route Directions

0.0 Park at the Four-Mile Trailhead or Swinging Bridge picnic area. *Supplies are available in Yosemite Village.*

0.9 Lower Yosemite Falls Trailhead. *Lock up your bike and walk the one-mile loop to the falls.*

1.5 Valley Visitor Center and Yosemite Village.

2.3 LEFT at fork (Curry Village to the right).

3.3 STRAIGHT for Mirror Lake at fork (Happy Isles and Curry Village to the right).

3.9 Mirror Lake. TURN AROUND.

4.5 LEFT toward Happy Isles; loop around Curry Village.

6.5 LEFT back to Yosemite Village.

8.2 Arrive at starting point.

4 MORAINES AND MEADOWS LOOP
east of Tioga Pass and west of Lee Vining

DIRT ROAD

Difficulty: 3

Riding Time: 2 hours

Total Distance: 11.4 miles

Elevation Gain: 1,200 feet

Summary: Two lovely meadows and the strange geology of Mono Craters and Mono Lake can be seen on this ride.

Wide views of Mono Lake are plentiful from the Moraines and Meadows Loop.

The Moraines and Meadows Loop starts by Highway 120 but quickly enters a world of alpine meadows and glacial moraines. The trail allows wide looks at giant-sized Mono Lake and neighboring Mono Craters, plus a visit to Upper and Lower Horse Meadows. An artificially constructed feature—one that has played a huge role in the history of California water rights—is also visible. That would be the Los Angeles Aqueduct.

The ride begins with a 1.6-mile connector trail (Road 1N15), which seems to be heading straight for Mono Lake. But long before approaching the lakeshore (or actually U.S. 395), you turn right and begin a counterclockwise loop, circling Williams Butte. That hill remains on your left for much of the ride.

A three-mile climb to Lower and Upper Horse Meadows will get you huffing and puffing. The lower meadow is not lined with delicate shooting stars, but rather sagebrush, rabbit brush, and a mix of grasses. The upper meadow is a more traditional, grassy alpine meadow. Just beyond it, at a saddle, is the high point of the ride (mile 4.9). Views of the June Lake area to the south and its surrounding craggy peaks are outstanding.

From the saddle, take Forest Service Road 1N18 due left (south), and over the next four miles enjoy losing all that elevation you've just gained. The final stretch of Road 1N18 crosses the Los Angeles Aqueduct road and then heads north, paralleling U.S. 395.

Note that this route is open to all-terrain vehicles. Although you probably won't encounter any on your ride, be alert for the high-pitched whine of their engines and get off the road if you hear one coming.

For more information, contact Mono Basin Scenic Area Visitor Center of Inyo National Forest, 760/647-3044, www.fs.fed.us/r5/inyo.

Driving Directions

From the Tioga Pass entrance station to Yosemite on Highway 120, drive east for 11 miles to just beyond the Forest Service ranger station (3 miles west of U.S. 395).

Route Directions

0.0 Park at the signed Moraines and Meadows Trailhead on Highway 120. Ride east on Highway 120 for a few yards and then turn off on Forest Service Road 1N15 (dirt). *Supplies are available three miles west in Lee Vining.*

1.6 RIGHT on Road 1N16 (Horse Meadows Road) at T-junction.

4.9 LEFT on Road 1N18 at saddle beyond Upper Horse Meadow.

7.1 STRAIGHT at junction with Road 1N17 (Aqueduct Road).

9.8 RIGHT on Road 1N15.

11.4 Arrive at starting point.

5 PANORAMA MOUNTAIN TRAIL
off U.S. 395 near June Lake

DIRT ROAD

Difficulty: 3   **Total Distance:** 10.7 miles

Riding Time: 2 hours   **Elevation Gain:** 1,100 feet

Summary: Get away from the eastern Sierra crowds on this ride on old jeep roads around ancient volcanic vents.

The Panorama Mountain Trail is a mountain bike route sanctioned by the Forest Service that consists of three consecutive loops on jeep roads and graded dirt roads. This is lonely sagebrush and big-sky country, where you probably aren't going to run into anybody else. Be entirely self-sufficient and carry plenty of water. The trail leads through sage and Jeffrey pines for the majority of the trip, with only occasional shade.

Because of the triple-loop formation, the number of junctions on this trail could drive you mad, but the Forest Service has very considerately signed the entire route. Just watch for their little brown markers and you'll be fine. Also, a few prominent landmarks will help guide you: U.S. 395, which is visible every time you climb a little; the distinct Mono Craters, a chain of barren-looking volcanic vents poking up from the surrounding sagebrush plains; and the Aeolian Buttes, where the most recent volcanic activity in this area occurred perhaps only 600 years ago. The third of the three loops circles the buttes, and will take you up high enough so that you get surprising views of Mono Lake and its neighboring craters to the northeast, plus the snowcapped, granite mountains of the eastern Sierra to the west. It's startling to see this juxtaposition of glacier-carved mountains and volcanic vents and tablelands all in one glance.

If you're new to riding in the Mammoth Lakes area, you may be a bit put off by the trail surface, even on these well-graded roads. The surface is a mix of pumice, gravel, and sand. You'll quickly learn to follow the line that looks the most hard-packed.

For more information, contact Mono Basin Scenic Area Visitor Center of Inyo National Forest, 760/647-3044, www. fs.fed.us/r5/inyo.

The sagebrush flats of the Panorama Mountain Trail give way to the snow-capped eastern Sierra.

Driving Directions

From the junction of U.S. 395 and Highway 158 (June Lake Junction), drive 150 yards north on U.S. 395 and turn right at dirt road 1S35. Drive 100 yards down the road to the signed trailhead.

Route Directions

0.0 Park at the Panorama Mountain Trailhead. *Supplies are available at June Lake Junction.* This ride is a combination of three loops with more than 25 turns and numerous possible junctions. Follow the Forest Service's small brown signs along the trail. *Maps are available at the Mono Basin Scenic Area Visitor Center just north of Lee Vining on U.S. 395.*

10.7 Arrive at starting point.

6 JUNE LAKE LOOP RAMBLE

June Lake, north of Mammoth Lakes

PAVED ROAD WITH MODERATE CAR TRAFFIC

Difficulty: 2

Riding Time: 2-3 hours

Total Distance: 28.8 miles

Elevation Gain: 1,000 feet

Summary: Some of the eastern Sierra's best scenery – multiple lakes, aspen groves, and soaring Carson Peak – can be viewed from your bike's saddle on the June Lake Loop.

Despite its name, this ride on the June Lake Loop is not a loop ride. The June Lake Loop is the main road through the June Lake area (Highway 158), but it's only a loop if you ride (or drive) a six-mile stretch on U.S. 395. It's much smarter, and more pleasurable, to ride the June Lake Loop as an out-and-back, and leave U.S. 395 to the giant tractor trailers hauling past at 70 mph.

Riding in this manner, you can plan on enjoying a couple of hours of some of the finest scenery in the eastern Sierra. You'll witness imposing granite peaks, the dancing leaves of aspen groves, and four sparkling, bright blue lakes. Because the route

JUNE LAKE LOOP RAMBLE

MONO BASIN NATIONAL SCENIC AREA

© ANN MARIE BROWN

Granite peaks tower over the June Lake basin.

has many places to stop for supplies or breaks, this ride is well within the abilities of most cyclists. Traffic is as you might expect: heavier on summer weekends, lighter the rest of the time. The ride outlined here bypasses the main downtown area of June Lake and travels on the alternative Northshore Drive. This will spare you the company of a lot of automobiles.

Note that June Lake is virtually deserted after Labor Day (first Monday in September), making early fall a fine time to ride. In late September and early October, the region's abundant aspens and cottonwoods don their golden headdresses for the annual autumnal dance.

The first 3.5 miles are all downhill or level and present pretty views of June Lake and Gull Lake. Then, with a right turn near the June Mountain ski lifts, you're on the official June Lake Loop. Traffic is busiest between miles 3.5 and 5.8 where numerous cabin resorts, shops, and private homes are located. There are dozens of places to stop for supplies along this stretch. You should certainly stop to admire granite Carson Peak, the predominant mountain towering over June Lake.

Beyond Silver Lake at mile 5.8, the road quiets down, but the wind may pick up in the next several miles as you near Grant Lake. You're leaving the shelter of granite peaks and entering wide-open sagebrush plains. The road follows the shoreline of Grant Lake for more than 3 miles; this is the largest lake on the June Lake Loop.

A good turnaround point is mile 14.4 at the Mono Craters Viewpoint; it's only another 1.2 miles to the road's end at U.S. 395 (you've seen the best scenery already). At the viewpoint, you get a good look at the barren, pumice-covered volcanic cones called Mono Craters, which were created by a series of volcanic eruptions as recently as 600 years ago.

Good news for the return trip: The views of Carson Peak are even more tremendous from the opposite direction. And after climbing that hill from the ski resort back up Northshore Drive, you can treat yourself to a swim at June Lake's beach.

Driving Directions

From U.S. 395 at the Highway 203/Mammoth Lakes turnoff, drive 15 miles north on U.S. 395 to Highway 158, the southern turnoff for the June Lake Loop. Turn west on Highway 158 and drive 0.9 mile to Northshore Drive (signed for Oh! Ridge and Pinecliff). Turn right and park at the overlook area.

Route Directions

0.0 Park at the overlook at the corner of Northshore Drive and Highway 158. Ride north on Northshore Drive. *Supplies are available in downtown June Lake, or at the store at the corner of U.S. 395 and Highway 158.*

0.7 Turnoff for June Lake beach on left.

2.7 Turnoff to head into downtown on left.

3.5 RIGHT at junction of Northshore Drive and Highway 158 (June Lake Loop).

5.8 Silver Lake Resort on the left; Silver Lake on the right. *The resort store is the last place to stop for supplies until the return trip.*

9.5 Grant Lake on right.

14.4 Mono Craters Viewpoint. TURN AROUND.

28.8 Arrive at starting point.

7 DEVILS POSTPILE
Mammoth Lakes to Red's Meadow

PAVED ROAD WITH MODERATE CAR TRAFFIC

Difficulty: 3   **Total Distance:** 19.6 miles (or 9.8-mile shuttle option)

Riding Time: 2-3 hours   **Elevation Gain:** 1,500 feet

Summary: Ride your bike instead of the bus on this scenery-filled tour of Devils Postpile National Monument.

If you want to earn the respect of all the hearty outdoor types in Mammoth, ride your bike from Mammoth Mountain down into Devils Postpile. Eat lunch at the resort at Red's Meadow and then ride back up, up, up. Then go brag about it at one of the local watering holes.

The paved road is narrow and has a 1,500-foot elevation change (down on the way in, up on the way back, with 1,000 feet of gain concentrated in a 2.5-mile stretch). Incredibly scenic throughout its entire length, the road travels near some of Devils Postpile National Monument's best features. Here's the best part: In summer, a mandatory shuttle bus system operates during daylight hours, so you'll encounter very few cars on the road. The winding, steep, sometimes one-lane road would not be rideable if it had the usual flow of national park traffic, so thank your lucky stars for the shuttle system.

The ride begins at Mammoth Mountain Ski Area, which is transformed into a mountain bike park in summer. You'll find a huge parking lot and ample opportunities to stock up on supplies. With a one-mile ascent to Minaret Vista, elevation 9,174 feet, you're at one of the finest viewpoints in the Sierra: a wide panorama of Mounts Ritter and Banner and the saw-toothed Minarets. Then you face a downward plunge into the forested canyon of Devils Postpile National Monument. Check your brakes before you go.

Once in the monument, plan on making a few stops. Stop at the ranger station and take the short walk to see the Devil's Postpile, a columnar basalt formation remaining from an ancient lava flow. Stop at the trailhead parking area just before Red's Meadow and take the one-mile walk to see 101-foot

Rainbow Falls, one of the Sierra's most picture-perfect waterfalls. Then stop at Red's Meadow and eat a big, high-energy lunch, because you have 1,500 feet to gain back on the way uphill. You probably don't need to be reminded that the alpine air is quite thin at this elevation.

For more information, contact Devils Postpile National Monument, 760/934-2289, www.nps.gov/depo; or the Mammoth Lakes Ranger District of Inyo National Forest, 760/924-5500, www.fs.fed.us/r5/inyo.

101-foot Rainbow Falls

© ANN MARIE BROWN

Options

Another plus to the bus shuttle system in Devils Postpile is that, if you choose, you can ride downhill into the national monument and then ride the shuttle bus back up the hill. You'll need to purchase an access pass for the bus ride, and the only place you and your bike can board the bus is at the end of Devils Postpile Road at Red's Meadow Resort. Riding between the peak visitation hours of 10 A.M. to 4 P.M. is not recommended. Also, fat-tire riders may take advantage of riding the Starkweather Trail in September and October, but only after the shuttle bus has stopped operating. The trail spans 2.5 miles from Minaret Vista, near the entrance station to Devils Postpile, downhill to Starkweather Lake.

Driving Directions

From U.S. 395 at Mammoth Lakes, take the Highway 203 turnoff and drive west for 4 miles, through the town of Mammoth Lakes, to the intersection of Highway 203 and Lake Mary Road. Turn right on Highway 203 (Minaret Road) and drive 4.5 miles to the main lodge area at Mammoth Mountain.

Route Directions

0.0 Park at Mammoth Mountain near the brass mammoth statue. Ride west on Highway 203. *Supplies are available at the mountain bike park and lodge.*

1.2 RIGHT at Minaret Vista overlook; enjoy the view then TURN AROUND.

1.8 RIGHT on Highway 203/Devils Postpile Road; begin steep descent.

4.3 Agnews Meadows turnoff on right.

8.4 Devils Postpile Ranger Station turnoff on right. *Ride 0.3 mile to ranger station, lock up your bike, and hike 0.4 mile to the Devil's Postpile. Then continue riding on Devils Postpile Road.*

9.7 Rainbow Falls Trailhead on right. *Lock up your bike and take the one-mile hike to Rainbow Falls.*

9.8 Red's Meadow Resort on left. TURN AROUND. *Supplies are available.*

19.6 Arrive at starting point.

8 MOUNTAIN VIEW TRAIL
Mammoth Lakes

DIRT ROAD AND SINGLE-TRACK

Difficulty: 3   **Total Distance:** 11 miles

Riding Time: 2 hours   **Elevation Gain:** 800 feet

Summary: Spectacular mountain views await on this fun, mostly single-track ride from Minaret Vista.

Mountain View Trail boasts 5.5 miles of single-track and jeep road, which winds its way from the Earthquake Fault overlook to Minaret Vista. It's a moderately challenging route through a dense forest of red firs, lodgepole pines, and Jeffrey pines. The route is packed with short but steep ups and downs, cambered turns, and plenty of loose and deep pumice. Keep watching for the brown Forest Service signs to keep you on track through several junctions.

Since you're starting at the Earthquake Fault parking area, you might as well take the short walk to see this phenomenon: a long, nearly straight fracture in hardened lava that is up to 60 feet in depth. Some scientists believe it was formed by a cooling volcanic fissure, while others claim it was caused by a small, local earthquake fault.

Ride back out the Earthquake Fault entrance road and pick up Mountain View Trail on the right 100 yards before Highway 203. Follow the trail uphill through big red firs to a nice view of Inyo Craters. After its first stint northward, the trail wends generally west toward Minaret Vista, alternating as stretches of single-track and jeep road. Where the trees thin out, you gain good views of Mammoth Mountain. The forest changes from firs and big pines to the sturdier, high-elevation whitebark pines. They are smaller and somewhat stunted looking, but it's no surprise considering what they have to deal with every winter at 9,100 feet.

Mountain View Trail ends at a dirt parking area on the entrance road to

Minaret Vista. Turn right on the pavement to gain the Minaret Vista overlook, a fine reward for all your efforts. Here you'll gaze at the jagged outline of the Ritter Range to the west, with Mount Banner and Mount Ritter leading the pack of saw-toothed peaks, and the Inyo and White Mountains to the east.

For more information, contact the Mammoth Lakes Ranger District of Inyo National Forest, 760/924-5500, www.fs.fed.us/r5/inyo.

Options

Note that if this single-track has worn you out, you can take the easy route back to the Earthquake Fault parking lot by riding on paved Highway 203 (Minaret Road). You'll cut a couple of miles off the round-trip,

The Mountain View Trail winds through dense forest on its way to Minaret Vista.

but more significantly, you'll be riding on smooth, descending pavement.

Driving Directions

From U.S. 395 at Mammoth Lakes, take the Highway 203 turnoff and drive west for 4 miles, through the town of Mammoth Lakes, to the intersection of Highway 203 and Lake Mary Road. Turn right on Highway 203 (Minaret Road) and drive 1.9 miles to the Earthquake Fault turnoff on the right.

Route Directions

0.0 Park at the Earthquake Fault parking lot, then ride back down the entrance road to the signed trail on the right, about 100 yards from Highway 203. (Watch for blue diamonds on the red fir trees and bike trail signs.) *Supplies are available in Mammoth.*

0.7 RIGHT at junction.

1.5 RIGHT at junction.

2.0 LEFT at junction with trail to Inyo Craters.

2.7 RIGHT then immediate LEFT at junction.

3.2 RIGHT at junction.

5.4 Dirt parking area. Turn RIGHT on pavement and ride uphill to Minaret Vista. TURN AROUND.

11.0 Arrive at starting point.

9 MAMMOTH LAKES BASIN AND HORSESHOE LAKE
Mammoth Lakes

**PAVED ROAD WITH MODERATE CAR TRAFFIC
(PLUS OPTIONAL DIRT SINGLE-TRACK)**

Difficulty: 1   **Total Distance:** 12.2 miles (or 13.9-mile option)

Riding Time: 1.5 hours   **Elevation Gain:** 700 feet

Summary: Bring your single-speed beach cruiser for a mellow, scenic ride around the Mammoth Lakes Basin.

This is an easy cruise in the Mammoth Lakes area that tours the Lakes Basin and its five gorgeous, alpine lakes. Many visitor services are found along the way (cabin resorts, stores, restaurants, and more), but the area retains its rustic feel; this part of Mammoth is by no means overrun with commercialism. Traveling through some of the eastern Sierra's most visually stunning, and easily accessible, scenery, this ride has long been popular for campers and vacationers staying in the Lakes Basin, but as of late 2011 it's even better for cyclists than before: Now you can ride most of the route on a paved bike path, separate from cars, rather than on the narrow shoulder of the road.

Start your ride at the north end of Twin Lakes Road and pedal past the Lower Twin Lake and Tamarack Lodge, a cabin resort known for its award-winning restaurant. Ride south, paralleling Twin Lakes Road, until it rejoins Lake Mary Road. Turn right here. Take the long loop around the south side of Lake Mary, enjoying more picturesque lakeside scenery. Leave the bike path here and follow the spur road up to Lake George, the most fetching of the five lakes. At 9,200 feet in elevation, Lake George is deep blue and lined with granite, but what sets it apart from its neighboring lakes is Crystal Crag, an exquisite chunk of rock that forms the lake's backdrop. If you have some free time, bring along a bike lock. Several short hikes can be taken from Lake George, including those to Crystal Lake, T.J. Lake, and Barrett Lake.

The final stretch of the ride passes lovely Lake Mamie and travels to the road's end at Horseshoe Lake. The lake's north shore is surrounded by dead trees, which met their end from carbon dioxide gas venting up through the soil, most likely from seismic action. If you're on a mountain bike, you can ride around the lake to the unaffected south side, which is lined with a thriving forest and plentiful wildflowers in midsummer (see *Options*).

Views of snow-capped peaks appear around every corner in the Mammoth Lakes Basin.

For more information, contact the Mammoth Lakes Ranger District of Inyo National Forest, 760/924-5500, www.fs.fed.us/r5/inyo. For a map of the Mammoth Lakes paved recreation trail system, go to www.mltpa.org.

Options

The newly constructed Lakes Basin Path connects to the paved Town Loop Trail at the parking area on Lake Mary Road just before Twin Lakes. You can easily add on another 12-plus miles of paved, car-free riding that will take you into the "downtown" of Mammoth Lakes for shopping, restaurants, and more. Or, if you're on a mountain bike, you can get off the pavement at the end of the ride and pedal the beautiful single-track loop around Horseshoe Lake. This trail is a great introduction to single-track riding. It is mostly level, presents no major obstacles, and is only 1.7 miles long.

Driving Directions

From U.S. 395 at Mammoth Lakes, take the Highway 203 turnoff and drive west for four miles, through the town of Mammoth Lakes, to the intersection of Highway 203 and Lake Mary Road. Continue straight on Lake Mary Road for two miles, then bear right on Twin Lakes Road.

Route Directions

0.0 Park at Twin Lakes in any of the day-use spots. Mileage starts at the northern junction of Twin Lakes Road and Lake Mary Road. Ride south on Twin Lakes Road. *Supplies are available at Twin Lakes Store, Lake Mary Store, or Pokenobe Lodge.*

1.8 RIGHT on Lake Mary Road.

2.6 LEFT to loop around Lake Mary.

4.1 LEFT to Lake George.

4.4 Lake George. TURN AROUND. *Several short hikes are possible from here.*

4.7 LEFT to continue loop around Lake Mary.

5.0 LEFT on Lake Mary Road to Lake Mamie.

6.1 End of the road at Horseshoe Lake. TURN AROUND. *Skinny-tire riders turn back now; mountain bikers can ride the 1.7-mile loop around Horseshoe Lake.*

12.2 Arrive at starting point (13.9 for mountain bikes).

MAMMOTH LAKES BASIN AND HORSESHOE LAKE

10 MAMMOTH CREEK PARK/ SHERWIN CREEK LOOP
Mammoth Lakes

DIRT ROADS AND PAVED BIKE PATH

Difficulty: 2   **Total Distance:** 6.3 miles

Riding Time: 1 hour   **Elevation Gain:** 500 feet

Summary: Enjoy Mammoth Lakes the way the locals do with this scenic ride on a paved bike path and dirt Sherwin Creek Road.

Downtown Mammoth Lakes has one of the most scenic paved recreation trails in all of Northern California, now made even better by its connection to Mammoth's Town Loop Trail and Lakes Basin Path (see ride 9, *Mammoth Lakes Basin and Horseshoe Lake*). The Mammoth Creek Park Trail offers expansive views of the frequently snowcapped Sherwins, and a sense that you are far from the hustle and bustle of downtown Mammoth, even though you aren't.

This mostly dirt loop gives you a short taste of that paved trail, then turns off onto dirt roads. By bypassing the first turnoff, as described below, you'll ride a short out-and-back on the pavement to a spectacular mountain overlook atop a sage-covered hill. Enjoy the view from the trailside wooden benches, then glide back down to that first turnoff, go left, and begin the dirt stretch of the ride.

Dirt road 3S09 follows the path of Mammoth Creek, passing by creekside aspen groves and offering great views of the surrounding mountains. (The best time to ride here is unquestionably in the fall, when the quaking aspens put on their fiery display.) After a right turn, a short but steep downhill, and a footbridge crossing

© ANN MARIE BROWN

The Sherwin Creek Loop provides great views of Mammoth's high peaks.

the creek, you'll find a maze of dirt roads; just continue straight and uphill for 0.3 mile until you reach the wide, graded Sherwin Creek Road. Turn right and follow the road past a campground and day-use area. You'll face a slow, gradual climb to the east, inspired by a head-on view of Mammoth Mountain. Eventually the road changes from gravel to pavement. Turn right on Old Mammoth Road and head back to your starting point at the park.

You may have to put up with some cars on Sherwin Creek Road; the dirt road extends east all the way to U.S. 395, and some people use it to access nearby hiking trails and a motocross track.

For more information, contact the Mammoth Lakes Ranger District of Inyo National Forest, 760/924-5500, www.fs.fed.us/r5/inyo.

Options

From Mammoth Creek Park, you can also connect to the Town Loop Trail, which leads all the way to the Lakes Basin Path. For more information and maps of the Mammoth Lakes paved recreation trail system, which as of 2011 is still in expansion, visit www.mltpa.org.

Driving Directions

From U.S. 395 at Mammoth Lakes, take the Highway 203 turnoff and drive west for 2.7 miles. Turn left on Old Mammoth Road and drive 1 mile to Mammoth Creek Park on the right.

Route Directions

0.0 Park at Mammoth Creek Park. Follow the paved trail from near the restrooms through the tunnel to the far side of Old Mammoth Road. *Supplies are available in Mammoth.*

0.5 Pass dirt road 3S09; note this junction.

0.9 Overlook of the Sherwins on paved bike path. TURN AROUND.

1.3 LEFT at previous junction with 3S09.

2.6 RIGHT on dirt road that quickly narrows and drops downhill.

2.9 Cross footbridge. Continue STRAIGHT on other side of creek.

3.2 RIGHT on Sherwin Creek Road (4S08) at a major junction of graded roads.

5.9 RIGHT on Old Mammoth Road.

6.1 LEFT into Mammoth Creek Park.

6.3 Arrive at starting point.

MAMMOTH CREEK PARK/SHERWIN CREEK LOOP

11 LOWER ROCK CREEK
south of Tom's Place on U.S. 395

BEST [

DIRT SINGLE-TRACK

Difficulty: 4

Total Distance: 7.9 miles (or 15.5-mile option)

Riding Time: 1.5 hours

Elevation Gain: 0 feet (2,000-foot loss)

Summary: Nearly eight miles of highly technical and sometimes treacherous single-track follow the path of Lower Rock Creek.

The single-track Lower Rock Creek Trail is more like two trails: the upper section, which is rideable by most mountain bikers with some single-track experience under their belt, and the lower section, which is extremely technical and for highly experienced (and gutsy) riders only. The trail varies greatly, consisting of rocky, narrow, and overgrown sections and less difficult, straight, and fast sections. The surface varies also: a mix of dirt, sand, loose gravel, and big and small rocks. This is a ride where you should expect the unexpected, from sharp turns and boulders lying in the middle of the path, to

willows and other brushy vegetation crowding the trail, to the possibility of encountering hikers and anglers around every curve. A warning about controlling your speed: At Lower Rock Creek, the stories are legion of riders crashing into rocks after riding too fast around a blind turn. Exercise caution.

Lower Rock Creek Trail's sandy single-track road parallels the lush riparian environment of Lower Rock Creek.

If all this starts to give you second thoughts once you've started riding, you can bail out at the first or second crossing of Rock Creek Road (mile 2.2 or 3.3), then ride back up the paved road to your starting point. Those who insist on continuing onward face the worst of the technical challenges beyond mile 3.5. There are no more bailouts beyond this point. Good luck.

The trail loses 2,000 feet from top to bottom, so many ride it as a shuttle trip by leaving a car at both ends. Another choice is to ride back uphill on the paved Lower Rock Creek Road (see *Options*). A third choice would be to ride back uphill on the single-track, but darn near nobody attempts it. You would carry your bike far too much of the time. Although the area around the start of this trail burned in a fire in August 2002, the trail itself was untouched. You'll leave all signs of the fire behind after the first couple miles.

If you've been riding around the Mammoth Lakes area prior to riding here, remember that you're not in Mammoth any more. Lower Rock Creek is in the arid, desert-like Owens Valley, quite a few miles from the nearest set of high mountain peaks. The sun can be hot and unforgiving. Still, the trail runs through Rock Creek's gorgeous stream canyon, which is surprisingly lush and filled with unusual geologic features, including columnar basalt like that found at nearby Devils Postpile National Monument. The entire ride follows the creek, often in the shade of aspens and Jeffrey pines (thankfully). This is a beautiful, pristine area, and it's a miracle that mountain bikers are allowed access to it. Let's mind our manners and keep it that way.

For more information, contact the White Mountain Ranger District of Inyo National Forest, 760/873-2500, www.fs.fed.us/r5/inyo.

Options

If you aren't lucky enough to be able to arrange a car shuttle, you are going to have to ride back to your starting point, and you sure as heck don't want to go back up the way you came down. So, at the end of the trail at Paradise Resort, start riding north on paved Lower Rock Creek Road. You'll face 7.6 mostly uphill miles, which can be extremely hot on summer days, with one particularly nasty, steep stretch. Total loop mileage is 15.5 miles with 2,000 feet of elevation gain.

Driving Directions

From U.S. 395 at the Highway 203/Mammoth Lakes turnoff, drive 15.5 miles south on U.S. 395 to Lower Rock Creek Road on the right, 1 mile south of Rock Creek Lakes Road. Turn right and park in the first available pullout. (To leave a shuttle vehicle at the southern end of the trail, continue south on U.S. 395 for 10.5 miles to the Paradise/Gorge Road exit. Turn right and drive 3 miles north on Lower Rock Creek Road to Paradise Resort; park across the road.)

Route Directions

0.0 Park at the start of Lower Rock Creek Road near its northern junction with U.S. 395. The trail begins directly across from the Lower Rock Creek Recreation Area sign, about 150 feet from U.S. 395 on the south side of the road. *Supplies are available in Tom's Place, one mile north on U.S. 395.*

2.2 RIGHT on Lower Rock Creek Road and pick up the single-track on the far side of the bridge (in the small parking area).

3.3 Cross Lower Rock Creek Road; trail becomes much more technically challenging from here on out.

7.2 Single-track widens into dirt road.

7.9 End of trail at Lower Rock Creek Road and Paradise Resort. *Supplies are available. If you have a shuttle car waiting for you, you're finished.*

RESOURCES

Bike Parks

The following downhill and cross-country ski resorts transform into mountain bike parks in summer. Mountain bikers pay a daily fee to ride all day on each park's specially designated trails. At some parks, your entrance fee includes one or more uphill shuttles on a chairlift or gondola, so if you choose your route carefully, all you have to do is coast back downhill.

Bear Valley
1 Bear Valley Road
Bear Valley, CA 95233
209/753-2834
www.bearvalleyxc.com

Kirkwood Resort
P.O. Box 1
Kirkwood, CA 95646
209/258-6000
www.kirkwood.com

Mammoth Mountain Bike Park
P.O. Box 24
Mammoth Lakes, CA 93546
800-MAMMOTH
www.mammothmountain.com

Northstar-at-Tahoe
5001 Northstar Drive
Truckee, CA 96161
530/562-1010 or 800/GO-NORTH
www.northstarattahoe.com

Bike Shops

REDWOOD EMPIRE
Arcata
Adventure's Edge
650 10th Street
707/822-4673
www.adventuresedge.com

Glover Bicycle Construction and Repair
860 11th Street
707/826-2118

Life Cycle Inc.
1593 G Street
707/822-7755
www.lifecyclearcata.com

New Outdoor Store
876 G Street
707/822-0321

Crescent City
Back Country Bicycles
1331 Northcrest Drive
707/465-3995

Eureka
Pacific Outfitters
1600 5th Avenue
707/443-6328
www.pacificoutfitters.com

Sport & Cycle
1621 Broadway Street
707/444-9274

Garberville
Allsport and Toys
776 Redwood Drive
707/923-2243

SHASTA AND LASSEN
Chester
Bodfish Bicycles
149 Main Street
530/258-2338
www.bodfishbicycles.com

Dunsmuir
The Third Wheel
5824 Dunsmuir Avenue
530/235-2453

Mount Shasta
The Fifth Season
300 North Mount Shasta Boulevard
530/926-3606
www.thefifthseason.com

Red Bluff
Fast Wheels Bike Shop
233 Main Street
530/529-1388

Redding
Bikes Etc.
2400 Athens Avenue
530/244-1954

The Bike Shop
3331 Bechelli Lane
530/223-1205
www.thebikeshop.cc

Chain Gang Bike Shop
1540 Division Street
530/243-9951
www.chaingangbikeshop.com

Sportmart/Sports Authority
1347 Churn Creek Road
530/222-9372
www.sportsauthority.com

Sports Limited Redding
950 Hilltop Drive
530/221-7333

Village Cycle
3090 Bechelli Lane
530/223-2320

Weaverville
Ellisons Bicycle Shop
31 Weaver Street
530/623-3377

Yreka
Badger Mountain Bike Shop
1525 Lucas Road
530/842-5420

MENDOCINO AND WINE COUNTRY

Calistoga
Calistoga Bike Shop
1318 Lincoln Avenue
707/942-9687
www.calistogabikeshop.com

Cotati
The Hub Cyclery
7885 Old Redwood Highway
707/795-6670
www.thehubcyclery.com

Fort Bragg
Fort Bragg Cyclery
301 North Main Street
707/964-3509
www.fortbraggcyclery.com

Healdsburg
Spoke Folk Cyclery
201 Center Street
707/433-7171
www.spokefolk.com

Mendocino
Catch-a-Canoe & Bicycles Too
44850 Comptche–Ukiah Road
707/937-0273
www.catchacanoe.com

Napa
Bicycle Madness
2500 Jefferson Street
707/253-2453

Bicycle Works
3335 Solano Avenue
707/253-7000

Fix-A-Bike
2965 Jefferson Street
707/255-2571

Napa River Velo
680 Main Street
707/258-8729
www.naparivervelo.com

Rohnert Park
Breakaway Bikes
5430 Commerce Boulevard
707/586-3400
www.breakawaybikes.org

Saint Helena
St. Helena Cyclery
1156 Main Street
707/963-7736
www.sthelenacyclery.com

Santa Rosa
The Bike Peddler
605 College Avenue
707/571-2428
www.norcalcycling.com

Cambria Bicycle Outfitter
2885 Santa Rosa Avenue
707/579-5400
www.cambriabike.com

Community Bikes
4009 and 4019 Sebastopol Road
707/579-5811

Norcal Bike Sport
425 College Avenue
707/573-0112
www.norcalcycling.com

REI
2715 Santa Rosa Avenue
707/540-9025
www.rei.com

Rincon Cyclery
4927 Sonoma Highway
707/538-0868
www.rinconcyclery.com

Sportmart/Sports Authority
1970 Santa Rosa Avenue
707/523-4700
www.sportsauthority.com

Sonoma
Goodtime Touring
18503 Highway 12
888/525-0453
www.goodtimetouring.com

Sonoma Valley Cyclery
20091 Broadway
707/935-3377
www.sonomacyclery.com

Ukiah
Dave's Bike Shop
163 East Gobbi Street
707/462-3230
www.davesbikeshop.com

Windsor
Windsor Bicycle Center
830 McClelland Drive
707/836-9111
www.windsorbikes.com

SACRAMENTO AND GOLD COUNTRY
Angels Camp
Mountain Pedaler
352 South Main Street
209/736-0771

Auburn
Auburn Bike Works
350 Grass Valley Highway
530/885-3861
www.auburnbikeworks.com

Cambria Bicycle Emporium
483 Grass Valley Highway
530/823-2900
www.bicycleemporium.com

Victory Velo Bike Shop
835 Lincoln Way
530/885-3986
www.victoryvelo.com

Carmichael
Carmichael Cycles
5142 Arden Way
916/488-5353
www.bicycleproducts.com

Chico

The Bicycle Wheel
130-B West East Avenue
530/897-0180
www.thebicyclewheel.com

Campus Bicycles
330 Main Street
530/345-2081
www.campusbicycles.com

Cherry Bikes
748 West Fifth Street
530/342-5295

Chico Bike and Board
845 Main Street
530/343-5506
www.chicobikeandboard.com

Cyclesport
148 Main Street
530/345-1910
www.chicocyclesport.net

North Rim Adventure Sports
178 East Second Street
530/345-2453
www.northrimadventure.com

North Valley Bicycle
2590 Cohasset Road
530/343-0636

Pullins Cyclery
801 Main Street
530/342-1055

Sports Ltd.
698 Mangrove Avenue
530/894-1110
www.chicosportsltd.net

The Third Wheel
2505 Esplanade
530/895-1116

Citrus Heights

City Bike Works
7885 Greenback Lane
916/726-2453
www.citybicycleworks.com

Davis

ASUCD Bike Barn
University of California Davis
1 Shields Avenue
530/752-2575
http://bikebarn.ucdavis.edu

B & L Bike Shop
610 Third Street
530/756-3540
www.blbikeshop.com

Davis Bike Exchange
612 Fourth Street
530/753-4600

Davis Wheelworks
247 F Street
530/753-3118
www.daviswheelworks.com

Freewheeler Bicycle Center
703 Second Street
530/758-5460
www.freewheelerbikes.com

Ken's Bike & Ski
650 G Street
530/758-3223
www.kensbikeski.com

Real Bicycles
P.O. Box 733
530/753-3043

Dixon
Fisk's Cyclery
539 North Adams Street
707/678-4330
www.fiskscyclery.com

Downieville
Downieville Outfitters
114 Main Street
530/289-0155
www.downievilleoutfitters.com

Yuba Expeditions
208 Main Street
530/289-3010
www.yubaexpeditions.com

Elk Grove
Elk Grove Cyclery
9632 Emerald Oak Drive
916/686-8020

Fair Oaks
Bob's Cycle Center
9920 Fair Oaks Boulevard
916/961-6700 or 916/967-5163
www.bobscyclecenter.com

Patriot Bicycles
4719 San Juan Avenue
916/961-9646
www.patriotbicycles.com

River Rat Mountain Bikes
4053 Pennsylvania Avenue
916/966-7777
www.river-rat.com

Folsom
Bicycle Planet
1760 Prairie City Road
916/355-1234
www.bicycleplanet.net

Bicycles Plus
705 Gold Lake Drive
916/355-8901
www.onlinecycling.com

REI
2425 Iron Point Road
916/817-8944
www.rei.com

Jackson
Jackson Family Sports
225 East Highway 88
209/223-3890

Lincoln
Gold Country Bicycles
150 G Street, Suite 103
916/645-3753

Lodi
City Bicycles
310 North Ham Lane
209/339-4371

Modesto
Valley Sporting Goods
1700 McHenry Avenue, Suite D50
209/523-5681

World of Wheels
1544 Standiford
209/522-0804

Nevada City
Tour of Nevada City Bicycle Shop
457 Sacramento Street
530/265-2187
www.tourofnevadacity.com

Oakdale
Oakdale Bicycle Shop
445 East F Street
209/847-5073

Oroville
Greenline Cycles
1911 Montgomery Street
530/533-7885
www.greenlinecycles.com

Paradise
The Bike Shop
6133 Skyway
530/872-9363

Placerville
Golden Spoke Bike Shop
679 Placerville Drive
530/626-8370
www.goldenspoke.org

Placerville Bike Shop
1307 Broadway
530/622-3015
www.placervillebike.com

Roseville
Bob's Cycle Center
378 North Sunrise Boulevard
916/784-2255 or 916/784-2257
www.bobscyclecenter.com

REI
1148 Galleria Boulevard
916/724-6750
www.rei.com

Sharp Bicycles
710 Pleasant Grove Boulevard
916/797-8894
www.sharpbicycles.com

Sportmart/Sports Authority
6740 Stanford Ranch Road
916/789-8436
www.sportsauthority.com

Sacramento

American River Bicycle
9203 Folsom Boulevard
916/363-6271
www.americanriverbicycles.com

The Bicycle Business
3077 Freeport Boulevard
916/442-5246
www.thebikebiz.com

Broadway Bicycles
3401 2nd Avenue
916/455-7721

City Bicycle Works
2419 K Street
916/447-2453
www.citybicycleworks.com

College Cyclery
2760 21st Street
916/456-2042
www.collegecyclery.biz

East Sac Bike and Board
5520 H Street
916/254-2453
www.esbnb.com

Ikon Cycles
1126 18th Street
916/441-1122
www/ikoncycles.com

Mad Cat Bicycles
2645 Marconi Avenue
916/488-8588
www.madcatbikes.com

Mike's Bikes of Sacramento
1411 I Street
916/446-2453
www.mikesbikes.com

Natomas Bike Shop
3291 Truxel Road
916/641-8640
www.natomasbikeshop.com

Performance Bike
919 Howe Avenue
916/614-9901
www.performancebike.com

Practical Cycle
114 J Street
916/706-0077
www.practicalcycle.com

REI
1790 Expo Parkway
916/924-8900
www.rei.com

Rex Cycles
1811 E Street
916/446-5706
www.rexcycles.com

Sacramento Bicycle Kitchen
1915 I Street
916/538-2725
www.sacbikekitchen.org

Shingle Springs
Gold Country Cyclery
3830 Dividend Drive
530/676-3305
www.tandems-recumbents.com

Sonora
JT Cycles
55 South Washington Street
209/536-9882
www.jtcycles.net

Sonora Cyclery
13867 Mono Way
209/532-6800

Stockton
Performance Bike
6555 Pacific Avenue
209/951-5665
www.performancebike.com

REI
5757 Pacific Avenue
209/957-9479
www.rei.com

Robby's Bike Shop
7931 Thornton Road
209/951-4371
www.robbysbicycles.com

Sportmart/Sports Authority
10536 Trinity Parkway
209/951-3650
www.sportsauthority.com

Vacaville
Precision Bicycles
630 Orange Drive
707/447-6399
www.precisionbikeshop.com

Ray's Cycles
400 Main Street
707/448-1911

Sportmart/Sports Authority
1071 Helen Power Drive
707/451-6800
www.sportsauthority.com

Winters
Velo City Bike Shop
41 Main Street
530/795-3454
www.velocitybicycles.com

Yuba City
Vans Bicycle Center
622 Gray Avenue
530/674-0179

TAHOE AND NORTHERN SIERRA
Bear Valley
Bear Valley Adventure Company
1 Bear Valley Road
209/753-2834
www.bearvalleyxc.com

Hope Valley
Hope Valley Outdoor Center
Highway 88 & 89 at Picketts Junction
209/878-7545
www.hopevalleyoutdoors.com

Incline Village
Village Ski Loft
800 Tahoe Boulevard
775/831-3537
www.villageskiloft.com

Kings Beach
Tahoe Bike and Ski
8499 North Lake Boulevard
530/546-7437
www.tahoebikeski.com

Kirkwood
Kirkwood Resort Adventure Center
1377 Kirkwood Meadows Drive
209/258-7218
www.kirkwood.com

Soda Springs
Java Summit Sports
21501 Donner Pass Road, Suite 19
530/426-3567

South Lake Tahoe
Sierra Cycle Works
3430 Lake Tahoe Boulevard
530/541-7505
www.sierraskiandcycleworks.com

South Shore Bikes
955 Emerald Bay Road
530/544-7433

www.southshoresnow.com
Watta Bike Shop
2933 Highway 50
530/544-7700
www.wattabike.com

Stateline
Shoreline Bikes
259 Kingsbury Grade
775/588-8777
www.shorelinesnowboards.com

Tahoe City
Alpenglow Sports
415 North Lake Boulevard
530/583-6917
www.alpenglowsports.com

Cyclepaths
1785 West Lake Boulevard
530/581-1171
www.cyclepaths.net

Factory Bike
3039 Highway 89
530/581-3399
www.factorybike.net

Gravity Shop
255 North Lake Boulevard
530/581-2558
www.tahoegravityshop.com

Olympic Bike Shop
620 North Lake Boulevard
530/581-2500
www.olympicbikeshop.com

Tahoe Vista
Enviro-Rents
6873 North Lake Boulevard
530/546-2780

Truckee
The Back Country
11400 Donner Pass Road
530/582-0909
www.thebackcountry.net

Cyclepaths Lake Tahoe
11073 Donner Pass Road
530/582-1890
www.cyclepaths.net

Northsport at Northstar
Highway 267 at Northstar Drive
800/466-6784
www.skinorthstar.com

Paco's Truckee Bike & Ski
11200 Donner Pass Road
530/587-5561
www.pacosbikeandski.com

Quincy
The Bike Shop
107 Leonard Avenue
530/283-4015

SAN FRANCISCO BAY AREA
Alameda
Alameda Bicycle
1522 Park Street
510/522-0070
www.alamedabicycle.com

Cycle City
1433 High Street
510/521-2872
www.cyclecityusa.com

Stone's Cyclery
2320 Santa Clara Avenue
510/523-3264

Alamo
Alamo Bicycles
1483 Danville Boulevard
925/837-8444

Albany
Solano Avenue Cyclery
1554 Solano Avenue
510/524-1094
www.solanoavenuecyclery.com

Antioch
Bikes 4 Life
1344 Sunset Drive
925/754-8025

Schwinn City
814 A Street
925/757-0664

Belmont
California Sports & Cyclery
1464 El Camino Real
650/593-8806

Berkeley
Berkeley Bikes & Skateboards
1227 San Pablo Avenue
510/356-4454
www.bikesandskateboards.com

Mike's Bikes
2161 University Avenue
510/845-2453
www.mikesbikes.com

Missing Link
1988 Shattuck Avenue
510/843-7471
www.missinglink.org

Recycle Bicycle
3121 Sacramento Street
510/666-1300
www.recyclebicycleshop.com

REI
1338 San Pablo Avenue
510/527-4140
www.rei.com

Solano Avenue Cyclery
1554 Solano Avenue
510/524-1094
www.solanoavenuecyclery.com

Velo Sport
1615 University Avenue
510/849-0437
www.velosportbicycles.com

Brentwood
REI
2475 Sand Creek Road
925/516-3540
www.rei.com

Burlingame
Summit Bicycles
1031 California Drive
650/343-8483
www.summitbicycles.com

Campbell
Performance Bike
1646 South Bascom Avenue
408/559-0495
www.performancebike.com

Tread
501 East Campbell Avenue
408/792-7191
www.treadbikes.com

Wheel Away Cycle Center
402 East Hamilton Avenue
408/378-4636
www.wheelaway.com

Castro Valley
AreaCycles
3052 Castro Valley Boulevard
510/589-7291
www.areacycles.com

Castro Valley Cyclery
20515 Stanton Avenue
510/538-1878
www.castrovalleycyclery.com

Eden Bicycles
3318 Village Drive
510/881-5000
www.edenbicycles.com

Endless Cycles
3300 East Castro Valley Boulevard
501/470-3551
www.endlesscyclesonline.com

Clayton
Clayton Bicycle Center
5411 Clayton Road
925/672-2522
www.encinabicyclecenters.com

Concord
REI
1975 Diamond Boulevard, B-100
Willows Shopping Center
925/825-9400
www.rei.com

Corte Madera
REI
213 Corte Madera Town Center
415/927-1938
www.rei.com

Spearhead Bicycle Excellence
79 Belvedere Street
415/342-7618
www.ride888.com

Cupertino
Cupertino Bike Shop
10493 South De Anza Boulevard
408/255-2217
www.cupertinobikeshop.com

Evolution Bike Shop
19685 Stevens Creek Boulevard
408/252-5202
www.evolutionbikeshop.com

Daly City
Mission Motion
7080 Mission Street
650/994-2456
www.missionmotion.com

Danville
California Pedaler
495 Hartz Avenue
925/820-0345
www.calped.com

Danville Bikes
115 Hartz Avenue
925/837-0966
www.danvillebikes.com

Pegasus Bicycle Works
415 Railroad Avenue
925/362-2220
www.pegasusbicycleworks.com

Dublin
Dublin Cyclery
7001 Dublin Boulevard
925/828-8676
www.dublincyclery.com

Livermore Cyclery
7214 San Ramon Road
925/829-4310
www.livermorecyclery.com

REI
7099 Amador Plaza Road
925/828-9826
www.rei.com

El Sobrante
El Sobrante Cyclery
5057 El Portal Drive
510/223-3440

The Pedaler
3826 San Pablo Dam Road
510/222-3420
www.theped.com

Fairfax
Fairfax Cyclery
2020 Sir Francis Drake Boulevard
415/721-7644
wwwfairfaxcyclery.com

Sunshine Bicycle Center
737 Center Boulevard
415/459-3334
www.sunshinebicyle.com

Fremont
The Bicycle Garage
5006 Mowry Avenue
510/795-9622
www.bicyclegarage.com

REI
43962 Fremont Boulevard
510/651-0305
www.rei.com

Half Moon Bay
The Bike Works
520 Kelly Street
650/726-6708

Hayward
Cyclepath
22510 Foothill Boulevard
510/881-5177
www.cyclepathhayward.com

Witt's Bicycle Shop
22125 Mission Boulevard
510/538-8771

Lafayette
Hank and Frank Bicycles
3377 Mount Diablo Boulevard
925/283-2453
www.hankandfrank.com

Sharp Bicycles
969 Moraga Road
925/284-9616
www.sharpbicycle.com

Larkspur
Village Peddler
1111 Magnolia Avenue
415/461-3091
www.villagepeddler.com

Livermore
Cal Bicycles
2053 First Street
925/447-6666
www.calbicycles.com

Livermore Cyclery
2752 First Street
925/455-8090
www.livermorecyclery.com

Los Altos
The Bicycle Outfitter
963 Fremont Avenue
650/948-8092 or 650/948-8126
www.bicycleoutfitter.com

Chain Reaction Bicycles
2310 Homestead Road
408/735-8735
www.chainreaction.com

Los Gatos
Crossroads Bicycles
217 North Santa Cruz Avenue
408/354-0555
www.crossroadsbicycles.com

Summit Bicycles
111 East Main Street
408/399-9142
www.summitbicycles.com

Menlo Park
Menlo Velo
433 El Camino Real
650/327-5137
www.menlovelobicycles.com

Mill Valley
Above Category
38 Millwood Street
415/389-5461
www.abovecategory.net

Studio Velo
247 Shoreline Highway
415/407-8960
www.studiovelomv.com

Tam Bikes
357 Miller Avenue
415/389-1900
www.tambikes.com

Milpitas
Sportmart/Sports Authority
111 Ranch Drive and 1200 Great Mall Drive
408/934-0280
www.sportsauthority.com

Sun Bike Shop
1624 South Main Street
408/262-4360
www.sunbikeshop.com

Morgan Hill
Sunshine Bicycles
16825 Monterey Road
408/779-4015
www.sunshinebicycles.com

Mountain View
The Off Ramp
2320 El Camino Real
650/968-2974
www.offrampbikes.com

Performance Bike
2124 West El Camino Real
650/964-1796
www.performancebike.com

REI
2450 Charleston Road
650/969-1938
www.rei.com

Novato

Classcycle
1531-B South Novato Boulevard
415/897-3288

Road and Tri Sports
366 Bel Marin Keys Boulevard, Suite A
415/786-9181

Oakland

Bay Area Bikes
2424 Webster Street
510/763-2453
www.bayareabikes.com

Bent Spoke
6124 Telegraph Avenue
510/652-3089

Cycle Sports
3530 Grand Avenue
510/444-7900
www.cyclesportsonline.com

Hank and Frank Bicycles
6030 College Avenue
510/654-2453
www.hankandfrankbicycles.com

Pioneer Bike Shop
11 Rio Vista Avenue
510/658-8981

Wheels of Justice
2024 Mountain Boulevard
510/339-6091
www.wojcyclery.com

Palo Alto

Bike Connection
2011 El Camino Real
650/424-8034
www.bikeconnection.net

Mike's Bikes
3001 El Camino Real
650/858-7700
www.mikesbikes.com

Palo Alto Bicycles
171 University Avenue
650/328-7411
www.paloaltobicycles.com

Petaluma

Bici Sport
143 Kentucky Street
707/775-4676
www.bicisportusa.com

Petaluma Cyclery
1080 Petaluma Boulevard North
707/762-1990

Pleasant Hill

Pleasant Hill Cyclery
1100-C Contra Costa Boulevard
925/676-2667
www.pleasanthillcyclery.com

Pleasanton

Bicycles Pleasanton
537 Main Street
925/461-0905
www.bicyclespleasanton.com

Reyes Station
Point Reyes Outdoors
11401 State Route 1
415/663-9164
www.pointreyesoutdoors.com

Redwood City
Chain Reaction Bicycles
1451 El Camino Real
650/366-7130
www.chainreaction.com

Go Ride Bicycles
2755 El Camino Real
650/366-2453
www.goridebicycles.com

San Anselmo
Caesar's Cyclery
29 San Anselmo Avenue
415/721-0111
www.marinbikeshop.com

City Cycle
702 San Anselmo Avenue
415/454-9534
www.citycycle.com

San Carlos
REI
1119 Industrial Boulevard
650/508-2330
www.rei.com

San Francisco
American Cyclery
510 Frederick Street
415/664-4545
www.americancyclery.com

American Cyclery Too
858 Stanyan Street
415/876-4545
www.americancyclery.com

Avenue Cyclery
756 Stanyan Street
415/387-3155
www.avenuecyclery.com

Big Swingin' Cycles
2260 Van Ness Avenue
415/441-6294
www.bigswingincycles.com

The Bike Hut
Pier 40
415/543-4335
www.thebikehut.com

The Bike Kitchen
650-H Florida Street
415/647-2453
www.bikekitchen.org

Box Dog Bikes
494 14th Street
415/431-9627
www.boxdogbikes.com

Citizen Chain Bicycles
2064 Powell Street
415/796-2925
www.citizenchain.com

City Cycle
3001 Steiner Street
415/346-2242
www.citycycle.com

DD Cycles
4049 Balboa Street
415/752-7980
www.ddcycles.com

Free Wheel Bike Shop
914 Valencia Street
415/643-9213
www.thefreewheel.com

Fresh Air Bicycles
1943 Divisadero Street
415/563-4824

Heavy Metal Bike Shop
82 29th Street
415/643-3929
www.heavymetalbikeshop.com

High Trails Cyclery
1825 Polk Street
415/814-3216
www.hightrailssf.com

Lombardi's Sports
1600 Jackson Street
415/771-0600
http://lombardisports.myshopify.com

Marin Bikes Factory Store
1090 Folsom Street
415/934-8000
www.marinbikes.com

Mike's Bikes
1233 Howard Street
415/241-2453
www.mikesbikes.com

Mission Bicycle
766 Valencia Street
415/683-6166
www.missionbicycle.com

Noe Valley Cyclery
4193 24th Street
415/647-0886

Nomad Cyclery
2555 Irving Street
415/564-3568
www.nomadcyclery.com

Ocean Cyclery
1935 Ocean Avenue
415/239-5004
www.oceancyclery.com

Pacific Bicycle
345 Fourth Street
415/928-8466
www.pacbikes.com

Pedal Revolution
3085 21st Street
415/641-1264
www.pedalrevolution.com

Performance Bike
635 Brannan Street
415/856-0230
www.performancebike.com

Refried Cycles
3804 17th Street
415/621-2911
www.refriedcycles.com

040 Brannan Street
415/934-1938
www.rei.com

Roaring Mouse Cycles
934 Old Mason Street, the Presidio
415/753-6272
www.roaringmousecycles.com

Sports Basement
1415 16th Street
415/437-0100
www.sportsbasement.com

Sports Basement
610 Old Mason Street, the Presidio
415/437-0100
www.sportsbasement.com

Treat Street Bicycle Works
Treat & 18th Streets
415/551-2453
www.treatstreetbicycle.com

Valencia Cyclery
1077 Valencia Street
415/550-6600 or 415/550-6601
www.valenciacyclery.com

Warm Planet Bikes
311 Townsend Street
415/974-6440
www.warmplanetbikes.com

San Jose
Bici Bike
5715 Cottle Road
408/225-0599

Bicycle Express
131 East William Street
408/998-1618
www.bicyleexpress.net

Calabazas Cyclery
6140 Bollinger Road
408/366-2453
www.calabazas.com

Fast Bicycle
2274 Alum Rock Avenue
408/251-9110
www.fastbicycleshop.com

Happy Trails Cyclery
4640 Meridian Avenue
408/265-8865
www.happytrailscyclery.com

Hyland Family Bicycles
1515 Meridian Avenue
408/269-2300
www.hylandbikes.com

La Dolce Velo
1280 The Alameda
408/244-8356
www.ladolcevelo.com

REI
400 El Paseo de Saratoga Shopping
Center
408/871-8765
www.rei.com

Slough's Bike Shoppe
260 Race Street
408/293-1616

Trail Head Cyclery
14390 Union Avenue
408/369-9666
www.trailheadcyclery.com

Willow Glen Bicycles
1016 Lincoln Avenue
408/293-2606
www.willowglenbicycles.com

San Leandro
Robinson Wheel Works
1235 MacArthur Boulevard
510/352-4663
www.robinsonww.com

Sports Authority
1933 Davis Street
510/632-6100
www.sportsauthority.com

San Mateo
Cyclepath
1212 South El Camino Real
650/341-0922
www.cyclepathsm.com

Talbots Cyclery
445 South B Street
650/931-8120
www.talbotscyclery.com

San Rafael
Mike's Bicycle Center
1601 Fourth Street
415/454-3747
www.mikesbikes.com

Performance Bike
369 Third Street
415/454-9063
www.performancebike.com

The Re-Cyclery
610 Fourth Street
415/458-2986

Summit Bicycles
1820 Fourth Street
415/456-4700
www.summitbicycles.com

Santa Clara
Calmar Bicycles
2236 El Camino Real
408/249-6907
www.calmarcycles.com

The Off Ramp
2369 El Camino Real
408/249-2848
www.offrampbikes.com

Sausalito
A Bicycle Odyssey
1417 Bridgeway
415/332-3050
www.bicycleodyssey.com

Mike's Bikes
1 Gate Six Road
415/332-3200
www.mikesbikes.com

...rt/Sports Authority
125 East El Camino Real
408/732-6400
www.sportsauthority.com

Sports Basement
1177 Kern Avenue
408/732-0300
www.sportsbasement.com

Walt's Cycles
116 Carroll Street
408/739-4287
www.waltscycles.com

Vallejo
Authorized Bicycles
1220 Georgia Street
707/648-1413

Walnut Creek
Encina Bicycle Center
2901 Ygnacio Valley Road
925/944-9200
www.encinabicyclecenters.com

Performance Bike
1401 North Broadway
925/937-7723
www.performancebike.com

Rivendell Bicycle Works
2040 North Main Street
925/933-7304
www.rivbike.com

MONTEREY AND BIG SUR
Aptos
Aptos Bike Station
36 Rancho Del Mar
831/688-4169
www.bikestationaptos.com

Carmel
Bay Bikes
3600 The Barnyard
831/624-7433
www.baybikes.com

Carmel Bicycle
26543 Carmel Rancho Boulevard
831/625-2211
www.carmelbicycle.net

Freedom
TNL Bikes
1916 Freedom Boulevard
831/722-1233

Gilroy
Sportmart/Sports Authority
6735 Camino Arroyo
408/847-5703
www.sportsauthority.com

Sunshine Bicycles
311 First Street
408/842-4889
www.sunshinebicycles.com

Hollister
Off the Chain Bikes
341 Tres Pinos Road, Suite 106
831/636-0802
www.offthechainbikes.com

Marina
Marina Cycle and Skate
214 Reservation Road
831/384-2453

Monterey
Adventures by the Sea
299 Cannery Row
and 201 Alvarado Street
831/372-1807
www.adventuresbythesea.com

Aquarian Bicycles
486 Washington Street
831/375-2144

Bay Bikes
585 Cannery Row
831/655-2453
www.baybikes.com

Joselyn's Bicycles
398 East Franklin Street
831/649-8520
www.joselynsbicycles.com

Pacific Grove
Winning Wheels
318 Grand Avenue
831/375-4322

Salinas
Bear Bikes
1288 North Main Street
831/444-8460

Bobcat Bicycles
141 Monterey Street
831/753-7433
www.bobcatbicycles.com

Santa Cruz
Another Bike Shop
2361 Mission Street
831/427-2232
www.anotherbikeshop.com

The Bicycle Shop
1325 Mission Street
831/454-0909
www.thebicycleshopsantacruz.com

The Bicycle Trip
1001 Soquel Avenue
831/427-2580
www.bicycletrip.com

The Bike Church
703 Pacific Avenue
831/425-2453

Dave's Custom Bikes
910 Soquel Avenue
831/423-8923
www.santacruzcustombikes.com

Electric Sierra Cycles
302 Pacific Avenue
831/425-1593

Family Cycling Center
914 41st Avenue
831/475-3883
www.familycycling.com

Recycled Bikes of Santa Cruz
2420 7th Avenue
831/465-9955

Spokesman Bicycles
231 Cathcart Street
831/423-5683
www.spokesmanbicycles.com

Sprockets
1420 Mission Street
831/426-7623
www.sprocketsbikes.com

Scotts Valley
Cyclesport
245-J Mount Hermon Road
831/440-9070
www.svcyclesport.com

Seaside
Sports Center Bicycles
1576 Del Monte Boulevard
831/899-1300
www.sportscenterbicycles.net

Watsonville
Watsonville Cyclery
25 East Fifth Street
831/724-1646
www.watsonvillecyclery.com

YOSEMITE AND MAMMOTH LAKES
Bishop
Aerohead Cycles
312 North Warren Street
760/873-4151
www.aeroheadcycles.com

Mammoth Lakes
Brian's Bicycles and Cross-Country Skis
3059 Chateau Road
760/924-8566
www.mammothbikesandskis.com

Footloose Sports
3043 Main Street
760/934-2400
www.footloosesports.com

Mammoth Mountain Bike Shop
1 Minaret Road
760/934-2571
www.mammothmountain.com

Mammoth Sporting Goods
1 Sierra Center Mall,
Old Mammoth Road
760/934-3239
www.mammothsportinggoods.com

Oakhurst
Yosemite Bicycle and Sport
40120 Highway 41
559/641-2453
www.yosemitebicycle.com

Index